Reading Strategies for
Nursing and Allied Health

Reading Strategies for Nursing and Allied Health

Ann B. Faulkner
Brookhaven College

Dana K. Stahl
El Centro College

Houghton Mifflin Company
Boston   New York

Senior Sponsoring Editor: Mary Jo Southern
Senior Associate Editor: Ellen Darion
Editorial Assistant: Kate O'Sullivan
Project Editor: Anne Holm
Production/Design Coordinator: Jennifer Meyer Dare
Manufacturing Manager: Florence Cadran
Senior Marketing Manager: Nancy Lyman

Cover design by Diana Coe
Cover photo copyright 1998 PhotoDisc Inc.

Credits

Selection 2-1: From Michael Pagliarulo, *Introduction to Physical Therapy.*
Copyright © 1996 Mosby. Reprinted with permission of the publisher.
Selection 2-2: This article is reprinted with permission of *Radiologic
Technology,* the official journal of the American Society of Radiologic
Technologists, © 1995. Photos on p. 41 from Grigg, E.R.N., *The Trail of the
Invisible Light,* 1964. Courtesy of Charles C. Thomas, Publisher, Ltd.,
Springfield, Illinois. Selection 2-3: Used with permission from *Nursing Into
the 21st Century,* 1996, © Springhouse Corporation, Springhouse, PA.
Selection 2-4: From Florence Nightingale, *Notes on Nursing: What It Is, and
What It Is Not,* pp. 95–105. Copyright © 1969 Dover Publications.
Reprinted with permission of the publisher. Selection 2-5: From R. Craven
and C. Hirnle, *Fundamentals of Nursing,* Second Edition. Copyright © 1996
Lippincott. Reprinted with permission of the publisher. From Lewis, Collier,
and Heitkemper, *Medical-Surgical Nursing* (5th ed.). Copyright © 1996
Mosby. Reprinted with permission of the publisher. From J. Needham,
Gerontological Nursing, p. 391. Copyright © 1993 Delmar Publishers, Inc.
Reprinted with permission of the publisher. From HEALTH ASSESSMENT
IN NURSING by Sims, et al. Copyright 1995 by Addison-Wesley Publishing
Company. Reprinted by permission. From Smith-Temple and Johnson,
Nurses' Guide to Clinical Procedures, Second Edition. Copyright ©
Lippincott-Raven Publishers. Reprinted with permission of the publisher.
Credits continue on page 298, which constitutes a continuation of the copyright page.

Printed in the U.S.A.

Library of Congress Catalog Card Number: 97-72465

ISBN: 0-395-77036-X

123456789-POO-02 01 00 99 98

To my husband, Bill Faulkner, without whose support and
understanding I would not have become myself.
ABF

To my mother, Evelyn G. Morse, R.N., encourager and
role model.
DKS

Contents

Unit 3   Pain 87

Unit 4 Ethical and Legal Issues 159

Unit 6 Review and Practice in Critical Thinking 251

Consultations 257

To the Instructor

Reading Strategies for Nursing and Allied Health grew out of several years of work with students and colleagues to make the reading of health-related texts an exciting challenge rather than an overwhelming hurdle. Our first effort was a grant-supported project partially funded by Carl Perkins Vocational Education Funds, awarded by the Texas Higher Education Coordinating Board and by the Dallas County Community College District. The need was clearly supported by reading and nursing faculty, who discovered a gap between the reading skill level at which students exit reading programs and that needed for success in entry-level nursing and allied health courses. Without this initial encouragement, the present work would still be unwritten. The intervening years have been filled with interesting students, supportive colleagues, and real learning about how to help students use reading strategies more effectively.

The publications chosen for use in *Reading Strategies for Nursing and Allied Health* come from textbooks and periodicals that beginning students in a health field might be asked to read. Whole articles and long sections of textbook chapters are included so that students may get authentic practice in reading professional literature. Various types of articles are represented, including research, reviews of research literature, historical overviews, first-person narratives, exposition, and persuasion. The textbook selections come from textbooks in physical therapy, medical-surgical nursing, and practical nursing.

The use of professionally relevant practice materials makes this book effective because students work harder on materials that engage their interest and challenge them. On the other hand, reading instructors need have no fear that they will be unable to work with the materials because they are too technically demanding. We provide information to assist both students and instructors with health-related content and terminology.

The periodical articles are primarily taken from nursing references; many allied health journals address subjects requiring a higher level of scientific knowledge than developmental reading students have. None of the selected publications is highly specialized; each focuses on issues of value to health industry consumers as well as educators. In fact, our intent is not to teach health subject matter but to use the subject matter to advance the reading proficiency and independence of students who are considering a health major.

This book has been designed for use by reading and study skills teachers who are generalists rather than specialists in the health fields. Indeed, learning strategies are not usually taught in health programs; it is expected that students arrive prepared to study efficiently and learn independently. The demands of health curricula prohibit faculty from remediating reading problems while they are initiating students into a new profession.

Occasionally, students who use this "real" material discover that they no longer want to pursue their original goal. In the process, however, they learn to read more effectively—whatever they eventually choose to do. Experience indicates that students with moderate-to-severe reading handicaps need a reading course or two before attempting to use this book. *Reading Strategies for Nursing and Allied Health* is designed for students at the pre-college level and for those who have no reading difficulties but want to brush up on strategies for successful reading and studying. It may be useful for individualized or small-group instruction as well as in a class setting.

Following their completion of an ESL program, students of English as a second language have used this text successfully, as the last phase of preparation before entering the professional sequence. Another group of students for whom this book may be appropriate is those who have not succeeded in a nursing or allied health program. Such students are often reassured that a reading course using *Reading Strategies* will not waste their time in preparing for readmission to the program. The familiarity of the material may, in fact, help rebuild their self-confidence.

Reading Strategies for Nursing and Allied Health emphasizes process in order to change a student's random or rigid approach to reading academic material into one employing a system. The first step involves an introduction to the demands of each assignment—the scope and difficulty of the material and the adequacy of the student's background knowledge and comprehension. The next step is to develop and carry out a plan for reading, which incorporates the information gained during assessment. Finally, the material that needs to be remembered so as to satisfy the purposes for reading is noted and prepared for periodic review. The reading process, like the writing process, is recursive—that is, to achieve a purpose, the learner may at any time go back to an earlier step and repeat part of the process. Knowing how to use the process can reduce wasted time resulting from inadequate preparation, unfocused reading, or ineffective review.

Reading Strategies for Nursing and Allied Health covers four topical units: Orientation, Pain, Ethical and Legal Issues, and Stress. These four units are preceded by a unit introducing students to the reading and remembering process. They are followed by a unit on critical thinking, which may be used as a supplement to the topical units or as a review for students preparing to take a comprehensive final exam.

Activities for each selection are rooted in the reading process; they teach strategies appropriate to the various stages in the process. The "Orientation" unit focuses on developing and practicing a variety of techniques to use *before reading*. Among the techniques introduced is previewing a new textbook, as well as chapters and articles, to assess background knowledge and the level of difficulty, to determine organization and structure, and to clarify the purpose for reading.

The next unit, "Pain," concentrates on *during-reading* techniques. Students are introduced to techniques for reading and understanding main ideas and details as well as for discerning the organizational patterns used by authors. The selections include a textbook chapter and journal articles of varying difficulty.

The emphasis in the "Ethical and Legal Issues" unit is on what to do *after reading*. In this critical phase of the reading process, techniques such as notemaking, paraphrasing, outlining, and summarizing are employed as aids to recall.

The final topical unit provides for extended practice and integration of techniques across all phases of the reading process, with special emphasis on review. Three selections focus on the topic of stress.

To support students' control of the reading process, we have marked many of the activities with a key symbol. This graphic indicates that the student should check the Consultations section at the end of the text before moving on to the next activity. This section offers suggestions and models through which students can judge their study effectiveness, and thus it helps keep students from feeling confused or uncertain about how they are doing. When the activity is a quiz requiring "right" answers, the Consultations section does not provide these. Instead, the *Instructor's Resource Manual* contains this information. We made the decision to move this type of information at the urging of some reviewers, and also to keep students from cheating themselves by looking rather than thinking.

We welcome your comments and questions. Learning is what makes it so much fun to teach!

Acknowledgments

We want to thank Mary Jo Southern, Senior Sponsoring Editor, who was the first person to show an interest in our work, and whose warmth and support has been crucial to our efforts. Senior Associate Editor Ellen Darion, Quica Ostrander of Lifland et al., Bookmakers, and Robin Hogan have done a wonderful job with formatting and editing.

Our reviewers are an absolute "Dream Team." They played a major part in shaping the version of *Reading Strategies* that you are reading today. Our sincere thanks go to Maxine Byers, Chemeketa Community College; Janice H. DeMots, Milwaukee Area Tech; Janice R. Ellis, Shoreline Community College; Richard McKnight, Blackhawk Technical College; Gail Platt, South Plains College; Debra Schulte, Monterey Peninsula College; and Diane Starkey, El Paso Community College.

An earlier version of this project was implemented with the support of a grant from the Texas Higher Education Coordinating Board. Three colleagues at Brookhaven College played key roles in its development: Linda Lee, Mary Brumbach, and Gloria Macklin. We are glad to have had the opportunity to work with them. Without that experience, this book would never have been written.

Friends and family have provided the love, concern, encouragement, and belief that enabled us to finish. Thanks to all of you!

Ann B. Faulkner, M.A.
Professor of Reading
Brookhaven College

Dana K. Stahl, R.N., M.S.
Professor of Nursing
El Centro College

Dallas County Community College District
Dallas, Texas

Reading Strategies for Nursing and Allied Health

Introduction

If you are reading this, you are probably planning a career in nursing or an allied health field. You are probably concerned about the amount and complexity of the reading you will do as a student in your chosen field. You may already be aware that casual reading techniques will not yield the grades you need for success in health sciences programs.

Reading Strategies for Nursing and Allied Health is designed to assist you as you prepare to enter a health sciences program. You will further develop your reading and learning skills using actual textbook and journal articles written for students studying nursing or one of the allied health fields. This approach will help you prepare for the actual requirements of your chosen field of study. If you master the techniques necessary to read the selections in this book effectively, you will find it easier to make the transition to the demanding program that you plan to enter. The ultimate goal is for you to develop the skills necessary for success in your health sciences courses.

This book is organized by topics and by phases of the reading process. Unit 1 introduces the reading process and provides a framework for understanding the rest of the book. The next four units focus on topics of interest to those entering the health care field: "Orientation to the Health Professions," "Pain," "Ethical and Legal Issues," and "Stress." The reading selections are taken from journals, textbooks, and reference books. The activities emphasize reading techniques in the different phases of reading: *before reading, during reading,* and *after reading.* You will notice a key symbol following certain activities. Once you've responded to them you can turn to the "Consultations" section at the end of the book for some possible answers. Unit 6 presents critical thinking questions for each of the reading selections in the topical units. You may use these questions when you finish each selection or to help you review the entire book in preparation for a final exam. All of these elements combine to make an interesting and challenging learning experience.

What if you decide, after using this book, that you want to change your major? The reading skills you learn here will apply to books and journals in other fields. The purpose of this book is to help you become a more independent reader and thinker.

This may be the most challenging book you have ever used. Our experience in using it with students indicates that this level of difficulty is necessary to prepare students for successful study in the health professions. Fortunately, our students tell us all the work is worth it; when they finish the course, they know how to study demanding material. We hope your experience is the same and welcome your comments and suggestions.

unit 1

The Reading and Remembering Process

This unit is designed to give you an overview of the reading process. It will introduce you to the three phases of the reading process—*before reading*, *during reading*, and *after reading*—and guide you in applying a wide range of reading and remembering techniques. Developing personal learning strategies by combining these techniques will help you not only to use this book but also to become a more effective and more independent reader and thinker.

Purpose for Reading

PROCESS GOAL: **To become acquainted with this book**

This unit offers an introduction to the reading process. Use it to become acquainted with the authors' organization of the topic and to develop a feel for how the authors present information.

OUTCOME GOAL: **To learn about the goals and techniques of the reading process**

The authors want you to have an overview of the techniques used by effective readers. The four topical units that follow will give you many opportunities to apply these techniques. Don't expect to master them at this point. Practice will help you become better, even if it doesn't make you perfect!

Before Reading 1

Goal: Get oriented to the text, the author, the assignment, and the scope and organization of the information

Technique: Preview new materials and assignment

To get an idea of how the authors present the reading process, look through the selection "The Reading and Remembering Process" and then answer the following questions:

1. How many phases are there in the reading process? _____
   What are they called?

2. How many process goals are there in each phase?

Before Reading 2

> Goal: Develop a study plan
> Techniques: Divide the assignment into manageable parts; decide
>   when to work on each part

Now that you've seen how long "The Reading and Remembering Process" is and how easy (or difficult) it looks, you're in a better position to make a decision about how and when you'll study it.

Think about your schedule and whether you can read all or part of the selection at one time, given your current reading rate and the other claims on your time.

Since there are three phases in the reading process, it might make sense to divide the selection into three parts for study. Decide how to divide the work and when you'll do each part. Write your plan here:

During Reading

> Goal: Monitor comprehension and achievement of purpose
> Technique: Stop periodically to check achievement of outcome
>   goals and to underline main ideas

When you have the time, read "The Reading and Remembering Process." Keep in mind that your purpose for reading the selection is to learn about the process so that you can use it throughout this book.

After Reading 1

Goals: Check initial recall of relevant material; organize relevant information for review

Techniques: Review the whole assignment by self-testing or answering review questions; think critically about what you have learned

---

If you studied the selection in more than one session, you will need to review all the material in order to remind yourself of the entire process.

Make notes during the review to draw attention to main ideas and to remind yourself of questions you'd like to ask in class.

After Reading 2

Goal: Check initial recall of relevant information

Technique: Review the whole assignment by answering review questions

---

When you have read and reviewed the selection, answer the following questions without looking at the text. See how much of the information stuck with you and which points you'll have to restudy.

1. Match each goal or technique with the appropriate phase in the reading process.

   a. Before reading   _____ Adjust reading rate to purpose for reading and to difficulty of the text
   b. During reading
   c. After reading   _____ Develop a study plan
                        _____ Periodically test recall of relevant material
                        _____ Underline, make notes, outline, summarize, and/or jot down questions
                        _____ Predict and answer possible test questions

2. Which of the techniques used during and after reading specifically relate to the recursive nature of the reading process?

3. Do any of the goals or techniques seem unclear to you? If so, do your best to write a question that you could ask your teacher.

Selection 1-1 *The Reading and Remembering Process*

As a college student, you may find that the casual approach to studying you have used in the past is not effective. In college, you are required to study a variety of textbooks and other materials. Whether these are fascinating or not, you'll need to be able to read them effectively and to remember what you have read. Unless you use a systematic approach to studying, your test grades may be lower than you hope or need them to be for admission into a health program.

As a student planning a career in the health sciences, you face special challenges in the amount and complexity of required reading. You must master a new vocabulary, and you must be able to remember and make connections between material covered in prerequisite courses and the courses in your major area of study.

Independence is another issue for health sciences students. You must be a self-directed, independent learner. Do not expect the instructor to tell you what to learn or how to study. Health sciences students are expected to be able to motivate themselves and to identify appropriate reading material independently once they enter a professional program. This does not mean, however, that you are expected to learn in isolation. Study groups are used effectively by many students, and working cooperatively is essential to success in most jobs.

The reading process can be divided into three phases: **before reading, during reading,** and **after reading.** Any process is a method for achieving a goal; in this case, the goal is effective reading and remembering.

The reading process, like the writing process, is *recursive;* that is, you may return to any earlier point in the process at any time in order to achieve your purpose. Reading and writing don't always proceed neatly from start to finish. For example, in the middle of drafting a paper, you may realize that you need more information to support an argument. You then must move back to an "earlier" stage, where you gather information. Similarly, you may come to the end of a reading assignment and realize that some concepts didn't stick with you. It is then essential that you go back to the point in the process where you stopped learning and restudy. This book explains the reading and writing processes in terms of sequence: what to do first, second, and last. In actual practice, though, you must be able to apply the techniques of any phase of the process at any time if they will help you achieve your purpose for reading.

To help you become comfortable with each of these reading techniques, we have designed this book so that you will use them while reading about topics often studied in health sciences programs. As you read the selections in this book, you will learn the information being presented as well as techniques to make your reading more effective. To give you practice in using a process-centered approach to reading, before-reading, during-reading, and after-reading activities that lead you through the reading process precede each selection. We've called these "process guides" because they guide you through a process for reading.

Purpose for Reading

A statement called "Purpose for Reading" appears before each selection to explain why you are reading the material. This statement discusses two different kinds of goals: process goals and outcome goals. *Process goals* refer to purposes for which you use the techniques in the three phases of the reading process. These goals include getting oriented to the assignment, monitoring comprehension, and checking recall of relevant information, among others. For easy reference, all the process goals discussed in this book are listed on page 16.

Outcome goals are the results required by the assignment. These results will vary widely from assignment to assignment. You may be asked to gather information, to summarize an article, to identify similarities and differences between two articles, or to understand the trends in research in a particular field. Thinking about what results you need to attain from studying is a crucial first step in process-based study.

You will use both process goals and outcome goals in all of your reading. By the time you finish this book, however, you will be comfortable enough with your options to select process goals without really thinking about them.

Phase 1: Before Reading

> Goal 1: Get oriented to the text, the author, the assignment, and the scope and organization of the information
> Techniques: 1. Preview new materials and assignment
> 2. Estimate the difficulty of the material, and improve your background knowledge
> 3. Ask questions or make predictions about the information
> 4. Look up significant terms that are not defined in the text
> 5. Check for bias in the author or reader
>
> Goal 2: Develop a study plan
> Techniques: 1. Decide which parts of the text relate to objectives
> 2. Divide the assignment into manageable parts
> 3. Decide when to work on each part

Before Reading

In this phase, there are two process goals: getting oriented and developing a study plan.

GOAL 1: **Get oriented to the text, the author, the assignment, and the scope and organization of the information**

Getting oriented is an essential part of the first phase of reading. Just as you pause at the door of an unfamiliar room to get an impression of its shape and contents, take time to get oriented to each new assignment. This will help you move smoothly through the text, without tripping over new ideas. Five techniques are useful for getting oriented.

1.1: Preview materials and new assignment. The first orientation technique is designed to give you a quick overview of your assignment. Previewing will vary, depending on whether you are working with a new textbook or a new assignment in a familiar text. When looking at a new textbook for the first time, pay attention to the parts that tell about the book, the author, the book's organization, and its supplements. When you preview a familiar book or periodical, look at these features: title, objectives, key word list, headings, words in any special style of type (such as **bold** or *italic*), photos and graphics, summary, and review questions.

1.2: Estimate the difficulty of the material, and improve your background knowledge. To estimate the difficulty of the material, look at the length of the selection and note how easy the print is to read. In some cases, the selection may be long, but the way the text is arranged on the page makes it easy to read. In other cases, the text is printed and arranged in such a way that you strain to read it. By estimating the level of difficulty in advance, you can allow the time needed to overcome such barriers.

You will also want to improve your background knowledge for any selection that appears to be difficult or unfamiliar. Learning builds on previous knowledge. If you have very little previous knowledge of a subject, you won't learn much from an advanced, technical article on the topic. To prepare yourself for such a technical selection, read an easier article with fewer technical terms. Encyclopedias often provide a nontechnical introduction. Even a dictionary may explain an idea well enough to get you started.

1.3: Ask questions or make predictions about the information. Can you predict what the author's intent is and what information might be especially important based on such things as headings and highlighted information? By making predictions, you are better able to keep the subject and possible conclusions in mind as you read. This orientation technique will help you focus on important points made in the text.

1.4: Look up significant terms that are not defined in the text. Some material is difficult to read because the author has used unfamiliar vocabulary. Occasionally, a text will highlight specialized terminology and actually define new terms. In many other cases, unknown words will not be defined. You will not only save time but also have a better grasp of the material if you look up these words before you begin to read.

1.5: Check for bias in the author or reader. As a reader, you need to raise questions about the author's slant on the topic, positive or negative. You should consider your own attitudes, too. Avoid making the error of accepting biased opinions as fact by asking questions such as these: "Who is this author, and what credentials does he or she have that make this work credible?" "How was the research conducted, and how was it funded?" "What is my own opinion of the topic, the author, and the findings?" and "Do I have beliefs or values that may influence my thoughts about this topic?"

GOAL 2: Develop a study plan

Three techniques will help you accomplish the second process goal of the *before-reading phase*.

2.1: Decide which parts of the text relate to objectives. First, identify objectives for reading the content. In college, the most important objectives are those provided by the instructor in a syllabus or when making an assignment. Textbooks often list objectives at the beginning of a unit or chapter. It is your responsibility to select the parts of the text that address the objectives of the instructor; fit his or her objectives to the text, even if they do not match exactly. If your instructor doesn't provide a clear purpose for reading, use the textbook objectives to guide your study. You may not need to read all of a chapter. Some sections will contain specific information to fulfill objectives. Other sections will provide related information. Material in a chapter that does not address the specific objectives provided by the instructor is of much lower priority. In some instances, it should be skipped altogether.

2.2: Divide the assignment into manageable parts. How long is the assigned selection? How much time do you have available for reading? How difficult is the material? Will it require more time because of the concentration necessary to grasp its meaning? By deciding how to divide the total assignment into shorter, more manageable parts, you put yourself in a stronger position to learn. Look for natural stopping points such as those provided by headings or section titles. Stopping in the middle of a paragraph or section often means that you must completely reread that portion of text to understand fully the information it provides.

2.3: Decide when to work on each part. When do you have enough time and the concentration necessary to read effectively? Can you do it now? Will you get better results if you wait until after work, after dinner, or after the children are put to bed? Don't try to follow someone else's plan; make one based on your own responsibilities and schedule. Keep in mind that if you are too tired, too rushed, or too anxious about other responsibilities, your reading will be less effective. By planning time that will be uninterrupted, you can better concentrate on learning new material. Then reviewing can be done in shorter amounts of time.

Phase 2: During Reading

Goal 3: Monitor comprehension and achievement of purpose

Techniques: 1. Look for main ideas, significant details, and paragraph organization

2. Stop periodically to check achievement of outcome goals and to underline main ideas

3. Use alternative strategies or return to an appropriate *before-reading technique*

Goal 4: Monitor reading efficiency

Techniques: 1. Adjust reading rate to purpose for reading and to difficulty of the text

2. Evaluate the efficiency of your study strategies

During Reading

GOAL 3:   Monitor comprehension and achievement of purpose

Successful students learn to ask themselves how effectively they are meeting their goals. They ask this question so frequently that going back to fill in knowledge gaps doesn't take much time.

3.1: Look for main ideas, significant details, and paragraph organization. Looking for main ideas and significant details will keep you from wasting time by merely passing your eyes over the words. Paragraph organizational patterns include lists, time or process order, cause and effect, and comparison/contrast. Looking for them will help you remember the main ideas and details more effectively.

3.2: Stop periodically to check achievement of outcome goals and to underline main ideas. Are you getting what you need to get from the reading? Ask yourself this question frequently. If you are sure that you are achieving your purpose in reading, you may begin to underline main ideas. However, some students prefer to wait until after reading to underline in order to avoid overmarking. With very difficult assignments, you may want to pause at the end of each paragraph to monitor your results. With easier material, stopping at the end of each section might be adequate.

3.3: Use alternative strategies or return to an appropriate *before-reading technique*. If you realize that you did not understand a particular paragraph or section, you may need to reorient yourself to that material. Maybe you need to build background knowledge or look up some key terms. Perhaps you are letting the complexity of the material overwhelm you. It might be a good idea to review your study plan. Back up to the last point at which you got what you needed from your reading, and review your outcome goals before you begin reading again.

GOAL 4:   Monitor reading efficiency

Reading efficiency involves both adequate comprehension and appropriate reading speed. Monitoring your efficiency is a crucial step in improving your reading rate and comprehension.

4.1: Adjust reading rate to purpose for reading and to difficulty of the text. In general, if you are reading easy material for your own pleasure, you will be able to read more rapidly. If you are mastering a new topic in a difficult textbook for a demanding course, you will have to slow down.

Two specialized types of reading—skimming and scanning—may be useful. *Skimming* is a rapid reading technique for getting the main ideas of the text. For example, skimming is used when you have limited time and just want to get a general idea of the contents of an article. *Scanning* is a selective search for specific information likely to be in the material. For example, you may scan for a specific name in a phone directory, and you may scan a textbook chapter to locate specific information about a medication. Both skimming and scanning can aid efficiency, but, if they are applied ineffectively, they will waste your time.

4.2: Evaluate the efficiency of your study strategies. You should check on whether you are using an appropriate reading rate for the material and for your outcome goals. Many students read everything at the same rate. Try monitoring how long it takes to complete various types of assignments. Be willing to speed up or slow down as necessary for comprehension. You'll soon become more flexible and efficient.

A strategy is a combination of techniques. Think about which techniques you used to reach this point in the reading process. If you are not yet proficient at certain techniques, give them more practice.

Phase 3: After Reading

Goal 5:   Check initial recall of relevant information
Techniques: 1. Review the whole assignment by self-testing or answering review questions
           2. To restudy, return to an appropriate *before-reading* or *during-reading technique*

Goal 6:   Organize relevant information for review
Techniques: 1. Underline, make notes, outline, summarize, and/or jot down questions
           2. Look up and learn new terms discovered during reading
           3. Think critically about what you have learned
           4. Apply principles to real-life situations

Goal 7:   Periodically test recall of relevant information
Techniques: 1. Review notes without rereading the text
           2. Predict and answer possible test questions

After Reading

Recall and review strategies are emphasized in the third phase of the reading process Many students think they are finished when they read the last word in an assignment, but the real work of remembering begins only *after reading*.

GOAL 5:   **Check initial recall of relevant information**

By testing your recall of material just read, you can assess specific knowledge gaps and then restudy the material more effectively.

5.1: Review the whole assignment by self-testing or answering review questions. If the author provided review questions, use them to quiz yourself. Try to answer from memory without using the text. If you don't know the answers, you may need to return to one of the techniques from an earlier phase of the reading process to restudy the material. After you have read the assignment in small sections, it is important to review the entire assignment. Otherwise, you may not be able "to see the forest for the trees." Whether you answer review questions in writing or orally, commit yourself to an answer and then find out whether your answer is correct. Don't kid yourself about whether you know the answer. Don't accept even a few wrong answers; expect yourself to do high-quality work.

5.2: To restudy, return to an appropriate *before-reading* or *during-reading technique*. If you can't remember important information, you'll need to study the material again. Think about why you are having difficulty with recall: Was the forgotten information very new to you? Should you read easier material on the topic or use the dictionary before rereading? Did you lose focus on your objectives? Did you read so slowly that you bored yourself? Review the *before-reading* and *during-reading techniques* and choose those that will make your restudying effective.

GOAL 6:   **Organize relevant information for review**

After you reach your goal of recalling the material accurately, the next step is to provide yourself with ways to review the material before the test.

6.1: Underline, make notes, outline, summarize, and/or jot down questions. Depending on your outcome goals, underlining parts of the text, taking separate notes, outlining, summarizing, and writing down questions may be effective ways to prepare to review. Learning to paraphrase the author's words, or translate them into your own words, is an important skill in notetaking and an excellent test of comprehension. You'll remember much more of the material if you have thought about it enough to paraphrase it.

Making it a habit to paraphrase also helps you avoid quoting without proper credit when you write about what you have read. Plagiarism, or taking credit for another's ideas (even if only by failing to credit the source of a paraphrase), is the scholarly equivalent of armed robbery.

6.2: Look up and learn new terms discovered during reading. Learning new words can best be accomplished either before reading (if the word becomes obvious to you during a preview) or after reading. If an unfamiliar word pops up during reading, circle the word, and then continue reading to the end of the paragraph. Unless your comprehension is completely blocked, it's best to keep concentrating on what you are learning. When you have finished reading, you can look up the new word and learn what it contributes to the author's meaning, without having to reread the entire section.

6.3: Think critically about what you have learned. Reconsider the predictions about the material or the judgments about possible bias that you made before reading. Think about your reactions to the ideas you just read. Could your reactions be biased? Were you able to read the information with an open mind? Do you disagree with the author? If so, on what basis? Is your disagreement based on emotion, on experience, or on a scientific rationale that supports your position?

6.4: Apply principles to real-life situations. If you have read about pain, think about how the principles you learned might apply to someone you know who has experienced a critical illness. Also think about the clinical implications of the concepts. Even if you do not have a job in the health fields, you can imagine situations that will help you review the information you gained from your reading.

GOAL 7:   Periodically test recall of relevant information

The notes you make and the thoughts you have after reading should be useful in testing your recall of the material.

7.1: Review notes without rereading the text. If you made marginal notes, use these to review without looking at the content of the textbook or article. Many students review by reading sections of the text over and over. Rereading leads to knowing *where* the right answer is on the page without knowing *what* the right answer is. Your notes should help you review the important information.

7.2: Predict and answer possible test questions. Think about the material in the way you'll have to use it on a test. This is an excellent way to confirm that you remember and can apply concepts you have studied. It is important to be honest with yourself as you use this technique. Don't say to yourself, "Oh, I'll remember that for the test" after you make a mistake. If you didn't remember it this time, you are unlikely to remember it later. A similar temptation is to peek at the paragraph with the right answer and pretend that you remembered the material. Don't fool yourself about what you know.

Consultations

Besides the various techniques discussed above, this book has another special feature. A picture of a key highlights many activities to remind you to look at the section of this book called "Consultations." This section provides answers to these activities with which you can compare your own answers before going on to the next step. A traditional answer key is often viewed as an absolute source of "right" answers. With a process-centered approach such as the one used in this book, right answers are less important than the pursuit of learning goals. You're learning about the process of reading, not just how to give correct answers to the specific questions asked here. Although it may be tempting to use the "Consultations" section to avoid making mistakes, it is more helpful to use it as an opportunity to evaluate your own progress while you are learning to judge the effectiveness of your study strategies.

Remember: Independent learning is crucial to success in your profession!

Because we advise you to look over a selection carefully before you start to read it, you may also want to read all of the process guides for that selection before you begin. In a few cases, activities are marked "Do not peek"; you should not read these until you're ready to do them. Please don't skip around in the activities or do the last ones first. Instead, focus your energy on doing the activities carefully, in the order in which they are presented. The sequence will help you develop the habit of approaching studying as a process. Promise yourself never to look at the Consultations section until you've done your best with each activity.

In a few cases, there really are "right" answers to questions, especially in activities that test your recall of material. At the request of our teacher colleagues, we have placed those answers in the *Instructor's Resource Manual,* which supplements this book.

A health-related topic links the readings in each unit. In addition, the units focus on different aspects of reading comprehension. Through practice and repetition, you will learn the reading skills just described.

The reading selections in this book may be more difficult than those you usually read. Some of these selections are long, and some are technical. All of them are the very same articles or book chapters used by students enrolled in programs leading to degrees in nursing or allied health occupations.

Keep in mind that the purpose of this book is to prepare you for other readings similar to these in complexity and difficulty. Your primary purpose here is not to learn everything about health occupations, pain, ethical and legal issues, and stress. It is to develop a group of skills that will help you become a more effective reader and learner.

A chart covering all three phases of the reading process is presented on the next page. Use it to review the goals and techniques for effective reading and remembering. To achieve each goal, the related techniques must be mastered. You will be given opportunities to learn more about these techniques and to use them as you work your way through the process guides in the units that follow. Each activity is labeled with the goal and technique being demonstrated. Feel free to refer to the chart often to see where you are in the reading and remembering process.

Reading and Remembering: A Three-Phase Process

Phase 1: Before Reading

Goal 1: Get oriented to the text, the author, the assignment, and the scope and organization of the information
Techniques: 1. Preview new materials and assignment
2. Estimate the difficulty of the material, and improve your background knowledge
3. Ask questions or make predictions about the information
4. Look up significant terms that are not defined in the text
5. Check for bias in the author or reader

Goal 2: Develop a study plan
Techniques: 1. Decide which parts of the text relate to objectives
2. Divide the assignment into manageable parts
3. Decide when to work on each part

Phase 2: During Reading

Goal 3: Monitor comprehension and achievement of purpose
Techniques: 1. Look for main ideas, significant details, and paragraph organization
2. Stop periodically to check achievement of outcome goals and to underline main ideas
3. Use alternative strategies or return to an appropriate *before-reading technique*

Goal 4: Monitor reading efficiency
Techniques: 1. Adjust reading rate to purpose for reading and to difficulty of the text
2. Evaluate the efficiency of your study strategies

Phase 3: After Reading

Goal 5: Check initial recall of relevant information
Techniques: 1. Review the whole assignment by self-testing or answering review questions
2. To restudy, return to an appropriate *before-reading* or *during-reading technique*

Goal 6: Organize relevant information for review
Techniques: 1. Underline, make notes, outline, summarize, and/or jot down questions
2. Look up and learn new terms discovered during reading
3. Think critically about what you have learned
4. Apply principles to real-life situations

Goal 7: Periodically test recall of relevant information
Techniques: 1. Review notes without rereading the text
2. Predict and answer possible test questions

unit
2

Orientation to the Health Professions

Phase 1 Before Reading

The two goals of the *before-reading phase* of the reading process are to get oriented to the assigned material and to develop a study plan. In this unit, you will learn the following techniques:

- Previewing an entire textbook
- Previewing chapters and articles
- Dividing long assignments into manageable parts
- Deciding when to work on each part of an assignment

You will most often use these techniques during the first phase of the reading process. However, they may be useful whenever you feel confused about what you are reading, frustrated by difficult material, or overwhelmed by long assignments.

The selections in this unit will help orient you to the health professions. An introductory chapter from a physical therapy textbook gives you an idea of the kinds of issues dealt with in the first chapter of many health occupations textbooks. A journal article that reviews the history of radiological technology for members of the profession allows you to read from the point of view of a colleague rather than that of a student. An essay by a respected journal editor invites you to think about the qualities health professionals will need in the future. Next, a selection from Florence Nightingale's best-known book gives you a chance to view the nursing profession in its infancy. The selection on using an index gives practice in choosing relevant textbooks to satisfy course objectives related to nurses as teachers and their clients as learners. The final selection of this unit consists of a pair of articles about cultural considerations in the health professions.

Selection 2-1　　*Introduction to Physical Therapy*

Purpose for Reading

PROCESS GOAL:　**Get oriented to a new textbook and preview a first assignment**

When you purchase new textbooks for a course, you probably look through them to get an idea of what is waiting for you. By getting an idea of the format and difficulty of a new textbook, you put yourself in a stronger position—better able to understand and respond to the author. The activities for this selection offer some ideas about what to do in your first contact with a textbook. In addition, you'll practice the technique of previewing an assignment in a textbook. Although this particular selection introduces students to physical therapy, introductory chapters are similar in many health occupations textbooks. Frequently, the author defines the profession and reviews its history.

OUTCOME GOAL:　**Answer the review questions at the end of the selection**

You will gain information about the definition and history of physical therapy by answering the review questions. If you have chosen to major in a different health field, you might compare the two professions.

Before Reading 1

Goal:	Get oriented to the text
Technique:	Preview new materials

Imagine you are having your first contact with the textbook *Introduction to Physical Therapy*. In addition to noticing the thickness and weight of the new book, you'll probably flip through it to look for colorful pictures or graphics. Since the whole textbook isn't included here, we'll give you these basic facts about *Introduction to Physical Therapy*. It is a slim 308 pages long (in some health fields, the basic textbook is nearly 2,000 pages long!). It is an attractive, paperbound volume with color photographs of people receiving physical therapy on the cover. There are no color graphics in the text. However, there are many clear, attractive black-and-white graphics and photographs.

There are several other features that you should check out during your first session with a new textbook. These features convey three types of information.

1. Information explaining the book to the reader is found in these features:

   - Title page (one of the first pages of a book, containing the title, author, and publisher)

- Copyright page (follows the title page and contains useful data on the date of publication)
- Introduction (a detailed guide to the book, written by the author)
- Foreword (a short introduction to the book, usually written by another expert in the field)
- Preface (the author's informal statement about the organization of the book)
- Acknowledgements (the author's expression of appreciation to those who helped in the preparation of the book; often included as part of the preface)

2. Information about the author is included in these features:

- Biography of the author (a short piece highlighting the author's qualifications for writing the text; usually located in the front of a textbook)
- Dedication (an offering of the book to someone whom the author loves or respects; located at the front of the book)

3. Organizational and supplementary information is given in these features:

- Table of contents (a listing of chapters and topical headings; located in the front of the book)
- Appendix (supplementary material at the end of the text, including conversion charts, lists of names and addresses, and other useful information)
- Glossary (listing of definitions of specialized terms used in the text; located at the ends of chapters or at the end of the book, usually before the index)
- Index (an alphabetical list of topics in the text with the page numbers on which they are discussed; located at the end of the book)

Look through the selection from *Introduction to Physical Therapy* in order to preview the entire textbook. Locate the following information, stating which features of the text (foreword, dedication, index, etc.) you used in each case. The first item is completed as an example.

1. The nature and scope of organizational and supplementary features
   The text includes an index and a glossary, but it has no appendices. The table of contents lists only chapter titles (it does not include section headings), but each chapter begins with a detailed outline of its contents.
   Features used: *Table of Contents, Glossary, Index, Chapter 1 outline*

2. The author's background, credentials, and family

Features used: _____

3. The organization of the book

Features used: _____

———————————— ⚷ ————————————

———— Before Reading 2 ————

Goal:	Get oriented to the assignment
Technique:	Preview new assignment

Now that you have an idea of how the entire textbook is organized and who the author is, you are in a better position to learn from this book.

Previewing each chapter before you begin to read it can provide you with vital information for understanding and remembering the author's ideas. This previewing involves looking at important elements of the chapter and reading a few paragraphs to get an idea of what the author wants you to know and how that information is organized.

Some of the study aids to consult during a chapter preview are the title, objectives, headings, bulleted items, **bold** or *italic* words, photos, graphs or charts, summary, and review questions. In addition, the introductory and concluding paragraphs are likely to contain important information and should be read carefully.

Page through the first chapter from *Introduction to Physical Therapy*, and put a check mark beside each feature it contains:

_____ Title
_____ Objectives
_____ Key word list or glossary
_____ Headings
_____ Bulleted items (list items introduced with a • instead of a number)
_____ Words in **bold** type
_____ Words in *italic* type
_____ Photos
_____ Graphs or charts
_____ Summary
_____ Review questions

_____ Other features: _____

_____

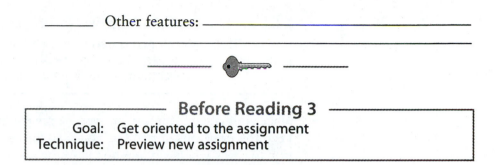

Before Reading 3

> Goal: Get oriented to the assignment
> Technique: Preview new assignment

Comparing the outline at the beginning of the chapter and the review questions at the end can help you determine which parts of the chapter are most important to the author.

Fill in the blanks to indicate which chapter section contains the answer to each review question:

Chapter Outline	Review Question Number
Definition	_____
Physical Therapy as a Profession	_____

Review Questions

1. How does the "definition" of physical therapy differ from the "philosophical statement" as defined and described, respectively, by the APTA?
2. Describe the practice vs profession of physical therapy, and identify the documents that describe each.
3. Define "profession" and apply its five characteristics to physical therapy. Is it a profession?

Don't expect to predict accurately every time; thinking about where you might be able to find the information is what's important at this point.

Before Reading 4

> Goal: Develop a study plan
> Technique: Decide which parts of the text relate to objectives

Did you notice that even though seven pages of the textbook chapter are omitted, you still have the information needed to answer the review questions? It is not always necessary to read a whole chapter in order to identify what is important. Once you have identified the parts of the chapter that relate to the objectives, focus your time and effort on those parts.

Students in the health professions rarely have time to do irrelevant reading because the relevant reading is so extensive! On the other hand, if course objectives are not covered by the textbook, you may have to read other materials to satisfy the objectives.

During Reading 1

Goal:	Monitor comprehension and achievement of purpose
Technique:	Stop periodically to check achievement of outcome goals and to underline main ideas

Since your assignment is to answer the review questions, you will want to keep the questions in mind as you read and stop at the end of each section to check whether a question has been answered in the material you've just read. If so, underline the information that answers the question.

During Reading 2

Goal:	Monitor reading efficiency
Technique:	Evaluate the efficiency of your study strategies

As you pause in your reading to underline material that answers the review questions, take a few seconds to evaluate your reading efficiency. Are you adjusting your reading rate to your ability to understand the material? Are you spending too much time on material that doesn't relate to the review questions? Remember: Always be aware of your reading rate and objectives.

Note how long it takes you to read to find the answers to the three review questions. Jot down the times you start and stop reading, then subtract to find the total time. If you plan to read more than the necessities, try to estimate the time you spend on the essential part: answering the review questions.

Stop time: _____

Start time: _____

Total time: _____

After Reading

Goals:	Check initial recall; organize relevant information for review
Techniques:	Self-test; make notes and underline

Mentally review your answer to each review question. Can you respond in your own words without looking at the book? If not, you need to restudy.

Make marginal notes that indicate where the answers are located in the chapter. Underline relevant details, and add to your marginal notes. Then try again to answer the review questions in your own words, either orally or in writing.

Introduction to Physical Therapy

Michael A. Pagliarulo, EdD, PT
Associate Professor
Department of Physical Therapy
Ithaca College
Ithaca, New York

with 94 illustrations

 Mosby

St. Louis   Baltimore   Boston   Carlsbad   Chicago   Naples   New York   Philadelphia   Portland
London   Madrid   Mexico City   Singapore   Sydney   Tokyo   Toronto   Wiesbaden

⋈ Mosby

Dedicated to Publishing Excellence

Publisher: Don Ladig
Executive Editor: Martha Sasser
Developmental Editor: Kellie F. White
Project Manager: Gayle Morris
Design and Layout: Chad Reidhead
Copyeditor: Linda K. Wendling
Manufacturing Supervisor: Betty Richmond
Cover Design: Kay Kramer

1996 EDITION

Printed in the United States of America
Composition by Wordbench

Mosby-Year Book, Inc.
11830 Westline Industrial Drive
St. Louis, Missouri 63146

International Standard Book Number: 0–8151–6714–8

95 96 97 98 99 / 9 8 7 6 5 4 3 2 1

Dedication

This book is dedicated to my father, Anthony, for his sense of responsibility and work ethic and my mother, Louise, for her complete unselfishness and commitment to our family.

As Italian immigrants to the United States with limited educational backgrounds, they survived the hard times of the Depression and World War II through perseverance and fortitude. I am grateful to their values, sense of pride in achievement, and insistence on advanced education.

Michael A. Pagliarulo

Preface

Physical therapists (PTs) and physical therapist assistants (PTAs) are members of an exciting profession with a proud heritage. As practitioners, we focus on the health needs of the public and maintain high clinical standards, while our academic programs sustain equally high standards to prepare the graduate for patient care. Yet, too frequently, the graduates know little about the evolution of this profession, or about the interdependence of PTs and PTAs, and begin their professional education with a narrow vision of our scope of practice.

Although there exist a variety of outstanding references to address the details of the techniques of practice, there is no comprehensive text at the *introductory* level. This text fills that void. It was designed to present a broad background on the profession and practice of physical therapy for the student beginning a PT or PTA educational program. It also serves students in other health-related programs who are interested in the roles and practices of PTs and PTAs.

The organization of the text is based on a logical approach to the subjects and consists of two components: Part I (Profession) and Part II (Practice). Part I begins with a chapter on the definition and evolution of the profession to serve as a foundation. Succeeding chapters describe the scope of activities and employment settings, the physical therapist assistant, the American Physical Therapy Association, regulations to practice, and concludes with current issues. Part II provides introductory level descriptions of primary practice areas with a somewhat chronological approach. That is, the section opens with a chapter on pediatric physical therapy and continues with chapters on neurological, orthopaedic, and cardiopulmonary physical therapy; these are followed by a chapter on physical therapy for the older adult. The section concludes with a chapter on selected topics not conveniently categorized by systems or chronology.

The beginning of each chapter includes a topical outline and list of key terms to provide the reader with an orientation to the subject. References are cited throughout the text, and suggested readings are briefly described to provide resources for further study. Study questions designed to promote analysis of issues conclude each chapter.

A distinct organizational plan was incorporated into the chapters in Part II to maintain a consistent approach. This includes a general description of the practice area, common clinical conditions, evaluation principles and techniques, and treatment principles and techniques. One or more case studies in each practice area provide a context and example of the evaluation and treatment activities in the given area. In accordance with the purpose of this text, the content of Part II was comprehensive, yet introductory in nature and not intended to provide details of skills for practice.

Other factors were consistent throughout the text. These included a "people first" approach to disabilities (e.g., "individual with cardiac dysfunction" rather than "cardiac patient"), and use of female as primary gender when referring to PTs or PTAs (This is consistent with current and historical distributions.). Every attempt was made to ensure current information (e.g., policies, issues) at the time of printing; however, with a rapidly evolving profession, updates must wait for further editions.

I believe this text will serve a distinct need for a comprehensive and introductory description of the profession and practice of physical therapy. It is a result of teaching an introduction to physical therapy course for over a decade without an adequate reference resource. I look forward to comments and feedback to enhance future editions.

Michael A. Pagliarulo, EdD, PT
Ithaca, New York

Acknowledgements

This text could not have been possible without the input and support of several individuals. This begins with hundreds of students who provided constructive feedback to enhance my teaching and classroom resources. I am grateful to Dr. Charles D. Ciccone, who encouraged me to transform an idea into reality. Each contributor provided an outstanding chapter in the respective content area. Dr. Katherine L. Beissner always provided thorough and helpful consultation in her reviews of the manuscript for the chapter on Physical Therapy for the Older Adult. The photographers, Dewey Neild and Bruce Wang, were sensitive to our needs and professional in their work. Subjects in the photos (patients, family, friends, colleagues, and students) were cooperative and generous with their time. Cheryl A. Tarbell and Debby Burris, who typed the manuscripts, and Bonnie DeSombre, who constructed the graphics, somehow maintained their sanity while providing timely documents. Personnel at Mosby Year-Book, Martha Sasser and Kellie White, were encouraging and informative throughout the project. Linda and Ken Wendling at Wordbench were efficient and creative in editing the manuscript and designing the layout. Finally, I am thankful to my wife, Tricia, and children, Michael, David, and Elisa, who always expressed an interest in and support of the text. They were an inspiration not only to complete this endeavor on time, but to do so with high standards.

Michael A. Pagliarulo, EdD, PT
Ithaca, New York

Table of Contents

CHAPTER 1

PHYSICAL THERAPY: DEFINITION AND DEVELOPMENT

Michael A. Pagliarulo

> "Physical therapy is knowledge. Physical therapy is clinical science. Physical therapy is the reasoned application of science to warm and needing human beings. Or it is nothing."[6]
>
> Helen J. Hislop, PT, FAPTA

Key Terms

American Physical Therapy Association (APTA)
American Physiotherapy Association (APA)
American Women's Physical Therapeutic Association
Division of Special Hospitals and Physical Reconstruction
National Foundation for Infantile Paralysis ("Foundation")
physiatrist
physical therapist
physical therapy
physiotherapists
physiotherapy
practice act
profession
reconstruction aides

DEFINITION
PHYSICAL THERAPY AS A PROFESSION

The profession of **physical therapy** currently enjoys a high demand for its services and an excellent outlook for growth. Although it has become popular and received substantial publicity, confusion remains regarding its unique characteristics. For example, how does physical therapy differ from occupational or chiropractic therapy? This chapter's first purpose, then, must be to present and define this profession.

But to define it thoroughly, it is essential to also present a brief history of the development of physical therapy. A review of the past will demonstrate how the profession has responded to societal needs and gained respect as an essential component of the rehabilitation team. It will also link some current trends and practices with past events.

DEFINITION

Part of the confusion regarding the definition of physical therapy results from the variety of legal definitions which vary from state to state. Each state has the right to define this field and regulate the practice in its jurisdiction. These definitions are commonly included in legislation known as a "Practice Act" which pertains to the specific profession.

To limit this variety, a model definition (Box 1-1) was created by the **American Physical Therapy Association (APTA)** and was recently amended by the Board of Directors of that organization in 1993.[7]

BOX 1-1

Model Definition of Physical Therapy
for State Practice Acts*

Physical therapy, which is the care and services provided by or under the direction and supervision of a physical therapist, includes:

1. Examining and evaluating patients with impairments, functional limitations, and disability or other health-related conditions in order to determine a diagnosis, prognosis, and intervention; examinations include but are not limited to the following:
   - aerobic capacity or endurance
   - anthropometric characteristics
   - arousal, mentation, and cognition
   - assistive, adaptive, supportive and protective devices
   - community or work reintegration
   - cranial nerve integrity
   - environmental, home, or work barriers
   - ergonomics or body mechanics
   - gait and balance
   - integumentary integrity
   - joint integrity and mobility
   - motor function
   - muscle performance
   - neuromotor development and sensory integration
   - orthotic requirements
   - pain
   - posture
   - prosthetic requirements
   - range of motion
   - reflex integrity
   - ventilation, respiration and circulation
   - self care and home management
   - sensory integrity

2. Alleviating impairments and functional limitations by designing, implementing, and modifying therapeutic interventions that include, but are not limited to:
   - therapeutic exercise (including aerobic conditioning)
   - functional training in self care and home management (including activities of daily living and instrumental activities of daily living)
   - functional training in community or work reintegration (including instrumental activities of daily living, work hardening, and work conditioning)
   - manual therapy techniques, including mobilization and manipulation
   - prescription, fabrication, and application of assistive, adaptive, supportive, and protective devices and equipment
   - airway clearance techniques
   - debridement and wound care
   - physical agents and mechanical modalities
   - electrotherapeutic modalities
   - patient-related instruction

3. Preventing injury, impairments, functional limitations, and disability, including the promotion and maintenance of fitness, health, and quality of life in all age populations.

4. Engaging in consultation, education, and research.

*From Model Definition of Physical Therapy for State Practice Acts, BOD 03-95-24-64, Alexandria, VA, 1995, American Physical Therapy Association.

This definition identifies several activities which are inherent in the practice of physical therapy. First and foremost, physical therapy begins with an evaluation to determine the nature and status of the condition. Findings from the evaluation are interpreted to establish the diagnosis, goals, and treatment plan. Treatment is then administered and modified in accordance with the patient's responses. The interventions used are physical and focus on the musculoskeletal, neurological, cardiopulmonary, and integumentary systems. Other activities which are also important for effective practice include: consultation, education, and research. Finally, it should be noted that physical therapists not only provide treatment to reduce physical disability, movement dysfunction, and pain, but also services which prevent these conditions. (See Chapter 2 for a more detailed description of the activities of a physical therapist.)

PHYSICAL THERAPY AS A PROFESSION

The model definition provides a comprehensive description of the *practice* of physical therapy. A companion document addresses the *profession* of physical therapy. This was adopted by the **House of Delegates** (policy-making body) of the APTA in 1983 (Box 1-2).[9]

Two significant features of this Statement which embellish the model definition are that physical therapy is a profession and that it promotes optimal health and function. The latter feature—promotion of optimal health and function—is a goal established with patient/client/family input. Optimal function may meet or exceed the level prior to injury/disease or may be severely diminished as a result of impairment. The former feature of this statement—that physical therapy is a profession—warrants further discussion.

It is generally agreed that a **profession** demonstrates three characteristics: knowledge in a specific area, social value and recognized autonomy.[11] Figure 1-1 indicates that these characteristics are the most valued features of a profession.[8] It also demonstrates that a hierarchy exists with two additional traits possessing lower values. In any case, they are all important to consider.

The first characteristic, a lifetime commitment, may seem formidable, requiring an individual's dedication to the profession. The second, a representative organization, provides standards, regulations, structure, and a vehicle for communication. In physical therapy, this is conducted by the APTA. Specialized education ensures competency to practice. For example, all licensed physical therapists must have a minimum of a four-year baccalaureate degree, and all physical therapist assistants must have an associate degree. The fourth characteristic, service to clients, is obvious in physical therapy. This provides a direct benefit to society. Finally, the last feature, autonomy of judgment, applies regardless of whether or not the therapist practices in a jurisdiction where a physician's referral is required by law. Independent and accurate judgment is inherent in every evaluation, goal, treatment plan, and discharge plan conducted by the physical therapist. This last criterion is frequently used to distinguish a professional from a technician (an individual who requires supervision).

As a profession, physical therapy emulates the criteria listed in Figure 1-1. This was not always true; therefore, the evolution of this profession

Philosophical Statement on Physical Therapy*

Physical therapy is a health profession whose primary purpose is the promotion of optimal human health and function through the application of scientific principles to prevent, identify, assess, correct or alleviate acute or prolonged movement dysfunctions. Physical therapy encompasses areas of specialized competence and includes the development of new principles and applications to more effectively meet existing and emerging health needs. Other professional activities that serve the purpose of physical therapy are research, education, consultation and administration.

*From Philosophical Statement on Physical Therapy (Position), HOD 06-83-03-05, Alexandria, VA, 1983, American Physical Therapy Association.

included significant change and varying degrees of recognition from other professions. The next section provides a brief overview of the history of physical therapy. . . . [Seven pages omitted.]

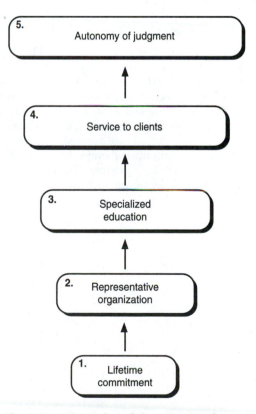

Fig. 1-1. Hierarchy of the criteria of a profession.

References

1. Beard G: Foundations for growth: a review of the first forty years in terms of education, practice, and research. Phys Ther Rev 41(11):843–861, 1961.
2. Davies EJ: The beginning of "modern physiotherapy". Phys Ther 56(1):15–21, 1976.
3. Davies EJ: Infantile paralysis. Phys Ther 56(1):42–49, 1976.
4. Granger FB: The development of physiotherapy. Phys Ther 56(1):13–14, 1976.
5. Hazenhyer IM: A history of the American Physiotherapy Association. Physiotherapy Rev 26(1):3–14, 1946.
6. Hislop HJ: The not-so-impossible dream. Phys Ther 55(10):1069–1080, 1975.
7. Model definition of physical therapy, for state practice acts. BOD 03-95-24-64, Alexandria, VA, 1993, American Physical Therapy Association.
8. Moore WE: The professions: roles and rules, New York, 1970. Russell Sage Foundation.
9. Philosophical statement on physical therapy (position). HOD 06-83-03-05, Alexandria, VA, 1983, American Physical Therapy Association.
10. Pinkston D: Evolution of the practice of physical therapy in the United States. In Scully RM, Barnes ML, editors: Physical Therapy, Philadelphia, 1989, JB Lippincott Company.
11. Purtilo RB, Cassel CK: Ethical dimensions in the health profession, ed 2, Philadelphia, 1993, WB Saunders Company.

SUGGESTED READINGS

American Physical Therapy Association: Healing the generations: a history of physical therapy and the American Physical Therapy Association, Lyme, CT, 1995, Greenwich Publishing Group, Inc. A comprehensive and detailed description of the history and evolution of the profession and practice of physical therapy in the United States.

The beginning: physical therapy and the APTA, Alexandria, VA, 1979, American Physical Therapy Association. An excellent anthology of selected articles which describe the history of physical therapy and the APTA.

Hazenhyer IM: A history of the American Physical Therapy Association: 2. Formative years, 1926–1930, Physiotherapy Rev 26(2):66–74, 1946. This article describes the pertinent issues confronting the profession during this period including first published curriculum and review of educational programs, controversy over technicians vs professionals, legislation to regulate practice, and growth of the journal.

Hazenhyer IM: A history of the American Physical Therapy Association: 3. Coming of age, 1931–1938, Physiotherapy Rev 26(3):122–129, 1946. Continues description of issues in previous article as they evolved during this pre-war period.

Hazenhyer IM: A history of the American Physical Therapy Association: 4. Maturity, 1939–1946, Physiotherapy Rev 26(4):174–184, 1946. In this final article in the series, the author describes issues which involved the membership rights, Chapter organizations, further curricular changes, impact of The National Foundation for Infantile Paralysis, activities in military service, and the journal.

Matthews J: Professionalism in physical therapy. In Matthews J: Practice issues in physical therapy, Thorofore, NJ, 1989, SLACK Incorporated. This chapter is a comprehensive review of aspects which contribute to physical therapy as a profession and physical therapists as professionals.

REVIEW QUESTIONS

1. How does the "definition" of physical therapy differ from the "philosophical statement" as defined and described, respectively, by the APTA?
2. Describe the practice vs profession of physical therapy, and identify the documents that describe each.
3. Define "profession" and apply its five characteristics to physical therapy. Is it a profession?

Glossary

accessory motion: Ability of the joint surfaces to glide, roll, and spin on each other.

acquired immunodeficiency syndrome (AIDS): Diagnosis based on both a positive test for the human immunodeficiency virus (HIV) and the presence of an opportunistic infection or malignancy.

active range of motion (AROM): Ability of the patient to voluntarily move a limb through an arc of movement.

active-assisted ROM: Joint movement in which the patient may be assisted either manually or mechanically through an arc of movement.

active-free ROM: Joint movement in which the patient does not receive any support or resistance through an arc of movement.

active-resisted exercise: Joint movement in which an external force resists the movement.

adaptive equipment/assistive device: Any device that enables an individual to accomplish a functional task with increased ease or independence.

aerobics training: Exercise program that uses oxygen as major energy source.

Affiliate Assembly: Component of the APTA that represents and is comprised of PTAs.

Affiliate Special Interest Group: Past component of the APTA; precursor to Affiliate Assembly.

akinesia: A poverty of movements.

alliance: Collaboration of several health care facilities and practices.

ambulatory center: Any facility in which health care is provided on an outpatient basis; the patient is able to walk into the facility, receive care, and walk out of the facility the same day.

American Board of Physical Therapy Specialities: Unit created by the House of Delegates to provide a formal mechanism for recognizing physical therapists with advanced knowledge, skills, and experience in a special area of practice.

American Physical Therapy Association (APTA): National organization that represents physical therapists in the U.S.A.

American Physiotherapy Association (APA): Organization (formerly called American Women's Physical Therapeutic Association) responsible for maintaining high standards and educational programs for physiotherapists. Precursor to APTA.

American Women's Physical Therapeutic Association: First national organization representing "physical therapeutics." Established in 1921 to maintain high standards and provide a mechanism to share information.

amyotrophic lateral sclerosis (ALS): Also known as "Lou Gehrig's disease"; rapidly progressive neurological disorder associated with a degeneration of the motor nerve cells.

angina: Condition in which chest pain occurs from ischemia.

angiography: Injecting radiopaque material into the blood vessels to better visualize and identify problems such as occlusion (blockage) of blood vessels, aneurysms, and vascular malformations.

angioplasty: The process of mechanically dilating a blood vessel.

annual conference: Yearly (June) meeting of the APTA, held in accordance with the Bylaws, and usually including an extensive program of presentations and activities.

aquatic physical therapy: Therapeutic use of water for rehabilitation or prevention.

arteriosclerosis: Hardening of the arteries.

assembly: Component of APTA whose purpose is to provide a means by which members of the same class may meet, confer, and promote the interest of the respective membership class.

assessment: Measurement or assigned value by which physical therapists make a clinical judgment.

assessment process: In pediatric physical therapy, close monitoring, evaluation and, if indicated, initiation of treatment.

Bad Ragaz method: Aquatic therapy technique using proprioceptive neuromuscular facilitation techniques while the patient is suspended by rings in the water environment.

Index

Selection 2-2   *The Birth of a New Profession*

Purpose for Reading

PROCESS GOAL: **Get oriented to a journal article written primarily for professionals rather than students**

Since students in a field are often required to read articles published in journals (professional magazines) and written for experienced professionals, you will need to be able to cope with the demands of these materials. However, you are likely to need some extra preparation to enable you to read as effectively as the intended audience would be able to do.

OUTCOME GOAL: **Learn about x-ray technology and the people who work with it**

Because the article reviews the history of the profession of radiologic technologist, you will be using techniques for learning history to meet the outcome goal. This article comes from the journal of the American Society of Radiologic Technologists. The journal featured a series of articles about the profession during the 100th anniversary of the discovery of x-rays. The focus of this article is on the early development of the profession; it presents a history lesson about a very popular allied health career.

Before Reading 1

Goal: Get oriented to the assignment
Techniques: Preview new assignment; check for bias in the author

---

To get an overview of the article, make sure that you preview these features:

- Series heading and article title
- Author identification
- Four introductory paragraphs
- Six headings
- Photographs and their captions
- Concluding paragraph

After your preview, you should be able to answer these questions:

1. This article is the _____ of a total of _____ articles in the series. (Use numbers to fill in the blanks.)
2. What is the authors' level of expertise in this topic? Does their presentation seem biased or balanced?

3. What historical period is covered by the *series* of articles? _____

4. Over what time span did "the birth of a new profession" occur? In other words, what period of time is covered by this particular article? _____

5. What changes in the profession can you infer from the photographs?

Before Reading 2

Goal:	Get oriented to the assignment
Technique:	Improve your background knowledge

Ask yourself how well prepared you are to understand this article. Do you know something about the medical use of x-rays? Do you know of a historical event that happened in 1895? In the 1920s, 1930s, 1940s, 1950s, or 1960s?

Although you can get something out of the article without having a lot of background knowledge, you'll get even more if you can relate the new concepts to something you already know. Try the following suggestions to put the evolution of x-ray technology in historical perspective:

1. Skim an encyclopedia article on x-rays, concentrating on the medical/allied health applications. See if you can find a reference to the "birth" of radiologic technology as a profession.

2. Use a reference book or talk with an older family member to identify either a historical event (preferably health-related) or a family milestone for each decade from the 1920s through the 1960s.

3. What are some other inventions that were discovered around 1895?

(*Hint:* A CD-ROM encyclopedia may make it easier to find answers to questions like those above. If you don't have one at home, try the school or public library. Raising and answering questions such as these is an important before-reading technique that you'll use more frequently if it's easy and convenient.)

During Reading 1

> Goals: Monitor comprehension and achievement of purpose; monitor reading efficiency
>
> Techniques: Look for main ideas, significant details, and paragraph organization; adjust reading rate to purpose for reading and difficulty of the text

Think back to how long it took you and the effort you made to locate answers to the review questions in "Introduction to Physical Therapy." Use that experience to plan for this one.

This article may be long enough to divide into two reading sessions— or maybe more, depending on your ability to concentrate on such material and on your available time. Make a plan for how you will read the article—when you'll read it, and how many sections you'll read during each session. It's more useful to plan your reading in terms of meaningful units (like a section) than to plan in terms of numbers of pages. Limiting a reading session to a certain number of pages might result in your breaking off in the middle of a paragraph, thus hurting your comprehension.

Plan to read this article about the birth of the profession of radiologic technology as you would any historical material: Understand the sequence of events, and remember at least one important event per decade.

After Reading 1

> Goal: Check initial recall of relevant information
>
> Techniques: Review the whole assignment by self-testing; restudy if necessary

Can you retell the story of the evolution of the profession of radiologic technology? Does your story include at least one event that happened in each decade between the 1920s and the 1960s? If not, go back to the sections covering the decades you are vague about, and restudy them.

After Reading 2

> Goal: Periodically test recall of relevant information
>
> Technique: Answer possible test questions

Do the events and dates you learned from reading the article help you answer possible test questions? Many of the blanks are to be filled in with a decade (1930s, 1940s, etc.). Try to answer these questions from memory first; look back if you have to, but make yourself a promise to get more useful results next time you read.

1. The need for a special uniform to distinguish x-ray personnel from other hospital workers was suggested in the _____ .

2. In the _____ , the need for training in testing equipment and making minor repairs became apparent.

3. Among the first x-ray operators was _____ , who made many contributions to the development of the profession although she died at age _____ because she failed to take the necessary precautions to prevent her own exposure.

4. By the 1940s, the job duties of the ideal radiologic professional were recognized as so complex and demanding as to suggest that anyone who fulfilled them deserved _____ .

5. The group now known as the American Society of Radiologic Technologists was founded in the _____ , with the assistance of Ed Jerman.

6. By the _____ , radiological professionals were required to receive training that provided both technical expertise and ethical understanding.

7. During the 1920s, various people in physicians' offices performed the job that came to be known as x-ray _____ .

—————— ⚷ ——————

THE BIRTH OF A NEW PROFESSION

From *Radiologic Technology*,
Vol. 66, No. 3 (January/February
1995), pp. 179–183.

Jack Cullinan
Angie Cullinan

Centennial Review is a seven-part series on the history of radiologic technology, commemorating the 100th anniversary of Roentgen's discovery of the x-ray. Series authors **Jack Cullinan**, R.T.(R), FASRT, and **Angie Cullinan**, R.T.(R), FASRT, have been radiologic technologists since the early 1950s. Mr. Cullinan was the clinical and technical support director for Eastman Kodak Company's Health Science Division until his retirement in 1991. Mrs. Cullinan was the program director for the Genesee Hospital School of Radiologic Technology in Rochester, N.Y., until her retirement in 1988. The Cullinans are the authors or coauthors of many articles and six textbooks, the latest of which is the second edition of *Producing Quality Radiographs*. Both have a strong interest in the history of radiologic technology and are collectors of old textbooks, photographs and artifacts.

Today's radiologic technologists are highly educated specialists who play a vital role on the medical team. Our background is in health care and our focus is on the patient.

Our predecessors, however, came from much more diverse backgrounds. Photographers, secretaries, engineers, chemists, physicists and nurses were the first radiologic technologists, paving the path for the diagnostic imaging experts of today.

Our growing status as a profession was reflected by our changing titles through the years. We evolved from "x-ray photographers" to "x-ray operators" to "x-ray technicians" before finally earning the modern title of radiologic technologist.

These shifts in the profession paralleled the increasingly important role of radiology itself, which within a short 100 years transformed itself from a scientific curiosity to a medical necessity.

The First X-ray Operators

Within months of Roentgen's discovery, charlatans and sideshow exhibitors were taking advantage of the public's interest in the new technology.[1] Studios conducting business in "Roentgen photography" sprung up in America and Europe, offering appointments for "small x-ray sittings."[2]

At one London exhibition, two elderly ladies asked the x-ray photographer to close and fasten the door to the x-ray demonstration room. They said they wanted to see each other's bones but asked the photographer not to exposure them below the waistline. A more practical young girl asked the x-ray photographer to look through her young man to see if he was quite healthy in his interior.[3]

Although it continued for years to be used as a form of photographic entertainment, the x-ray also was put to work immediately for diagnostic and therapeutic purposes. Besides photographers, other early operators included physicists, chemists, engineers, electricians, nurses, hospital orderlies, porters and handymen.

In the early 1900s, quite a few resourceful businessmen purchased their own x-ray equipment and opened independent establishments. Physicians would send patients to these x-ray operators for diagnostic and therapeutic services.[4]

During that era, it was acceptable for the x-ray operator to straddle the line between physician and technician, partly because it was believed that x-ray pictures were as simple to interpret as photographs.[5,6(702)] Thus, many owners of x-ray equipment—despite a lack of knowledge of anatomy and pathology—tried to enter the practice of medicine by attempting to interpret Roentgenograms.

Compounding the problem was the willingness of some salesmen to place x-ray equipment in the hands of anyone willing to buy.[7] Despite these doubtful beginnings, the profession and its practitioners soon began to gain respect, largely due to the dedication of pioneers such as Elizabeth Fleischman Ascheim.

Born in 1859, Ascheim was working as a bookkeeper in San Francisco when she first heard about x-rays. Intrigued, she enrolled in a six-month course in electrical science and borrowed money from her father to purchase an x-ray machine, which she installed in the home of her brother-in-law, a physician, in 1897. This likely was one of the first privately-owned x-ray establishments in California.[8(43-49)]

During the Spanish-American War, Ascheim x-rayed ambulatory patients at her lab and nonambulatory patients at the Army Hospital at the Presidio in San Francisco. Ascheim's early efforts were confined to locating bullets and other foreign objects, but later her work became important in determining the extent of bone injuries, including those of the skull.

Ascheim's work was of such quality that she helped overcome the skepticism and fear surrounding x-ray equipment and convinced the military's surgeon-general of the value of x-ray examinations. An example of her remarkable work was published in the 1900 book *The Use of Roentgen Rays in the Medical Department of the U.S. Army in the War with Spain*. (See Fig. 1.)

Ascheim continued to work in her office following the war and, despite warnings, failed to protect herself from radiation. She exposed herself needlessly during experiments and examinations to

Fig. 1. Radiograph of the shoulder made by Elizabeth Fleischman Ascheim during the Spanish-American War. The radiograph, remarkable in its balance of contrast and detail considering the x-ray equipment of the day, reveals a Mauser bullet that had passed through the patient's spine.
From Borden WC. The Use of Roentgen Rays in the Medical Department of the U.S. Army in the War with Spain. Washington, DC: The Government Printing Office; 1900.

assure her patients that the procedure was painless. She suffered serious radiation damage to her hands, eventually dying in 1905 of metastasis to the pleura and lungs.[8(43-49)]

From 'Operators' to 'Technicians'

As the technology gained popularity in the 1910s and '20s, most medical x-ray equipment was operated by the physician, who was his own technician. When one person could no longer handle the job, however, the office receptionist or secretary was recruited to turn the handle of the static machine, pose as a subject, rock the developer pan and so on, until she evolved into what eventually was called the x-ray technician.

In the beginning, the technician was simply a handy person to have around to push the button, with no knowledge of the principles involved.[9] Some believed that anyone familiar with human anatomy should be able to "take x-ray pictures."[10] A physician speaking at a meeting of the American Association of Radiological Technicians in the 1920s stated that a well-trained nurse usually made a much more valuable technician because of her training in ethics. He also believed that women made better technicians than men.

Throughout the 1920s, most radiologic technicians were nurses or young women who had some training in radiologic technique.[11] (See Figs. 2 and 3.) Some believed that technicians who were nurses or who had the advantages of college training were conversant with the fundamental psychology of the sick.[12]

In 1936, the editor of the *X-Ray Technician* was asked in a letter if any distinguishing cap or uniform was available to designate a registered technician. The writer claimed to be often confused with other departmental service personnel.[13] Others, including nurses, suggested that more nurses should enter the profession because the average technician school served only to familiarize students with Roentgen ray terminology and rarely prepared x-ray students to assume positions as qualified technicians. In many instances, technicians were "a friend of a friend of a friend" and, thus, were employed in an office or hospital to learn Roentgen technology by rule of thumb.[14]

Initially, men were not advised to enter the profession due to its poor salaries and female management. However, they began to enter radiography in great numbers after World War I. During the war, the U.S. Army Medical

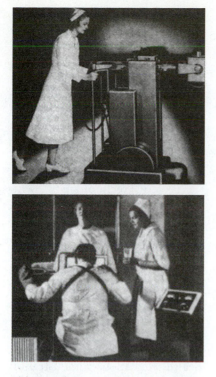

Fig. 2 and Fig. 3. These photos from the 1930s reflect the role of the nurse as an x-ray technician. In Fig. 2 (top) a nurse/technician moves a mobile x-ray unit. In Fig. 3 (bottom) a nurse assists a radiologist during a fluoroscopic study. Note that she is unprotected from radiation.

Both photos from Grigg ERN. The Trail of the Invisible Light. 1964. Reprinted courtesy of Charles C. Thomas Publisher, Springfield, Ill.

School at Camp Greenleaf, Ga., trained inductee assistants in technique, apparatus and patient positioning. These assistants were called "x-ray manipulators"[7] by the Army.

During World War II, women were not admitted into the Army or Navy as x-ray technicians. They could, however, be employed as civilian x-ray technicians in service hospitals. In 1942, an officer's ranking for registered x-ray technicians, similar to registered nurses, was not available because no governmental provisions existed.[15]

More than 400 registered technicians enlisted in the armed services during World War II, and the services trained another 9000. Upon discharge, many veterans sought formal training as x-ray technicians and found employment in the profession in civilian life.[5]

Duties of Early Technicians

In the late 1920s, the x-ray technician in a radiologist's office had a heavy load to bear. She was expected not only to operate the x-ray equipment, but also to answer the telephone and keep the doctor's books. On quiet days, she was responsible for filing, card indexing and cleaning the department—especially the equipment that could not be trusted to a janitor. There were gloves and instruments to sterilize, color photographs to file and classify, and lantern slides to clean. She also was responsible for keeping the radiologist on schedule, keeping him supplied with clean white coats and making sure that his hair, possibly askew from the removal of a lead apron or red goggles, was combed before he confronted a patient.[16]

By the 1940s, some in the profession began to question this unreasonable depiction of the ideal technician. "Outside the Bible, which gives space to a chapter on the perfect woman, I have never seen such a list of characteristics and abilities demanded from one poor human being," wrote Verna Thompson, B.A., R.T., in a 1941 issue of the *X-Ray Technician*.[17]

According to Ms. Thompson, the ideal technician of the era was expected not only to be a scientific expert, but also a hostess, housekeeper, cleaning woman, secretary, file clerk, bookkeeper and telephone operator—and be willing to take the blame for everything that could possibly go wrong. In addition, she was supposed to be clean, neat and orderly; courteous, tactful and sympathetic; loyal to the radiologist, the institution, her fellow technicians and her patients; and as self-effacing as a piece of office furniture. All of this for less than $60 a week!

"If any of you feel that you fill all these requirements, just put your hands up, and we'll give you your wings now. There's no reason why you should have to wait for them until you reach Heaven," Ms. Thompson wrote.[17]

During the profession's early days, the technician also was expected to assemble the x-ray machines and perform routine maintenance. As late as 1929, an hour or two was required daily to check the machine, check the oil level in the transformer, fill the oil cups, clean the brushes, look for and tighten loose connections, check the overhead electrical system and clean and adjust every part carefully. The technician had to be familiar with every part so that if trouble arose, it could be located quickly, eliminating the need for a serviceman and avoiding hours of delay.[18]

In the 1950s, it was suggested that even though many technicians felt incapable of adjusting and repairing x-ray equipment, most breakdowns were sufficiently simple in nature that considerable time and expense could be saved if the technician was able to carry out a few fundamental tests and make minor repairs.[19] These early attempts at quality control might have avoided the situation described in 1956 by an equipment repair manager.[20] One evening, a message came from a hospital located 180 miles from the office of the service company, demanding that a serviceman be sent at once. It was the middle of winter, roads were hazardous, and a large body of water had to be crossed by ferry boat. The serviceman had to spend the night at a motel after making the repairs. The total charges came to $102.70—equal to the weekly paycheck of the average chief technician—just to throw the external line switch.[20]

Early Technician Training

Ed Jerman, pivotal in the 1920 founding of the organization that eventually would become known as the American Society of Radiologic Technologists, was instrumental in developing training programs for the first x-ray technicians. As a representative of medical equipment manufacturers, Jerman witnessed a trial-and-error approach to training while he traveled the country.[21] Thus, when he organized the Jerman Medical Electric Company to supply x-ray equipment to physicians, he took on the responsibility of personally instructing the physicians and their staffs in x-ray technique.[22] He was a pioneer in advocating proper training for technicians and organized the first service department for educational purposes in the commercial field.[23]

When x-ray training schools were formed, formal or theoretical instruction often was second in importance to technique learned on the job. Those in charge of these schools frequently made comments such as "We try to meet the students in class once or twice each week, if the work isn't too heavy and we can find the time"; or "We had to start a school in order to have enough help."[24]

Many x-ray technicians also were trained in areas other than diagnostic radiology, doing double duty as nurses, laboratory technicians or EKG technicians. For many years, x-ray technician training also included assisting with radiation treatments and the localization of radium implants.

Radiation Safety

The first technicians worked in a climate of indifference to radiation protection. They often held difficult patients for each other and in some instances were allowed to perform x-ray exposures on each other.[25] As late as 1943, there were reports of x-ray workers who had not been educated in radiation protection. This class of workers primarily was comprised of self-taught technicians, usually working in small offices or hospitals, more or less on their own. Some were dental assistants who held films in the mouths of their patients and received radiation burns on their hands.[26]

In the 1940s and '50s, it was recommended that x-ray technicians participate in outdoor recreation, with the amount of time spent in the open air proportionate to the amount of time in the x-ray department.[11] In the 1950s, some hospitals required that technicians undergo a complete blood count monthly to monitor their exposure to radiation. For treatment and prevention of anemia, they were required to eat liver at least once a week.

The Transition to Radiologic Technologist

The x-ray technician gradually advanced from a pseudo mechanic-electrician-physicist to a skilled, well-trained medical assistant. By the 1960s, technicians were required to have a well-rounded knowledge of their work and related equipment and an ethical understanding of relationships with patients, physicists, radiologists and management.[5] To this day, however, technologists in rural areas or small hospitals still may be required to perform electrocardiograms, clinical laboratory studies and general office work.[27]

In 1964, Dr. E.R.N. Grigg reported, "It is gratifying to see that x-ray technicians are receiving greater recognition, not only in monetary ways, but also by adequate job designations. In some places, the more deserving are granted academic faculty status. This is all the better; in a scientific team the stature given to each individual should not be determined by his rank but by the degree of responsibility."[6(703)]

A few technologists who achieved this status included Richard Olden, who became technical director at Johns Hopkins Hospital in Baltimore, and John Cahoon, who achieved similar status at Duke University in North Carolina.

Today, radiologic technologists hold associate, baccalaureate, master's and doctorate degrees in health, education, administration and other specialties.

A classic example of success was William A. Williams, who first learned to operate an x-ray machine at the age of 14. He later graduated from Georgia Tech with a bachelor of science degree in engineering and joined the Victor X-Ray Corporation, training under Professor Ed Jerman. He went on to work for Eastman Kodak Company, Picker X-Ray Corporation and Agfa-Ansco. Mr. Williams received the first National Electrical Manufacturers Association award in 1956.[28]

In the early 1960s, when hospitals discoverd that they needed managers as well as technical specialists in their radiology departments, they began to promote radiologic technologists to positions as administrative assistants, radiology managers, business managers and technical specialists. Many chief technologists were promoted into these new positions.

In 1965, former ASRT President Clark Warren, R.T., predicted that radiologists eventually would entrust technical responsibility and technical decisions to quali-

42

fied technical associates. He also expected that this change would occur because younger radiologists, who were without the technical experience of their elders, would have no wish to assume resonsibility for technical operation.[29]

At the 1968 ASRT Annual Conference, Dr. Reynold F. Brown predicted the evolution of x-ray technology into an allied health profession with several categories of professional titles.[30] This began to occur in the early 1970s, when specialists with business degrees took over management of many radiology departments in conjunction with a technical manager, usually the chief technologist, who once again assumed more technical responsibilities. Many large institutions now have a support team that includes QA technologists, medical physicists and highly trained, certified technologists. The specialized categories of technologist envisioned by Dr. Brown in 1968 have become a reality.

References

1. Dewing SB. *Modern Radiology in Historical Perspective.* Springfield, Ill: Charles C Thomas; 1962:83.
2. Fuchs AW. Evolution of Roentgen film. *AJR.* 1956;74:30–47.
3. Glasser O. *William Conrad Röntgen and the Early History of the Roentgen Rays.* Springfield, Ill: Charles C Thomas; 1934:45.
4. Trostler IS. Agency in law as it applies to nurses and technicians and their relations to physicians. *The X-Ray Technician.* 1936;8:76–78.
5. Greene AB. The American Registry of X-Ray Technicians: Twenty-two years of achievement. *Radiol Technol.* 1989;60:543–545. (Reprinted from *The X-Ray Technician,* November 1945).
6. Grigg ERN. *The Trail of the Invisible Light.* Springfield, Ill: Charles C Thomas; 1964.
7. Klawon MM. Present facilities for collegiate education in schools for x-ray technicians. *The X-Ray Technician.* 1956;27:313–321.
8. Brown P. *American Martyrs to Science Through the Roentgen Rays.* London, England: Bailliére, Tindall & Cox; 1936.
9. Bell ME. Science and art in Roentgenography. *The X-Ray Technician.* 1948;20:146–148.
10. Brecher R, Brecher E. *The Rays.* Baltimore, MD: Williams and Wilkins Company; 1969:103.
11. Cushway BC. The ethical relationship of the x-ray technician. *The X-Ray Technician.* 1929;1:29–32.
12. Williams KE. Psychology applied in the x-ray room. *The X-Ray Technician.* 1929;1:47–50.
13. From out around. *The X-Ray Technician.* 1936;7:133.
14. Graham D, Dreher AC. *The Nurse-Technician.* New York State Council of Roentgen Ray Technicians Inc: 1945:17.
15. Women technicians not admitted in the armed forces. *The X-Ray Technician.* 1942;13:269.
16. Allen KDA. The ideal x-ray technician. *The X-Ray Technician.* 1951;23:72–83.
17. Thompson V. The code of the x-ray technician. *The X-Ray Technician.* 1941;12:205–210.
18. Kretzmann AC. The effect of minor detail on good radiography. *The X-Ray Technician.* 1930;1:73–74.
19. Olden RA. Preventive maintenance. *The X-Ray Technician.* 1950;21:280–283.
20. DePriest HJ. What to do before calling the serviceman. *The X-Ray Technician.* 1957;28:236–240.
21. Widger JI. Is excellence still respectable? *Radiol Technol.* 1970;41:219–230.
22. Idstrom LG. New images in radiology. *Radiol Technol.* 1976;47:357–363.
23. In memoriam. *The X-Ray Technician.* 1936;8:83.
24. Anger MA. Educational progress in radiologic technology during the past twenty-five years. *The X-Ray Technician.* 1956;28:72–91.
25. White EW. The complete technologist. *Radiol Technol.* 1967;39:138–146.
26. Chaussee M. Why x-ray technicians should know the safety factors. *The X-Ray Technician.* 1943;14:194–195.
27. Basart JA. Rural radiologic health care, Nebraska style. *Radiol Technol.* 1975;46:452–456.
28. Who's who in ASXT. *The X-Ray Technician.* 1956;28:25.
29. Warren CR. Changing concepts in chiaroscuro. *Radiol Technol.* 1965;36:218–228.
30. Brown RF. Goals for radiologic technology and alternative means of achievement. *Radiol Technol.* 1969;40:381–384.

Selection 2-3   *Blessed Are the Flexible . . .*

Purpose for Reading

PROCESS GOAL: **Get oriented to the text and the author**

This essay is one of a collection of writings by Leah Curtin, the editor of the journal *Nursing Management*. The foreword to the book of essays, written by well-known nursing author Margretta Madden Styles, is included to help you reach the process goal. For Styles, Curtin's writing is a source of amusement and education.

OUTCOME GOAL: **Learn about an important (and entertaining) author**

Since you, like Styles, would probably be reading this essay for personal rather than course-related goals, your outcome goal will be to learn a few bits of new information while enjoying yourself. Curtin's topic is flexibility, which she sees as the essential quality nurses need in adapting to unending change.

Before Reading 1

         Goal: Get oriented to the author
Technique: Improve your background knowledge

Read Styles's foreword to get an idea of Curtin's position in the nursing profession.

Before Reading 2

         Goal: Get oriented to the text
Technique: Preview new assignment

Preview the article by doing the following:

- Look at the title and headings.
- Read the introductory material that comes between the title and the first heading.
- If you see a list, determine the topic of the list without reading each item carefully. (Usually, the sentence in the text just before a list tells you what the list is about.)
- Read the last couple of paragraphs to get an idea of the author's conclusion.

Don't take more than a minute or so to complete your preview; you need only a brief time to get oriented to the author's ideas.

Before Reading 3

         Goal: Get oriented to the text
Technique: Make predictions about the information

Previewing means that you haven't read the whole essay, but you have read some headings and a few paragraphs. In this essay, you probably noticed some of these words and phrases: *flexible, change, manager, good old days, (1905) Rules for Nurses,* and *change agent.*

Make a guess about what Curtin's main point, or thesis, is. Don't worry about what you haven't read; concentrate on what you did glean from your preview.

Write one sentence that captures Curtin's main point.

_____

_____

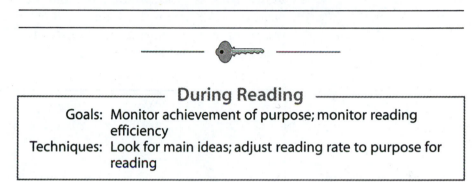

During Reading

Goals:	Monitor achievement of purpose; monitor reading efficiency
Techniques:	Look for main ideas; adjust reading rate to purpose for reading

Your purpose for reading this essay is to inform and entertain yourself. Since you'll be asked to list three or four issues from the essay, to explain the title, and to recall two or three amusing points, it won't be necessary to look for details while you read. Plan your reading so that you read as efficiently as you can to achieve these outcomes.

After Reading 1

Goal:	Check initial recall of relevant information
Technique:	Review the assignment by self-testing

List three or four issues in nursing history that you didn't know before.

Why do you think Curtin titled her essay "Blessed Are the Flexible . . ."?

List two or three points in the article that amused you.

After Reading 2

Goal: Organize relevant information for review
Technique: Look up and learn new terms discovered during
           reading

Did you encounter any unfamiliar words in the article? Now is a good time to look them up. If you don't already know any of the following words (that is, you couldn't use the word comfortably in speech or writing), take time to look the word up in a collegiate dictionary. Use the dictionary to learn about the word's etymology (history) and the meaning of its parts.

	Word Meaning	Prefix, Meaning	Root, Meaning	Suffix, Meaning
accommodate				
innovator				
incredulous				
obsolete				
gyroscope				
dictum				
status quo				
interventions				

FOREWORD

Leah Curtin's pen just gets better and better.

When I am too busy to keep up with the professional literature, I steal time to read her editorials and articles. And when I vow to cut down my journal subscriptions, as I do periodically, *Nursing Management* reigns at the top of the protected list. Why? Because I know for sure I will find a gem of information on some breaking development and a point of view I need to know. And I will be amused to boot. Moreover, I never want to discard what I have read. So what could be better than a collection of Curtin's writings?

Leah is a prolific author. The selections in *Nursing into the 21st Century* cover a wide range of topics from practice and leadership to health care reform and restructuring. But Leah is no dilettante skimming the surface of a vast pond. Nor is she solely a gadfly pricking the professional conscience and then flitting off in search of another target. And, although she has the uncanny ability to point out the crux of a situation, she is more than an analyst and commentator. Leah Curtin is a seminal thinker. She is a source of new ideas. She plants new seeds in the field of ethics, which nursing and all of the health professions would do well to cultivate.

Leah may be best known to nurse managers, who have clung to her words of wit and wisdom for years. She deserves and is receiving a wider audience, because she has an important message for all who are caught up in the delivery and politics of health care. For those of us who are her followers, this compendium will serve as a ready source of refreshment. For others, it is a good introduction to a national treasure, to a fine writer, pundit, and sage.

Margretta Madden Styles

Leah Curtin

Earlier in this century, when the architect Frank Lloyd Wright was at the peak of his profession, he designed and built a cluster of office buildings around a central green. When the construction was complete, the landscape crew asked him where he wanted to place the sidewalks. He responded, "Don't put in any sidewalks just yet. Plant grass solidly between the buildings, and we'll know where to put them soon enough." The buildings were rented and as people moved in and out and all about, paths of trodden grass laced the lawns between the buildings. These paths turned into gentle curves and were sized according to traffic flow. When Mr. Wright saw them, he said, "Pave the paths." Not only were the paths graceful, but they also responded directly to users' needs. *He adapted changes to the natural patterns of the people affected by them.*

Perhaps the greatest problem in the days ahead will not be AIDS or aging or healthcare reform. It probably will be the acceptance of change *as a way of life.* And the key to successfully managing change just might lie in Frank Lloyd Wright's approach to it: *accommodate the natural pattern of those affected by it.*

Change as Torture?

In 1532, Machiavelli wrote, "There is nothing more difficult to take in hand, more perilous to conduct, or more uncertain in its success, than to take the lead in the introduction of a new order of things. . . . The innovator makes enemies of all those who prospered under the old order, and only lukewarm support is forthcoming from those who would prosper under the new . . . because men are generally incredulous, never really trusting new things unless they have tested them in experience."

Actually, Machiavelli *understates* the difficulties you face in introducing change. Even those who have not prospered under the old ways of doing things want to cling to the familiar! Almost 30 years ago a Canadian neurosurgeon conducted some experiments that revealed the intensity of this problem: when people are forced to change viewpoints, the brain undergoes a series of changes that are biochemically similar to those experienced by individuals who are being tortured. Is it any wonder that people resist change, *particularly when it is forced?*

Even Winston Churchill, one of the most daring men in the 20th century, said, "When it is not necessary to change, it is necessary not to change." He wanted to conserve what had proved effective in the past; he was prepared to strike out in new directions only if the old ways had to be abandoned.

The Manager's Role . . .

And what is a problem for the individual becomes a problem for the organization. We recently polled a sampling of *Nursing Management*'s readership and every response had to do with effecting change, managing change, overcoming resistance to change and surviving change. As one nurse manager put it, "When I go to bed at night, I don't know whether or not my job will have become obsolete by morning. Change is a daily thing with us."

Between our reluctant departure from the womb (resisting change from the start!) to our equally reluctant departure for the tomb, we live under a pro tem set up that is constantly shifting—like a ship at sea. And, like an ocean liner, we need a gyroscope—an instrument *that adjusts the ship to the natural rhythm of the sea and the rise and fall of the winds*—to keep us on an even keel. The manager's role, *i.e.*, to be a gyroscope, maintaining balance and perspective, adapting changes to suit the pace and personalities of staff whenever possible. That is, like a ship, the organization has a goal, but it will not reach its goal unless *it adjusts to the natural patterns of* the personnel who are the organization. Just as the organization expects employees to be flexible, so it also must be flexible.

The Good Old Days . . . ?

Years ago, as a student of philosophy, I was "led down the garden path" by an ancient Greek by the name of Heraclitus who said: "What is, is. And what is not, is not." That seemed an eminently reasonable dictum to me, until Heraclitus' inexorable logic continued: "Therefore, what is always was and always will be, and what is not never was and never will be." Slowly, step by step, he led me to what was to become his most famous and most often quoted "law", i.e., "The only constant is change." Your institution is going to change. Your job is going to change. The people around you are going to change; your environment, your tools of living, your community is going to change. Society, culture and technology are going to change. (And I might add, while thumbing my nose at Heraclitus, *not* always for the better.)

Not, let me hasten to add, that I am against change. When I find myself longing for the "good old days," I read over a list of "Rules for Nurses" posted in 1905 by a hospital in the northeast:

1. Nurses will fill lamps, clean chimneys and trim wicks.
2. Each nurse will fetch a bucket of water for scrubbing and a scuttle of coal to stoke the fire before beginning her rounds.
3. Each nurse is to record her observations carefully and legibly. She must make her pens carefully, and she may whittle nibs to her individual taste.
4. The nurses will be given one evening off each week for courting purposes, or two evenings if they go to church regularly and the superintendent of nurses gives her approval.
5. After 13 hours of work, the nurses should spend their remaining time reading the Bible and other good books.
6. Every nurse should lay aside from her pay each week a goodly sum of her earnings for her declining years so that she will not become a burden on society.
7. The nurse who has performed her duties faithfully and without fault for five years will be given an increase of $.05 per day in her pay, providing the hospital's situation permits.

I do not know about you, but reading that list makes the thought of change warm the cockles of my heart.

The Nurse As Change Agent

Regardless of how individual nurses may react to change, by the very definition of their role, nurses are change agents. That is, a nurse is brought into a situation precisely because the patient's *status quo* is not acceptable. As perceived by the patient, the role of the nurse is to bring about a desired change.

49

Moreover, it is through observation and analysis that the nurse is expected to bring about that change.

Ultimately, what really counts is your ability to understand how you relate to the change process—be you staff nurse or manager. Over 100 years ago, Florence Nightingale said: "What the nurse has to do is to put the patient in the best frame possible for nature to act upon him." To determine what needs to be done, how quickly it can be done, what constitutes "the best frame possible," and who (patient or nurse) ought to do what are matters for critical analysis. Over 30 years ago, Hildegard E. Peplau (who was proclaimed a *living legend* by the American Academy of Nursing last fall) suggested just how/when this analysis is done: "The nurse is a participant observer in most relationships in nursing. This requires that she use herself as an instrument and as an object of observation at the same time that she is participating in the interaction between herself and a patient or a group. The more precise the nurse can become in the use of herself as an instrument for observation, the more she will be able to observe in relation to performances in the nursing process."

Only on the basis of such critical self-examination can clinical nurses be effective "gyroscopes" for patients, matching interventions with the patients' natural patterns. And only on such a basis can nurse managers be effective "gyroscopes" for the organization, matching change with the natural pattern of patient, staff and institution.

Blessed are the *flexible*, for they shall *change* the earth!

March 1995

Selection 2-4   *Chattering Hopes and Advices*

Purpose for Reading

PROCESS GOALS: **Estimate difficulty of the material, and improve background knowledge; make predictions about the information**

The process goals for this selection will extend the orientation techniques you have been practicing. Leah Curtin's essay refers to Florence Nightingale as the founder of modern nursing. Now you will have a chance to meet Miss Nightingale as an author. "Chattering Hopes and Advices" is a chapter from her book *Notes on Nursing,* which was originally published in England in 1859 and appeared in the United States in 1860. It will give you a look at a writing style and a perspective that come from a different era and another country.

OUTCOME GOAL: **Contrast current nursing practice with Florence Nightingale's perspective on patient care**

Although some aspects of patient care have changed dramatically over the last 140 years or so, many have remained the same. Nursing students are often assigned to read some or all of *Notes on Nursing* to help them develop an appreciation for the changes—and unchanging principles—in caring for the sick.

Before Reading 1

Goal: Get oriented to the text
Technique: Preview new materials

Glance through the selection quickly to see what it looks like, how the pages are laid out, and how challenging the author's language seems to be.

Before Reading 2

Goal: Get oriented to the text and the author
Technique: Improve your background knowledge; make predictions about the information

---

There aren't any pictures. The headings are in the margin and are often several lines long. The footnotes run on and on. Yet you still need to understand this selection. Don't panic! You might even be inspired if you get yourself ready to read it. To prepare yourself, find out something about the author and the time in which she wrote. Use the headings in the chapter to raise questions or make guesses about the author's ideas.

Recall what you already know about Florence Nightingale; then do some background reading. Consider using an easy, accessible source such as an encyclopedia article or even a child's biography of Nightingale.

When you have adequate background knowledge about Florence Nightingale, you should be able to answer these questions:

1. When was Florence Nightingale born? _____ How old was she when she died? _____
2. When and where did the Crimean War take place? What was Nightingale's role in it?

3. What are Nightingale's major contributions to the development of nursing?

4. Label each event as happening BN (before Nightingale was born), DN (during her lifetime), or AN (after her death):

_____ Invention of the hot air balloon

_____ Declaration of Independence

_____ U.S. statehood for Alaska

_____ First flight by the Wright brothers at Kitty Hawk

_____ First associate degree programs in nursing

_____ U.S. Civil War

Before Reading 3

Goal: Get oriented to the text
Techniques: Ask questions about the information; look up significant terms that are not defined in the text

Asking questions about the author's organization of the material is an important technique for getting oriented. Headings and subheadings can be of great help in focusing on the organization. To prepare to read assignments that "look" difficult, provide yourself with a good map, or outline, of the author's ideas before you begin to read. Jot down the headings in order, and then think about the author's plan, which caused the ideas to be presented in this order.

Some marginal headings from Nightingale's chapter are listed below. Look through the chapter to fill in the blanks with the missing marginal headings. Note that two of the headings are indented here to show their lower level of importance, which is signaled by the fact that they accompany footnotes in the selection.

XII. CHATTERING HOPES AND ADVICES
   Advising the sick.

_____

Patient does not want to talk of himself.

         Absurd statistical comparisons . . . (This heading
         accompanies the footnote that begins on p. 58)

_____

Wonderful presumption of the advisers of the sick

Advisers the same now as two hundred years ago.

_____

_____

         Two new classes of patients peculiar to this generation.

To prove to yourself that you have a good idea of the topic of each heading, try paraphrasing each one; that is, translate Nightingale's words into your own. Write your paraphrase below each heading.

If some of the headings are hard to understand or paraphrase, you may need to employ one or both of these strategies:

1. Read a few words of the text near the heading. If they don't make the meaning clear, skim through the whole section, looking for clues to the author's meaning.
2. Use the dictionary to look up any words you don't understand in the marginal headings or in the text you read or skimmed while trying to get the meaning of the headings.

Before Reading 4

Goal:	Develop a study plan
Techniques:	Divide the assignment into manageable parts; decide when to work on each part

---

As you have seen, there are eight main headings in this chapter. For most students, reading this material will be more difficult and slower than reading most textbook assignments. Decide how many sections you can read in your first session; then use that estimate to plan your reading of the rest of the chapter.

During Reading

Goal:	Monitor comprehension
Techniques:	Look for main ideas, significant details, and paragraph organization; use alternative strategies

---

If an unfamiliar word pops up during your reading, circle the word and try to finish the section (or at least the paragraph) in which it occurs. If you can't even make sense of the sentence without the definition, stop and use the dictionary. However, if you can get a reasonable sense of the meaning, don't interrupt your reading. Wait until the end of the section to go to the dictionary. But don't forget to go back to clarify the meaning of the sentences in which circled words occur.

You'll need a clear understanding of what Nightingale has to say about each of the headings in this chapter. If you encounter a difficult sentence, try isolating the core sentence (subject, verb, completers), and then adding the modifiers for complete understanding.

Footnotes are a particular challenge in writings from Nightingale's era. Today, writers are encouraged to put all the important information in the text, leaving footnotes for references and sidelights. In the nineteenth century, many writers used footnotes to communicate important ideas via a less formal channel than the main text. It is known that Nightingale put some of her most strongly held beliefs in her footnotes, so don't skip them. When to read footnotes is a matter of personal preference. Some readers go directly to the bottom of the page when they see an asterisk; others finish the main sentence before reading a footnote. Many fail to see the footnote indicator and get totally confused as they read from the main text into the footnote. If that happens, look back in the main text to find the asterisk, so that you are clear about what ideas go together.

After Reading 1

Goal:	Check initial recall of relevant information
Technique:	Review the whole assignment by self-testing

Look back at the list of marginal headings you made for this selection. Can you add clarifying comments for each one? If you cannot remember anything from a particular heading, glance back at the text to discover the main idea.

After Reading 2

Goal:	Organize relevant information for review
Technique:	Learn new terms discovered during reading

Here are ten words that Nightingale used to express her ideas in "Chattering Hopes and Advices." Try using each in a sentence of your own.

1. extant

2. bane

3. cursory

4. seraphic

5. *viva voce*

6. obstinately

7. benevolent

8. lachrymose

9. vegetate

10. pluck (noun)

After Reading 3

Goal: Organize relevant information for review
Technique: Think critically about what you have learned

What do you think of Nightingale's opinions about what to do and what not to do when visiting the sick? To clarify your thoughts, write a paragraph in which you (1) indicate your general reaction (positive or negative) to the ideas in the chapter, (2) list specific examples of Nightingale's dos and don'ts that determined your general reaction, and (3) indicate any other reactions you had to particular parts of Nightingale's chapter.

Florence Nightingale

Advising the sick.

The sick man to his advisers.

"My advisers! Their name is legion. Somehow or other, it seems a provision of the universal destinies, that every man, woman, and child should consider him, her, or itself privileged especially to advise me. Why? That is precisely what I want to know." And this is what I have to say to them. I have been advised to go to every place extant in and out of England—to take every kind of exercise by every kind of cart, carriage—yes, and even swing (!) and dumb-bell (!) in existence; to imbibe every different kind of stimulus that ever has been invented. And this when those *best* fitted to know, viz., medical men, after long and close attendance, had declared any journey out of the question, had prohibited any kind of motion whatever, had closely laid down the diet and drink. What would my advisers say, were they the medical attendants, and I the patient left their advice, and took the casual adviser's? But the singularity in Legion's mind is this: it never occurs to him that everybody else is doing the same thing, and that I the patient *must* perforce say, in sheer self-defence, like Rosalind, "I could not do with all."

Chattering hopes the bane of the sick.

"Chattering Hopes" may seem an odd heading. But I really believe there is scarcely a greater worry which invalids have to endure than the incurable hopes of their friends. There is no one practice against which I can speak more strongly from actual personal experience, wide and long, of its effects during sickness observed both upon others and upon myself. I would appeal most seriously to all friends, visitors, and attendants of the sick to leave off this practice of attempting to "cheer" the sick by making light of their danger and by exaggerating their probabilities of recovery.

Far more now than formerly does the medical attendant tell the truth to the sick who are really desirous to hear it about their own state.

How intense is the folly, then, to say the least of it, of the friend, be he even a medical man, who thinks that his opinion, given after a cursory observation, will weigh with the patient, against the opinion of the medical attendant, given, perhaps, after years of observation, after using every help to diagnosis afforded by the stethoscope, the examination of pulse, tongue, &c.; and certainly after much more observation than the friend can possibly have had.

Supposing the patient to be possessed of common sense,—how can the "favourable" opinion, if it is to be called an opinion at all, of the casual visitor "cheer" him,—when different from that of the experienced attendant? Unquestionably the latter may, and often does, turn out to be wrong. But which is most likely to be wrong?

Patient does not want to talk of himself.

The fact is, that the patient* is not "cheered" at all by these well-meaning, most tiresome friends. On the contrary, he is depressed and wearied. If, on the

Absurd statistical comparisons made in common conversation by the most sensible people for the benefit of the sick.

*There are, of course, cases, as in first confinements, when an assurance from the doctor or experienced nurse to the frightened suffering woman that there is nothing unusual in her case, that she has nothing to fear but a few hours' pain, may cheer her most effectually. This is advice of quite another order. It is the advice of experience to utter inexperience. But the advice we have been referring to is the advice of inexperience to bitter experience; and, in general, amounts to

one hand, he exerts himself to tell each successive member of this too numerous conspiracy, whose name is legion, why he does not think as they do,—in what respect he is worse,—what symptoms exist that they know nothing of,—he is fatigued instead of "cheered," and his attention is fixed upon himself. In general, patients who are really ill, do not want to talk about themselves. Hypochondriacs do, but again I say we are not on the subject of hypochondriacs.

Absurd consolations put forth for the benefit of the sick.

If, on the other hand, and which is much more frequently the case, the patient says nothing, but the Shakespearian "Oh!" "Ah!" "Go to!" and "In good sooth!" in order to escape from the conversation about himself the sooner, he is depressed by want of sympathy. He feels isolated in the midst of friends. He feels what a convenience it would be, if there were any single person to whom he could speak simply and openly, without pulling the string upon himself of this shower-bath of silly hopes and encouragements; to whom he could express his wishes and directions without that person persisting in saying, "I hope that it will please God yet to give you twenty years," or, "You have a long life of activity before you." How often we see at the end of biographies or of cases recorded in medical papers, "after a long illness A. died rather suddenly," or, "unexpectedly both to himself and to others." "Unexpectedly" to others, perhaps, who did not see, because they did not look; but by no means "unexpectedly to himself," as I feel entitled to believe, both from the internal evidence in such stories, and from watching similar cases; there was every reason to expect that A. would die, and he knew it; but he found it useless to insist upon his own knowledge to his friends.

In these remarks I am alluding neither to acute cases which terminate rapidly nor to "nervous" cases.

By the first much interest in their own danger is very rarely felt. In writings of fiction, whether novels or biographies, these death-beds are generally depicted as almost seraphic in lucidity of intelligence. Sadly large has been my experience in death-beds, and I can only say that I have seldom or never seen such. Indifference, excepting with regard to bodily suffering, or to some duty the dying man desires to perform, is the far more usual state.

The "nervous case," on the other hand, delights in figuring to himself and others a fictitious danger.

But the long chronic case, who knows too well himself, and who has been told by his physician that he will never enter active life again, who feels that every month he has to give up something he could do the month before—oh! spare such sufferers your chattering hopes. You do not know how you worry and weary them. Such real sufferers cannot bear to talk of themselves, still less to hope for what they cannot at all expect.

So also as to all the advice showered so profusely upon such sick, to leave off some occupation, to try some other doctor, some other house, climate, pill,

---

nothing more than this, that *you* think *I* shall recover from consumption because somebody knows somebody somewhere who has recovered from fever.

I have heard a doctor condemned whose patient did not, alas! recover, because another doctor's patient of a *different* sex, of a *different* age, recovered from a *different* disease, in a *different* place. Yes, this is really true. If people who make these comparisons did but know (only they do not care to know), the care and preciseness with which such comparisons require to be made, (and are made,) in order to be of any value whatever, they would spare their tongues. In comparing the deaths of one hospital with those of another, any statistics are justly considered absolutely valueless which do not give the ages, the sexes, and the diseases of all the cases. It does not seem necessary to mention this. It does not seem necessary to say that there can be no comparison between old men with dropsies and young women with consumptions. Yet the cleverest men and the cleverest women are often heard making such comparisons, ignoring entirely sex, age, disease, place—in fact, *all* the conditions essential to the question. It is the merest *gossip*.

---

powder, or specific; I say nothing of the inconsistency—for these advisers are sure to be the same persons who exhorted the sick man not to believe his own doctor's prognostics, because "doctors are always mistaken," but to believe some other doctor, because "this doctor is always right." Sure also are these advisers to be the persons to bring the sick man fresh occupation, while exhorting him to leave his own.

Wonderful presumption of the advisers of the sick.

Wonderful is the face with which friends, lay and medical, will come in and worry the patient with recommendations to do something or other, having just as little knowledge as to its being feasible, or even safe for him, as if they were to recommend a man to take exercise, not knowing he had broken his leg. What would the friend say, if *he* were the medical attendant, and if the patient, because some *other* friend had come in, because somebody, anybody, nobody, had recommended something, anything, nothing, were to disregard *his* orders, and take that other body's recommendation? But people never think of this.

Advisers the same now as two hundred years ago.

A celebrated historical personage has related the commonplaces which, when on the eve of executing a remarkable resolution, were showered in nearly the same words by every one around successively for a period of six months. To these the personage states that it was found least trouble always to reply the same thing, viz., that it could not be supposed that such a resolution had been taken without sufficient previous consideration. To patients enduring every day for years from every friend or acquaintance, either by letter or *viva voce,* some torment of this kind, I would suggest the same answer. It would indeed be spared, if such friends and acquaintances would but consider for one moment, that it is probable the patient has heard such advice at least fifty times before, and that, had it been practicable, it would have been practised long ago. But of such consideration there appears to be no chance. Strange, though true, that people should be just the same in these things as they were a few hundred years ago!

To me these commonplaces, leaving their smear upon the cheerful, single-hearted, constant devotion to duty, which is so often seen in the decline of such sufferers, recall the slimy trail left by the snail on the sunny southern garden-wall loaded with fruit.

Mockery of the advice given to sick.

No mockery in the world is so hollow as the advice showered upon the sick. It is of no use for the sick to say anything, for what the adviser wants is, *not* to know the truth about the state of the patient, but to turn whatever the sick may say to the support of his own argument, set forth, it must be repeated, without any inquiry whatever into the patient's real condition. "But it would be impertinent or indecent in me to make such an inquiry," says the adviser. True; and how much more impertinent is it to give your advice when you can know nothing about the truth, and admit you could not inquire into it.

To nurses I say—these are the visitors who do your patient harm. When you hear him told:—1. That he has nothing the matter with him, and that he wants cheering. 2. That he is committing suicide, and that he wants preventing. 3. That he is the tool of somebody who makes use of him for a purpose. 4. That he will listen to nobody, but is obstinately bent upon his own way; and 5. That he ought to be called to a sense of duty, and is flying in the face of Providence;—then know that your patient is receiving all the injury that he can receive from a visitor.

How little the real sufferings of illness are known or understood. How little does any one in good health fancy him or even *her*self into the life of a sick person.

Means of giving pleasure to the sick.

Do, you who are about the sick or who visit the sick, try and give them pleasure, remember to tell them what will do so. How often in such visits the sick person has to do the whole conversation, exerting his own imagination and memory, while you would take the visitor, absorbed in his own anxieties,

60

making no effort of memory or imagination, for the sick person. "Oh! my dear, I have so much to think of, I really quite forgot to tell him that; besides, I thought he would know it," says the visitor to another friend. How could "he know it"? Depend upon it, the people who say this are really those who have little "to think of." There are many burthened with business who always manage to keep a pigeon-hole in their minds, full of things to tell the "invalid."

I do not say, don't tell him your anxieties—I believe it is good for him and good for you too; but if you tell him what is anxious, surely you can remember to tell him what is pleasant too.

A sick person does so enjoy hearing good news:—for instance, of a love and courtship, while in progress to a good ending. If you tell him only when the marriage takes place, he loses half the pleasure, which God knows he has little enough of; and ten to one but you have told him of some love-making with a bad ending.

A sick person also intensely enjoys hearing of any *material* good, any positive or practical success of the right. He has so much of books and fiction, of principles, and precepts, and theories; do, instead of advising him with advice he has heard at least fifty times before, tell him of one benevolent act which has really succeeded practically,—it is like a day's health to him.*

You have no idea what the craving of sick with undiminished power of thinking, but little power of doing, is to hear of good practical action, when they can no longer partake in it.

Do observe these things with the sick. Do remember how their life is to them disappointed and incomplete. You see them lying there with miserable disappointments, from which they can have no escape but death, and you can't remember to tell them of what would give them so much pleasure, or at least an hour's variety.

They don't want you to be lachrymose and whining with them, they like you to be fresh and active and interested, but they cannot bear absence of mind, and they are so tired of the advice and preaching they receive from everybody, no matter whom it is, they see.

There is no better society than babies and sick people for one another. Of course you must manage this so that neither shall suffer from it, which is perfectly possible. If you think the "air of the sick room" bad for the baby, why it is bad for the invalid too, and, therefore, you will of course correct it for both. It freshens up a sick person's whole mental atmosphere to see "the baby." And a very young child, if unspoiled, will generally adapt itself wonderfully to the ways of a sick person, if the time they spend together is not too long.

If you knew how unreasonably sick people suffer from reasonable causes of distress, you would take more pains about all these things. An infant laid upon the sick bed will do the sick person, thus suffering, more good than all your logic. A piece of good news will do the same. Perhaps you are afraid of "disturbing" him. You say there is no comfort for his present cause of affliction. It is perfectly reasonable. The distinction is this, if he is obliged to act, do not "disturb" him with another subject of thought just yet; help him to do what he wants to do; but, if he *has* done this, or if nothing *can* be done, then "disturb" him by all means. You will relieve, more effectually, unreasonable suffering from reasonable causes by telling him "the news," showing him "the

---

*A small pet animal is often an excellent companion for the sick, for long chronic cases especially. A pet bird in a cage is sometimes the only pleasure of an invalid confined for years to the same room. If he can feed and clean the animal himself, he ought always to be encouraged to do so.

baby," or giving him something new to think of or to look at than by all the logic in the world.

It has been very justly said that the sick are like children in this, that there is no *proportion* in events to them. Now it is your business as their visitor to restore this right proportion for them—to show them what the rest of the world is doing. How can they find it out otherwise? You will find them far more open to conviction than children in this. And you will find that their unreasonable intensity of suffering from unkindness, from want of sympathy, &c., will disappear with their freshened interest in the big world's events. But then you must be able to give them real interests, not gossip.

Two new classes of patients peculiar to this generation.

NOTE.—There are two classes of patients which are unfortunately becoming more common every day, especially among women of the richer orders, to whom all these remarks are preeminently inapplicable. 1. Those who make health an excuse for doing nothing, and at the same time allege that the being able to do nothing is their only grief. 2. Those who have brought upon themselves ill-health by over pursuit of amusement, which they and their friends have most unhappily called intellectual activity. I scarcely know a greater injury that can be inflicted than the advice too often given to the first class to "vegetate"—or than the admiration too often bestowed on the latter class for "pluck."

Selection 2-5   *Using an Index*

Purpose for Reading

PROCESS GOALS: **Get oriented; develop a study plan**

These process goals are familiar ones for the *before-reading phase*, but the materials will be new. You will be looking at the indexes from several textbooks used by beginning students in nursing, though you will not actually be reading the textbooks. You will be searching the indexes for the topic "patient teaching," which is often covered in introductory nursing courses because teaching clients and their families is an important responsibility of nurses.

OUTCOME GOAL: **Choose the most useful textbooks to master course objectives**

In many allied health programs, especially in nursing, students work with syllabi that indicate course objectives but do not list specific pages to read or textbooks to use. Students are expected to make these decisions and be responsible for the results.

> ―――――――――――― **Before Reading 1** ――――――――――――
>
> | | Goal: | Get oriented to the assignment |
> | Technique: | Preview new assignment |

Learning to use course objectives effectively is an important step in improving the efficiency of your studying. Course objectives tell what you need to know to complete a course successfully; they define the relevant information.

The following is a list of course objectives relating to teaching clients. Read through the list to understand the scope of the assignment.

- Identify the significance of the nurse's role as a health teacher.

- Give examples of these three types of learning: cognitive, psychomotor, and affective.

- Recognize certain principles of learning and the effect of each on health teaching.

- Identify external factors affecting the teaching/learning process.

- Describe four major steps in the teaching process.

- Recall relevant factors to be considered in the assessment of a patient's learning needs.

- Write appropriate learning objectives for specific situations.

- Apply various teaching methods in patient care situations.

- Recognize the appropriate use of teaching aids.

- Select methods of evaluating the teaching/learning process.

- Identify the influences of cultural diversity on the teaching plan.

Before Reading 2

Goal:	Get oriented to the scope and organization of the information
Technique:	Ask questions about the information

Before you can scan an index effectively, you must have in mind terms or phrases for which you want to search. Even if an index doesn't list "patient teaching," it might contain useful information listed under a related topic. You need to be flexible when searching an index.

List three other terms or phrases that you might use to search for information related to "patient teaching" (*Hint:* think of synonyms for "patient" and for "teaching"):

1. _____

2. _____

3. _____

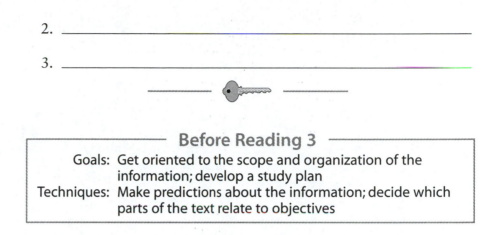

—— **Before Reading 3** ——

Goals: Get oriented to the scope and organization of the information; develop a study plan
Techniques: Make predictions about the information; decide which parts of the text relate to objectives

Scan the index pages to locate relevant material. Decide which textbooks provide information to address each course objective listed in Before Reading 1. For each course objective, write the first author's name and page numbers (for example, Craven, 33) of the textbook where relevant information *seems* to be found. Feel free to make guesses; there's time to correct mistaken impressions about content later.

—— **Before Reading 4** ——

Goal: Develop a study plan
Technique: Decide when to work on each part

Now that you have matched the course objectives to information in the textbooks, decide which sources are most important to read.

Use numbers (1, 2, 3, . . .) to indicate the order in which you'll read the sources. Explain why you ranked each source as you did and why you may have decided to omit a source.

_____ R. Craven & C. Hirnle. *Fundamentals of nursing* (2nd ed.).
Explain:

_____ S. Lewis, I. Collier, & M. Heitkemper. *Medical-surgical nursing* (5th ed.).
Explain:

_____ J. Needham, *Gerontological nursing.*
Explain:

_____ L. Sims, D. D'Amico, J. Stiesmeyer, & J. Webster. *Health assessment in nursing.*
Explain:

_____ J. Smith-Temple & J. Johnson. *Nurses' guide to clinical procedures* (2nd ed.).
Explain:

—————— ⚷ ——————

S. Lewis, I. Collier, M. Heitkemper

J. Needham

L. Sims, D. D'Amico
J. Stiesmeyer, J. Webster

*J. Smith-Temple
J. Johnson*

Selection 2-6   *Cultural Considerations*

Purpose for Reading

PROCESS GOAL: **Develop a study plan for a two-part assignment**

There are two articles in this selection, both of which come from the same issue of *Imprint,* the journal of the National Student Nurses' Association. Both deal with health care for specific ethnic groups, a critical issue for the health professions today, as both clients and care-givers represent increasingly diverse populations.

OUTCOME GOAL: **Read both articles, looking for similarities and differences between the two client populations**

Articles like these are often assigned to prepare students for discussions of important issues concerning working directly with patients. These articles relate to course objectives on client teaching in transcultural settings.

> ───────── **Before Reading 1** ─────────
> Goals: Get oriented; develop a study plan
> Techniques: Preview new materials; decide when to work on each part

When you have more than one selection to read, your first task is to decide which article you will read first. Both must be read to complete the assignment of preparing for a class discussion of similarities and differences in the health considerations for two culturally diverse groups. Consider some of the following questions as you decide where to start:

- Which article looks most interesting to you?
- Which article looks easiest to understand?
- Does either article offer a method of organization or analysis that could be applied to the other?

Look through both articles to answer these questions and to pick up any other information that will help you decide where to start.

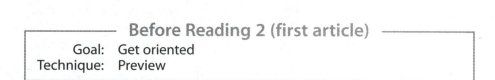

> ───────── **Before Reading 2 (first article)** ─────────
> Goal: Get oriented
> Technique: Preview

Once you have chosen the article you'll read first, preview it extensively in order to get a clear idea of the author's organization of the material.

Before you begin to actually read, either underline or make notes on separate paper so as to develop a tentative outline of the author's main points.

During Reading 1 (first article)
Goal: Monitor achievement of purpose
Technique: Look for main ideas, significant details, and paragraph organization
---

Read the first article to complete the tentative outline you developed during the preview. Keep in mind that your goal is to find points of similarity and difference in the health care advice given in the two articles.

After Reading 1 (first article)
Goal: Organize relevant information for review
Technique: Make notes

Underline or add notes to your outline to provide yourself with a thorough guide to the author's ideas. Don't forget that you have another article to read, so budget your time accordingly.

Before Reading 3 (second article)
Goal: Get oriented
Techniques: Preview new materials; improve your background knowledge; ask questions about the information
---

Preview the second article thoroughly, looking specifically for points at which the two authors deal with similar information. If you think it would be helpful to use an encyclopedia or atlas before reading about unfamiliar cultures, take the time now—it will improve your comprehension later!

Write out a tentative outline of the author's ideas in this before-reading phase.

During Reading 2 (second article)
Goal: Monitor achievement of purpose
Technique: Look for main ideas, significant details, and paragraph organization
---

Read the second article, giving it as much attention as you gave the first. Take time to absorb new concepts before jumping to conclusions about similarities or differences between the two articles.

After Reading 2 (second article)
Goal: Organize relevant information for review
Technique: Make notes

Take time to complete your notemaking on the second article. Again, remember to give this author's ideas your full attention before moving on to the comparison/contrast stage.

After Reading 3

Goal: Organize relevant information for review
Technique: Think critically about what you have learned

Review both sets of your notes, looking for similarities and differences between the two groups. Make a third set of notes, which include observations and questions that you can't answer for yourself.

After Reading 4

Goal: Test recall of relevant information
Technique: Answer possible test questions

When you have prepared yourself as well as you can, use your notes to respond to the following questions, which might be raised in a discussion of the two articles. Of course, you may look back at the actual articles. Without having annotated the articles or made separate notes, you will have a much slower response time than will students who really made the ideas their own.

1. What is a "culturally competent nurse," according to Douglas? Do you think Louie would agree with that definition? Why?

2. Douglas includes three examples of cross-cultural differences that might cause misunderstandings between African-American clients and majority-culture health care providers. Explain each one.

3. One culturally related risk factor clearly affects the health of many African-Americans. Explain.

4. List four significant health issues for the African-American population, and indicate the health care response proposed by Douglas.

5. List four significant health issues for Asian-Americans and Pacific Islanders as a group. Where possible, indicate the health care response proposed by Louie.

6. List six different subgroups within the AAPI group, and indicate a distinguishing health problem for each subgroup.

7. What are some similarities in nursing interventions to provide culturally appropriate care, as suggested by Douglas and Louie?

8. What are some differences in the two authors' approaches to nursing interventions for the two groups? What's your explanation for the differences?

9. Does socioeconomic status affect the health status of African-Americans and Asian-American/Pacific Islanders equally, according to the two authors?

10. Do you have any questions, based on your reading of the two articles? What are they?

CULTURAL CONSIDERATIONS FOR THE AFRICAN-AMERICAN POPULATION

From *NSNA/Imprint*, November/ December 1995, pp. 57–59.

Charlene Y. Douglas, PhD, RN

The decade of the 90's will perhaps be best known as the decade of cultural awareness, following unprecedented demographic shifts in the United States.[1]

While the African-American population is currently the largest ethnic group in the United States, by the year 2010 the Hispanic population will outnumber African-Americans and, with their current 100% increase every decade, Asians will become a more prominent piece of the demographic picture in this country.

Any crosscultural interaction can result in misinterpretations and misjudgments. The health care system of one culture interacting with a population from another is an important example of a cross-cultural interaction. Nurses are in the front-line of this daily interaction, and their preparation to be culturally competent, that is, able to function effectively across cultures, is crucial to their role as advocates for their clients.[2]

A culturally competent nurse: 1) acknowledges and appreciates cultural differences and how they affect the caring process of nursing and 2) makes a genuine effort to understand clients' behavior within their cultural context. Like psychosocial, managerial and technical skills, cultural competence has become a cornerstone of quality nursing practice, vital to every nurse, not just those practicing in coastal or urban areas. Becoming culturally competent is a developmental process born of a commitment to provide quality care to all and a willingness to risk.[3]

> The word culture "implies the integrated patterns of human behavior that includes thoughts, communication, action, customs, beliefs, values and institutions of racial, ethnic, religious, or social groups." These values, beliefs, norms and life practices are borne out of patterns of social interactions, religious practices, historical context, and geographic region of origin.

African-Americans are often the most acculturated of the diverse populations in the United States; that is, they have assumed many of the traits of the mainstream culture. This acculturation increases with education level and employment where contact with the mainstream culture is consistent and parallel. Many members of diverse populations are bicultural; that is, they are able to function effectively in mainstream society, while holding onto manifestations of their own culture.[4]

The word culture "implies the integrated patterns of human behavior that includes thoughts, communication, action, customs, beliefs, values and institutions of racial, ethnic, religious, or social groups.[5]" These values, beliefs, norms and life practices are borne out of patterns of social interactions, religious practices, historical context, and geographic region of origin.

The meeting of cultures in the health care system is exemplified by an African-American client with a nurse from the majority culture. Both bring culturally-prescribed patterns of communication and problem-solving, and both may bring distinct feelings about helping or being helped by someone who is different. They also bring to the nurse-client relationship the history of the relationship between their groups.[6]

The use of first names in the clinical setting, and the issue of eye-contact provide good examples of misjudgments and misrepresentations that may result due to crosscultural differences.

Nurses often use adult and elderly client's first names in an attempt to appear friendly and approachable. In my view this is poor clinical practice for anyone, not to mention a sign of disrespect. Moreover, for African-Americans, this practice is laden with a history of racism and humiliation. There was a time not too long ago when African-Americans would only be addressed by their first names or derogatory synonyms such as "boy" or "gal."

Becoming culturally competent includes being sensitive to cultural differences and changing a behavior which is offensive to another, although it may seem harmless.

What is said during a nurse-client interaction is important, but never as powerful as nonverbal communication. In any given communication exchange, only 7% of the message conveyed is verbal, 38% is vocal and 55% is facial. Body language and vocal intonation will always betray true motivation. Disdain, condescension and contempt are instantly conveyed without a word being spoken. Understanding and appreciation of the power of nonverbal communication is even more important in a cultural context that is already susceptible to misunderstanding.[7]

For many African-American youths, maintaining eye contact when speaking to someone is a learned skill. As an adolescent working for the first time, I was informed that not maintaining eye contact would be misunderstood. It would be assumed that one felt subservient, afraid or embarrassed if eye contact was not maintained during a verbal exchange.

In general, when the client's behavior is incongruent with the nurse's own behavior, it is important for the nurse to ask "What does the client's behavior signify in his or her cultural context?" This will be helpful to the nurse in avoiding an inaccurate assessment of a client from a different cultural group.[8]

When hospital visits are limited to family only, the role of the extended family in the African-American community can cause conflict with the nursing staff. Many nurses consider the nuclear configuration of mother, father and child as the complete family. However, extended family plays a major role in all ethnic minority communities. A client's definition of family will include the nuclear family, as well as those members who provide instrumental support (e.g., child care, care of the elderly, money) and emotional support (e.g., counseling and advice).[9] An aunt or cousin can be intimately involved in the structure and function of a family system that is strong enough to ward against the stresses of poverty and discrimination.

Though in absolute numbers, more whites live in poverty than do African-Americans, nearly a third of the African-American population (compared to 11% of whites) live below the poverty line. In the United States, race is often used as a marker for poverty in terms of health outcomes.

> **Without regard to race or culture, the death rate for those earning less than $9,000 per year is three to seven times higher than for those earning more than $25,000 per year.**

Without regard to race or culture, the death rate for those earning less than $9,000 per year is three to seven times higher than for those earning more than $25,000 per year. This is due in part to lack of access to health care and the definitions of what constitutes illness. For the poor, illness may not be attended to until it reaches advanced stages. Primary prevention and early treatment remain a challenge to the health care system.[10]

While the incidence rates for some cancers, heart disease and stroke are lower for African-Americans than for whites, age-adjusted death rates remain as much as 40% higher.[11]

One risk factor for cancer and heart disease that can be attributed directly to cultural influences is diet.[12] Prior to World War II, 75% of the African-American population lived in the south.[13] Southern diet, including high-fat diets with fried meats and vegetables flavored with pork, has been handed down for generations, and many diseases resulting from this diet may not develop for twenty to forty years.

Culturally diverse populations are also becoming geographically diverse, so much so, that if you are reading this article, you have probably been involved in the care of someone from a cultural background different from your own. Cultural sensitivity and competence is a choice. As stated in Cross et al., "The first task in developing cross-cultural skills is to acknowledge cultural differences and to become aware of how they affect the helping process."[14]

Nurses starting their careers are often very concerned about making mistakes. A safe, point of practice is to treat all clients with the same respect and compassion that you would like shown to your own family members.

Aside from cultural considerations, there are specific health issues that impact the African-American community.

The infant mortality rate of any population is an indicator of that population's access to and utilization of health care. Approximately 18 of every 1,000 African-American babies born die within the first year of life, and 12.5 percent had low birth weight ($\leq$ 2.5 kg.). These rates are nearly double the rates for white births, a disparity that has existed for forty years. The key to closing this gap, and lowering the infant mortality rate for the entire nation, is to encourage all expectant mothers to enter prenatal care early, and maintain a consistent pattern of care.[15]

Nursing students are not in a position to fund prenatal programs or make them more accessible. However, when developing

78

health education programs for expectant African-American mothers, students should stress the importance of early and regular prenatal care in preventing a low birth-weight delivery and protecting against infant mortality.

Acquired immune deficiency syndrome (AIDS) has had a significant impact on the African-American community. Women are now the fastest growing group at risk for AIDS, and this is especially true for women of color. The mode of transmission is primarily heterosexual contact with infected men (IV drug use is a major source of infection in this male population).[16]

Health education programs focused on any aspect of sexual contact (birth control, STD control) must include, in addition to abstinence, a discussion of the correct and consistent use of latex condoms as protection against the AIDS virus. Because of the heterosexual nature of the spread, latex condoms must be correctly used during every sexual contact, even when another form of birth control is in use.

In addition to contributing to the spread of AIDS, substance abuse has had a negative and far-reaching impact on ethnic communities, and communities as a whole in this nation when alcohol is factored in as a drug of abuse. Because alcohol, marijuana and other drugs of abuse have become epidemic by adolescence, intervention strategies should begin in elementary school. Community-based prevention programs that involve the church and other significant community leaders will have a far-reaching effect.

Nurses who present health education programs to clergy on the effect of chemical dependence on the human body and strategies for how churches can become involved in prevention, intervention and treatment refer-

ral efforts will have gained a very important point of entry into a large segment of the African-American community.[17]

Hypertension is a major risk factor for heart disease, stroke and end-stage renal damage. African-Americans experience excess mortality compared with whites as a result of the high level of hypertension found in this community. Traditionally, screening for high blood pressure has been a part of many African-American church programs. In many protestant denominations, lay members of the church provide first aid and may form a "Nurse Guild." Teaching these lay church members the proper techniques for taking blood pressure, and parameters for referral with the names of community health care agencies is an effective strategy for surveillance and referral for cases of hypertension.[18]

> **Culturally diverse populations are also becoming geographically diverse, so much so, that if you are reading this article, you have probably been involved in the care of someone from a cultural background different from your own.**

Culturally sensitive, well developed and well placed (eg, in the church) health education efforts will make the greatest strides in closing the disparity in the health outcomes between African-Americans and whites. Early and consistent prenatal care, the effective management of hypertension, the prevention of substance abuse and the prevention of the spread of the AIDS virus are important goals that will significantly

improve the health outcomes of the entire nation, and begin the process of closing the gap between the health outcomes of different ethnic groups.

The author is commonwealth associate professor, George Mason University College of Nursing & Health Science, Fairfax, VA.

REFERENCES

1. Isaacs, M.R. and Benjamin, M.P. *Towards a Culturally Competent System of Care, Vol. II.* Washington, D.C., National Institute of Mental Health, 1991, p. 5.
2. Cross, T.L., Bazron, B.J., Dennis, K.W. and Isaacs, M.R. *Towards a Culturally Competent System of Care, Vol. I.* Washington, D.C., National Institute of Mental Health, 1989, p. 13 and 20.
3. Cross, T.L., Bazron, B.J., Dennis, K.W. and Isaacs, M.R. *Towards a Culturally Competent System of Care, Vol. I.* Washington, D.C., National Institute of Mental Health, 1989, p. 21.
4. Locke, D.C. *Increasing Multicultural Understanding.* Newbury Park, California, Sage, 1992, p. 6.
5. Cross, T.L., Bazron, B.J., Dennis, K.W. and Isaacs, M.R. *Towards a Culturally Competent System of Care, Vol. I.* Washington, D.C., National Institute of Mental Health, 1989, p. 13.
6. Cross, T.L., Bazron, B.J., Dennis, K.W. and Isaacs, M.R. *Towards a Culturally Competent System of Care, Vol. I.* Washington, D.C., National Institute of Mental Health, 1989, p. 20.
7. Locke, D.C. *Increasing Multicultural Understanding.* Newbury Park, California, Sage, 1992, p. 8.
8. Cross, T.L., Bazron, B.J., Dennis, K.W. and Isaacs, M.R. *Towards a Culturally Competent System of Care, Vol. I.* Washington, D.C., National Institute of Mental Health, 1989, p. 34.
9. Paniagua, F.A. *Assessing and Treating Culturally Diverse Clients.* Thousand Oaks, California, Sage, 1994, p. 14.
10. Cassetta, R.A. RNs work against cultural barriers to improve

health care access. *The American Nurse* 25:8:p. 14, Sept. 1993.

11. U.S. D.H.H.S., U.S. Public Health Service. *Healthy People 2000.* Washington, D.C., Government Printing Office, DHHS Publication No. DHS 91-50213, 1991, p. 418.

12. U.S. D.H.H.S., U.S. Public Health Service. *Healthy People 2000.* Washington, D.C., Government Printing Office, DHHS Publication No. DHS 91-50213, 1991, p. 392–395.

13. Locke, D.C. *Increasing Multicultural Understanding.* Newbury Park, California, Sage, 1992, p. 15.

14. Cross, T.L., Bazron, B.J., Dennis, K.W. and Isaacs, M.R. *Towards a Culturally Competent System of Care, Vol. I.* Washington, D.C., National Institute of Mental Health, 1989, p. 32.

15. Braithwaite, R.L. and Taylor, S.E. (eds.). *Health Issues in the Black Community.* Jossey-Bass Publishers, San Francisco, California, 1992, p. 39.

16. *Op. Cit.,* p. 39.

17. *Op. Cit.,* p. 43.

18. *Op. Cit.,* p. 96.

CULTURAL CONSIDERATIONS: ASIAN-AMERICANS AND PACIFIC ISLANDERS

From *NSNA/Imprint*, November/ December 1995, pp. 41—45.

Kem B. Louie, PhD, RN, CS, FAAN

The classifications of five racial/ethnic groups are defined by the Office of Management and Budget.[1] Asian-American and Pacific Islanders comprise one of the five groups identified. The term "Asian-Americans" refers to those of Asian descent who are citizens or permanent residents of the United States. The 1990 Census designations of Asian-Americans include, but are not limited to, approximately 23 subgroups: Asian-Indian, Cambodian, Chinese, Filipino, Hmong, Japanese, Korean, Laotian, Thai or Vietnamese, or they may become classified as "other Asian." Pacific Islanders refer to many different populations ranging from the indigenous Hawai'ians (preferred spelling among people of Hawai'i); Chamorros, the indigenous people of the Mariana Islands (including the island of Guam); American Samoans and the native peoples of the many islands in the Pacific Ocean. As defined, this broad racial/ethnic group represents many cultures, religions and languages.

The population of Asian-Americans has grown considerably. Between 1960 and 1970, this growth has increased 75.3 percent. This increase reflects the reclassification of Asian-Indians from white to Asian-American.[2] Between 1970 and 1980, the rate of increase was 127.5 percent and between 1980 and 1990, the Asian-Americans and Pacific Islanders increased 108 percent.

In 1990, this population was 7.3 million.[3] Presently, Asian-Americans comprise 3 percent of the U.S. population and is projected to increase to 11 percent by the year 2050.[4] Chen and Hawks reported that this unprecedented growth in a single U.S. Bureau of the Census designation was unusually rapid and unanticipated.[5]

The largest percentage of increase in population of AAPIs occurred in the following five states: Rhode Island, New Hampshire, Georgia, Wisconsin, and Minnesota. Yet, the largest number of Asian-Americans continue to reside on the West and East coasts.

In 1985, a landmark document identified the health status of minority groups, including AAPIs. The 1985 Secretary's "Task Force Report on Black and Minority Health" concluded that, as a group, "the Asian/Pacific Islander population in the United States is at lower risk of early death than the white population.[6]" Since these conclusions were published, newer findings on the health status of AAPIs reveal an even poorer profile. For example, Chen and Hawks reported that the mortality rates for AAPIs with lung cancer and possibly cardiovascular disease will probably exceed those of other U.S. racial groups in the next 20 years. Such findings may be due to the inadequacies of the data that have been collected on this heterogeneous group.

Specifically, there has been misclassification, paucity, and lack of ethnic specificity in the data.[7]

HEALTH STATUS PROFILE OF AAPIs

A survey of the prevalence of male smoking in California revealed that Asian-American and Pacific Islander smoking rates exceed the total male California smoking rate.[8]

Cancer is the second leading cause of death for AAPIs. In Hawai'i, incidence rates are among the highest for thyroid cancer. This disease is also found to have the highest rates for Chinese men and Filipino women.[9]

- Filipinos have the lowest survival rates for kidney and renal cancers. The Chinese have the highest incidence of nasopharyngeal cancer and the lowest survival rates for leukemia, as well as the highest incidence of liver cancer and the highest liver cancer mortality.[10]
- Hepatitis B prevalence rates are the highest among AAPIs, higher than for any other racial or ethnic group. It is estimated that 8–15 percent of Asian, African, and Pacific Islander populations are chronically infected with hepatitis compared to less than 2 percent of the total population.[11]
- It is reported that AAPIs' risk of tuberculosis is highest (17 percent) of all racial or

81

ethnic groups and 9.9 times greater than nonHispanic whites.[12]

- Parasitic infestations disproportionally affect Southeast Asian refugees. Of all the malaria in the United States, 45 percent occurs among Southeast Asians.[13]
- There are genetic, maternal, and child health care services that need special attention. These disorders include hemoglobin E, alpha-thalassemia-1, beta thalassemia and G-6PD deficiency.[14] Studies have shown a high prevalence of sudden infant death syndrome (SIDS). In a survey conducted in California, researchers found that among 62 Chinese SIDS cases (1.3 per 1000) SIDS was approximately 38 times more likely to occur in Chinese in California than Chinese in Hong Kong.[15]
- Sudden unexpected nocturnal death syndrome (SUNDS) has also been found to be high. It has been reported that many young Southeast Asian males die unexpectedly. Stress and depression have been suspected risk factors.[16]
- Stress and post-traumatic stress syndrome, particularly among the Southeast Asian refugees, have been documented. The Cambodian refugees now in the United States are recent survivors of mass violence and torture.

SELECTED ETHNIC/ CULTURAL GROUPS

Southeast Asian Refugees

The refugees from Southeast Asia represent the countries of Vietnam, Cambodia, and Laos. There is tremendous diversity among these groups in relation to language, education, and health care beliefs. The diversity of languages and dialects may necessitate having a number of different translators available.

The religious beliefs include Buddhism, Confucianism and Taoism. Some are animists (who believe that things animate and inanimate possess an innate soul) and supernaturalist who believe in demons and spirits. There are also refugees who are Catholics.

Beliefs about health and illness are strongly influenced by religion. In general, good health is regarded as a state of physical and spiritual harmony. Like other AAPI groups, Southeast Asian refugees believe health results from a balance between the forces of Yin (male, positive energy, lightness) and Yang (female, negative energy and darkness). Disease can be produced by an excess of one force over another. For example, diarrhea is thought to be a cold illness that must be treated with hot foods or medicines. This is referred to as beliefs in the hot and cold theory of illnesses.

Health problems are generally defined in terms of physical symptoms and medical care is thought to provide relief of symptoms. Descriptions of these symptoms may not be translated correctly if interpreters and health care providers do not understand certain cultural subtleties. For example, among some refugees, some complain of "feeling hot," which means that they are not feeling well or may have a disease considered to be a "hot illness."[17]

Among refugees from Southeast Asia, where illness is considered an imbalance of forces, the health care practices of Cao gio (Vietnamese) or kos khyal (Cambodian) mean "to scratch or rub the wind." This involves massaging the skin with a lubricant and then rubbing it with a coin in symmetrical patterns until fever results. This treatment is commonly applied to the neck, back, chest and arms, and is thought to bring the toxic "wind" to the surface of the body. Other treatments or cures among southeast Asian refugees include pinching the skin (bat gio), inhalation of herbal steam while the body is wrapped in heavy blankets, applications of balms and oils, medicinal herbs, and massages.

The most common diseases among Southeast Asian refugees are tuberculosis, parasitic infections and hepatitis B. Most refugees have not been immunized as children and attempts at immunizations are made in resettlement camps.

Vietnamese

The Vietnamese comprise eight percent of the AAPI population. In a study conducted by Filiozof et al., Vietnamese immigrants' perceptions of important health problems and services were identified.[18] One hundred-twenty households were sampled. The health problems reported included dental (82 percent), eye (57 percent) and high blood pressure (56 percent). In relation to needed health care services, prenatal care (68 percent), family planning (52 percent), and alcohol prevention (46 percent) ranked high. Ninety-three percent of the sample identified language as a barrier to accessing health care and more than 50 percent identified transportation problems as a barrier.

Chinese

Within the category of Asian-Americans, the Chinese currently comprise 24 percent of the AAPI category, the largest proportion of AAPIs. Chinese-Americans have important differences based upon generational status with first generation Chinese (born in Asia) and those subsequent generations born and raised here in this country. The differences among Chinese-Americans are based on:

1. place of origin, e.g., China vs. Taiwan
2. language/dialect, e.g., Mandarin vs. Cantonese
3. political allegiances in Asia
4. whether first-generation immigrant or American-born
5. place of birth, e.g., U.S. or Asia
6. degree of acculturation

Reports on the health status of AAPIs have stated that the Chinese have been observed to be disproportionally affected by tuberculosis.[19] The most common ethnically-related risk factor that affects the Chinese and other AAPIs is hepatitis B. Hepatitis B is a principal risk factor for chronic liver diseases including cancer. The Chinese have the highest incidence and mortality rates for liver cancer and nasopharyngeal cancers among all U.S. racial/ethnic populations.

The prevalence of adult male Chinese who smoke (28 percent) exceeds the total male California smoking rate of 21 percent. Chinese-American women are choosing to smoke at higher rates than Asian-born women. Acculturation may also account for the changes in the incidence of cardiovascular disease and increasing rates of diet-related cancers among the Chinese.

Generally, Chinese women are less likely to have a mammogram than California women. Nearly three out of every four Chinese women aged 40 never had a mammogram. Chinese men are the least likely among all racial/ethnic groups to see a physician (42 percent did not visit a physician in the last twelve months versus 33.4 percent for whites).

Kanaka Maoli
Kanaka Maoli (full-blooded indigenous Hawaiians) continue to have the worst health and socioeconomic indicators in Hawaii. As a result, it is estimated that by 2043, the last full-blooded Hawaiian will have disappeared.[20]

Cardiovascular disorders, cancers, diabetes, obstructive lung disease, maternal and infant ill health and mental distress are prominent health problems.[21] Tobacco smoking, a high-fat diet, alcohol, and hyperlipidemia and obesity are the major lifestyle risk factors.

Asian Indians
One million Asian-Indians live in the United States and are about 11 percent of the AAPI population. It is documented that high rates of coronary artery disease (CAD) are not influenced by a vegetarian diet.[22] About 50 percent of all Asian-Indians are vegetarians, but their excessive risk for CAD varies from 4 times that of Americans and Europeans to almost 20 times that of the Japanese. Risk factors such as high blood pressure, high total serum cholesterol level, cigarette smoking, high fat diet and obesity consistently fail to fully explain these unusual incidences of CAD. Insulin resistance and abdominal obesity found in Asian-Indians may contribute to the high prevalence rate of CAD. Also, high levels of lipoprotein suggest a genetic predisposition.

Koreans
Another Asian-American group which until recently had been ignored by health reports are Koreans. One of the fastest growing Asian-American groups in the United States, Koreans comprise about 11 percent of the AAPI population.

Korean-Americans are a heterogeneous group composed of (1) Korean immigrants of whom 82 percent are foreign-born, (2) Korean-Americans born of Korean parents, (3) Korean children adopted by American families, and (4) children of bicultural families (where one partner is Korean). The four groups of Koreans differ in language, culture and religion. The largest number of Koreans live in Los Angeles, New York and Honolulu.

Special health problems among Koreans include stomach, lung, and liver cancer, cigarette smoking, and hepatitis, tuberculosis, and mental health issues, such as stress, anxiety, and alienation resulting from the cultural disruption of recent Korean immigrants.[23]

Koreans use a combination of Western medical practices and traditional remedies. Acupuncture and a plethora of Korean home and folk remedies are available for various complaints.

Previously reported research findings on AAPIs indicate that lifestyle and cultural factors far outweigh socioeconomic status in accounting for differences in health care status among ethnic and racial groups.[24] Furthermore, applying United States norms and standards to health care practices with AAPIs has been questioned. A recent example involves medication dosages. Lin-Fu points out that frequently the prescribed dosages are inappropriate, since many AAPIs tend to weigh less than the average European-American. In addition, genetic differences between ethnic groups may influence pharmacokinetics of a drug. Different acetylation rates (metabolism process in the liver) for drugs such as procainamide, isoniazid and hydralazine have been found in Chinese as compared to other racial groups.[25]

For example, one study showed that one half the dose of chlorpromazine usually will produce signs of extrapyramidal symptoms for Asian-Americans compared to about two-thirds the dose for whites.[26]

The specific ethnic/cultural groups within the broad category

83

of Asian-American and Pacific Islanders must be examined. Within each specific ethnic/cultural group, other determinants such as generation, immigrant status, gender and place of birth need to be taken into consideration.

IMPLICATIONS FOR NURSING INTERVENTION

An American Academy of Nursing Expert Panel on Cultural Diversity reported that "... more than at any other time in the history of the United States, it is imperative that we give special attention to these clients by developing a health care system oriented to cultural diversity. Nurses are central to the potential of developing and maintaining programs that deliver culturally competent health care.[27]"

Access

Primary health care services need to be located in neighborhoods where the clients/families reside. The On Lok Senior Services in San Francisco and the International District Community Health Center in Seattle, Washington serve as models of cost-effective primary care to Asian-American and Pacific Islanders. At both centers, interdisciplinary teams of physicians, nurses, cross-cultural health and mental health specialists, and family health workers provide cultural care.

Availability

The health status profile of Asian-American and Pacific Islanders is poorer than previously identified. The nursing care provided should involve health promotion and disease prevention. Several strategies are recommended:

1. Screening for tuberculosis, particularly for the foreign-born and new immigrants.
2. Educational programs about cancer risk factors

and gender-relevant cancer screening practices, e.g., mammograms, breast self-examination and prostate screening.
3. Screening and vaccination for Hepatitis B and treatment.
4. Efforts to reduce behaviors such as smoking.
5. Special attention for maternal and child health care services as well as genetic counseling for AAPIs.
6. Educational and treatment programs for mental health problems affecting immigrants and recent refugees including alcohol and drug abuse.
7. Educational programs on lifestyle factors such as diet which contribute to cardiovascular diseases, diabetes, and so on.
8. Incorporating traditional methods of healing and beliefs on health in the design of educational programs.

Mental Health

Asian-American immigrants and refugees are at high risk for mental disorders. The stress of immigration, relocation, and separation from family; loss of status and self-esteem due to discrimination and trauma associated with forced evacuation, refugee camps and war all are contributing risk factors. Flaskerud and Soldevilla concluded that staff were most successful when using a culture-compatible approach which addressed health care needs of AAPIs and involved: (1) shared language and culture of therapist and clients, (2) appropriate treatment modalities, (3) use of adjunctive services and caregivers and (4) community outreach.[28]
A study by Donnelly concludes that psychiatric nurses are held in high esteem by Korean clients and that Koreans have a

psychotherapeutic relationship similar to the special teacher-disciple relationship in Korea.[29] The author advocates that the cultural concepts of mental health be integrated in the Western concepts of psychotherapy.

In one of my reports, I suggested special considerations in the mental health assessment of clients.[30] One must be aware that many standardized psychological tests have not been normed on the AAPI population and test results must be loosely interpreted. When interviewing clients, nurses should provide a brief period of social talk before asking questions. Cultural factors in the interviewing process include various meanings of words and terms, nonverbal responses, proximity or physical distance of clients to the interviewer, and possible limited English proficiency.

Utilization

The utilization of health care services by Asian-American and Pacific Islanders depends on how culturally relevant the services are. Reports indicate that AAPIs underutilized available health care services.

A cultural assessment examines various aspects of the client's cultural beliefs about health and illness. This assessment will assist nurses in identifying specific ways to make the plan of care culture relevant for the client/family. Various assessment tools are available in nursing textbooks and generally include beliefs about health and disease, use of traditional treatments, ceremonies or rituals performed as well as religious preferences and language and dialect spoken.[30]

It is reported that 21 percent of AAPIs do not have health insurance.[31] Those who do have health care access and insurance coverage may not utilize health care services because of lack of linguistically appropriate and culturally competent services.

CONCLUSION

According to the 1990 census, 30.3 percent of AAPIs in the United States are monolingual or have limited English proficiency.[32] Since AAPIs are composed of many different ethnic and cultural groups speaking many languages and dialects, the need for translation is obvious.

In addition, it is important for nurses to work on developing good communication skills to better understand the client's perspectives on health and illness. The client-practitioner negotiation model of care is helpful in identifying health needs and solutions.[33]

It calls for the nurse to:

1. create a dialogue with clients on care-related issues.
2. establish mutual understanding with clients.
3. identify a common goal in care.
4. establish a plan to work towards the common goal.

Health professionals who display respect by adopting a more personal approach, use clear, jargon-free language and pay attention to individual cultural needs can increase their ability to provide care.

Traditional health belief practices such as acupuncture, use of herbs and teas, and personal dietary food choices must be incorporated into a care plan. For example, herbs are widely accepted in the treatment of a variety of symptoms and illnesses. The classification of herbs is by their function or actions on parts of the body and is based on the Yin and Yang energies. Pharmacologically, these include emetics, purgatives, perspiration and heat inducers, supplementary tonics, diuretics, detoxins and neutralizers.

Until recently, there has been a paucity of information on the health status of specific Asian-American and Pacific Islanders. Several of the groups identified in this article require additional health care resources and health care providers to deliver culturally relevant interventions. Furthermore, members of the community must participate in designing programs which meet their own health care needs. This will help to ensure appropriate planning for culturally relevant health promotion strategies.

The author is nursing instructor, College of Mount St. Vincent, Bronx, N.Y.

REFERENCES

1. Office of Management and Budget. Directive No. 15: Race and ethnic standards for federal statistics and administrative reporting. In: *Statistical Policy Handbook*. Washington, D.C.: Office of Federal Statistical Policy and Standards, US Dept of Commerce, 1978, pp. 37–38.
2. US Bureau of the Census. *1980 Census population. Vol. 1. Characteristics of the population*. Chapter A. Washington, D.C., April 1983, pp. 1–34.
3. Forget Zero Population Growth. *U.S. News and World Report*, 14:18, December 1992.
4. Lin–Fu, J.S. Asian and Pacific Islander Americans: An overview of demographic characteristics and health care issues. *Asian American and Pacific Islander Journal of Health*, 1:1:20–36, Summer 1993.
5. Chen, M.S., and Hawks, B.L. A debunking of the myth of the healthy Asian Americans and Pacific Islanders. *American Journal of Health Promotion*, 8:4:261–268, March/April 1995.
6. U.S. Dept of Health and Human Services. *Report of the Secretary's Task Force on Black and Minority Health. Volume I.* Executive summary. Washington D.C.: U.S. Dept of Health and Human Services, 1985.
7. Chen and Hawks, *op. cit.*, pp. 261–268.
8. Centers for Disease Control. Behavioral risk factor survey of Chinese–California, *MMWR*, 41:16:266–270, 1989.
9. Goodman, M., Yoshizawz, D., and Kolonel, L. Descriptive epidemiology of thyroid cancer in Hawai'i. *Cancer*, 61:6:1272–1281, 1988.
10. American Cancer Society. *Cancer facts and figures for minority Americans*. Atlanta: American Cancer Society, 1991.
11. Margolis, H.S., Alter, M.J., and Hadler, S.C. Hepatitis B: Evolving epidemiology and implications for control. *Semin Liver Disease*, 11:2:84–92, 1991.
12. Centers for Disease Control. Screening for tuberculosis and tuberculosis infection in high–risk populations and the use of preventive therapy for tuberculosis infection in the U.S. *MMWR*, 39:RR–8,5, 1990.
13. Hann, R.S. Parasitic infestations. In: Nolan, W.S., Zane, D.T., Takkeuchi, K.N., et al. eds. *Confronting critical health issues of Asian and Pacific Islander Americans*. Thousand Oaks, CA: Sage Publications, 1994, pp. 302–315.
14. Lin–Fu, J. Meeting the needs of Southeast Asian refugees in maternal and child health and primary care programs. *MCH Technical Information Series*, March 1987, 2–7.
15. Grether, J., Schulman, J., Croen, L. Sudden infant death syndrome among Asians in California. *Journal of Pediatrics*, 16:525–8, 1990.
16. Centers for Disease Control. Update: Sudden unexplained death syndrome among Southeast Asian refugees–United States. *MMWR*, 1989, 37:37:568–570.
17. Poss, J.E. Providing health care for southeast Asian refugees. *Journal of the New York State Nurses Association*, 20:2:4–6, June 1989.
18. Filiozof, E.M., Miner, K., Schmid, T.L., King, D., and Ebberwein, A. Perceived health

care problems, needs and barriers of Vietnamese immigrants in metropolitan Atlanta. *Asian American and Pacific Islander Journal of Health,* 3:1: 18–27, Winter 1995.

19. Chen, M.S. Health status of Chinese Americans: Challenges and opportunities. *Asian American and Pacific Islander Journal of Health,* 3:1: 8–17, Winter 1995.

20. Mike, L.H. Who is Hawaiian today? *Honolulu Sunday Star–Bulletin–Advertiser,* Feb 14, 1993, p. 1., 1:2: 116–160.

21. Blaisdell, R.K. Health status of Kanaka Maoli (Indigenous Hawaiians). *Asian American and Pacific Islander Journal of Health,* Autumn 1993.

22. Enas, E.A. The coronary artery disease in Asian Indians (CADI) study. *Asian American and Pacific Islander Journal of Health,* 1:2:161–162, Autumn 1993.

23. Koh, H.K., and Koh, H.C. Health issues in Korean Americans. *Asian American and Pacific Islander Journal of Health,* 1:2:176–193, Autumn 1993.

24. Williams, D.R. Socioeconomic differential in health: A review and redirection. *Social Psychology Quarterly,* 53:2: 81–99, 1990.

25. Quock, C.P. Health problems in the Chinese in North America. *Western Journal of Medicine,* 156:557–558, 1992.

26. Hui, K.K., Yu, J.L., and Kitazai, L. How to avoid pitfalls in the drug treatment of the Chinese patient. In: *Proceedings of the Sixth International Conference on Health Problems Related to the Chinese in North America,* June 1992, San Francisco.

27. American Academy of Nursing. *Expert panel report: Culturally competent health care.* Washington, D.C.: American Academy of Nursing, 1992.

28. Flaskerud, J., Soldevilla, E.Q. Filipino and Vietnamese clients: Utilizing an Asian mental health center. *Journal of Psychosocial Nursing and Mental Health Services,* 24:8: 32–36, August 1986.

29. Donnelly, P.J. The impact of culture on psychotherapy: Korean clients expectations in psychotherapy. *Journal of the New York State Nurses Association,* 23:2:12–15, June 1992.

30. Louie, K.B. Cultural issues in psychiatric nursing. In Iego, S., ed., *American Handbook of Psychiatric Nursing.* Philadelphia: JB Lippincott, 1985, pp. 608–615.

31. Louie, K.B. Providing health care to Chinese clients. *Topics in Clinical Nursing,* 7:18–25, October 1985.

32. U.S. Bureau of the Census, *1990 census of the population.* Washington, D.C.: Government Printing Office.

33. Chen and Hawks, *op. cit.,* pp. 261–268.

unit
3

Pain

Phase 2   During Reading

As you continue to practice what you learned about the *before-reading phase,* this unit will help you focus on what you do during reading. While you are reading an assigned chapter in a textbook or an article in a journal, you should have two goals in mind. One goal is to monitor your comprehension of the information you are reading. Techniques to help you achieve this goal include reading for main ideas and noting how paragraphs are organized. The second goal is to monitor your reading efficiency by setting your pace according to the difficulty of the material you are reading. Evaluating and improving your reading efficiency is an important study strategy.

You will practice these reading techniques as you read about a subject that concerns everyone—pain. The first selection in this unit is a textbook chapter that introduces the topic of pain in relation to patients and their care. The remaining selections are periodical articles that present a variety of perspectives on pain. First, you will read an article that compares two approaches to relieving pain—one that wasn't helpful and another that was. You will also read about a group of patients who can't describe their pain but still need help—newborns. Also included in this unit are an article about cultural influences on the response to pain and one on nurses' concerns about a dangerous complication of medications given for pain.

Selection 3-1   *Care of Patients with Pain*

Purpose for Reading

PROCESS GOAL: **To monitor comprehension and achievement of purpose**

While monitoring your comprehension, you will practice underlining main ideas and significant details and noting paragraph organization.

OUTCOME GOAL: **To master the chapter objectives provided by the textbook author**

"Care of Patients with Pain" is a chapter from a medical-surgical nursing textbook that could be used in licensed practical nursing (LPN) programs or with licensed vocational nurses (LVNs), as they are called in some states. The objectives in this textbook chapter provide a guide to key concepts that will be presented in this unit on pain. Unless your teacher provides more specific guidelines, use the chapter objectives as your outcome goals. When you are studying a new topic, reading a textbook chapter first can provide an effective introduction, making it easier to understand more specialized journal articles.

Before Reading 1

Goal: Get oriented to the text
Techniques: Preview new materials; ask questions about the information

---

To get a feeling for the format of this textbook, preview the chapter by looking through all the pages for headings, graphic aids, and study aids. Keep these questions in mind during your preview:

1. How long is the chapter? _____
2. How many objectives does it cover? _____
3. How difficult does the chapter appear to be? Is the content so detailed that you must take more time to understand what you are reading?

Before Reading 2

Goal: Develop a study plan
Technique: Decide which parts of the text relate to objectives

---

Developing your ability to read for main ideas and significant details is one of the main purposes of this unit. Using the chapter objectives to preview is an especially helpful technique for locating main ideas in a textbook.

For each chapter objective, list the page numbers on which the topic is covered. Don't spend too much time reading; just skim the headings, bold type, and graphic aids. If you're not sure, make a guess and go on to the next objective.

Page Number(s)	Objective
_____	1. Define pain.
_____	2. Describe physiologic and psychological reactions to pain stimuli.
_____	3. Compare and contrast three different types of pain.
_____	4. Describe common biases and myths about pain.
_____	5. Assess pain in assigned patients, fully appreciating the subjective nature of pain.
_____	6. List at least seven nursing interventions other than the administration of analgesics for the relief of pain.
_____	7. Select nursing interventions appropriate for each type of pain experience.
_____	8. Evaluate the effectiveness of measures used for the management of pain in assigned patients.

Before Reading 3

Goal:	Get oriented to the text
Technique:	Look up significant terms that are not defined in the text

Do you need to look up any of the terms used in the chapter objectives or in the vocabulary list? If so, write the terms and their definitions here.

Before Reading 4

Goal:	Develop a study plan
Technique:	Decide when to work on each part

Make a plan for reading the chapter, taking into account your assessment of its difficulty and your schedule. The assignment is to underline the main idea in each paragraph in order to *master* the chapter objectives. Casual reading will not get these results.

You might decide to scan the whole chapter to locate each objective and then go back and read to address the objectives. Or you might plunge in and study each section of text thoroughly to learn what it says about each objective. In either case, it will take a large block of time to master the chapter. Therefore, it's probably unrealistic to plan to read it in one sitting. Instead, make a plan to do parts of the assignment at various times (before the due date). Allow time to review the entire assignment after you've completed the parts.

Write your tentative study plan, using the following format:

<u>Date/Time</u>   <u>Text Headings/Objectives to Be Covered</u>

_____   _____

_____   _____

_____   _____

_____   _____

_____   _____

_____   _____

_____   _____

_____   _____

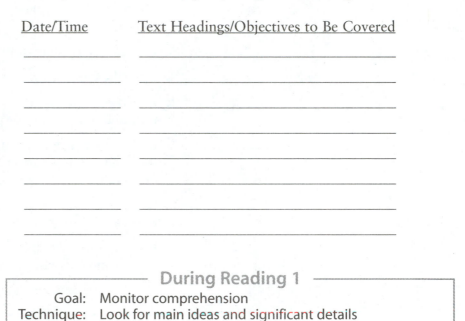

+--+
| ───────── **During Reading 1** ───────── |
| |
| Goal: Monitor comprehension |
| Technique: Look for main ideas and significant details |
+--+

When reading this selection, you'll practice locating main ideas and significant details that directly relate to chapter objectives. Read with a pencil in your hand; if you use a highlighter, you'll be making permanent marks too early in the reading process.

Do you mark too much? Do you "paint" your textbooks yellow or pink with highlighter without being sure that you have marked the important information? If so, don't even pick up your pencil until you have read to the end of a paragraph. Underline lightly *only one sentence* in the paragraph. Then put your pencil down until you finish reading the next paragraph. The point of this assignment is to practice finding main ideas, not to practice drawing lines.

If a paragraph doesn't seem to relate to any of the objectives, underline nothing. If it doesn't seem to have an "underlineable" sentence but does convey an important idea related to an objective, jot the idea in the margin, using your own words. You'll have an opportunity later to decide which details are important. For now, just concentrate on main ideas.

Notice while you're reading that the author used several different *organizational patterns* to present the information in this textbook chapter. Among the most frequently found patterns are the following:

Comparison/contrast: showing similarities and differences
Cause/effect: showing causes and/or results
Process/time order: showing the sequence of steps in a procedure or of events in a series
Listing: presenting examples of a principle or concept in a more or less arbitrary order (at least not organized by one of the other patterns)

As you read the chapter, find examples of paragraphs or sections organized in each pattern.

During Reading 2

Goal: Monitor reading efficiency
Technique: Evaluate the efficiency of your study strategies

Before you end each study session, ask yourself how you're doing with your study plan. Are you able to complete each part of the assignment within the allotted time? If not, revise your goals before the next study session.

After Reading 1

Goal: Organize relevant information for review
Technique: Make notes

Now look back at the chapter to find the examples of paragraphs or sections organized in the following patterns. Use the chart to indicate where each pattern can be found.

Pattern	Section	Page Number
Comparison/contrast	_____	_____
Cause/effect	_____	_____
Process/time order	_____	_____
Listing	_____	_____

After Reading 2

Goal:	Organize relevant information for review
Technique:	Underline

Review the underlined sentences and marginal notes you made during reading. Make any changes that seem necessary now that you're looking at the big picture, rather than focusing on one paragraph at a time. Now is the time to decide which details support the main idea and thus deserve to be underlined and remembered.

When you're satisfied with your underlining efforts, look at the Consultations section.

After Reading 3

Goal:	Check initial recall of relevant information
Technique:	Review the whole assignment by self-testing

During reading, you looked for main ideas in paragraphs and thought about the organizational patterns used by the author. Now it's time to find out how successful your efforts to master the information have been by seeing whether you can address the eight chapter objectives.

Mastery of the information in the chapter is your goal, and you may need to try a variety of approaches to achieve it. If you learn best by listening, you may prefer to recite aloud the information related to each objective. If you learn best by writing things down, you may want to add marginal notes to the text, indicating where the information for an objective can be found. Experiment with different strategies even if they seem a little awkward at first. No matter which methods you use, hold yourself responsible for a complete understanding of each objective. *Mastery* is your goal.

Do your best to provide a response for each objective without looking back at the chapter. It's okay to look back if you have trouble, but test your recall first to see how much of the material you know without looking. (For the "assigned patients" in Objectives 5 and 8, use the Clinical Case Problems, p. 106.)

1. Define pain.

2. Describe physiologic and psychological reactions to pain stimuli.

3. Compare and contrast three different types of pain.

4. Describe common biases and myths about pain.

5. Assess pain in assigned patients, fully appreciating the subjective nature of pain.

6. List at least seven nursing interventions other than the administration of analgesics for the relief of pain.

7. Select nursing interventions appropriate for each type of pain experience.

8. Evaluate the effectiveness of measures used for the management of pain in assigned patients.

CHAPTER 10

Susan deWit

Vocabulary
abduction
addiction
aversion
endogenous
endorphin
enkephalin
euphoria
polypeptide
receptor

Upon completion of this chapter the student should be able to:

1. Define pain.
2. Describe physiologic and psychological reactions to pain stimuli.
3. Compare and contrast three different types of pain.
4. Describe common biases and myths about pain.
5. Assess pain in assigned patients, fully appreciating the subjective nature of pain.
6. List at least seven nursing interventions other than the administration of analgesics for the relief of pain.
7. Select nursing interventions appropriate for each type of pain experience.
8. Evaluate the effectiveness of measures used for the management of pain in assigned patients.

PHYSIOLOGY OF PAIN

Dictionary definitions of pain usually describe it as a feeling of distress, suffering, or agony that is caused by stimulation of specialized nerve endings scattered throughout the body. Pain is a universal symptom, which means that it is not specific to any one disease or type of injury. Its purpose is to act as a warning that tissues are being damaged and to motivate the sufferer to remove or withdraw from the source of the pain or otherwise seek relief.

Anyone who is trying to help a person cope with pain must be careful not to be judgmental and decide whether the pain actually exists. We can define pain in a somewhat detached and limited way for the purposes of study and communication, but the person experiencing pain is the most reliable source of information about how it feels, where it is located, and what provides relief.

> **McCaffrey says that pain is whatever the person who is experiencing it says it is, and it exists and is real whenever he says so (McCaffrey, 1989).**

Reception and Transmission of Pain Signals

All receptors for painful stimuli are free nerve endings that are specially designed to perform their function of receiving and relaying pain impulses.

Pain receptors are abundantly distributed throughout the skin, as well as in deeper structures such as the peritoneum, the surfaces of joints, walls of arteries, and in parts of the cranial cavity. Mucous membranes lining the gastrointestinal tract also contain an abundant supply of pain receptors, as do the bile ducts, bronchi, and parietal pleura of the respiratory system. The eye has more pain receptors than any other body structure, because it is the most vulnerable and sensitive of all external organs.

> **Pain receptors do not adapt or become less sensitive to repeated stimulation as do other kinds of receptors. In fact, under some conditions the receptors become even more sensitive over a period of time.**

This concept is important to an understanding of the assessment and management of chronic pain. The assumption that a person gets used to having continued pain simply is not true. Specialists who work with those suffering chronic pain almost all agree that instead of becoming accustomed to long-standing pain, patients seem, if anything, to become more sensitive and to suffer more as time passes.

A few pain receptors are so specialized they respond only to a specific stimulus (for example,

94

histamine); however, most are sensitive to more than one kind of excitation. Pain is felt when tissues are damaged, because the hurt cells release chemicals such as histamine, potassium ions, acids, prostaglandins, and acetylcholine. These chemicals stimulate the chemosensitive pain receptors and also can damage the nerve endings themselves. If there is an inadequate supply of oxygen to a group of cells (ischemia)—as, for example, in coronary occlusion ("heart attack")—the ischemic tissue releases chemicals that stimulate the pain receptors, and the patient feels intense pain. Muscle spasm is another cause of pain, probably because it has the indirect effect of causing ischemia and stimulation of chemosensitive pain receptors.

Once pain stimuli have been recognized by the specialized nerve cells, the impulses travel to the spinal cord and then go upward along thin nerve fibers to the brain. Some go directly to the posterior part of the thalamus, which is the sensory relay station of the brain. Others go to the brain stem and from there are sent along to the thalamus.

Because of its role in recognizing pain impulses, the thalamus is sometimes called the *pain center*. However, the thalamus can only recognize the impulse as uncomfortable or disagreeable. It cannot tell where the pain is coming from. This must be done by the cerebral cortex, whose role is to "decide" where the pain is and how intensely it will be felt. Hence if the connections between the thalamus and cerebral cortex are broken, as in a frontal lobotomy, the person may report pain but will not feel it to an intense degree or be able to tell exactly where it is.

Perception of and Reaction to Pain

The *physiologic recognition* or *biologic perception* of stimuli by pain receptors is essentially the same for all persons with an intact and normally functioning nervous system. However, the reaction to the sensation of pain is highly individualized and depends on a number of factors within and outside of the individual. *Reaction* is used here in the sense of what the total person thinks, feels, and does when he is experiencing injury or any other stimulus to the pain receptors.

> **The way in which humans react to pain can vary widely from person to person and in the same individual under different circumstances.**

There are many stories of people who have been severely injured but have not been aware of pain or complained of feeling distress. Soldiers injured in battle, young men undergoing unbelievably painful rituals during tribal initiations, and seriously injured athletes caught up in the excitement of a game have all provided examples of unusual or unexpected reactions to pain.

There are two major kinds of reaction to pain: physiologic and psychological. *Physiologic reactions* usually are automatic, involuntary responses that result from stimulation of the sympathetic and parasympathetic nervous systems. Objective signs of pain that are manifestations of physiologic reactions are presented in the section on assessment of pain later in this chapter.

Psychological reactions to pain are extremely complex. As mentioned previously, one can be so distracted by an external event or concentrate so completely on what he is doing that he does not seem to be aware of the pain and does not react to it as would be expected. On the other hand, fear and anxiety can make a person more sensitive to pain, thereby increasing his suffering.

Some psychological factors that are believed to influence an individual's reaction to pain are (1) his previous experience with pain, (2) the coping mechanisms he has developed, (3) training and cultural guidelines for acceptable responses to pain and discomfort, (4) his state of mental and physical health, and (5) his level of fatigue. As previously mentioned, distracting a person's attention from the pain also can influence how he reacts to it.

A person does not "get used to" pain, at least not in a purely biologic sense. As was stated earlier, pain receptors are the only receptors in the body that do not adapt or become less responsive to repeated stimulation. However, a person's experience with personal suffering can affect his attitude toward it and his ability to handle it. For some of us, memories of a previous pain experience trigger feelings of fear and anxiety, which make the current experience of pain more intense. Anyone who has been to a dentist and felt pain can appreciate how much the experience influences his attitude toward future visits to the dentist and his reaction to even mild discomfort while in the dentist's chair.

Some patients with chronic pain have learned to live with it and find ways to have some control over it. In other words, they have developed coping mechanisms and adapted to the pain in such a way that they have some measure of relief. Two important therapeutic goals for the person who has continuous or repeated experience with pain are to maintain some control over it and to find some meaning in their suffering.

A person's cultural background influences his feelings about pain and his overt reaction to it. In various cultures it is acceptable to complain bitterly, moan, thrash about, or otherwise bring attention to the fact that one is experiencing pain. In other cultures the admirable attitude is one of stoic and uncomplaining acceptance. A person with this cultural background and training may often be reluctant to talk about his pain and embarrassed to ask for relief lest it indicate a personal weakness or a flaw in his character. A high tolerance for pain is valued in Western culture, and this value often is expressed in a nurse's reluctance to give medication for relief and in her disapproval of patients who complain of pain.

Coping with pain and trying to find some relief so that it is at least tolerable takes a lot of energy. Patients who are debilitated are less able to withstand pain than are healthy, robust people. However, even those who are physically strong can become fatigued with the struggle and therefore likely to react more intensely to pain.

Physiologic Control of Pain

Pain is a highly complex phenomenon and remains for the most part a mystery to those who study it. Nevertheless, in recent years there has been intense research to try to unravel the mystery. The results of research have given us a better understanding of pain and have contributed to more effective ways to manage it.

Among the most widely known theories is the *gate-control* theory proposed by Melzack and Wall in the early 1970s. They assumed that pain impulses travel along thin nerve fibers that convey the message to synapses in the dorsal horn of the spinal cord. The synapses act as gates that open and close and in so doing allow some impulses to pass through while others are prevented from entering the gate and going on to the brain. Signals for other kinds of stimulation, especially touch and pressure, travel along larger nerve fibers and compete with pain signals for passage through the gate.

If there are more tactile impulses than pain signals arriving at the gate at the same time, the tactile impulses will prevail and pass through. Thus the pain signals are prevented from getting through and ascending the spinal cord to the thalamus. When this occurs, the person is not aware that the pain receptors have been stimulated. However, if there are many more pain impulses than tactile signals arriving at the gate, the gates will allow them to pass through, and the person will feel pain. Tactile signals can be created by massage, contrastimulation, acupressure, and other noninvasive techniques used for the management of pain.

Although the above explanation is a vast simplification of the gate-control theory, it does help explain the effectiveness of measures that have been used for centuries and with varying degrees of success in the relief of pain.

Those who study pain also believe that the brain plays some role in mediating pain impulses that do manage to pass through the gates and ascend the spinal cord. It is thought that signals arising in the brain can travel downward toward the dorsal horn of the spinal cord and block or significantly reduce upward progress of pain signals on their way to the thalamus. This could account for the effectiveness of mental imagery, distraction, and other techniques that require activity of the cerebral cortex to mitigate awareness of the sensation of pain.

A third means by which pain might be controlled is by signals from the cerebral cortex. For example, simply knowing when pain will end or how it can be relieved can inhibit full transmission of the pain impulses and awareness of the presence of pain.

Enkephalins and Endorphins   In their research on pain, scientists found that certain neural tissues in laboratory animals contain receptor sites for opiates such as morphine. They concluded that these sites would not be present unless there were some endogenous chemical (i.e., one that is produced internally) in the tissues of the animals' bodies. In other words, why would there be receptor cells for something that would not naturally be present in the body and for which there would be no use?

The first endogenous chemical found to attach itself to the opiate receptors was a large polypeptide called enkephalin, which means "substance in the brain." Later, larger polypeptides having similar properties were found. These were called *endorphins,* a combination of the words *endogenous* and *morphine.*

The discovery of endorphins raised many more questions than it answered. However, researchers suspect that they modify and inhibit unpleasant stimuli, reduce anxiety, relieve pain, and sometimes produce euphoria and a feeling of well-being.

ASSESSMENT OF PAIN

As you know, assessing involves the gathering of subjective and objective data. In assessing the problem of pain, the subjective data far outweigh the objective data in importance and significance. You cannot see pain, and you cannot feel the pain of someone else.

The more you know about a patient, the better able you will be to assess his pain. His beliefs, values, and attitudes will influence his behavior and his ability to communicate to you what you need to know to make a more accurate assessment. You also need to examine your own biases and personal feelings about complaints of pain and how you deal with the problem of pain in others.

96

> **Because pain is a subjective phenomenon, you must rely on the person who has the pain to tell you where it is, what it feels like, what makes it worse, and what gives him relief.**

Biases and Myths About Pain

Since the attitudes of nurses and doctors are basic to the way in which they treat patients who say they have pain, it might be well to look at some values, misconceptions, and biases that have been identified through research. Not all nurses and physicians have these biases and counterproductive attitudes, of course, but perhaps by reviewing them you might avoid some of the more common pitfalls that prevent accurate assessment and effective management of pain.

Myth: If pain is really present, there must be a demonstrable cause.

Fact: *Pain can be very real to the patient even though no cause can be found. Cellular damage need not be present for pain to occur.* Although damage to the cells does lead to the release of chemicals that stimulate the pain receptors, in many cases no cellular abnormality can be found, but there is, nevertheless, pain. There is as yet no test or instrument that can precisely and objectively measure the degree of pain that is being felt. The search for evidence that pain exists is, in the words of Hackett, "fruitless and irrelevant." The patient with a tension headache may or may not suffer less than one with a brain tumor. We cannot say that just because the brain tumor can be shown on a brain scan and the tension headache cannot, the person with the brain tumor has pain and the person with the tension headache does not.

Myth: The person who has a low tolerance for pain has no self-control and probably is emotionally immature or childish.

Fact: *Pain tolerance is a physiological response to pain that is made more complex by psychosocial factors, many of which can be beyond the control of the patient.* Tolerance for pain is defined as that duration or intensity of pain the person is *willing* to endure without seeking relief.

Pain tolerance varies greatly from one individual to another and in the same individual from time to time. Nurses often place a high value on a patient's ability to feel pain without complaining or asking for relief, and those who value a high pain tolerance usually impose their own values on their patients by ignoring or belittling their reports of pain. The person who should decide how willing he ought to be to tolerate pain is the one who is suffering.

Myth: Reactions to acute pain and chronic pain are the same.

Fact: *In general, acute pain is more often associated with anxiety and chronic pain with reactive depression.* This does not mean that the emotional reaction is the cause of the pain but that it often occurs with and intensifies pain. Physiologic reactions to acute and chronic pain also can differ; therefore management of acute and chronic pain is not the same. The differences between acute and chronic pain are explained further under Planning and Intervention later in this chapter.

Myth: Addiction to pain-relieving drugs is always a hazard, and for the sake of the patient, nurses often must withhold a drug even though the patient asks for it.

Fact: In spite of an abundance of evidence to the contrary, this mistaken belief about the dangers of addiction persists. Studies have repeatedly shown that *a very small percentage of patients (roughly 1% to 3%) become addicted to drugs administered for the purpose of relieving acute pain.*

Myth: Placebos are very useful in assessing whether a patient actually has pain.

Fact: The relationships of placebos and pain relief are perhaps the most misunderstood of all concepts related to the problem of pain. The question of how placebos affect people and why they have a positive response in some and not in others is still not completely understood. However, there has been sufficient study of the subject to show that *there is no basis for believing that a patient who finds relief from pain after receiving a placebo is pretending to have pain or that it is "all in his mind."* Because placebos and the placebo response are so relevant to the management of pain, a more detailed discussion of the topic is presented later under Selecting Measures for Pain Relief (McCaffrey, 1989).

Subjective Data

Although there is a wide variation in how individuals react to pain and the ways in which it is reported when it occurs, there are some specific questions one can ask to help a patient communicate more effectively when he reports pain. Assessment tools developed by nurses for more accurate evaluation of pain usually include information about location, quality, intensity, onset and precipitating or aggravating factors, and measures that bring relief.

Location Perhaps the question most frequently asked about pain is, "Where does it hurt?" Sometimes the patient can answer this question without hesitation. If not, he might be able to point to the area that is painful. There is, however, the problem of *referred pain,* which means that the pain is felt at a distance from its source. This could be because branches of pain fibers leading from the viscera (large interior organs in the body cavities) enter the spinal cord at the same point as do neurons that receive pain sensations from the skin. When pain sensations from the viscera spread to the neurons that normally conduct only cutaneous pain sensations, the brain interprets sensations from the viscera as being from the skin, and the person has the feeling that the pain is originating in the skin itself.

There are many examples of referred pain. Kidney stones that have traveled down a ureter and become trapped there cause a sensation of pain in the flank above the ureter, and the pain "radiates" down the thigh to the groin or scrotum. Cardiac pain is referred to the neck and jaw, over the shoulders, to chest muscles, and down the arms. Gastric pain is usually felt in the front of the chest or upper abdomen. Liver and gallbladder pain might be felt at the shoulder under the tip of the right scapula (Fig. 10-1).

When assessing referred pain, it is sometimes helpful to have the patient trace the course of his pain or point to the areas where the pain is localized.

Quality Patients do not always describe their pain in the same way, nor do they use the words nurses often use to describe pain. In answer to the question, "How does it feel?" they might say "crushing," "throbbing," "stabbing," "gnawing," "cramping," or any of a number of descriptive words or phrases.

Knowing the quality of a patient's pain can help in identifying its cause and can provide a sounder basis for effective management. Cardiac pain often is described as "crushing," "suffocating," "like a vise," or "like a steel band." Gastric pain related to ulcers or hyperacidity usually causes a burning or gnawing sensation. Muscle pain is typically called cramping, while pain in the viscera is described as dull and aching. Whatever words the patient uses to describe his pain, his exact words should be recorded.

Intensity A common practice in recording a patient's report of pain is the nurse's use of words like "mild," "moderate," and "severe." These terms really don't mean very much in an in-depth assessment, because they are subject to a variety of interpretations. The nurse might evaluate a patient's pain as mild because he does not exhibit outward behavior indicative of extreme discomfort. However, if the patient were asked to evaluate the pain on a scale of 0 to 10, he might rank the pain as a 7 and want very much to have something for relief, even though he has not explicitly asked for it.

Although we continue to use the terms *mild, moderate,* and *severe* when writing or talking about the intensity of pain, a thorough assessment should go beyond these general terms to more specific measurements such as the scale mentioned above.

Onset and Precipitating or Aggravating Factors There are several reasons why the nurse should know when pain is first noted by the patient and whether there are any precipitating or aggravating factors that he is aware of. In acute pain assessment, information about onset can help determine the cause of the pain and assist in surgical diagnosis. For example, if the pain occurs after the patient eats a meal with a high fat content, this could indicate gallbladder disease. Severe muscle pain in the legs after the patient walks a short distance could mean that he has a circulatory disorder affecting the blood vessels supplying the leg muscles.

In the management of chronic pain it is helpful to know what time of day the pain usually recurs or is noticed, whether there are any physical activities or emotional upsets that seem to bring it on or make it worse, and how long the pain usually lasts.

Nurses should not assume that if a patient needs relief from pain he will ask for it. The nurse must be actively involved in assessing the patient's pain and in helping him decide when he needs relief. Sometimes the nurse may need to intervene, take an authoritative approach, and administer a prescribed analgesic when objective data indicate the patient is indeed having pain that is interfering with rest and healing.

Measures That Bring Relief Information from a patient or relative about the effectiveness of drugs, rest and relaxation techniques, massage, and any other activity that gives relief can provide significant help in determining the cause of the pain, as well as in planning for its control. For example, if rest reduces the pain, this could mean that the heart or blood vessels or both are not functioning properly. Cardiac pain (angina) typically is relieved by rest, as are muscle cramps resulting from poor blood supply.

In the case of acute pain related to surgical disorders, it is important that the nurse know whether the analgesic a patient is receiving is actually providing relief and allowing the patient to achieve as much rest as he needs for healing and recovery. Drugs affect people differently. Giving a patient an analgesic does not always guarantee removal of pain. The best way to find out if a drug has provided relief is to ask the patient. The second best is to observe him closely for objective signs of pain.

Objective Data

> **Objective signs of pain should *not* be used to "prove" that a patient does or does not have pain.**

98

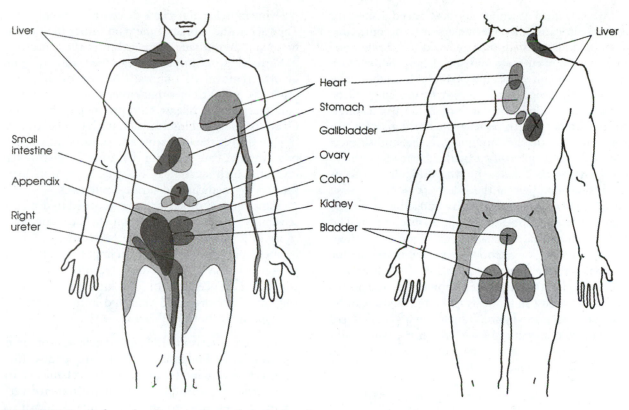

FIGURE 10-1   Referred pain, anterior and posterior views.

Objective signs are valuable additions to subjective data from the patient, and they are helpful when a patient is either unwilling or unable to report his pain. Hospitalized patients most often are in acute pain. However, often a patient with chronic pain is admitted to a hospital, where the pain continues or is made worse by hospitalization and by the condition that required his admission.

Objective signs of acute pain include some but not necessarily all of the following physiologic and behavioral indicators. *Physiologic signs* of low to moderate or superficial pain are related to response of the sympathetic nervous system. They include rapid, shallow, or guarded respirations, pallor, diaphoresis, increased pulse, elevated blood pressure, dilated pupils, and tenseness of the skeletal muscles.

When pain is severe or when it is located deep in the body cavities, stimulation of the parasympathetic neurons can produce a drop in blood pressure, slowing of the pulse, pallor, nausea and vomiting, weakness, and even loss of consciousness.

Behavioral signs of pain might include crying, moaning, tossing about in bed, lying quietly but tensely in one position, drawing up the knees (as with pain in the groin), rubbing the painful part (for example, a cramping muscle), and a pinched facial expression, or grimacing. The person in pain also might have difficulty concentrating and remember-ing or might become self-centered and preoccupied with his pain.

Elderly patients are particularly in need of a thorough and accurate assessment of their pain. Older adults often have a diminished sense of touch (tactile loss), in which case the protective mechanisms of pain are not fully operative. In her assessment of the elderly person, the nurse may notice bruises and cuts or pressure sores that the patient has not mentioned because the injury is not accompanied by the expected discomfort or pain.

Pain is very complex, and it is difficult to separate organic pain from emotional pain. Contrary to popular belief, many older patients have never been hospitalized before, and when they are admitted to an acute-care setting they experience fear, anxiety, and a sense of losing control. Although they could manage fairly well at home, the strange environment in the hospital threatens their sense of independence. In her assessment of the elderly patient, it is extremely important that the nurse find out what the patient was able to do for himself at home, how he coped with pain, and the measures that he used to find relief. This will help avoid erroneous assumptions about an elderly patient's physical and mental health status that are based solely on his appearance and behaviors while he is in the hospital.

Admission to a strange and fast-paced acute-care setting can cause the elderly person to become confused and disoriented; thus he has difficulty describing his pain accurately and specifically. Some older patients may not report their pain because they have mistakenly accepted it as a part of growing old or are afraid to admit they are not doing well enough to go home. Elderly patients in hospitals also are sometimes afraid they are going to die, and so their physical pain is intensified by their fear of death.

Whatever the reason for the difficulty in accurately assessing pain in the elderly person, the nurse is obligated to look for objective and subjective signs that indicate a problem of pain or discomfort. The patient might become noticeably more irritable, short-tempered, or uncooperative. He may resist or be unable to do some things for himself that he was previously able to do either at home or in the hospital. Depression can intensify pain, but it also can be a sign of unreported pain. If the patient becomes less inclined to communicate with the nurse, this could mean that he is withdrawing and using his available energy to try to cope with his pain.

PLANNING AND INTERVENTION

Acute and chronic pain differ in their causes and the reactions they can produce, and so measures employed for the management of acute and chronic pain are not always the same.

Acute pain is usually of short duration, has a sudden onset, is intense or severe, and eventually will subside with, or sometimes without, treatment. *Chronic pain* has a gradual onset, is prolonged and continuous, persists or recurs for an indefinite period, and is more difficult to manage successfully. Because of the nature of chronic pain, those who have it and those who try to relieve it are often frustrated in their attempts to control it.

A comparison of the characteristics of acute and chronic pain is shown in Table 10-1.

Among the measures employed for the relief, management, and control of pain are surgical and medical interventions and general nursing measures, including noninvasive techniques.

Medical and Surgical Treatment

Medical and surgical treatments for relief of pain are usually done either (1) to remove the cause of pain or if that is not possible (2) to decrease sensibility to pain. In the first category are drugs that act on the injured tissues producing the pain. For example, an antiinfective is given to reduce infection in a person with bacterial pneumonia, thereby making it easier and less painful for him to breathe, or a muscle relaxant is prescribed to relieve spasms, thereby

relieving muscle pain. These drugs are *not* analgesics. They act at the source of the pain rather than in the brain and other tissues removed from the source.

Surgical procedures to treat the cause of pain involve removal of tumors, diseased organs, and other abnormal tissues that either cause pressure on pain receptors or release pain-producing chemicals. Of course, surgical intervention itself can be a cause of pain during the operative and postoperative periods. Another cause of pain that often is overlooked is that which accompanies diagnostic tests performed for medical and surgical purposes.

Some surgical procedures are designed to decrease sensibility to pain and thus belong to the second category of pain treatment. These procedures are done to interrupt transmission of pain impulses so that the person is not aware that pain receptors are being stimulated. Procedures of this kind (for example, vagotomy) are discussed later and in more detail in appropriate sections in this text.

Analgesics   Also in the second category of interventions are analgesics, which are drugs that decrease sensibility to pain. The mechanisms by which analgesics bring about their effect are very complex and not completely understood. It is known, however, that narcotic and non-narcotic analgesics relieve pain in completely different ways. There also are drugs that enhance the pain-relieving effect of analgesics. That is why combinations of drugs often work better than any one drug alone.

In the administration of injectable analgesics, McCaffrey (1989) suggests two general guidelines for nurses: First, select the drug and dosage on the basis of each patient's *individual needs;* and second, practice *preventive* treatment, rather than crisis management of pain. These guidelines can apply to administration of analgesics by oral and other means, as well as to injectables.

Individualize Drug and Dose   Although the physician is responsible for prescribing analgesic drugs, his choice of drugs for a particular patient can be made more wisely if the nurse provides information about the effects of the drug and the patient's response to it. First of all, does the drug relieve pain so that the patient has adequate rest and also is able to perform some necessary activities? Coughing, ambulating, and exercise are important activities for the prevention of problems and promotion of recovery from surgery. If these activities cause pain that is not relieved, the patient will not be inclined to do them.

Failure of an analgesic to work as expected could be due to too low a dose or too long an interval between doses. If the pain is not sufficiently relieved but the patient seems oversedated, increasing the dosage probably isn't the answer. Another

100

TABLE 10-1 Acute and Chronic Pain

	Acute	Chronic
Duration	Hours to days	Months to years
Prognosis for relief	Good: may occur spontaneously or in response to routine analgesic therapy.	Poor unless complicating factors are removed; spontaneous relief rarely occurs.
Cause	Relatively easy to identify.	Sometimes easy to find but diagnosis usually complex.
Psychosocial effects	Usually transient or none. Sometimes interferes with social activities but only temporarily.	Can affect ability to earn a living, enjoy social interactions, maintain self-esteem.
Effect of therapy	Medication usually beneficial. Surgery often helpful.	Medication may be addictive. Surgery can worsen condition but is sometimes helpful.

drug or combination of drugs probably should be tried.

On the other hand, the dose may be too high. The nurse should note whether the patient is so sedated that he is drowsy and unable to participate in his care. The drug could depress respirations to a potentially dangerous level. The physician should be notified if there is a drop of more than four or five respirations per minute after a patient has been given an analgesic.

Patient-Controlled Analgesia Intravenous patient-controlled analgesia (PCA) machines are a common site in most hospitals today. The PCA pump is programmed to allow the patient to control administration of a narcotic analgesic with the push of a button. The physician writes his orders so that a bolus of the medication may be given at set intervals. The machine is designed so that no more than the physician-ordered amount may be given within a particular time period. This prevents the possibility of overdosage. Research has shown that most patients use less narcotic analgesic with this method than when the medication is ordered by "prn" intramuscular injection.

Epidural or Intrathecal Analgesia Administration of narcotics such as morphine or fentanyl via a catheter that is placed into the epidural or intrathecal (subarachnoid) space is another new approach to pain control. The medication can be given by intermittent bolus or continuous infusion pump. Duration of pain relief by this method is quite long: about 5 to 15 hours with the epidural route and up to 36 hours for the intrathecal route.

Practice Preventive Pain Control Practicing preventive pain management is primarily the responsibility of the nurse. This means treating acute pain before it becomes so severe that no anal-

gesic will safely and completely relieve it. (Note that this practice may not be effective in the relief of chronic pain, which requires a different approach.) Patients should not have to wait until they are in trouble before something is done to help them. Perhaps the patient needs to be told to ask for medication when his pain first returns, or if he is hesitant to "bother the nurse," he should be looked in on frequently and asked if he feels the need for something before his pain gets too bad.

Nurses frequently hesitate to offer pain medication when a patient does not ask for it or try to stretch out the intervals between doses because they are afraid the patient will become addicted. As previously stated, the chances for creating addiction in patients who receive narcotics for short-term acute pain are very remote. Larkins presents two reasons why addiction is not likely to develop:

- The patient receiving the narcotic experiences *pain relief*, which is not the reinforcement ordinarily associated with addiction. The sensation that usually is responsible for addiction is euphoria due to a decrease in ungratified drives.
- The person who is *given* a narcotic has less control over reinforcement and is less apt to become addicted than the person who has possession of the narcotic and can inject himself whenever he wants to do so (Larkins, 1977).

General Nursing Measures: Planning and Intervention

Since before the time of Florence Nightingale, nurses have used positioning, back rubs, applications of heat and cold, and similar measures to relieve pain and discomfort (Fig. 10-2). It is only

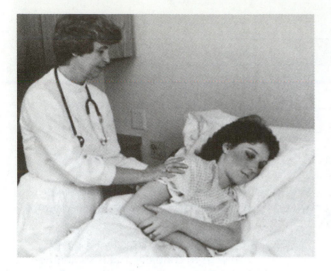

FIGURE 10-2 Gentle massage, back rubs, and other noninvasive techniques traditionally used by nurses can provide relaxation and relief from discomfort. (Photo by Ken Kasper.)

since the discovery of endorphins that a physiologic basis for the effectiveness of these measures has been suggested. However, regardless of whether endorphins are responsible for relief of pain and discomfort when nursing measures are employed, experience has shown that the nurse can do much in addition to administering drugs to help her patient in pain.

An important aspect of any pain-relieving measures employed by the nurse is the use of her "self" to reduce or relieve the anxiety associated with pain or the anticipation of pain. She can be with the patient, listen to him, assure him that everything possible is being done, and teach him ways to relax, divert his attention from the pain, or otherwise control it.

Nursing care plans for the management of pain should, whenever possible, be developed *with* the patient rather than *for* him. Once the plan has been developed, it must be communicated and followed by everyone involved in implementing it. In the case of chronic pain, persistence in looking for the most effective therapies, in spite of frustration or failures, is probably the most important factor. The patient needs to feel that whatever his problem with pain, he will not be abandoned to deal with it alone, and if he needs encouragement or instruction in accepting and carrying out his plan of care, he must know that that too, will be provided (see Nursing Care Plan 10-1).

Selecting Measures for Pain Relief The specific measures chosen to help a patient deal with his problem of pain are selected according to the type of pain he is experiencing, his medical diagnosis or mode of surgical intervention, his experience with pain and knowledge of measures that work well for him, and the nurse's knowledge of and ability to use a particular measure effectively. Some techniques require more experience and expertise than others. Repositioning, back rubs, applications of heat and cold, and use of self (*being there* with the patient) are familiar to the average staff nurse. Relaxation techniques, meditation, mental imagery, and acupressure require more knowledge and skills than would be expected for one who has not specialized in pain control. Some of the more commonly used measures for pain management and some additional information about each are summarized in Table 10-2.

Managing Cancer Pain The management of pain for the cancer patient requires a team approach. A combination of narcotic and non-narcotic drugs may work the best. It is very important that the nurse develop a trusting relationship with the patient in order for pain control measures to be maximally effective. There is a fine line between providing sufficient pain control and preventing severe side effects such as a decreased level of consciousness, respiratory depression, and constipation. Often, combining antidepressants, sedatives, or tranquilizers with the pain medications makes pain control more effective. Patient-controlled analgesia gives the patient a feeling of control over his pain. Whatever type of delivery system of pain medication is used, medication should be scheduled at regular intervals and not just given on an as-needed basis.

Whatever chemical means of pain control are utilized for the cancer patient, the nurse must also employ all of the nonchemical interventions she can. Relaxation, music distraction, imagery, and humor therapy can be most beneficial.

Pain-inducing activities or procedures should be scheduled during peak analgesic effect. Rest periods after such activities are vitally important.

Managing Other Chronic Pain The patient who has chronic pain should become familiar with all the nonchemical methods for pain control that are available. Electrical stimulation devices, massage, whirlpool baths, applications of alternating heat and cold, yoga, meditation, distraction, imagery, relaxation, and music therapy can all be helpful. Biofeedback techniques help many patients.

Physicians hesitate to heavily medicate the chronic pain patient with narcotics because of the addictive nature of most of these medications. The chronic pain patient is not going to die of his condition; he needs pain control that will not cease to work over time.

Stress reduction and regular exercise can be very beneficial to improvement of pain management in these patients. If the patient is obese, weight loss can be very beneficial in reducing certain types of pain. Weight loss can improve the patient's self-

102

Selected nursing diagnoses, goals/outcome criteria, nursing interventions, and evaluations for a patient with pain

Situation: Patient is a 58-year-old black female admitted for bilateral total hip replacement. She is hesitant to ask for pain relief and frequently denies pain altogether, even though it is apparent that she is having moderate to severe pain. She has voiced her concern about becoming addicted to pain medication (Demerol).

Nursing Diagnosis	Goals/Outcome Criteria	Nursing Intervention	Evaluation
Ineffective individual coping related to cultural taboos about asking for something for pain. SUPPORTING DATA Black female; states that she feels that it's better to "tough it out."	Patient will accept analgesics when needed. Patient will ask for pain medication before pain becomes intense.	Establish trusting relationship. Encourage discussion of beliefs about pain and medication for control of pain. Explain that she must move about, cough, and deep breathe in order to prevent complications and that these activities will be easier if she is not in pain. Explain that she needs pain medication for a few days in order to hasten healing by preventing complications. Use alternative methods of pain relief as much as possible: positioning, music, relaxation exercises, heat and cold.	Discussed how decreasing her pain will allow her to move, cough, and deep breathe better, promoting quicker healing; taught relaxation exercise; she is practicing; had pain med at 8 and 1; continue plan.
Fear related to belief that narcotics are addicting. SUPPORTING DATA States that she has a brother who got hooked on drugs when he was treated with narcotics for back pain. "I don't want that to happen to me."	Patient will verbalize acceptance of analgesics as appropriate after surgery.	Encourage verbalization of beliefs about addiction. Explain that addiction to the small amounts of pain medication needed for a few days after surgery is unlikely. Observe nonverbal signs of pain; facial expressions, body tension, mood changes, etc. Encourage to take pain medication before pain becomes severe. Utilize distraction and diversion to ease pain. Reinforce need for pain medication after surgery.	Discussed narcotics and addiction; expresses more willingness to take medication for a few days postop; had pain med at 8 and 1; continue plan.

image, thereby giving him a new outlook on life that might decrease his chronic pain.

Acupressure and acupuncture are other effective therapies for some patients with chronic pain. Therapeutic touch is also proving to be beneficial to many.

TABLE 10-2   Interventions for the Management of Pain

Measure	When appropriate/General effects
Narcotic analgesics—e.g., morphine, codeine, meperidine (Demerol), oxycodone (in Percodan, Tylox)	Moderate to severe pain; acute or chronic. Postoperative pain.
Non-narcotic analgesics— e.g., aspirin, acetaminophen, ibuprofen (Datril, Tylenol, Motrin)	Mild to moderate pain. In combination with narcotics or alone. Oral medications act less quickly but are appropriate when injections are to be avoided because of age, emaciation, hemophilia, etc.
Combinations of tranquilizers, antidepressants, and narcotics	Chronic pain.
Cold packs	Reduce swelling, relieve pressure, provide cutaneous stimulation.
Menthol ointments	Probably provide cutaneous stimulation; could have some positive placebo effect.
Positioning and repositioning	Reduce muscle tension and fatigue from immobility; increase blood supply; relieve pressure on body parts.
Massage	Promotes relaxation, relieves muscle cramps.
Contralateral stimulation: stimulation of skin in area opposite area of pain or itching	When painful or itching area cannot be reached— e.g., when under a dressing or cast.
Relaxation techniques—e.g., Lamaze, rhythmic breathing	Particularly suited for ongoing pain. Provide relief of muscle tension and fatigue; reduce anxiety. Can give patient periods of rest, increase effectiveness of analgesics.
Distraction	Brief periods of acute pain.
Talk, conscious suggestion, conversation	A form of distraction; allays fright, can provide assurance in emergency situation; relieves loneliness.
Biofeedback	Helpful for coping with chronic pain to promote relaxation, relieve anxiety. Usually used with other pain-relief methods.
Hypnosis	Acute, short-term pain.
Transcutaneous electrical nerve stimulator (TENS)	Can relieve both acute and chronic pain. Enhances healing, increases blood flow, reduces muscle spasm.

Whatever the type of pain, a thorough, detailed nursing assessment of the pain and the patient's habits is essential in providing the best pain control plan.

Placebos   The word *placebo* is taken from the Latin word meaning "I will please." The term was once used in reference to inert or inactive substance only—for example, a "sugar pill" or an injection of normal saline. This limited definition of a placebo has undergone significant change in recent years because of extensive drug research that was begun in the 1940s. During their research scientists needed to know whether it was the actual pharmacologic effect of the drug being studied or psychological reactions that produced the beneficial effects they observed. This led to studies of how and under what conditions a placebo effect takes place. There still are no concrete answers to these questions, but the research has shown that there are many misconceptions of the phenomenon known as the *placebo effect* or response. Because this is true, there are many abuses of the placebo in the practice of medicine and nursing.

Placebos can have both positive and negative effects. They can be addictive, produce pronounced physical and psychological side effects, mimic the action of a drug, and even reverse the action of potent drugs. Additionally, placebos have been shown to change brain chemistry and alter the physiology of bodily organs.

A study completed in 1978 led researchers to the conclusion that placebo-positive responders—those who benefit from placebos—release endorphins in response to the placebo. These endorphins are believed to account for the pain relief placebo-positive persons report when they are given a placebo for pain (Beyerman, 1982).

Nurses should be aware of both positive and negative effects of the placebo response. Negative effects could account for the unpleasant side effects patients report after receiving a drug. In other words, administration of the drug not only produces the expected effect of the drug but also an accompanying placebo response to its administration. Whether they realize it or not, nurses use the placebo response almost daily in their interaction with their patients. When a nurse says with honesty and conviction, "This will make you feel better," or "This lotion will clear up your rash," she is using the placebo effect.

Research indicates that between 30% and 40% of patients given placebos will consistently react to them. However, there is no group of people with certain personality traits who consistently react to placebos. Those who have a placebo response are no more gullible, suggestible, or emotionally unstable than those who do not react to placebos. Additionally, reactions to placebos can vary in an individual person, depending on the conditions under which they are given.

Another interesting result of placebo research that has great significance for the nurse is the conclusion that *how* the placebo is given and *by whom* has more influence on the outcome than the personality traits of the person receiving it. In other words, if the nurse truly believes that what she is doing will make a patient feel better and improve his condition, then the patient will usually have a favorable response to her actions. By her verbal and nonverbal behavior she tells the patient that she has faith in what she is doing for him. When that faith is conveyed to the patient he does indeed benefit from what she does. This is true of a back rub, repositioning, lowering the blinds, administering a drug, or whatever else the nurse does when she intervenes on her patient's behalf.

There are some complex and difficult moral and ethical issues associated with the administration of placebos, especially those intended to "trick" or "fool" the patient. The nurse must look at her own attitudes toward the use and abuse of placebos and learn more about them so as to correct any misconceptions she might have. Then she must make decisions from day to day about how she will use the placebo effect. Guidelines for the use of the placebo response are as follows:

- Always try to be honest in your dealings with patients. If you are uncomfortable with lying, deceiving, or "tricking" your patient into thinking he is receiving a drug when he is actually being given an injection of normal saline, your basic instincts are correct. You should do what you know and feel is the right thing to do. However, you should never tell him he is receiving a placebo.
- Do not use placebos to assess the severity of a patient's pain or to find out if the pain is real or imaginary. The issue is not that simple. A patient can have very real and intense pain and get relief from a placebo if he happens to be placebo-positive.
- Remember that being placebo-positive is not the same as being suggestible or having some personality defect or psychiatric disorder.
- Use the placebo effect for the benefit of your patients. When you are doing something that you honestly believe will help, say so. Be sincere and communicate to your patient your faith in the nursing measure, drug, or procedure. Help the patient use the healer that is in him and in you.

Concerns for the Elderly Pain is not an inevitable part of aging, as was once thought. However, the elderly are at risk for many chronic disorders that result in pain, such as arthritis, osteoporosis, cardiovascular disease, and cancer. Research has failed to show any age-related difference in pain perception. Lack of pain expression in the elderly patient does not necessarily mean lack of pain. Many older people have experienced pain for a long time and have learned to minimize the expression of that pain for various reasons.

Narcotics can be effectively and safely used in the elderly if the person's response to the medication is evaluated closely and dosages are adjusted as needed.

Several factors affect the distribution of drugs in the elderly patient. Changes in the proportion of body fat may affect the way fat-soluble drugs are handled by the body. Heart, kidney, and muscle mass decrease with age, and elderly patients need to be monitored more closely for signs of drug toxicity. If the patient is protein deficient, which is common in the elderly, many drugs may build to higher than usual concentrations because of lack of protein binding, thereby causing toxicity.

The elderly do metabolize acetaminophen much more slowly than younger patients, and there should be longer intervals between doses in this age group to prevent toxic damage to the liver. Drugs that are excreted unchanged by the kidneys may also remain in the body longer than usual because of the decreased glomerular filtration rate that occurs with advanced age. Meperidine (Demerol) may quickly accumulate in the patient with renal insufficiency, causing central nervous system excitation. Morphine remains in the body longer in the elderly, and therefore its effects may be greater and will last longer than in the younger patient.

After surgery, narcotics should be used carefully in the early postoperative period and should be given orally or intravenously, as slowed circulation makes intramuscular or subcutaneous injection absorption erratic. Quality of perfusion should be kept in mind any time an intramuscular or subcutaneous injection is to be given to an elderly patient.

Chronic pain can best be handled by around-the-clock dosage schedules. It may be helpful to schedule the doses in relation to daily activities, rather than by specific hours of the clock, as this makes it easier to remember for most elderly patients.

Constipation and confusion are often caused by the total combination of drugs an elderly patient is taking, rather than by analgesics alone. Many experience considerable pain on a daily basis from chronic disease, and it is up to the nurse to see that comfort is obtained for these patients. Safe pain control means medicating before the pain becomes severe, using an around-the-clock dosage schedule, monitoring very closely for effect and signs of toxicity, and titrating the dosage as needed.

BIBLIOGRAPHY

Baquil, M. L.: What matters most in chronic pain management? RN, March, 1989, p. 46.

Beare, P. G., and Myers, J. L.: Principles and Practice of Adult Health Nursing. St. Louis. C. V. Mosby, 1990.

Beyerman, K.: Flawed perceptions about pain. Am. J. Nurs., Feb., 1982, p. 302.

Chalupka, S., and Gillon-Allard, B.: Home care: When your patient has an epidural catheter. RN, Dec., 1989, p. 70.

Doehring, K. M.: Relieving pain through touch. Adv. Clin. Care, Sept./Oct., 1989, p. 32.

Empting-Koschorke, L. D., et al.: When pain is intractable. Patient Care, June, 1989, p. 107.

Gropper, E. I.: Your Jewish patients in pain. Adv. Clin. Care, Sept./Oct., 1990, p. 39.

Guyton, A. C.: Human Physiology and Mechanisms of Disease, 8th ed. Philadelphia, W. B. Saunders, 1991.

Hansberry, J. L., et al.: Managing chronic pain with a permanent epidural catheter. Nursing 90, Oct., 1990, p. 53.

Jones, J., and Brooks, J. The ABCs of PCA. RN, May, 1990, p. 54.

Larkins, F. R.: The influence of one's culture on pain response. Nurs. Clin. North Am., Dec., 1977, p. 663.

Mast, D., et al.: Relaxation techniques: A self-learning module for nurses. Cancer Nurs., June, 1987, p. 141.

McCaffrey, M.: Nursing Management of the Patient with Pain, 4th ed. Philadelphia, J. B. Lippincott, 1989.

McCaffrey, M.: Would you administer placebos for pain? Nursing 82, Feb., 1982, p. 80.

McCaffrey, M., et al.: Giving narcotics for pain: The secrets to giving equianalgesic doses. Nursing 89, Oct., 1989, p. 68.

McGuire, D. B., and Yarbro, C. H., eds.: Cancer Pain Management. Orlando, Grune & Stratton, 1987.

McGuire, L., et al.: Managing pain: In the young patient . . . in the elderly patient. Nursing 82, Aug., 1982, p. 52.

McGuire, L.: The power of non-narcotic pain relievers. RN, April, 1990, p. 28.

Meyer, T. M.: TENS—relieving pain through electricity. Nursing 82, Sept., 1982, p. 57.

Porterfield, L. M.: Narcotic analgesics. Adv. Clin. Care, July/Aug., 1990, p. 30.

Powell, A. H., et al.: How do you give continuous epidural fentanyl? Am. J. Nurs., Sept., 1989, p. 1197.

Thiederman, S.: Stoic or shouter, the pain is real. RN, June, 1989, p. 49.

Witte, M.: Pain control. J. Gerontol. Nurs., March, 1989, p. 32.

STUDENT STUDY AIDS

Clinical Case Problems

Read each clinical situation and discuss the questions with your classmates.

1. Anne Mays, age 27, has suffered from muscle tension pain in her neck and shoulders for several years. Her physician has prescribed a muscle relaxant for her when the pain becomes particularly severe, but Anne does not want to continue taking "drugs that I might become addicted to."
   - What is the intended action of a muscle relaxant?
   - How would you respond to Anne's statement regarding her fear of addiction to a muscle relaxant?
   - What other measures could you suggest for management of Anne's problem with pain?

- If you did not know how to teach these techniques to Anne, where would you go for the information you need?
2. At the change of shift the nurse going off duty says, "Mr. Abernathy was given two placebos of normal saline during the day and slept for a couple of hours after each injection. It is obvious that he doesn't have pain. Mr. Davis probably could use the same kind of treatment for his pain, too. If he complains, I'm sure Dr. Evans will order a placebo if you just ask him."
- What do you think is the best response to the nurse's statements?
- Would you ask Dr. Evans for an order for a placebo for Mr. Davis?
- How could you use the placebo response to help Mr. Davis while giving him a back rub and preparing him for sleep?
- What are some other ways you could stimulate endorphin release for your patients?

Study Outline

I. **Physiology of pain**
   A. Pain is a feeling of distress, suffering, or agony resulting from stimulation of pain receptors.
   B. The person experiencing pain is the most reliable source of information about whether pain exists and what it means.
   C. Reception and transmission of pain signals.
      1. All pain receptors are specialized nerve endings abundantly distributed throughout the skin, mucous membranes, peritoneum, coverings of joints, eye, and other structures.
      2. Pain receptors do not become less sensitive to repeated stimulation.
      3. Damaged tissues release chemicals that stimulate chemosensitive receptors. Resulting pain serves as a warning that the body is injured.
      4. Pain impulses travel upward along the spinal cord from the source to the thalamus, the so-called pain center.
      5. The cerebral cortex interprets pain signals.
   D. Perception of and reaction to pain.
      1. Physiologic recognition (biologic perception) of stimuli by pain receptors is essentially the same for all persons.
      2. Reaction to sensation of pain is highly individualized.
      3. *Reaction* refers to what the total person thinks, feels, and does when he feels pain.
      4. Physiologic reactions are automatic responses to stimulation of the sympathetic and parasympathetic nervous systems.
      5. Psychological reactions are extremely complex. They include:
         a. Previous experiences with pain.
         b. Coping mechanisms the person has developed.
         c. Cultural background and training.
         d. State of health.
         e. Level of fatigue.
      6. A person does not "get used to" pain.
      7. Two important goals for the person with chronic pain:
         a. To maintain control over it.
         b. To find some meaning in suffering.
II. **Physiologic control of pain**
   A. Gate-control theory.
      1. Pain impulses do not travel along the same nerve fibers as other signals.
      2. Synapses between neurons act as "gates" to admit or prohibit passage of signals.

3. When tactile signals predominate at the "gate," they are allowed to pass through, while pain impulses are not.
   B. Brain also plays some role in mediating pain impulses, possibly by blocking their transmission to the thalamus.
   C. Enkephalins and endorphins: endogenous morphinelike polypeptides that modify and inhibit unpleasant stimuli, reduce anxiety, relieve pain, and produce a sense of well-being.

III. **Assessment of pain**
   A. Biases and myths influence assessment. The *facts* are that:
      1. Cellular damage need not be present for pain to occur.
      2. Pain tolerance is a physiologic and psychosocial response; it may or may not be under the person's control.
      3. There are differences between acute and chronic pain.
      4. Placebos can be effective even though the patient's pain is real.
   B. Subjective data:
      1. Location: Where is the pain? Is it referred pain?
      2. Quality: How does it feel? What does it feel like?
      3. Intensity: More accurately measured on a scale of 1 to 10.
      4. Onset and precipitating or aggravating conditions that bring on pain.
      5. Measures that bring relief: What, if anything, helps the person find relief?
   C. Objective data:
      1. Physiologic signs:
         a. Low to moderate pain produces symptoms of rapid, shallow, or guarded respirations, pallor, diaphoresis, increased pulse, elevated blood pressure, dilated pupils, tenseness of skeletal muscles.
         b. Severe pain or pain located in deeper structures can produce drop in blood pressure, slowing of pulse, pallor, nausea and vomiting, weakness, loss of consciousness.
      2. Behavioral signs: crying, moaning, tossing about in bed, lying quietly but tensely in one position, drawing up knees (groin or abdominal pain), rubbing the painful part. Patient also may have difficulty in concentrating and remembering or may become preoccupied with pain.
      3. Elderly persons require a more in-depth assessment to determine behaviors prior to hospitalization. Fear, anxiety, and threats to their independence can intensity pain. New environment can cause confusion and difficulty in describing pain.

IV. **Planning and intervention**
   A. Acute and chronic pain require different approaches.
      1. Comparison of acute and chronic pain shown in Table 10-1.
   B. Medical and surgical treatment.
      1. Done for one of two reasons:
         a. To remove cause of pain by treating injured tissues with drugs or removing them surgically.
         b. To decrease sensibility to pain through surgical interruption of pain impulses.
      2. Analgesics: drugs that decrease sensitivity to pain. Narcotic and non-narcotic analgesics do not have the same action.
         a. Guidelines for giving analgesics:
            (1) Individualize drug and dose to meet patient's needs.
               (a) Evaluate effectiveness on basis of whether patient has relief and is able to rest and also can perform necessary activities to avoid problems of immobility.

(b) Dose may be too high, causing drowsiness or lowering respiratory rate to dangerous levels. Notify physician if respiratory rate drops by more than four or five per minute after drug is administered.

(2) Patient-controlled analgesia given intravenously allows the patient control over his pain.

(3) Epidural or intrathecal analgesia provides much longer pain relief.

(4) Practice preventive pain control, especially for acute pain. Treat pain before it becomes severe.

   (a) Patients should be assessed frequently for need for pain relief.

   (b) Nurse may need to take authoritative approach if patient shows objective signs of pain but does not ask for medication.

(5) Addiction to drug given for relief of acute pain likely in only 1% to 3% of patients.

   (a) Pain relief not the reinforcement ordinarily associated with addiction.

   (b) Person who is given a narcotic has less control over reinforcement than one who can take the drug whenever he wants to.

C. General nursing measures: planning and intervention.

1. Nurses can do much besides administer analgesics for pain relief.

2. Nurse uses her "self" to:

a. Be with the patient, and check on him frequently.

b. Listen to him.

c. Assure him everything possible is being or will be done.

d. Teach him ways to deal with his pain.

3. Care plans must be developed *with* the patient whenever possible.

a. Plan is communicated to everyone responsible for implementing it.

b. Patient must know he will not be abandoned to deal with his pain alone, that others have not given up on him. Most important factor in dealing with chronic pain is persistence in looking for most effective therapies.

c. Sample care plan for patient with cultural biases in regard to pain.

4. Selecting measures for pain relief (see Table 10-2).

5. Managing cancer pain requires a team effort.

a. Use combination of narcotic and non-narcotic medications.

b. Adding antidepressants, sedatives, or tranquilizers with pain medications provides more effective relief.

c. Pain medication should be given on a regular schedule, rather than "prn", for the cancer patient.

d. All nonmedication methods of pain relief—relaxation, music, distraction, imagery, humor, biofeedback—should be combined with pain medication also.

6. Managing other chronic pain requires diligent use of nonchemical methods.

a. Electrical stimulation devices, massage, whirlpool baths, applications of heat and cold, yoga, meditation, distraction, imagery, relaxation, and music therapy can all help.

b. Stress reduction and regular exercise are also beneficial.

c. Weight loss may be beneficial for the obese chronic pain patient, as it can improve self-esteem and well-being.

      d. Acupressure and acupuncture are effective therapies for some patients with chronic pain; therapeutic touch helps others.
7. Placebos:
    a. Word means "I will please."
    b. Placebos can have both positive and negative effects.
      (1) Can be addictive.
      (2) Produce pronounced physical and psychological side effects.
      (3) Mimic the action of a drug.
      (4) Reverse the action of potent drugs.
    c. Placebo-positive persons (those who have positive effects) are believed to produce endorphins that are responsible for positive effects.
    d. Between 30% and 40% of persons will consistently react to them.
    e. How and by whom a placebo is given has *more* influence on the outcome than the personality traits of the person receiving it.
    f. Guidelines for use of placebo effect:
      (1) Always try to be honest in your dealings with patients. Do what you know and feel is the right thing to do.
      (2) Do *not* use placebos to assess the severity of pain or determine whether it actually exists.
      (3) Being placebo-positive is not the same as being suggestible or gullible.
      (4) Use the placebo effect for the benefit of your patient whenever you do something you honestly believe will help.
D. Concerns for the elderly
  1. Pain is not an inevitable part of aging.
  2. No difference in pain perception between elderly and young patients.
  3. Chronic diseases often cause pain in the elderly.
  4. Lack of pain expression does not necessarily mean lack of pain.
  5. Narcotics can be safely and effectively used in the elderly.
  6. Factors that may affect distribution of drugs in the elderly: proportion of body fat; decreased heart, kidney, and muscle mass; decreased kidney function; and decreased protein levels.
  7. Elderly metabolize acetaminophen more slowly.
  8. Meperidine (Demerol) may quickly accumulate in the patient with decreased renal function and cause CNS excitability.
  9. For safe pain control, medicate before pain becomes severe, monitor side effects closely, use round-the-clock scheduling, and titrate dosage as needed.

Selection 3-2   *Nurses Plunged Me Into the Pain Cycle; Nurses Pulled Me Out*

Purpose for Reading

PROCESS GOAL: **To monitor comprehension and reading efficiency**

The author's organization of the material deserves special attention in this article. Because the article is not as difficult as some, you may find that you can read it more quickly than other, more demanding articles or chapters.

OUTCOME GOAL: **To clarify pain concepts introduced in the textbook chapter "Care of Patients with Pain"**

This article from a popular journal for registered nurses might be posted in a classroom or recommended as optional outside reading. It emphasizes and clarifies many ideas about pain relief.

Before Reading 1
> Goal: Get oriented to the text
> Technique: Make predictions about the information

Before you even glance at the article, you may be able to predict the author's organizational pattern by reflecting on the title: "Nurses Plunged Me Into the Pain Cycle; Nurses Pulled Me Out." Which organizational pattern do you think the author used? Circle one (or two) choices that seem most likely:

Comparison/contrast

Cause/effect

Process/time order

Listing

Knowing how the author has organized the material will help you decide which details are most significant.

Before Reading 2
> Goal: Get oriented to the text
> Techniques: Preview new materials; look up significant terms that are not defined in the text
---

As you preview the article, seek evidence to confirm your prediction. Were you right or wrong about the organizational pattern(s) used? Be sure to include in your preview the title, the introduction in bold print to the left of the article, the information about the author, headings, and concluding paragraphs.

After your preview, you should be able to fill in the blanks in this statement:

The author is identified as a _____ who uses a _____ pattern to present her experiences with _____

If you found unfamiliar words during your preview, look them up before reading. Otherwise, mark such words as you come across them while reading, and look them up afterwards.

———— ○—— ————

During Reading 1

> **Goal:** Monitor comprehension
> **Technique:** Underline main ideas

While you are reading this article, you may become involved in the experience of the writer. However, pause occasionally to check your understanding of what you have read and underline main ideas as you go. Remember to avoid underlining more than one sentence per paragraph unless you can justify doing so.

During Reading 2

> **Goal:** Monitor reading efficiency
> **Technique:** Adjust reading rate to difficulty of the text

What is your impression of the article's difficulty level after previewing it? It's about three pages long and has a number of headings. Do you find this article reader-friendly? If so, you can plan to read it somewhat faster than you did the textbook chapter (Selection 3-1).

Plan a time when you can read the article, estimating your reading time before you start and timing yourself while you read. There are approximately 2,300 words in the article. A reading time of just under 10 minutes would be about average (250 words per minute), but you might find that you can go faster.

After Reading 1

> **Goal:** Check initial recall of relevant information
> **Technique:** Review the whole assignment by self-testing

As soon as you finish reading, mentally summarize the article. Your mental summary should take advantage of the organizational structure by explaining how the pain cycle was affected by the author's treatment in both the "bad" and the "good" facilities. After first summarizing from memory, go back to the article to add any details that you didn't recall.

After Reading 2

Goal:	Organize relevant information for review
Technique:	Make notes

Making notes that reflect the organizational pattern often aids your recall of the material. In this case, since there were contrasting experiences, you can use two columns to record the major details of the article. For an extra challenge, see how many of the five psychological factors listed on p. 95 of the textbook chapter "Care of Patients with Pain" you can identify in the article. The five factors are (1) previous experience with pain, (2) coping mechanisms, (3) training and cultural guidelines for acceptable responses, (4) mental and physical health, and (5) fatigue level.

Use this form if it provides enough space; otherwise, make a chart of your own.

Orthopedic Hospital	Rehabilitation Facility	Psychological Factor
fear of "trouble-maker" label	initial expression of concern met with smile, analgesia	training and cultural guidelines for acceptable responses

continued

Orthopedic Hospital	Rehabilitation Facility	Psychological Factor

After Reading 3

> Goal:　Organize relevant information for review
> Techniques:　Look up and learn new terms discovered during reading; think critically about what you have learned

According to the author, the nurses in the orthopedic hospital experienced an "exaggerated sympathy" (paragraph 6) toward her. However, they became angry when they learned that she had complained even though they'd "empathized" (paragraph 16) with her pain. Which of these two terms would you use to describe the reaction of the nurses—empathy or sympathy? _____

Health professionals have specialized definitions of these terms that are slightly different from their definitions in general usage. Look up *empathy* and *sympathy* in both a collegiate dictionary and a nursing or medical dictionary to get a clear understanding of the distinction between the two terms.

Did the nurses in the orthopedic hospital "empathize" or "sympathize" with the author? Defend your choice of terms by referring to the specialized definitions.

After Reading 4

Goal:　　 Organize relevant information for review
Technique:　 Look up and learn new terms discovered during reading

Did you mark any unfamiliar words during your reading? Have you looked them up? If not, take time to do so now. Then take the following vocabulary quiz about words used in the article.

Match the words and meanings. If you'd like to look back at a word in context before choosing an answer (the location is indicated by the paragraph number in parentheses following the word), you might increase your accuracy!

_____ 1. fibrotic neuroma (2)

_____ 2. inappropriate (3)

_____ 3. exaggerated (6)

_____ 4. intractable (6)

_____ 5. irony (10)

_____ 6. shun (14)

_____ 7. retaliation (14)

_____ 8. demoralized (17)

_____ 9. recuperating (18)

_____ 10. physiotherapy (19)

_____ 11. grasped (27)

_____ 12. analogy (27)

_____ 13. inhibited (28)

a. an outcome of events opposite to what was expected
b. treatment by physical remedies such as massage, exercise
c. to return injury for injury
d. not suitable
e. resisting treatment
f. to keep away from or avoid
g. abnormally magnified
h. recovering health
i. to be deprived of spirit or courage
j. condition where there are tumors on the peripheral nerves
k. understood, comprehended
l. blocked, prevented
m. a comparison based on similarities

NURSES PLUNGED ME INTO THE PAIN CYCLE; NURSES PULLED ME OUT

From *RN*, August 1988, pp. 22–25.

Angelika Schulze Owen, RN

This nurse experienced the worst and the best of her colleagues' responses to patients' pain. She concluded that confidence makes the difference, and she tells you how to get it.

The author has worked as an orthopedic nurse in Toronto. She is presently relocating to British Columbia, where she will seek assignment in a pain clinic.

Produced by David Anderson

1   "I can't endure this pain a minute longer. My medication is an hour late, and it's 20 minutes since I rang the call bell. Should I ring again? If I do, the nurses may put me down as a troublemaker."

2   After almost a decade of knee problems I was trying to recover from yet another complicated surgery, this time for the removal of a fibrotic neuroma. The physician had prescribed 300 mg of acetaminophen with 30 mg of codeine (Tylenol 3) q3h to control my pain—from within the bone and from bone rubbing against bone, muscle-wasting, tendon tears, and arthritis. But the nurses seldom brought it on time. Even when I went to the nurses' station and reminded them, it was often an agonizing hour before I got the pill.

3   I was experiencing firsthand how nurses' common but inappropriate responses can trap patients in a hellish cycle of pain and self-doubt. Eventually, I would need weeks in another hospital—one where the nurses did everything right—to get free from the pain cycle these nurses helped create. My contrasting experiences in the two institutions would teach me much about the nurse's crucial role in pain control. They would enable me to better manage my own pain and help others manage theirs.

Neglect drove me inward

4   "Are they too busy? Responding to an emergency? Or have they simply forgotten about me? Someone could at least have talked to me on the intercom, but they just turned the light off. I can't endure this. I'll ring again. It hurts, oh, it hurts."

5   I knew these nurses—in fact I'd worked with some of them on this very floor. Surely they must have some good reason for letting me suffer. Because I knew they were understaffed, it was easy to make excuses for them.

6   Indeed, I had seen how intense was one nurse's sympathy for me. Her hand shook as she stood, half turned away from me, preparing an injection. When I asked her what was wrong, she blurted out, "I don't know how to cope when I see patients in pain!" Ironically, exaggerated sympathy coupled with a sense of helplessness often makes nurses avoid patients who have intractable pain. As a result, they fail to administer effective pain control.

7   Sensing the nurses' discomfort, I tried to conceal my pain. I endured it until nothing else existed in the world—for fear that they would discard their compassion, stop respecting me, avoid coming near me. Each time I finally gave in and reminded them about my medication, I shuddered.

8   My worst fears seemed to come true one afternoon when I heard two nurses talking just outside my door. One was saying to the other, "You go in. She just wants more pain medication."

9 All my responses were typical of desperate patients who are neglected by nurses. So was my feeling of isolation—that I must be the only one with such problems.

10 Irony piled on irony. Because my chart reflected that I received medication every four to five hours instead of every three as ordered, the doctor assumed that I only asked for it that often. As a result, he rewrote my order for q4h.

I became a "situation"

11 One afternoon, Joanne, my physiotherapist, came to my room looking concerned. She pointed out that my knee wasn't recovering strength as fast as it should, and asked me what the cause might be. I admitted that I cheated on my exercises because the pain was so great.

12 "Other patients on this floor are having similar problems," Joanne told me. "It's the worst in the hospital for pain management."

13 Learning that I was not alone gave me the courage to take action. Thinking it best to deal with the problem colleague-to-colleague, I requested a meeting with the head nurse. Without singling anyone out, I told Mrs. Harding I believed that her nurses felt uncomfortable and helpless in the face of their patients' pain. Like all nurses in this situation, they could use some extra support.

14 Mrs. Harding said little, took notes, and left. The only apparent result of our talk was that Mrs. Harding, too, began to shun me. She'd wait until I was out of the room to come in and talk to my roommate. As I was unhappily to find out, she was an insecure manager who responded to problems with threats and retaliation instead of support and solutions.

15 After waiting a week, I wrote a note to the supervisor of nursing, again taking care not to name any names. The supervisor talked to me and then to Mrs. Harding. This time Mrs. Harding called a meeting of the nursing staff—and declared that I'd cited each of them for poor performance, putting all of their jobs on the line.

16 The staff nurses naturally became angry at me. They felt betrayed, too, because even if they had not been prompt in bringing my medications they had empathized with me. Now they began to ignore my schedule altogether and brought me medication, with sulky looks, when they got around to it.

17 One nurse who knew me well enough not to believe Mrs. Harding told me what had happened at the meeting. Shattered, I became the "perfect" patient for demoralized nurses—passive, depressed, withdrawn, never asking for anything. I lost weight and color. I lay as still as possible because every move caused pain.

I was lucky to be dumped

18 Three weeks later, Mrs. Harding told the doctor that I would probably be better off recuperating at home. Having failed to face up to the problem I represented, she was anxious to be rid of me.

19 My doctor was ready to discharge me on Mrs. Harding's advice, over my objections. But once again Joanne intervened in my behalf. She pointed out that my knee was still so weak that I would have trouble taking care of myself at home. Besides, I lived too far from the hospital to make it in for my daily physiotherapy sessions. The doctor decided to transfer me to a rehabilitation facility.

20 One rainy afternoon eight weeks after my surgery I taxied across town to the rehab facility. When I saw it, my spirits sank. The building was old, heavy, and dark—a disheartening contrast to the shiny new orthopedic hospital I was coming from. I was certain it would be full of old, unfeeling, burned-out nurses.

21 "Oh, what am I getting myself into?" I groaned. It seemed that Mrs. Harding had finished me off.

22 But smiling faces met me at the door, and from that moment on everything began to get better.

Caring nursing turned the corner

23 I gave short answers to the nurse who conducted my admission interview and assessment. With my experience at the other hospital still fresh in mind, I was afraid details would irritate her.

24 Instead, she took my hand and said, "It's apparent that you've been through a rough time. I hope we can make your stay here more comfortable. If there's anything I can do, please let me know." She left the room only to return immediately with an analgesic.

25 I was so touched by her concern I began to cry.

26 The staff nurses were equally thoughtful. They put my daily itinerary on my chart and the medication chart so they would always know where to bring my pills. My experiences in the first hospital made it difficult for me to put my faith in them right away, and for the first week I went looking for them every time my medication was more than a couple of minutes overdue. Only when they had delivered the medication promptly for a week was I able to take the first step in breaking the pain cycle.

How we broke the pain cycle

27 The physiology of the pain cycle is complicated and incompletely understood, but the basic idea is easily grasped. The mind receives painful sensations and interprets them as signals that something needs to be done. When the mind finds no way to stop the signals, it sends a message through the nervous system to intensify the signals—and the pain sensations peak higher. As an analogy, imagine yourself turning up a radio during a civil defense broadcast so that you'll be sure to catch any important instructions. You pick a volume at which you can hear and leave it there. But with the pain cycle, the "louder" the pain gets, the more the mind turns up its receiver.

28 I entered the pain cycle in the first hospital because unreliable analgesia left me with no control over painful sensations. As a result, I became increasingly focused on my pain—to the point where I was aware of nothing else. Even when my analgesics were at peak effectiveness, the tension of knowing they'd probably run out well before my next dose inhibited relief.

29 I began to emerge from the pain cycle when I realized that my medication really would arrive when scheduled. With that assurance, I was able to start learning how to further break the cycle by diverting myself temporarily with relaxation techniques and by minimizing my level of discomfort with secondary measures such as a TENS unit.

30 All my caregivers now combined their efforts to restore my control over painful sensations. The doctor, head nurse, and I worked out a medication schedule that delivered the greatest analgesia during physiotherapy sessions, when I needed it most. Because I knew analgesics would be at the nursing station in case I needed them, it was easy to try other ways of managing my pain first. I set target dates for cutting back on medication, and

---

TENS: Push-Button Pain Relief

The TENS—transcutaneous electric nerve stimulator—can help many patients manage pain. It's a pocket-sized machine that transmits current through electrodes attached to the skin on or near the painful area. The patient feels tingling or throbbing sensations the first couple of minutes he uses TENS, but continued use often produces increasing relief.

TENS is most commonly employed during and after minor procedures such as suture removal, dressing changes, and injections. Doctors sometimes order it to decrease the need for postoperative narcotics, especially when patients are elderly, debilitated, or have respiratory problems, and TENS can help control chronic pain.

Many TENS models are available. Some have two electrodes, others have four; the latter are usually more effective because the patient can criss-cross the current over a painful area. Some TENS units have only one setting for wavelength and intensity; others have several settings for each. If the hospital owns a number of machines, offer your patient the chance to try a unit for two weeks, then switch to another if there's no improvement.

Once the patient begins using his TENS, assess for skin rashes, minor burns, and muscle cramps. These side effects most often come from setting the voltage too high, using too little gel to attach the electrodes, or leaving the machine on longer than the recommended limit—which can vary from half an hour to three hours.

Several theories attempt to explain how TENS combats pain. It may stimulate the body to release natural pain-relieving substances called endorphins, increase local tissue temperature and circulation, or block impulses to the brain. Whatever the reason, many patients testify to its effectiveness.

---

although I didn't make all of them, I made steady progress.

Following basics brings confidence

31 When I think back on these experiences, it seems to me that the nurses in the second hospital had a critical advantage. They used a methodical approach that gave me—and themselves—confidence that my pain could be controlled.

32 The nurses in the rehab facility didn't rely solely on *my* assessment of my pain. They knew that personal and cultural factors can make some patients deny pain even when it's extremely severe. Therefore, they watched closely for the objective signs of pain—pallor, facial tension, increased blood pressure and heart rate, withdrawal or depression, protection of a body part.

33 When they did ask for my assessment, they didn't ask simply if I was in pain. I was asked to describe the pain, rate it on a scale of zero to 10, say whether it was constant or intermittent, and tell of anything that alleviated it.

34 Once you've assessed the patient's pain, help draw up a plan to manage it. Have the doctor schedule medications for those times when the patient experiences the greatest discomfort—such as during physiotherapy sessions. Hot packs, cold packs, and elevating a painful part can also improve the effectiveness of the analgesics that are prescribed. Reassess your plan daily.

35 Work with the patient to set dates by which he'll achieve goals of increased activity, greater facility with relaxation techniques, and less and less reliance on analgesics. Don't expect that your patients will achieve every goal the first time: Most won't. Discuss the reasons the goals were not attained, adjust the plan, and set new time frames.

36 If a patient has gotten into the pain cycle, explain it to him. Stress that he can interrupt the cycle by learning not to fret and focus on the pain. Offer a range of diversionary strategies—hobbies, hypnosis, or massage. They'll increase the effectiveness of medications; they'll also minimize discomfort if drug levels fall off at the end of a dosing period.

37 Stress your determination to aid the patient. Prove it by bringing medications punctually and returning within a reasonable time to monitor the effects. Consistent analgesia is the all-important first step in freeing any patient from the pain cycle—and it's up to you.

Selection 3-3   *Nurses' Judgments of Pain in Term and Preterm Newborns*

Purpose for Reading

PROCESS GOAL: **To monitor comprehension and reading efficiency**

Three reading methods will be considered: skimming, selective reading, and comprehensive reading. Making decisions about which method to use will make you a more efficient reader.

OUTCOME GOAL: **To gather material for an oral report**

The following article appeared in the "Clinical Studies" column of the *Journal of Gynecological and Neonatal Nursing*. It reports research on pain assessment of infants. Students are often called upon to give oral reports about what they have read. Therefore, it is worthwhile to develop your self-confidence about this form of public speaking. An article like this would be a good choice as the basis for an oral report to a class or seminar.

Before Reading 1

Goal: Get oriented to the text
Technique: Make predictions about the information

If you glance quickly at the first page of the article, you'll see that there is an outline summarizing the contents in the first column on the left. The outline headings are reproduced in the left column below.

<u>Journal's</u> <u>Outline</u> <u>Format</u>	<u>Author's</u> <u>Headings</u> and <u>Subheadings</u>
Objective	Purpose of the Research
	Literature Review
Design	Methods
	Population and Setting
Setting	Instrumentation
	The instrument
Participants	Establishing validity and consistency
	Procedure
Interventions	Results
	Hypothesis 1
Main Outcome Measures	Hypothesis 2
	Discussion and Nursing Implications
Results	Limitations
	Recommendations for Further Research
Conclusions	Conclusions
	Acknowledgment
	References

Looking through the whole article, you'll note that there are many headings and subheadings. The wording used in the outline is not the same as the wording of the headings. The outline format is used by the journal's editors for every research article; a standard format like this helps the publication's readers to preview articles. The author of this article has used similar, but not identical, headings and organization.

Listing the author's headings and subheadings to the right of the outline headings, as we did on page 120, makes a comparison easier. Draw lines to connect the outline entries with the author's headings and subheadings having similar meaning.

Before Reading 2

Goal:	Get oriented to the text
Technique:	Look up significant terms that are not defined in the text

Read the article's summary outline carefully to get a clear idea of the author's research. If there are terms in the outline that you don't understand, look them up before proceeding.

In previewing the article, you probably noticed tables of numerical data and a detailed statistical analysis of the results. Unless you have had a statistics course, you may find these numbers a little scary. Don't panic. Practice reading the text for the author's main ideas; you don't need to understand all the data in order to get the author's ideas.

During Reading 1

Goal:	Monitor reading efficiency
Technique:	Adjust reading rate to purpose for reading and to difficulty of the text

Since there seem to be no large gaps in the summary outline's coverage of the contents of the article, you may decide that you don't need to do a careful reading of every section of the article. Instead of having to discover the main idea of every section as you would in a textbook, you can use the summary outline to guide your reading.

Make a plan, deciding when you'll read the article as well as what strategy you will use for reading. Be sure to choose a strategy appropriate to your purpose:

- Skimming—rapid coverage of the whole article to confirm the main ideas presented in the summary outline, focusing on high-yield locations such as first sentences, last sentences, the introduction, and the conclusion
- Selective reading—thorough reading of only certain parts of the article, omitting those that are unlikely to yield information related to the purpose for reading

- Comprehensive reading—careful reading of the entire text when thorough understanding and recall are the goals

Keep in mind that your purpose for reading is to gather material for an oral report to the class. Even if your report is going to be short, it must meet the following criteria:

- Accuracy (Even if the instructor has not read the article, he or she will have enough expertise to pick up on dubious-sounding terms, procedures, or conclusions.)
- Selectivity (Only the *most* important information should be included, but be sure that you don't leave the audience wondering about any essential ideas.)
- Interest (Besides the facts of the study, include one or two pieces of information that you found particularly colorful, unusual, or dramatic. When you are reporting on research, your audience will welcome information that makes your report more interesting and memorable.)

During Reading 2
Goal:	Monitor comprehension
Technique:	Stop periodically to underline main ideas

As you come to the end of each section in the article, stop to review mentally the ideas you have just read. Underline the most important information in each section.

During Reading 3
Goal:	Monitor reading efficiency
Technique:	Evaluate the efficiency of your study strategies

Evaluate the effectiveness of your study plan. Did you read accurately and selectively? Did you find interesting tidbits of information to make your report special? If not, make the necessary changes as soon as you realize they are needed.

After Reading 1
Goal:	Check initial recall of relevant information
Technique:	Review the whole assignment by self-testing

Remember these headings from the summary outline and from the article? Without looking back at the article, write a statement expressing the main idea of each section.

Objective/Purpose

Design/Methods

Interventions/Instrumentation, Procedure

Results

Conclusions/Implications, Limitations, Recommendations

If you left any blanks (or you're sure that what you wrote isn't accurate), reread the appropriate section. Then rewrite your sentence—but not while you're looking at the text. Do it from memory!

After Reading 2

Goal:	Organize relevant information for review
Technique:	Think critically about what you have learned

Certain kinds of items (along with personal opinions, clearly labeled) are often useful to introduce a report or to conclude it.

List a couple of ideas or facts from the article that you found particularly interesting or surprising.

What did you especially like about this article? Did you question or disagree with any of the conclusions in the article?

From *JOGNN*, January/February 1993, pp. 41–47.

Carla R. Shapiro, RN, MN

Objective: To examine neonatal intensive-care unit nurses' judgments of pain intensity in term and preterm newborns and to describe the cues used to assess the possible presence of pain in newborns.

Design: A combination of quantitative and qualitative approaches that included both parametric and nonparametric statistical procedures and a content analysis.

Setting: A large, university-affiliated, tertiary-care hospital in central Canada.

Participants: Forty-five registered nurses employed in the neonatal intensive-care unit.

Interventions: Nurses viewed videotapes of term and preterm newborns and written vignettes. Visual analogue scales and open-ended questions were used.

Main Outcome Measures: Pain intensity ratings of full-term and preterm newborns and the cues identified as indicative of pain in newborns.

Results: Nurses gave significantly higher pain intensity ratings to the full-term group than to the preterm group of newborns. Some differences were found in the cues identified by the nurses in assessing pain in term versus preterm newborns.

Conclusions: Nurses' judgments of pain intensity in newborns are influenced by the vigor and richness of the newborn's behavior response. Neonatal nurses must be provided with continuing education that focuses upon recognition of the signs and symptoms of pain in newborns.

Accepted: July 1992

Technologic advances are enabling neonates with life-threatening conditions to survive. However, the numerous life saving treatments, invasive procedures, and therapies are often accompanied by pain. Every day, children are born who will have to endure pain within the 1st minutes, hours, days, and even months of their lives.

Although newborns historically have been regarded as incapable of experiencing and interpreting pain, current evidence refutes such a thesis and indicates that newborns—including premature neonates—have the neurologic capacity to perceive and experience pain (Anand & Hickey, 1987). However, the assessment of pain in the neonatal population is no easy task: The subjective nature of the experience and the limited number of clinically applicable, valid, and reliable instruments available for measuring the level of pain in newborns are barriers the nurse must overcome. In premature newborns, a further complicating factor is the varying level of neurodevelopmental sophistication when compared with full-term newborns (Als, 1986). The behavioral patterns and physiologic responses manifested by preterm neonates in response to stressful or painful stimuli may differ from those evidenced by full-term newborns. The failure of a premature neonate to respond to a stimulus may merely indicate a temporary inability to respond, not the lack of any perceptual faculty (Franck, 1989).

Purpose of the Research

The purpose of this research was twofold: to examine nurses' judgments of pain intensity in full-term and preterm neonates and to describe the cues that neonatal nurses use to assess the possible presence of pain. The study combined both quantitative and qualitative approaches.

The conceptual framework that guided the research was derived from the work of Davitz and Davitz (1981). They stated that "An inference made from observations requires a cognitive process that either explicitly or implicitly takes the following general form: observation of cues; interpretation of these cues in terms of experience of suffering; judgment of the other person's suffering" (p. 12).

Two hypotheses were examined in this descriptive study:

- There is no difference in nurses' pain intensity ratings of full-term and preterm newborns undergoing the same procedure.
- There is no difference in the cues identified by NICU nurses as indicative of pain in full-term versus preterm neonates.

> To date, no research has been reported that has considered whether differences exist between how nurses judge and interpret pain in preterm versus full-term neonates.

Literature Review

Knowledge about pain in the neonatal population to date has been relatively limited. Because it is unethical to inflict pain intentionally on a newborn child for the sake of study, researchers have used an alternative methodology to study acute pain in this population: naturalistic observation of neonates undergoing painful procedures in the course of routine medical care. Among the neonatal behavioral signs that observers have suggested are measures of pain such as crying, facial expression, and body movement (Franck, 1986; Grunau & Craig, 1987; Johnston & Strada, 1986). Physiologic variables such as heart rate, oxygenation status, palmar sweat response, and serum hormone levels also have been examined (Anand, Sippell, & Aynsley-Green, 1987; Beaver, 1987; Harpin & Rutter, 1982).

Although the researchers' studies have contributed important baseline information on healthy full-term newborns and infants beyond the neonatal period who have been exposed to brief procedural pain, the studies did not extend beyond this population and were carried out by social scientists, physicians, and nurses, but not staff nurses. In contrast to earlier works, one recently published study has explored the behavioral symptoms and physiologic signs of pain in newborns from a staff nurse perspective (Jones, 1989).

Jones (1989) distributed a pain sensitivity questionnaire to a group of neonatal nurses in a tertiary-care hospital in the American midwest. The nurses were provided with a list of 34 physiologic signs and behavioral symptoms suggestive of the possibility of pain in a newborn. A large number of these were identified by the nurses as useful; however, only 3 of the 34 symptoms were selected with high frequency: fussiness, crying, and grimacing.

In another study, Pigeon, McGrath, Lawrence, and Mac-Murray (1989) used a questionnaire to examine neonatal nurses' perceptions of the indicators and causes of different intensities of pain in neonates under their care in the NICU. They reported that nurses use similar classes of behavior (e.g., general state, crying, and limb movement) to identify pain in neonates, but the frequency of each varies for different levels of pain.

The work of Penticuff (1989) was based upon content analysis of interviews of 20 nurses in three NICUs over a 6-year period. The nurses all reported experiencing emotional distress when the therapies that newborns under their care received resulted in suffering without proportional benefit.

No research has been reported that has considered whether differences exist between how nurses judge and interpret pain in preterm versus full-term neonates. It is this important and neglected area that the current study addresses.

Methods

The study used a new methodology developed by the investigator for assessing nurses' inferential judgments of pain intensity. This methodology involved the following:

1. Videotaped segments of the behavior of 5 term and 5 preterm newborns, who all underwent a common painful stimulus (heel lance). The videotapes provided a consistent, multidimensional experience of real neonates in the clinical setting that included color, sound, and motion.
2. Written vignettes that provided a brief history of and important contextual information (e.g., gestational age, health, and mode of delivery) about each neonate.
3. Visual analogue scales to measure intensity of inferred pain.
4. Open-ended questions about the cues that led to the nurses' judgments of pain for each of the 10 neonates in the videotape.

In addition, every nurse participant completed a demographic information form at the end of the testing period.

> This study used a new methodology for assessing pain intensity in newborns: videotapes accompanied by written vignettes, visual analogue scales, and open-ended questions about pain cues.

Written informed consent was obtained for both the videotape development phase and the observational phase of the study. The consent forms stressed that participation was voluntary and that confidentiality would be maintained.

Population and Setting

All registered nurses employed full time or on a permanent part-time basis in the NICU of a large university-affiliated, tertiary-care hospital in Winnipeg, Canada, were invited to participate. This group was selected for study because it is regularly involved in the care of newborns who undergo painful procedures.

Of the 55 nurses who were eligible, 45 volunteered to participate, a response rate of 82%. There was a wide range of ages

TABLE 1 Characteristics of Sample

Demographic Variables	Range	Mean	SD
Nurses' age (years)	20–52	31.2	7.4
Nursing experience (years)	0.5–29	9.1	7.4
NICU experience (years)	0.25–18	6.4	5.5

and levels of experience among the participants (Table 1). The majority of the subjects ($n = 38$) were diploma prepared and had no higher level of education. Only seven subjects had a baccalaureate degree in nursing.

Instrumentation

The Instrument

Each of the 10 vignette-videotape combinations was accompanied by a visual analogue scale. The 45 respondents were asked to use the scale to estimate the intensity of the pain experienced by the 10 neonates described and viewed. The scale consisted of a 10-cm horizontal line with anchors at each end. The end points represented the extremes along the continuum of the concept being measured (pain intensity). A score of 0 indicated an absence of pain, whereas 10 indicated the most intense pain possible.

The respondents were asked to put a stroke through the line to indicate the intensity of the pain they believed each newborn was experiencing. The actual score was obtained by the investigator, who used a ruler to measure the distance in centimeters from the "no pain" anchor to the point on the scale where the mark was placed.

Finally, accompanying each vignette-videotape and visual analogue scale was the question, "What are the cues that lead you to that judgment? (Please include any visual, auditory, and written clues)," which the participants were expected to answer.

Establishing Validity and Consistency

To establish content validity of the instrument, the videotape segments and accompanying vignettes were evaluated by a panel of three clinical nursing experts. The individual segments were edited by the investigator to ensure consistency in the content, presentation, and duration of each of the 10 segments.

The instrument was pretested by a second group of three neonatal nursing experts, and revisions were incorporated based upon their critique. The tool was then pilot tested by a third group of nurses employed at a different hospital from that at which the data would be collected. This group confirmed that the videotapes were clear and interesting and that 30 seconds of viewing per neonate provided adequate exposure to elicit the information needed to answer the research questions.

Procedure

Data for the study were collected over a 2-week period in February 1990. The data were hand-scored by the investigator, coded, and transferred into a computer file. The computer package SAS was used to analyze the results (SAS Institute, 1979). Statistical significance for the study was set at the .05 level.

Results

Hypothesis 1

A two-tailed, paired t-test was used to determine whether there was a statistically significant difference in pain intensity scores assigned to term and preterm neonates. The full-term group had a mean score of 3.73, and the preterm group had a mean score of 2.55 ($t = 8.37$, $df = 8$, $p < 0.001$).

Nurses gave significantly higher pain intensity ratings to the full-term group than to the preterm group of newborns.

The range of pain intensity scores for both groups of neonates was wide (see Table 2). All 10 newborns received at least one score of zero, corresponding to a rating of "no pain" on the visual analogue scale. One full-term and one preterm neonate each received one rating of 10, indicative of "pain as bad as it could possibly be."

Pearson correlation coefficients were derived to discover whether the pain intensity scores correlated with nurses' ages, years of experience, levels of nursing education, or parental status. The results of this analysis indicated that none of these factors was relevant to the pain intensity scores.

> NICU nurses attributed a greater intensity of pain to a group of full-term neonates than to a group of preterm neonates.

Upon scrutiny of the data, it was noted that some nurses had a tendency to score all 10 newborns on the upper end of the visual analogue scale, whereas others consistently gave scores on the lower end. To address this concern, Friedman two-way analysis of variance by ranks was used to consider magnitudes, rather than absolute scores, of pain intensity (Marascuilo & McSweeney, 1977).

The 10 pain intensity scores assigned by each of the 45 participating nurses were ranked from

TABLE 2   Pain Intensity Scores

Subject ID	Range	Mean	Median	S.E.
Full-term Neonates				
A	0–8.2	2.43	2.2	0.28
C	0–9.4	3.78	3.9	0.31
D	0–8.8	3.74	3.6	0.32
H	0–10	4.87	5.0	0.39
J	0–8.2	3.91	4.2	0.36
Preterm Neonates				
b	0–4.8	1.22	0.7	0.19
e	0–5.9	1.26	1.0	0.19
f	0–10	3.84	3.3	0.37
g	0–7.7	3.27	3.2	0.33
i	0–7.6	3.2	3.2	0.32

S.E. = standard error.

1 (for the neonate with the lowest score) to 10 (for the neonate with the highest score). In the event of a tie, those neonates were ranked equally.

In this study, 39 of the 45 nurses surveyed (86.6%) ranked the group of full-term newborns as perceiving more intense pain, on average, than did the group of preterm newborns, and a statistically significant difference was found between the ranking of the groups (X^2 (1, $N = 45$) = 22.2, $p = 0.05$).

In sum, both a parametric and a nonparametric analysis indicated that differences occurred in nurses' determinations of pain intensity in a group of preterm neonates, compared with a group of full-term neonates. The nurses assigned higher pain intensity scores and rankings to the full-term group.

Hypothesis 2

To address the second hypothesis, a content analysis was carried out on the data collected from the 45 respondents' answers to the open-ended questions. Seven categories of cues indica-tive of pain in newborns emerged from the data: vocalization, facial expression, body movement and posture, general behavioral state, physiologic signs, context, and other attributes.

A chi-square analysis was used to determine differences present in full-term versus preterm neonates for the frequency of the cues identified in each of the seven categories. Three cues—body movement, context, and other attributes (e.g., hunger)—showed statistically significant differences in their frequency of identification by nurses in term versus preterm neonates (see Table 3).

As reported in the literature, vocalization, body movement, and facial expression were the most frequently cited cues reported by nurses as indicative of pain in new-borns. References were made to several types of vocalization: cry-ing, screaming, sobbing, whimper-ing, and groaning. Different aspects of crying were described: pitch, intensity, quality, and pat-tern. Body movements were men-tioned in approximately 49% of the nurses' responses to the ques-tionnaire. Included among body movements were references to movement of the limbs, movement of the hands and fingers, and movement of the torso and head, as well as body posture and posi-tion. Examples of direct comments from the data in this category are "waving arms," "kicking," "fists clenched," "fingers splayed," and "arching."

Facial expressions were noted approximately one quarter of the time (28.2%), with references to grimacing, quivering of the lip, chin, or tongue; clenching of the eyes; and facial expressions such as frowning, scowling, and a fur-rowed brow.

Other attributes also were mentioned 25% of the time. The most common explanation for a neonate's crying was hunger. Other reasons for crying were frustration, distress, anger, agita-tion, and sadness.

References to a neonate's general behavioral state often included comments about self-calming behaviors, such as suck-ing and rooting, and changes in activity level, such as falling asleep, being fussy, or being active.

Context and physiologic signs were recorded with the least fre-quency in this study. Contextual cues noted included references to the newborn's overall health, the presence of a noxious stimulus, and the neonate's gestational age. Examples of comments in this category are "Healthy pre-mie with no apparent noxious stimulus" and "History doesn't indicate painful treatments."

Among the physiologic signs cited by the nurses were skin color, as in "looks dusky" or "turned red in the face," and respiration pat-tern, including holding the breath and hyperventilating.

In sum, content analysis con-firmed that, generally, the cues identified by the group of nurses who were the subjects of this

128

TABLE 3 Frequency of Cues Used to Identify Pain in Full-Term versus Preterm Neonates

Cue	Full Term		Preterm		Total*	
	n	%	n	%	n	%
Vocalizations	160	(71.1)	166	(73.7)	326	(72.4)
Body movements[†]	126	(56.0)	93	(41.3)	219	(48.6)
Facial expressions	62	(27.5)	65	(28.8)	127	(28.2)
Other attributes[†]	72	(32.0)	41	(18.2)	113	(25.1)
General behavioral state	44	(20.0)	62	(27.5)	106	(23.5)
Context[†]	50	(22.2)	30	(13.3)	80	(17.7)
Physiologic signs	21	(9.3)	17	(7.5)	38	(8.4)

*Based on 450 potential observations per cue.
[†]Denotes statistically significant difference, $p < 0.05$.

study were similar to those reported in the literature. Vocalizations, body movements, and facial expressions were the cues most frequently cited in judging whether a neonate was experiencing pain. Some differences were found in the cues identified by the nurses in assessing pain in term versus preterm neonates.

Discussion and Nursing Implications

In this study, a statistically significant difference was found in the scores assigned by nurses as indications of the intensity of pain in full-term newborns, compared with scores for preterm newborns. Specifically, higher mean pain intensity ratings were assigned to the full-term neonates, on average, than to premature neonates.

The most logical explanation of this finding is that, in general, the full-term newborns were more vigorous and vocal: They cried louder and harder and, as a group, were much more active than their premature counterparts. If this is so, then it would appear that nurses' judgments of the intensity with which newborns feel pain are influenced by the vigor and richness of the neonate's behavioral response.

This would confirm the finding previously reported by von Bayer, Johnson, and McMillan (1984) in their study of consequences of nonverbal expression of pain and observer concern that high nonverbal expressiveness yielded significantly higher ratings of pain in patients.

> **Neonatal nurses must be provided with continuing education that focuses upon recognition of the signs and symptoms of pain in newborns.**

This phenomenon has important clinical implications, suggesting that the more vocal neonates get more attention. If so, premature neonates might be deemed to be suffering less when in fact that may not be the case. A corollary of this potential misperception is that premature newborns may not be receiving adequate analgesia because they are not able to communicate their suffering to their caregivers.

The failure to recognize pain in premature neonates may result in other consequences, aside from the neonates' suffering. Acute episodes of pain with associated physiologic changes are not without potential risk. Fluctuations in blood pressure resulting in hypertension or swings in blood sugar and osmolarity brought about by metabolic shifts may result in detrimental consequences to newborns, such as an increased incidence of intraventricular hemorrhage (Anand et al., 1987; Arant & Gooch, 1987). Moreover, short-term pain may affect newborns' activities, such as feeding, ability to interact in a positive way with parents, and sleep-wake cycles.

The long-term effects of pain on a still developing premature neonate are not yet known. However, animal research indicates that there may be harmful effects from inappropriate sensory stimulation during critical periods of neurodevelopment (Duffy, Mower, Jensen, & Als, 1984; Spinelli & Jensen, 1979). Furthermore, research into the new field of psychoneuroimmunology suggests that ongoing stress and pain can heighten the immune system's susceptibility to infection and illness (Glaser et al., 1985).

Surprisingly, no correlation was found between pain intensity scores and nurses' ages, years of experience, levels of education, or parental status. One might surmise that the longer a nurse worked and the greater the nurse's level of clinical experience, the more adept she or he would be at recognizing pain in patients. Perhaps the process of arriving at the pain intensity scores differed among nurses of different ages or levels of experience, but it made no difference to the findings. The wide range and variability in pain scores and responses among the nurses may be a reflection of the difficulty they have in recognizing pain in newborns.

One implication of the current study is that neonatal nurses must be provided with continuing education that focuses on recognizing the signs and symptoms of pain in newborns, on neurobehavioral development in premature newborns, and on pain management techniques for neonates.

Limitations

The generalizability of the study is limited by the fact that all data were collected in one hospital from a small group of nurses. Thus, the findings may be applicable only to this particular population, although there may be a limited degree of generalizability to other groups of neonatal nurses in central North America.

All the premature neonates in the study were relatively healthy newborns between 34 and 37 weeks' gestational age. The findings are, therefore, limited to neonates within a gestational age range of 34–40 weeks. A bigger sample of newborns (e.g., 10 term and 10 preterm neonates) might have yielded different results.

Recommendations for Further Research

A number of recommendations for future nursing research arise from this study. The study could be replicated with nurses from NICUs throughout the United States, Canada, and overseas. This would enhance the sample size and determine whether the findings could be generalized to the broader population of neonatal nurses. Going yet further, the study could be replicated with a number of other groups, including nurses employed in normal and intermediate-care nurseries, nursing students, and physicians.

Another area of study would be to examine nurses' behavior in response to their perceptions of

> **Replication of this study with nurses from other neonatal units would determine whether the findings can be generalized to the broader population of neonatal nurses.**

pain in neonates. For example, do more expressive newborns actually receive more attention, more medication, or different nursing care than the quieter, less expressive neonates? Is there a correlation between ratings of pain intensity and the amount of time a nurse devotes to a newborn?

Finally, long-term studies are needed to assess the effects that pain in the neonatal period may have upon the child's future development, personality, and perception of pain.

Conclusions

The study presented in this article used a new methodology for assessing nurses' judgments of pain intensity in newborns: videotapes accompanied by written vignettes, visual analogue scales, and open-ended questions about pain cues. This methodology was developed to increase the validity of the data derived in comparison to data from other studies using questionnaires.

The chief finding of the study is that NICU nurses attributed a greater intensity of pain to a group of full-term neonates than to a group of preterm neonates. Even though the newborns underwent the same procedure (heel lance), they exhibited individual variability in response to the painful stimulus. Some were vigorous and expressive, whereas others were less active or expressive. Nurses based their inferential judgments about the neonates'

experience of pain on the behavioral and contextual cues that they picked up from each newborn.

This finding lends tentative support to the belief that nurses attribute a greater intensity of pain to full-term than to preterm neonates. It also contributes important baseline data in an area of research that is relatively unexplored.

Several implications for nursing practice, education, and research have been identified. Further refinement and use of the methodology will help provide answers to future questions about the assessment and management of pain in newborns.

Acknowledgment

This study was supported by the National Association of Neonatal Nurses, RG #179.

References

Als, H. (1986). A synactive model of neonatal behavioral organization. *Physical and Occupational Therapy in Pediatrics, 6,* 3–55.

Anand, K.J., & Hickey, P.R. (1987). Pain and its effects in the human neonate and fetus. *New England Journal of Medicine, 317,* 1322–1329.

Anand, K., Sippell, W., & Aynsley-Green, A. (1987). Randomized trial of fentanyl anesthesia in preterm babies undergoing surgery: Effects on the stress response. *Lancet, 1*(8524), 62–65.

Arant, B.S., & Gooch, W.M. (1987). Effects of acute hyperglycemia on the central nervous system of neonatal puppies. *Pediatric Research, 12,* 549.

Beaver, P.K. (1987). Premature infants' response to touch and pain. *Neonatal Network, 6,* 13–17.

Davitz, J.R., & Davitz, L.L. (1981). *Inferences of patients' pain and psychological distress.* New York: Springer Publishing Co.

Duffy, F., Mower, G., Jensen, F., & Als, H. (1984). Neural plasticity: A new frontier for infant development. In H. Fitzgerald, B. Lester, & M. Yogman (Eds.), *Theory and research in behavioral pediatrics* (pp. 67–90). New York: Plenum.

Franck, L. (1986). A new method to quantitatively describe pain behavior in infants. *Nursing Research, 35,* 28–31.

Franck, L. (1989). Pain in the nonverbal patient: Advocating for the critically ill neonate. *Pediatric Nursing, 15,* 65–68.

Glaser, R., Koecolt-Glaser, J., Stout, J., Tarr, K., Speicher, C., & Holliday, J. (1985). Stress-related impairments in cellular immunity. *Psychiatry Research, 16,* 233–239.

Grunau, R., & Craig, K. (1987). Pain expression in neonates: Facial action and cry. *Pain, 28,* 395–401.

Harpin, V., & Rutter, N. (1982). Development of emotional sweating in the newborn infant. *Archives of Disease in Childhood, 57,* 691–695.

Johnston, C., & Strada, M. (1986). Acute pain response in infants: A multidimensional description. *Pain, 24,* 373–382.

Jones, M.A. (1989). Identifying signs that nurses interpret as indicating pain in newborns. *Pediatric Nursing, 15*(1), 76–79.

Marascuilo, L., & McSweeney, M. (1977). *Nonparametric and distribution-free methods for the social sciences.* Monterey, CA: Brooks/Cole Publishing Co.

Penticuff, J.H. (1989). Infant suffering and nurse advocacy in neonatal intensive care. *Nursing Clinics of North America, 24*(4), 987–997.

Pigeon, H., McGrath, P., Lawrence, J., & MacMurray, S. (1989). Nurses' perceptions of pain in the neonatal intensive care unit. *Journal of Pain and Symptom Management, 4*(4), 179–183.

SAS Institute. (1979). *SAS User's Guide.* Cary, NC: Author.

Spinelli, D., & Jensen, F. (1979). Plasticity: The mirror of experience. *Science, 203,* 75–78.

Von Bayer, C., Johnson, M., & McMillan, M. (1984). Consequences of nonverbal expression of pain: Patient distress and observer concern. *Social Science and Medicine, 19,* 1319–1324.

Address for correspondence: Carla R. Shapiro, RN, MN, 619 Niagara St., Winnipeg, Manitoba, Canada, R3N OV9.

Carla R. Shapiro is a clinical nurse specialist in the Department of Maternal/Child Nursing at St. Boniface General Hospital in Winnipeg. She is a member of AWHONN (formerly NAACOG).

Selection 3-4   *Review of Literature on Culture and Pain of Adults with Focus on Mexican-Americans*

Purpose for Reading

PROCESS GOAL: **To use your understanding of the structure of an article to look for main ideas in each section**

The article "Nurses' Judgments of Pain in Term and Preterm Newborns" is a report of one research study with a brief review of the related literature. The following article from the *Journal of Transcultural Nursing* reviews a number of research studies on pain, with a focus on Mexican-Americans. The authors present a critical evaluation of many different research studies with this group.

OUTCOME GOAL: **To read the article to meet the course objective "describe how culture affects the patient's experience of pain"**

Reading literature reviews can help you develop an understanding of trends in research. The authors of such articles summarize a number of studies, pointing out areas of agreement among researchers and also suggesting areas where further study is needed. Don't expect yourself to master the details of the research reviewed by these authors; just focus on deciding which parts of the text address the course objective.

Before Reading 1

Goal: Get oriented to the text
Techniques: Preview new assignment; make predictions about the information

---

A preview is an especially important first step when reading a research article. A professional seldom reads a research article in sequence. Instead, he or she previews the introductory paragraphs and the conclusion to get an idea of the usefulness of the information in the article.

The authors of this article have made previewing easy by including an introductory summary of the article (often called an *abstract*). In addition, the headings help you focus on the authors' organization of the material.

Read the abstract to find the main idea for each heading in the article. Since a summary should include *only* main ideas, you should expect to find a related heading for most of the sentences in the abstract. Write each main idea following its heading. Leave a blank for any headings you don't think are included in the abstract.

Introduction (heading omitted): purpose of the article

Conceptual framework: culture and pain

Definition of terms

Transcultural pain studies

Pain response in Mexican-Americans

Evaluation of pain response by nurses

Implications for transcultural nursing practice

Recommendations for future research

Conclusion

Which sentences in the abstract are *not* related to one of the headings?

Which headings are not explained in the abstract?

Before Reading 2

Goal:	Develop a study plan
Technique:	Decide which parts of the text relate to objectives

---

Assess your position after previewing the article.

> Do you know the authors' purposes and conclusions for three of the major sections of this literature review? (If not, preview the article again.)
>
> Are you curious about the specific research studies on which the conclusions are based? (If so, you'll read more closely for details. If not, you're looking for main ideas only.)
>
> Do you already know the definitions of the terms used by the authors? (If not, allow time to learn the definitions as you read.)
>
> Do you need to know about the implications the authors see for transcultural nursing practice and the recommendations they make for future research? (If not, do you need to read the article at all?)

Develop a plan for when and how you'll satisfy your curiosity about specific issues and terms and learn about implications and recommendations from the last sections of the article.

During Reading

Goal:	Monitor comprehension
Technique:	Stop periodically to check achievement of outcome goals and to underline main ideas

---

Stop at the end of each section to review what you have learned. If you don't recall what you just read, reread and then recheck your memory.

Since the abstract does not include information from two important sections of the article, "Implications for transcultural nursing practice" and "Recommendations for future research," you will need to decide for yourself what the main points of these sections are. To do so, start by underlining sentences that express the main idea of each paragraph in these sections. Hold yourself to one or two sentences for each paragraph.

After Reading 1

Goal: Check initial recall of relevant information
Technique: Review the whole assignment by self-testing

Now that you have learned what you needed to and satisfied your curiosity about other issues, review the main ideas of the article.

Use the following activity to test your recall of the main points. If you cannot remember the main idea of a section, skip it and go on to the next section; return to the sections you left blank when you've completed the others.

In your own words, state the main idea of each of these sections of the article:

Introductory paragraphs (purpose of the article)

Conceptual framework: culture and pain

Definition of terms (Don't try to be comprehensive here, just list the terms you were curious to learn.)

Transcultural pain studies

Pain response in Mexican-Americans

Evaluation of pain response by nurses

Implications for transcultural nursing practice

Recommendations for future research

Conclusion

—————— ⚷ ——————

```
┌──────────────────────────────────────────────────────┐
│ ───────── After Reading 2 ─────────                  │
│       Goal:   Organize relevant information for review│
│  Technique:   Think critically about what you have    │
│               learned                                 │
└──────────────────────────────────────────────────────┘
```

Look at the references included on the last page of the article. How many familiar names of authors can you find?

—————— ⚷ ——————

REVIEW OF LITERATURE ON CULTURE AND PAIN OF ADULTS WITH FOCUS ON MEXICAN-AMERICANS

From *Journal of Transcultural Nursing,* Vol. 2, No. 2 (Winter) 1991, pp. 16–23.

Evelyn Ruiz Calvillo, M.S.N., R.N.
Jacquelyn H. Flaskerud, Ph.D., R.N., F.A.A.N.

The purposes of this paper are to review the literature on culture and pain in adults, and specifically on Mexican-American beliefs about pain, and nurses' responses to patients' pain. Nurses and other health caregivers in the United States often characterize various ethnocultural groups according to their reaction to pain and their ability to tolerate pain. Cross-cultural studies have demonstrated that White Americans of Northern European origin react to pain stoically and as calmly as possible, choosing to withdraw if pain becomes intense. This response to pain has become the cultural model or norm in the United States. It is the behavior expected and valued by health caregivers.

Mexican-Americans are often described as complainers who want immediate relief for their pain. Yet studies of Mexican-American culture and cross-cultural studies of the pain experience and responses of Mexican-Americans do not support this characterization.

Nurses and patients assess pain differently regardless of cultural background. Both nurses and physicians tend to underestimate and undertreat the pain of their patients when compared to patients' assessment of pain. However, the ethnicity and culture of the patient influence the extent of difference between the patient's and nurse's assessment. The culture of the nurse also influences the inference of patients' physical pain and psychological distress.

Based on the studies reviewed, implications are drawn for transcultural nursing practice and recommendations are made for future nursing research.

Evelyn Ruiz Calvillo, M.S.N., R.N., Associate Professor, Department of Nursing, California State University, Los Angeles, California
Jacquelyn H. Flaskerud, Ph.D., R.N., F.A.A.N., Professor, School of Nursing, University of California, Los Angeles California
© University of Tennessee, Memphis, 1991

Cultural groups in the United States are sometimes characterized according to their ability to tolerate pain. These characterizations often approach stereotypes in statements such as "Mexican Americans have a low pain tolerance" or "Italian Americans are very dramatic about their pain" or "Jewish Americans complain a lot about pain" or "Asian Americans do not express their pain." Because nurses are often in primary contact with patients, they may be the most likely of all health professionals to make assessments of patients' pain and to manage their pain. Nurses are in a position to make judgments about the severity of the patient's pain and whether or not the patient should receive pain medication. Often these judgments are influenced by ethnic stereotypes and the clock. That is, nurses make their decisions based on their own impressions of what a person's pain threshold ought to be (related to their own cultural values) and on when the patient received his or her last pain medication. It is important, therefore, that nurses understand both the phenomenon of pain and the role that culture plays in the perception and expression of pain. This understanding is necessary to the nurse's accurate and appropriate assessment and management of patients' pain.

The purposes of this paper are to review the general research literature on culture and pain in adults in the United States; specific studies of Mexican-American responses to pain; and studies of nurses' evaluation of patients' pain. Implications are drawn for transcultural nursing practice and suggestions are made for future transcultural nursing research among Mexican-Americans based on the studies reviewed.

Conceptual framework: culture and pain

The role that culture plays in the perception of pain both by people from different cultures and nurses may be conceptualized by integrating concepts of transcultural nursing (Leininger, 1976, 1977, 1979, 1984), traditional beliefs about health and illness of a specific ethnocultural group, and the gate control theory of pain (Melzack, 1983). Transcultural nursing draws from the framework of the relationship between culture and pain. Leininger states that culture is the "blueprint for thought and action" (1976, p. 9) and is a dominant force in determining health and illness behaviors. Transcultural nursing focuses on comparative studies of caring behaviors in cultures throughout the entire world. Culture can determine the best interventions based on beliefs, values, and past experiences within a specific group. The meanings of care such as nurturance, compassion, empathy, comfort, support, and other constructs identified by previous transcultural nursing studies is not the same for all cultures (Leininger, 1984). Nursing observations of behaviors closely related to caring provide valuable insights on how best to intervene based on what the person, as part of a culture, views, understands, and has experienced.

Traditional beliefs provide culture-specific examples of values, attitudes and experiences. Indigenous or traditional beliefs affect the perception of health and illness which often includes expected behaviors in response to illness and pain. Beliefs are important constructs which lie at the core of "culture" and which are seen as antecedents of behavior (Castro et al., 1984). Investigation of indigenous or traditional beliefs that take into account different acculturation levels may point to factors that can be used to provide meaningful transcultural care.

For example, in many Hispanic cultures the value of suffering and the concept of fatalism are accepted beliefs with religious undertones. Many Hispanic persons believe that life has many difficulties which must be accepted without complaints. One's fate is to suffer in this world and "submit with patience to one's allotted measure of suffering" (Calatrello, 1980). If a person is ill, that person bears the illness with dignity and courage.

Many are able to progress through an illness or through a recovery period with this attitude because "everything is in the hands of God" (Calatrello, 1980).

The gate control theory of pain proposed by Melzack and Wall (Melzack, 1983) provides an explanation of the relationship between pain and culture. These investigators established that pain is not just a physiological response to tissue damage, but that psychological variables such as behavioral and emotional responses expected and accepted by one's cultural group influence the perception of pain. These expectations are stored in the brain and in cultural experiences and are capable of influencing the transmission of painful stimuli throughout the individual's life.

Gate control theory suggests that transmission of pain impulses can be modulated or altered by a gating mechanism composed of blocking cells all along the nervous system. When these cells are activated, the gate is closed and pain impulses do not flow to the brain. If these cells are not stimulated, impulses get through the open gate to the brain. Similar pain-inhibiting mechanisms exist in descending nerve fibers in the thalamus and the cerebral cortex. These areas of the brain regulate processes related to thoughts, emotions, and past experiences. These structures send messages to open or close the gate. When pain is occurring, the individual's thoughts, cultural beliefs and values, and memories can influence whether pain impulses reach the level of awareness (Meinhart & McCaffery, 1983).

Although pain is held to be basically a physiological phenomenon, the meaning and responses to pain may be determined by cultural experiences and beliefs. Culture is an important variable in

determining an individual's behavioral response to pain. Leininger (1979) states that a person's reaction to illness, health maintenance, bodily discomforts, and caring and curing practices are linked with cultural beliefs, values, and experiences. A person learns what is expected and accepted by his or her culture; this learning includes reactions to painful experiences. Perception, expression, and management of pain are all embedded in a cultural context. The definition of pain, just like that of health and illness, is culturally determined (Ludwig-Beymer, 1989). According to Meinhart and McCaffery (1983) cultural expectations may specify: (a) different reactions according to age, sex, and occupation, (b) what treatment to seek, (c) the intensity and duration of pain that should be tolerated, (d) what responses should be made, (e) who to report to when pain occurs, and (f) what types of pain require attention. It is possible that a patient's cultural background influences not only attitudes towards pain but the overt response to it as well.

Much of the literature on pain in adults includes the caveat that culture may have a significant influence on the pain response; however, major studies or replications of outdated studies which examine the influence of culture have not been conducted recently. There is a paucity of literature on the relationship of culture or ethnicity to the pain response; there are even fewer studies which focus on Mexican-Americans. There is also a scarcity of cross-cultural studies which include the nurses' evaluation of pain. This review begins with a summary of studies dealing with culture and pain in the United States and then focuses on studies dealing with Mexican-Americans and pain. Finally, the literature on nurses' evaluation of patients' pain is summarized. The

138

literature review is limited to studies of pain in adults.

Definition of terms

Several terms related to ethno-cultural identity are used with frequency in the literature. For purposes of clarity they are defined here. Anglo-American refers to White non-Hispanic people of Northern European origin in the United States. They are variously referred to in the studies reviewed as Whites, Old Americans, Anglo-Saxons and Yankees. Hispanic refers to Spanish origin or Spanish-speaking peoples of the Western Hemisphere. Mexican-American refers to people of Mexican origin in the United States, both those born in Mexico and those born in the United States. In the review of literature that follows, the terms used for ethnocultural identity by the investigators of the study being reviewed are used here also.

Transcultural pain studies

In the United States, the cultural beliefs of Anglo-Americans are considered dominant in spite of the fact that there is little social research done on them (Harwood, 1981). This group is selected as the reference group in transcultural comparison studies because their social and cultural behaviors represent the accepted pattern (Castro, et al., 1984; Winsberg & Greenlick, 1967; Zborowski, 1952, 1969). Zborowski (1952) conducted a classic and the best known study of pain in European-origin ethnic groups. The study described the dominant culture values of pain experience which are still used today. The Anglo-American patient reports pain and is able to give a detailed description of it; however, the person usually demonstrates few emotional side reactions to pain. When in pain, the Anglo-American tries to remain calm, avoiding complaining, crying, screaming, or other manifestations of pain.

Meinhart and McCaffery (1983) reported that among Anglo-Americans vocalizations are viewed as useless but an occasional jerk or "ouch" are considered acceptable. When the patient is in severe pain, an attempt is made to withdraw in order to minimize pain and reduce pity. Stoicism is valued; there is pride in being the good patient, i.e., one who does not annoy anyone with his or her pain experience. The pain reaction of this group is the cultural model for the dominant society. Ideal patients are expected to behave and react to pain based on this model whether or not they are of Anglo-American origin.

Zborowski's early study, conducted in 1952, has been pertinent to subsequent cross-cultural studies on the influence of culture on pain. The study described the pain response patterns in "Old Americans" (those of Anglo-Saxon origin), Italians, Jews, and Irish. Age, education, occupation, socioeconomic status, the disease causing the pain, and ethnicity were compared. Zborowski found differences in the pain response among the four groups and concluded that culture and social conditioning played an important role in pain behavior. He suggested that patterned attitudes toward pain exist in every culture. Appropriate and inappropriate expressions of pain are culturally prescribed. Cultural traditions dictate whether to expect and tolerate pain in certain situations and how to behave during a painful experience (Ludwig-Beymer, 1989).

Hospital staff in Zborowski's study tended to support the "Old American" (Anglo-Saxon) response to pain and to characterize the other groups as overreacting, emotional, and complaining. Zborowski dis-agreed with this interpretation, considering it too simplistic. He reached two conclusions based on his study: 1) similar reactions (behaviors, vocalizations) to pain demonstrated by members of different ethnocultural groups do not necessarily reflect similar attitudes toward pain; and 2) reactive patterns similar in their manifestations (e.g., crying, moaning or stoicism) may have different functions in various cultures (Zborowski, 1952).

Using Zborowski's hypotheses and the same four ethnic groups, Sternback and Tursky (1965) conducted threshold, magnitude estimation, and physiological reactivity studies of responses to electric shock. The groups were controlled on a number of physical and social variables (sex, age, height, weight, social class). They differed in religion and generation of immigration (although all subjects were U.S. born). The groups did not differ in pain threshold (ability to perceive and report the pain sensation); however, they differed significantly in pain tolerance (magnitude or severity of pain tolerated). "Yankees" had the highest pain tolerance mean scores followed by Jews, Irish, and Italians, in that order. The investigators concluded that there were attitudinal differences in the four groups, which accounted for the differences in pain sensitivity and tolerance.

Wolff and Langley (1979) reviewed all relevant studies on cultural factors and the response to pain up to that date. Results of the various studies they reviewed were equivocal. Often studies were difficult to compare because of: 1) the different methods used to induce pain, 2) laboratory versus field conditions, and 3) lack of controls. For example, an early study which found differences in the pain response of Black and White Americans was contradicted by another study of these same groups when social class was controlled. A study by Flannery and colleagues (1981) supported the importance of controlling social class. They found no difference in response to episiotomy pain among Black, Italian, Jewish, Irish, and Anglo-Saxon Protestant patients when education was controlled. As a further example of methodological problems, two studies which used a thermal technique to induce pain did not control for the temperature of the room in comparing the responses of Alaskan Indians, Eskimos, and Whites.

Despite the plethora of methodological problems found in cross-cultural studies of pain, Wolff and Langley (1979) reached the conclusion that culture plays a role in response to pain. They found that role to be attitudinal. Their summary was that none of the studies allows a definitive conclusion about basic differences in pain sensation among ethnic groups. However, they found strong experimental evidence that attitudinal factors influence the pain response (the reaction to pain or expression of pain) of different cultures. Cultural values, beliefs, and conditions all contribute to the development of attitudes in a group.

Pain response in Mexican-Americans

Mexican-Americans are a diverse group and there are many intragroup differences among them that could affect responses to pain. Harwood (1981) noted that adherence to traditional ethnic health beliefs and practices is related to the degree of acculturation. There are a large number of today's Mexican-Americans who no longer believe or practice the folk medicine of their forefathers (Gonzalez-Swafford & Gutierrez, 1983). Still there is a large percentage of Mexican-Americans who hold traditional beliefs. There seems to be evidence that a more intense adherence to the Mexican culture produces a more traditional health behavior (Castro et al., 1984; Harwood, 1981). In a study examining health-illness beliefs among Mexican, Mexican-American, and Anglo-American women, Castro et al. (1984) hypothesized that the acceptance of folk or traditional beliefs would vary with the level of acculturation. Their findings revealed that the Mexican women differed significantly from the Anglo-American women. Those women with a more intense adherence to the Mexican culture believed in the traditional folk beliefs of that culture.

The traditional beliefs of Mexican-Americans provide one part of a conceptual framework for understanding that relationship of culture and pain in this group. As noted earlier, Calatrello (1980) examined the traditional health beliefs of Hispanics. He noted that when an individual is ill, the person bears the illness with dignity and courage; this is because many Hispanics believe that difficulties are part of life and must be accepted without complaints. Stoicism is valued, and many times signs and symptoms of pain are not acknowledged because lack of stamina is considered a sign of weakness.

Most newly arrived, first-generation, and many elderly Mexican-Americans believe a healthy person is one who function adequately, is well-fleshed or robust, and is free of pain (Harwood, 1981; Meinhart & McCaffery, 1983). Functioning adequately means being able to do routine everyday tasks even if a person has symptoms such as a sore throat or pain. If a person is able to perform normally that person is considered healthy regardless of the symptoms.

Gonzalez-Swafford and Gutierrez (1983) investigated the ethnomedical beliefs and practices of Mexican-Americans in a primary care setting in Texas. These family nurse practitioners discovered that usually two symptoms are considered in determining the severity of an illness: pain and the appearance of blood. If these symptoms subside, the person may stop treatment altogether even when continuation of treatment is considered important to the nurse.

Self-control is a practice common to the Mexican-American who is experiencing pain. Castro and colleagues (1984) examined health-illness beliefs in 102 Mexican, Mexican-American, and Anglo-American women. They found that the concept of self-control is an important element in the Mexican culture. Self-control (controlarse) includes: 1) the ability to withstand stress in times of adversity (aguantarse); 2) a passive resignation in which the person accepts his or her fate (resignarse); or 3) a more active cognitive coping which means working through a problem (sobreponerse). Cognitive-behavioral techniques such as self-monitoring and self-control have been found to be useful for guiding behavior change in patients with pain if these are done in conjunction with cultural norms.

Many Mexican-American patients, especially women, moan when uncomfortable. Consequently, they are often identified by the nursing staff as complainers who cannot tolerate pain (Orque et al., 1983). These investigators stated that in the Mexican culture, crying out with pain is an acceptable expression and not synonymous with an inability to tolerate pain. Crying out with pain does not necessarily indicate either that the pain experience is severe or that the person is experiencing a loss of

140

self-control. Neither does it mean that the patient expects the nurse to intervene. Some patients may react to mild pain by crying or moaning and others may suppress overt behaviors with severe pain. Neither expression or behavior is a demand for nursing management of the pain without further nursing assessment of the situation. Zborowski's (1952, 1969) conclusions are especially relevant to this situation. He made the point that similar patterns do not necessarily have the same function. Nurses operating from the dominant culture model of response to pain might interpret the pattern of crying and moaning as an inability to tolerate pain and a request for intervention. In the Mexican culture, however, the pattern of crying and moaning might have the function for the patient of relieving pain rather than the function of communicating a request for intervention. This example points out clearly that any attempt to delineate cultural factors in the pain response should be made within the wider context of cultural attitudes and behaviors.

In cross-cultural studies which included Hispanic subjects, differences were found between them, Anglo-Americans, and other ethnic/racial groups in how patients viewed and described their pain (Kalish & Reynolds, 1976; Meinhart & McCaffery, 1983). The descriptions by the Hispanic subjects were consistent with the beliefs of fatalism, stoicism and self-restraint reported as valued in the Hispanic culture. In a study conducted by Lipton and Marbach (1980), ethnic differences in 166 patients with chronic facial pain of unknown origin were studied. The groups studied included Hispanics, Blacks, Jewish, Italian, Irish, and White Protestant patients. The emotional response to pain such as tears or moans were similar but there were distinct differences in how patients viewed and described their pain. In this study, Hispanics were less willing to admit loss of control and less likely to describe their pain as unbearable (Meinhart & McCaffery, 1983). Their descriptions were consistent with the beliefs of the Hispanic culture that stoicism and self-control are valued.

Kalish and Reynolds (1976) studied the expression of emotions during the loss of a significant other in four cultural groups. One question asked may be considered relevant to the pain experience or to emotional suffering. In answer to the question "Would you try very hard to control the way you showed your emotion in public?", 64% of Mexican-Americans responded "yes" as compared to 54% of Anglo-Americans. This finding seems to support the concept of self-control in the Mexican-American culture.

Among Anglo-Americans and especially Anglo-American nurses, the stereotype exists that Mexican-Americans can not stand pain. Despite the lack of any evidence to support it, Perez-Stable (1987) notes that Mexican-American patients are often characterized as dramatic, emotional and complainers. A failure to understand culturally learned attitudes and reactions to pain might account for this misperception.

Evaluation of pain response by nurses

Health caregivers' views of pain have been analyzed in many studies in which the culture of the patient and the nurse did not differ or in which culture was not considered as a variable. There have been consistent differences between patients and health care staff in assessing the severity of patients' pain (Teske et al., 1983). Among studies of nurses, it has been shown that the nurses' perceptions of pain did not coincide with the patients, which generally resulted in more suffering for the patient (Cohen, 1980; Jacox, 1979; Teske et al., 1983). Regardless of culture, nurses gave less medication for pain than ordered and less medication than patients needed to alleviate their pain. Both nurses and physicians had a limited understanding of long term narcotic use; they lacked knowledge of current pain management techniques; and they overestimated the potential for addiction to prescription narcotics (Rankin & Snider, 1984).

Some of the important conclusions of these studies of nurses' assessment and management of patients' pain are summarized here. Rankin and Snider (1984) found that for about 58% of the nurses in their study, the goal was to reduce the patient's pain, not to relieve it. This objective was realized in their actual practice as 67% of the patients in their study (and 76% in a parallel study) continued to experience moderate to severe pain.

Teske and colleagues (1983) reported that there was little relationship between patients' self-reports of pain and observers' (nurses') inferences of pain based on observation of nonverbal behaviors. They noted that there is not a good reason to believe that observed behaviors are a better (or worse) measure of pain than self-report.

Dudley and Holm (1984) found that nurses tended to infer a greater degree of psychological distress than pain. They made the observation that such an inference can lead to inappropriate management of suffering; that is, patients will be given psychological support but not pain intervention.

Winsberg and Greenlick's (1967) ethnocultural study of the pain response in obstetrical

141

patients investigated the consistency of pain evaluations by people occupying different professional roles. The study specifically investigated if Black and White women responded differently to childbirth pain, and if there were discrepancies in the evaluations of that pain response by the various health care professionals. There were no observed differences in the two racial groups and the medical personnel tended to evaluate the patients the same way. However, both patient groups evaluated the pain experience as being more severe than did their nurses and physicians.

Streltzer and Wade (1981) studied post-cholecystectomy pain in Whites, Hawaiians, and Asians. They noted that nurses commonly limited the amount of analgesic administered to all their patients. However, some patients received fewer analgesics than others. This difference seemed to be based on ethnicity, with less vocal ethnic groups (Asians) receiving the least medication. Several investigators have given explanations for nurses' underestimation and undertreatment of their patient's pain (Jacox, 1979; Meinhart & McCaffery, 1983). With repeated exposure to patient pain and suffering, nurses gradually become less sensitive to patients' complaints of pain. In addition, nurses fear causing respiratory depression in their patients and addiction. They also lack knowledge of basic pharmacology or fail to apply their knowledge.

Nursing staff in the studies cited tended to uphold the dominant culture values which strongly encourage stoicism during pain experiences and to believe that patients exaggerate their pain experiences. Davitz and Davitz (1981) studied nurses' attitudes toward pain and found that the patient's ethnicity was related to how much physical and psychological distress the nurse believed the patient was experiencing. Nurses thought that Jewish and Spanish-speaking patients expressed the most distress with pain and Anglo-Saxon patients the least. The nurses' own cultural background also influenced how much distress they thought patients were experiencing with pain. Nurses of Northern European and United States backgrounds thought patients were experiencing less physical pain and psychological distress, whereas nurses of Eastern and Southern European or African backgrounds thought patients were experiencing more pain and psychological distress. This was true regardless of the nurses' years of experience, position, and area of practice. These investigators concluded that nurses' judgments about the pain and distress suffered by patients are influenced by their own beliefs about suffering. Cultural factors, social class, religion, education, and ethnic background all played a role in nurses' inferences of patients' pain. Regardless of cultural background, however, all studies reviewed here showed that nurses and other medical staff consistently underestimated pain when compared to their patients' reports of pain.

Implications for transcultural nursing practice

The studies reviewed here reveal a need among nurses for general knowledge of the concepts of culture and pain, and for specific knowledge of various cultures and their traditional beliefs, values, and practices as these relate to pain and its treatment. These studies also suggest a need among nurses for transcultural knowledge of pain assessment and management. The implications for nursing practice discussed here will focus on Mexican-Americans but the same ideas might apply to other cultures with whom the nurse is working. In making an assessment of a Mexican-American and his or her potential response to pain, the cultural beliefs, values and practices of the client must be assessed with respect to illness, suffering and pain. The extent to which traditional beliefs are held and adhered will give the nurse information about the value of fatalism and suffering, stoicism, and self-control and how these are expressed during pain experience.

An assessment of actual responses to pain should include gathering data on what a particular behavior and/or vocalization might mean in response to pain. For example, does it mean the pain is merely perceived or recognized? Or does it mean the pain is intolerable? Secondly, an assessment of actual response to pain should include gathering data on the function of particular behaviors and vocalizations, for example, crying and moaning. Is the function of these behaviors and vocalizations to relieve the pain? Or is the function to signal the nurse that pain intervention is being requested? Or is it something else?

The management of the patient's pain should include an assessment of the type of intervention the person desires. Does the patient wish traditional interventions, expressions of nurturance and compassion, psychological support, physical interventions (soothing, having brow wiped, relaxation)? cultural support? medication? or a combination of these? Does the patient value self-control and can the nurse assist the patient in practicing self-control if this is desired? The role of the family or social support network in providing any of these interventions should be assessed as well and accommodations made for family, friends and clergy to provide

142

interventions. These are a few of the most obvious implications for transcultural nursing practice based on the studies of Mexican-Americans reviewed in this paper.

Recommendations for future research

It should be emphasized that nurses and other health care workers need a working knowledge and understanding of specific cultures in order to conduct research with these populations. Studies included in the review of literature have provided information on traditional values, health beliefs and practices, and the role of culture and responses to pain among Mexican-Americans and Anglo-Americans. In addition, some studies on how nurses respond to patients in pain have provided a basis for further research. Nurses who wish to pursue research of the kind reviewed here should be aware of the methodological problems that characterize these studies and make cross-cultural comparisons difficult. These problems are common to quantitative approaches and involve issues of validity, reliability, control, sampling, and setting. Questions which occurred frequently in the studies reviewed included: 1) Questions of validity, such as were the investigators measuring the pain response or an emotion such as anxiety? 2) Questions of reliability, such as would the findings be similar in a replication study or with a larger sample? 3) Questions of control, such as would the pain response be different if age, education, sex and social class were controlled? and 4) Questions of setting, such as would a laboratory setting provide more control and valid results than a hospital setting? For all of these questions, nurses need to weigh the credibility and applicability to practice of findings resulting from a laboratory setting where pain is induced in subjects randomly assigned to an experimental group against findings emerging from a hospital setting where patients are experiencing cholecystectomy pain. Their decisions will be influenced inevitably by the real life world in which they study and practice.

Research with various cultures and the application of that knowledge to the improvement of client care are the goals of transcultural nursing. The focus of research recommendations here, however, is limited to Mexican-Americans and Anglo-Americans. Suggested areas for study involving Mexican-Americans and Anglo-Americans include both qualitative and quantitative approaches to the development of knowledge. Qualitative studies are needed which explore and describe various cultures' beliefs, values and practices with respect to the pain experience, that is, the value of pain, the perception of pain, the response to pain, and the management of pain. For Mexican- and Anglo-Americans these include: 1) descriptions of traditional health beliefs and practices in the two groups related to pain, suffering, fatalism and stoicism; 2) description of the meaning and function of behaviors and vocalizations associated with pain in the two groups; 3) identification of traditional practices or self-control practices to alleviate pain used by individuals from the two groups; and 4) identification of home and folk remedies used for pain by persons from the two groups. Quantitative studies needed include: 1) comparison of pain perception between the two groups in clinical settings; 2) comparison of pain perception between nurses and patients from the two groups; 3) investigation of different nursing interventions with patients from each of the two groups; and 4) comparison of requests for medication and the amount of medication provided by the nursing staff to patients from the two groups for the same source of pain. Finally research is needed which focuses on development of pain assessment tools that nurses can use with different cultures; and development of reliable and valid research tools that can be used in cross-cultural populations.

Conclusion

Pain is a subjective sensation affected by many variables which include cultural values, beliefs, practices and response style; social characteristics like education, age, sex, and social class; and psychological reactions like depression and anxiety (Calatrello, 1980; Leininger, 1977; Teske et al., 1983). The person experiencing pain has developed attitudes, influenced by social and cultural factors, which affect how the pain experience should be reacted to and reported. Because pain is a subjective sensation, it is difficult for nurses to objectively evaluate the pain response. It may well be that the best measure of pain is the patient's subjective experience. Therapeutic relationships and interactions may be affected negatively by the tendency for nurses to rely on values largely derived from dominant Anglo-American cultural values and behavioral expectations. For this reason, nurses should not minimize the significance of patients' traditional values, health beliefs and practices learned from being a member of a specific culture.

References

Calatrello, R.L. (1980). The Hispanic concept of illness: An obstacle to effective health care management? *Behavioral Medicine, 7*(11), 23–28.

Castro, F.G., Furth, P., & Karlow, H. (1984). The health beliefs of Mexican, Mexican-American, and Anglo-American women. *Hispanic Journal of Behavioral Sciences, 6*(4), 365–368.

Cohen, F.L. (1980). Postsurgical pain relief: Patients' status and nurses' medication choices. *Pain, 9*(1), 265–274.

Davitz, J.R., & Davitz, L.J. (1981). *Influences on patients' pain and psychological distress.* New York: Springer-Verlag.

Dudley, S.R., & Holm, K. (1984). Assessment of the pain experience in relation to selected nurse characteristics. *Pain, 18*(2), 179–186.

Flannery, R.B., Sos, J., & McGovern, P. (1981). Ethnicity as a factor in the expression of pain. *Psychosomatics, 22*(1), 34–39, 45, 49–50.

Gonzalez-Swafford, M.L., & Gutierrez, M.G. (1983). Ethnomedical beliefs and practices of Mexican-Americans. *Nurse Practitioner, 8*(10), 29–34.

Harwood, A. (1981). *Ethnicity and medical care.* Cambridge: Harvard University Press.

Jacox, A.K. (1979). Assessing pain. *American Journal of Nursing, 79*(5), 895–900.

Kalish, R.A., & Reynolds, D.K. (1976). *Death and ethnicity: A psycho-cultural study.* Los Angeles: Ethel Percy Andrus Gerontology Center/University of Southern California.

Leininger, M. (1976). *Transcultural health care issues and conditions.* Philadelphia: F.A. Davis.

Leininger, M. (1977). Cultural diversities of health and nursing care. *Nursing Clinics of North America, 12*(1), 5–18.

Leininger, M. (1979). *Transcultural Nursing.* New York: Masson.

Leininger, M. (1984). Transcultural nursing: An overview. *Nursing Outlook, 32*(2), 72–73.

Lipton, J.A., & Marbach, J.J. (1980). Pain differences, similarities found. *Science News, 118,* 182–183.

Ludwig-Beymer, P. (1989). Transcultural aspects of pain. In J.S. Boyle and M.M. Andrews (Eds.), *Transcultural concepts in nursing care.* Glenview, IL: Scott-Foresman.

Meinhart, N.T., & McCaffery, M. (1983). *Pain: A nursing approach to assessment and analysis.* Norwalk, CT: Appleton-Century-Crofts.

Melzack, R. (1983). *Pain measurement and assessment.* New York: Raven Press.

Orque, M., Bloch, B., & Monrroy, L.S. (1983). *Ethnic nursing care: A multicultural approach.* St. Louis: Mosby.

Perez-Stable, E.J. (1987). Issues in Latino healthcare. *Western Journal of Medicine, 139,* 820–828.

Rankin, M.A., & Snider, B. (1984).

Nurses' perception of cancer patients' pain. *Cancer Nursing, 7*(2), 149–155.

Sternbach, R.A., & Tursky, B. (1965). Ethnic differences among housewives in psychophysical and skin potential response to electric shock. *Psychophysiology, 1,* 241–246.

Streltzer, J., & Wade, T.C. (1981). The influence of cultural group on the undertreatment of postoperative pain. *Psychosomatic Medicine, 43*(5), 397–403.

Teske, K., Daut, R.L., & Cleeland, C.S. (1983). Relationships between nurses' observations and patients' self-reports of pain. *Pain, 16*(3), 286–296.

Winsberg, B., & Greenlick, M. (1967). Pain response in Negro and White obstetrical patients. *Journal of Health Social Behavior, 8,* 222–227.

Wolff, B.B., & Langley, S. (1979). Cultural factors and the response to pain. In D. Landy (Ed.), *Culture, disease, and healing* (pp. 313–319). New York: McMillan.

Zborowski, M. (1952). Cultural components in responses to pain. *Journal of Social Issues, 8,* 16–30.

Zborowski, M. (1969). *People in pain.* San Francisco: Jossey-Bass.

Selection 3-5 *Avoiding Opioid-Induced Respiratory Depression*

Purpose for Reading

PROCESS GOAL: **To monitor comprehension and reading efficiency**

The topic of this article is of such importance and current interest that the journal in which it appeared offered continuing education credit for nurses who passed a test about the article. RNs who read this article could answer the questions to update their knowledge about the subject and could register to receive required continuing education units.

OUTCOME GOAL: **To evaluate reading efficiency by passing a test**

Although the offer of continuing education credit is not available to you as a student, you will get a good idea of how well you are thinking like a health professional when you prepare for and take the test that accompanies the article.

Before Reading 1

Goal: Get oriented to the text
Techniques: Preview new assignment; make predictions about the information; estimate the difficulty of the material

---

Think about the article's title: "Avoiding Opioid-Induced Respiratory Depression." What is "respiratory depression"? Why is avoiding it important enough to offer continuing education credit to nurses mastering the article?

In your preview, confirm your guesses and get an idea of the organization of the article as well as a sense of the expertise of the authors. Estimate the difficulty of the article.

Before Reading 2

Goal: Get oriented to the assignment
Technique: Preview new assignments

If you haven't already done so, preview the test that follows the article. Note that the authors' objectives are included on the test page.

It's a good idea to get as much information as you can before reading. Although you probably can't remember specific test questions as you read, knowing the type of question you'll have to answer can focus your reading very effectively. Since you'll be reading to locate information that you can then reread as you answer each question, it's not necessary to try to remember details.

Before Reading 3

Goal:	Develop a study plan
Technique:	Decide which parts of the text relate to objectives

---

Make a plan for reading, considering your knowledge of and interest in the topic. Your goal is to be able to answer the test questions with the confidence that comes from a thorough understanding of the material.

When you encounter a term you don't know, mark it, but don't interrupt your reading unless your comprehension is completely blocked.

Note: Answering the test questions is *not* considered part of the reading. In fact, there are some other questions to be answered *after reading,* before you take the test.

During Reading 1

Goal:	Monitor comprehension
Technique:	Use alternative strategies or return to an appropriate before-reading technique

---

Be aware of how well you are understanding the article as you read. If you find yourself finishing a section that you don't understand, go back to an earlier technique that you think will help you get back on track.

During Reading 2

Goal:	Monitor reading efficiency
Technique:	Evaluate the efficiency of your study strategies

Are you able to recognize when you have learned something that will be useful after reading? Losing yourself in your reading is only acceptable in leisure reading. When studying for an assignment, you need to be aware of your studying efficiency as you read.

After Reading 1

Goal:	Organize relevant material for review
Technique:	Look up and learn new terms discovered during reading

---

Now is the time to clarify any new terms or concepts that you don't understand. In addition, answer the following questions before taking the test:

1. What (exactly) do these abbreviations stand for?
   COPD _____
   NSAID _____
   PACU _____
   PCA _____
   PRN _____
   Where can you look up such abbreviations?

2. Use the chart on opioid characteristics on page 151 to answer these questions:
   a. Which opioid has the quickest onset time using the intravenous route?

   _____

   b. Which opioid takes the longest time to reach peak effectiveness? Using which route?

   _____

   c. If the goal is delayed onset of analgesia, which medication and route would you recommend?

   _____

3. If the "incidence of clinically significant respiratory depression in hospitalized adults receiving opioids in therapeutic doses is approximately 0.09%," how many people are affected? _____ (Yes, this is a reading text, not a math text, but you must understand what you are reading even when it includes numbers.)
   a. 9 of 100
   b. 9 of 1,000
   c. 9 of 10,000
   d. 9 of 100,000

4. Have you mastered the authors' objectives? Although the test at the end of the article will assess your mastery, you should be able to address the three objectives. For example, what is your response to the second objective: "Identify two factors that increase the risk for opioid-induced respiratory depression"?

After Reading 2

Goal:	Test recall of relevant information
Technique:	Answer test questions

When you're satisfied with your level of comprehension, begin answering the thirteen test questions at the end of the article. Note that you are not required to do this from memory. You are welcome to look back at the article as often as you like. A good technique to use is to mark the section of the article that answers a question with the number of the question. This allows you to double-check the information that supports your answer before you turn in the test.

Review your answers before checking the Consultations section. If you can't decide between two answers, double-check the information in the article until you can choose one best answer. Make this a real test of your comprehension; don't undercut its usefulness by allowing yourself to think you "almost" picked the right answer, or that you "really meant" an answer that you didn't write down. *Do your best!*

From *AJN*, April 1994, pp. 25–31.

Christine L. Pasero, RN, BSN
Margo McCaffery, RN, MS, FAAN

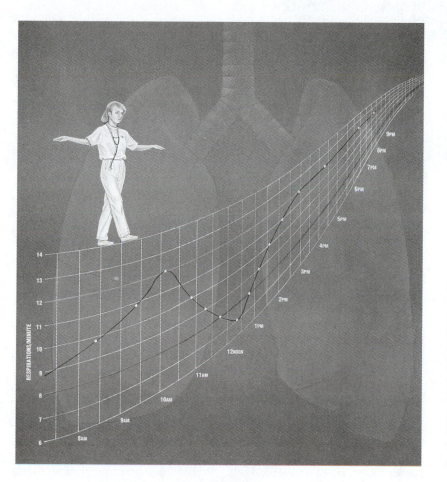

Fear of respiratory depression needn't result in poor pain management. Understanding how to prevent, assess, and manage respiratory depression will help you walk that fine clinical line that ensures both safe and effective pain relief.

Christine L. Pasero is an independent pain management education consultant in Rocklin, CA, and a co-founder and past president of the American Society of Pain Management Nurses. Los Angeles–based Margo McCaffery is a consultant in the nursing care of patients with pain.

John Stewart has lung cancer with widespread metastases. He's been admitted to the hospital for some tests. While he's in the hospital, Mr. Stewart's physician also would like to get his pain under better control. At home, Mr. Stewart has been taking oral morphine daily for three months. For the last week he's been taking 200 mg of morphine orally every four hours around the clock, plus 50 mg between doses for breakthrough pain. Mr. Stewart's physician has ordered an increase to 300 mg orally every four hours around the clock beginning with the next dose, which is due now.

Betty Lewis was sent to your surgical unit from the emergency department following an automobile accident. She's just been medically cleared for head injuries and will be taken to the operating room to repair her lacerations and a fractured wrist. She's reporting severe pain and hasn't received analgesia yet. Her physician has ordered 10 mg of morphine IM every three hours as needed for pain. When you ask Mrs. Lewis if she's allergic to any pain medication, she mentions having tolerated injections of pain medications well following her cesarean section two years ago.

Michael Thomas is scheduled for surgery tomorrow for repair of a knee injury. During your medication history-taking in the admission assessment, Mr. Thomas tells you that when he was given an injection of pain medication after abdominal surgery last year, he became so sedated he couldn't even sit up in bed. He recalls that his nurses gave him another drug to wake him up and help him breathe better. The surgeon is planning to use intravenous PCA to manage Mr. Thomas's postoperative pain.

Like the three preceding examples, each of your patients' pain management needs poses a unique challenge. Opioids, like morphine and fentanyl, are the most effective drugs to relieve pain because they directly affect the body's ability to feel pain. But they also raise the specter of adverse effects—primarily respiratory depression. How would you assess the risk levels of the three patients above?

Although research shows that clinically significant opioid-induced respiratory depression rarely occurs, many clinicians are very concerned about it and feel powerless to prevent it or ineffective in managing it. But when you apply the guidelines we'll discuss here for assessment, prevention, and management, you'll become confident that you can guard against respiratory depression without compromising pain relief.

When is respiratory depression clinically significant?

Respiratory depression is assessed on the basis of what's normal for a particular individual. Respiratory depression associated with opioid use is a decrease in rate or depth of respirations, not necessarily a specific number of respirations per minute. This means that in some cases even patients breathing less than 10 times per minute may not have respiratory depression if they're breathing deeply.

Respiratory depression is considered clinically significant only when it's severe enough to require intervention, such as stopping an analgesic infusion, providing physical stimulation, or administering an opioid antagonist (naloxone [Narcan]) to reverse it and prevent progression to respiratory arrest. The incidence of clinically significant respiratory depression in hospitalized adults

receiving opioids in therapeutic doses is approximately 0.09%.

Because even more opioid is required to produce respiratory depression than is required to produce sedation, patients with clinically significant respiratory depression are usually also sedated. This is why monitoring of sedation level is as important as monitoring respiratory status, if not more so. As we'll see later, you can prevent respiratory depression by taking actions when you detect an increasing level of sedation. Patients who have acceptable sedation levels don't suddenly succumb to respiratory depression.

> **Patients who have acceptable sedation levels don't suddenly succumb to respiratory depression.**

Why opioids depress respiration

Opioids may cause respiratory depression because they reduce the responsiveness of carbon dioxide chemoreceptors located in the respiratory centers of the brain (primarily in the medulla). That means increasing blood levels of carbon dioxide no longer produce an increase in respiratory rate. When the CO_2 receptors are desensitized by opioids, the body must rely on the oxygen-driven respiration regulating mechanism, which is less sensitive. Brain centers that regulate the rhythm of respirations are also depressed, which can disrupt the pattern of breathing.

Even in doses that relieve pain without adverse effects, opioids depress all phases of respiratory activity—rate, minute volume, and tidal exchange—to some extent. Some decrease in respiration is normal with opioids and requires no treatment.

Your patient's relative risk

To manage your patient's pain with confidence, one of the first things you need to do is assess his relative risk of opioid-induced respiratory depression. There's no set dose of an opioid that will be safe or effective for all patients. Generally, patients are at greatest risk for respiratory depression when they receive their first dose of an opioid. So sedation and respiratory rate, quality, and patterns should be monitored closely until a safe dose and interval are determined. Pulse, blood pressure, and any adventitious sounds (crackles and wheezes) can be assessed routinely.

Some patients are at greater risk than others. For example, infants younger than six months have difficulty eliminating opioids and an increased susceptibility to respiratory depression because of slower liver metabolism (due to liver immaturity). But older infants and children who don't have predisposing complications have no higher risk of respiratory depression than adults. Elders may be more sensitive to sedation and respiratory depression because of their bodies' altered drug distribution and slower rate of drug excretion.

Concurrent use of certain medications may increase the risk of respiratory depression. For example, postoperative patients who've been given large amounts of anesthesia and sedative drugs during surgery are at increased risk until those effects wear off. Whenever patients receive drugs with sedative effects, such as promethazine (Phenergan) or midazolam (Versed), any time during the postoperative period, their risk increases.

Preexisting conditions may affect the likelihood of respiratory depression. Because opioids exert a direct effect on the respiratory centers of the brain,

Characteristics of Commonly Prescribed Opioids

Opioid	Route	Onset* (min.)	Peak* (min.)
morphine	oral	30–60	90–120
	IM	15–45	30–60
	IV	10–20	15–30
	E	30	30–60
hydromorphone	IM	15	30–60
	IV	5	10–20
	E	15	25
meperidine	IM	15	30–60
	IV	5–15	20–45
	E	10	20
fentanyl	IV	1	1–5
	E	5	10–20

IM = intramuscular; IV = intravenous; E = epidural

*Remarkably little research has been done to establish onset and peak effects of opioids. The numbers above are based on clinical experience and sources listed in Selected References (see Jaffe, Hord, and Willens).

patients with already compromised pulmonary status (by lung cancer, COPD, or heavy smoking, for example) are at higher risk. Patients who have renal dysfunction, impairing their ability to excrete drugs, are also at higher risk for opioid-induced respiratory depression.

Whether your patient is opioid naive or tolerant is also a factor to consider even in otherwise healthy adults. Opioid naive means that the patient hasn't used opioids for at least a week and is at higher risk than someone who's been using opioids for a while.

Opioid tolerant means that the patient has developed tolerance to the drug's effects. The time to develop tolerance will vary among patients, but usually takes a week or longer. It's apparent when a patient's dose of pain medication needs to be increased to give the same relief. In general, the greater a patient's tolerance is, the less risk of respiratory depression.

Respiratory depression is dose-related—higher doses cause increased respiratory depression. The first 24 hours after surgery is considered a risky phase because the amount of opioid the patient receives is likely to be greatest during that time. But a "high" dose will differ from one individual to another. For example, 300 mg of oral morphine isn't too much for Mr. Stewart, but it would very likely be high for Mrs. Lewis or Mr. Thomas.

Patients like Mr. Thomas should be considered at increased risk because they've reported a history of opioid sensitivity. For reasons that aren't fully understood, some patients have a profound reaction to opioids. There isn't an easy way to identify them except that adults will often report such a reaction during history-taking.

Betty Lewis is opioid naive because she hasn't received opioids recently enough to have tolerance to respiratory depression. Most patients you'll encounter having surgery are opioid naive and therefore at normal risk for opioid-induced respiratory depression. John Stewart has the smallest risk because he's been taking opioids for a long time and has developed tolerance to

opioid analgesia and respiratory depression.

When respiratory depression is most likely to occur

One rule of thumb is that the most important time to observe carefully for respiratory depression is from onset through peak of the first opioid dose given to an opioid-naive patient. (See box at left.)

The initial dose of an opioid for pain relief usually is given to the patient in the PACU. But patients are very often discharged from this specialty unit as soon as they've recovered consciousness and are breathing normally. In many cases they will still be experiencing effects of intraoperative sedatives and anesthetics when they reach the clinical unit. Establishing a safe dosage and dosing interval that effectively relieves pain will largely be done after the patient leaves the PACU.

During the remainder of the 24-hour postop period, opioids accumulate. Most, like morphine and hydromorphone (Dilaudid), reach a steady state within 24 hours. Throughout this phase, your patient is at risk for respiratory depression. Sedation and respiratory status still need monitoring approximately every one to two hours. After the first 24 hours, if no problems have occurred, the frequency of monitoring can be reduced to every two to four hours.

Demand patient-controlled analgesia (PCA), contrary to what you might assume, can be useful to avoid opioid-induced respiratory depression. Because sedation precedes clinical significant respiratory depression and demand PCA doesn't automatically deliver a dose, the patient is unlikely to self-administer enough doses to produce clinically significant respiratory depression or arrest.

Watching for sedation

As we noted earlier, you can prevent respiratory depression by taking action when you detect an increasing level of sedation, which precedes it. In our experience, nursing observation is the best method of monitoring sedation level and respiratory status. In fact, a recent survey of over 16 medical facilities reports that pain management services only use pulse oximetry outside of the PACU or ICU if a patient has a preexisting condition that requires it.*

Pulse oximetry and blood-gas analysis aren't the best ways to avoid clinically significant respiratory depression because sedation will, in most cases, precede any change in blood gases. Most patients in the acute setting won't require blood gas monitoring. The same is true of pulse oximetry, and both are expensive.

Assessment guidelines

Preparing for the possibility of opioid-induced respiratory depression begins before the patient receives his first dose. This includes ensuring that an opioid antagonist is ordered along with the analgesic, so it's available if you need it. On admission, baseline information about a patient's normal respiratory rate, quality, and patterns, as well as pupil size, sedation level, and arousability, should be obtained and documented. There are many sedation scales available, but for this discussion, we'll refer to a simple numeric scale with "S" denoting normal sleep. (See *Sedation Scale* on opposite page.)

Arousability is the key to determining your patient's sedation level. Be aware that a sleeping patient isn't necessarily sedated. It's normal and recom-

*C. Pasero, Unpublished data, 1994.

NINE WAYS TO PREVENT OPIOID-INDUCED RESPIRATORY DEPRESSION

Clinically significant respiratory depression is preventable. In fact, its prevention is easier than its management. Here are nine suggestions to prevent respiratory depression from reaching clinical significance:

1. *Assess risk.* Determine on admission if your patient is at high or low risk for opioid-induced respiratory depression. During the admission interview, ask your patients to describe past experiences with surgery, anesthesia and analgesics, and current opioid use. Ask specific questions about the effects of the analgesics they've taken, including the level of pain relief and the adverse effects. Make sure that an opioid antagonist is ordered along with the analgesic in case it's needed.

2. *Communicate.* The information you obtain in the admission interview is very important for everyone involved in managing your patient's pain. If your patient has a history of sensitivity, inform the pain service nurse, the PACU, the anesthesiologist, and the physician of this opioid sensitivity so that less-sedative drugs can be used before, during, and after surgery, and so the postoperative opioid dose can be reduced.

3. *Anticipate pain.* Whenever possible, address your patients' postoperative analgesic needs during preoperative preparation. Nonsteroidal anti-inflammatory drugs (NSAIDs), for example, are capable of producing analgesia without sedation and respiratory depression. When NSAIDs are administered in combination with opioids, the opioid dose often can be reduced. Patients then will experience pain relief but with less risk of sedation and respiratory depression. If your patient is at high risk for opioid-induced respiratory depression, request an order from the physician to administer at NSAID preoperatively and to continue the administration of the NSAID around the clock postoperatively, using an opioid to provide additional analgesia if needed.

4. *Watch for additive effects.* Be aware of other drugs that your patient is receiving. For all patients receiving opioid analgesia, carefully assess the need for antiemetics and sedatives. Avoid routinely adding phenothiazines (promethazine/Phenergan) and benzodiazepines (midazolam/Versed or diazepam/Valium). These drugs provide little, if any, pain relief but they can increase respiratory depression, sedation, and hypotension—effectively limiting the dose of opioid you can safely give.

5. *Adjust initial doses.* If your patient is at risk for respiratory depression and a range of dosage has been prescribed, administer the lowest amount and titrate upward to effectiveness. If your patient isn't at high risk, start in the middle of the range for your patient and titrate upward to effectiveness. Remember, the first dose will reveal your patient's ability to tolerate opioids. It's up to you to evaluate these effects and make arrangements to adjust the dose or interval if needed. Continue to assess the appropriateness of dose and interval for as long as your patient is receiving opioid analgesia.

6. *Act on response, not amount.* Increase or decrease the dose of opioid based on your assessment of the patient's response. Patients' responses and therefore their requirements vary widely, even when they have identical diagnoses or surgical procedures, so it's less important to focus on the amount given. To determine what dose your patient needs after the initial dose, always look at the effect the opioid has had on your patient's pain rating, sedation level, and respiratory status.

7. *Adjust maintenance doses.* The safest way to increase the dose of opioid is gradually, by percentage of the previous dose or the current opioid infusion dose, and after the peak effect. If your patient isn't at high risk for respiratory depression, reports pain, and has no intolerable adverse effects, the dose can be increased by 50% to 100%. If your patient is at high risk for opioid-induced respiratory depression, reports pain, and has no intolerable adverse effects, increase the dose by only 25%.

continued

8. *Be aware of pharmacokinetic differences.* Learn the peak times for the various opioids and other sedative drugs you administer and monitor your patient closely when those peak times are reached. It's also wise initially to stagger the times you give other sedative drugs as much as possible so that all the effects don't peak at the same time.

9. *Plan ahead.* Known high-risk patients need more frequent monitoring. The busiest times on surgical units are when the majority of the patients are in their first 24 postoperative hours. These busy times are often predictable because most major surgeries are done on a known, regular schedule. Whenever possible, work with your nursing administrators to ensure adequate staff on those days that are the busiest and require the closest patient monitoring.

Communicate staffing needs as soon as you're aware of them. Accountability for providing patients with effective, safe pain relief begins at the administrative level in the hospital, but they need information from the front line in order to provide support. Also, be willing to be part of the team to manage the demands on nurses caring for high-risk patients. Through teamwork, nurses can protect their patients from developing clinically significant respiratory depression.

mended for patients to sleep, and a sleeping patient's sedation level is acceptable if he's easily aroused. If possible, check your patient's baseline arousability. He or she may be a sound sleeper and normally difficult to arouse.

For nurses working during the night, who may be justifiably reluctant to awaken their patients, one easy way to assess the level of sedation without disturbing sleep is to observe the patient's response when you enter the room or touch their shoulder lightly. Most patients will stir, indicating an acceptable level of sedation. In any case, if the patient's respiratory rate and depth are acceptable, you don't need to arouse him. But if your patient doesn't stir or his respiratory rate is below his baseline rate, he should be aroused so that you can better determine the sedation level, especially during the first 24 hours after surgery.

Like the normal sleep rating, sedation levels of 1 and 2 are reassuring. When patients have a sedation level of 1, they're fully awake and able to perform all activities of recovery at the time

of your assessment. Patients with a sedation rating of 2 may report feeling "groggy" and that their eyelids are heavy, but they're able to participate fully in their recovery. Most patients progress to these sedation levels when the effects of anesthesia wear off if their opioid dose is at or below their requirement for adequate pain relief.

Patients with acceptable levels of sedation who are taking opioids will usually have mild, if any, respiratory depression. The respiratory rate will usually be within acceptable limits and breathing may be slightly shallower than normal. Their pupil size may be slightly constricted but still more than 2 mm in size. Normally, pupil diameter is from 3 to 7 mm.

Managing clinically significant respiratory depression

Taking a moment to strike up a conversation with your patient is an excellent way to confirm a sedation level of 3. If your patient can't complete a sentence without falling asleep or perform activities such as sitting at the bedside doing range of motion

exercises as requested, he has a sedation level of 3.

Respiratory depression may be evident with shallow respirations, irregular or periodic breathing, and a rate of 10 or less, though some patients maintain a higher respiratory rate. Your patient may also have apneic episodes during sleep. Pupils may be constricted; usually they are no more than 2 to 3 mm in size.

With a sedation level of 3, it's very important to inform the physician of the need to cut the opioid dose by at least half or, in some cases, to discontinue the infusion. Increase the frequency of sedation and respiratory status monitoring of your patient to every 15 minutes. You should also attempt to arouse him every 15 minutes with reminders to take deep breaths, which he should be able to do.

When the effect of the opioid begins to wear off, the patient will become more alert and need monitoring less frequently. When you notify the physician of the need to decrease the opioid dose, ask him for an order for an NSAID around the clock to stay ahead of the pain as you reduce the amount of opioid. If taken promptly, these actions can prevent a clinically significant episode of respiratory depression and maintain pain relief.

SEDATION SCALE
S Sleep, easily aroused
1 Awake and alert
2 Occasionally drowsy, easy to arouse
3 Frequently drowsy, arousable, drifts off to sleep during conversation
4 Somnolent, minimal or no response to stimuli

Patients with a sedation rating of 4 are difficult to arouse and require immediate attention. They'll have shallow respirations and more frequent apnea. Their respiratory rates may be less than eight breaths per minute (though some patients may have a higher rate). Pupil size will usually be less than 2 mm (pinpoint).

If your patient has a sedation rating of 4 and is receiving an analgesic infusion, the first action you should take is to stop the infusion. Stay with your patient and have a colleague notify the physician and bring an opioid antagonist, naloxone. If your patient is receiving PCA, set the PCA button aside or remove it so that it can't inadvertently be pressed.

Next, determine if physical stimulation and withholding the opioid are sufficient treatment. If the patient arouses when shaken and spoken to loudly, opens his eyes briefly, and possibly groans before lapsing back into profound sedation, physical stimulation with reminders to breathe deeply every one to two minutes may be acceptable. But you must remain with the patient. If a patient with a sedation rating of 4 is unresponsive when shaken and spoken to loudly, you'll need to administer an opioid antagonist. Always notify the physician when your patient has a sedation rating of 4.

Reversing opioid-induced respiratory depression

Naloxone is an opioid antagonist that will reverse the sedative and respiration-depressing effects of opioids. Administering naloxone correctly is crucial because if you give too much or give it too quickly, analgesia will also quickly be reversed.

To ensure that you reverse the adverse effects while minimizing analgesia reversal, administer a dilute solution of naloxone (0.4 mg in 10 mL in normal saline) intravenously using the titration-to-effect technique. To do this, observe your patient closely as you push the naloxone solution very slowly (0.5 mL over two minutes) into your patient's IV access. Naloxone will begin to reverse sedation within one to two minutes and your patient should then be able to open his eyes and talk to you.

The IV route is ideal, but if naloxone can't be given IV it can be given IM or subcutaneously. With either of these two routes, you'll see a response within two to five minutes.

The amount of naloxone needed to reverse opioid-induced sedation and respiratory depression will vary among patients. So remember, the effect you achieve from naloxone is more important than the amount you administer. When your patient is awake and able to respond to your questions, you've achieved the desired effect. However, naloxone has a shorter duration than most opioid analgesics, so you may need to administer a repeat dose in 30 to 60 minutes, depending on the duration of the opioid analgesic you've given.

Once reversal has begun, continue monitoring your patient's recovering sedation level and respiratory status every one to two minutes and, if necessary, provide physical stimulation.

Instituting other methods of pain relief is especially important for patients who've been given naloxone because it will reverse analgesia to some degree. Request an order to administer an NSAID around the clock as soon as possible. If your patient was receiving an analgesic infusion before the incident, with the physician's order it may be resumed under close supervision at 25% to 50% of the prior dose when the patient's respiratory rate is greater than nine breaths per minute and sedation level is less than 3.

Documentation and follow-up

As soon as possible, document the incident, your assessment, actions, the patient's response to your actions, and the physicians' responses. Later, as part of the follow-up to an incident of respiratory depression, the staff members involved in caring for the patient and in managing his sedation and respiratory depression should meet. The purpose of this is to emphasize aspects of the incident that were handled appropriately and to determine if care can be improved, not to blame or find fault.

At the meeting review the following information:

- Doses, onset, and peak times of analgesics including nurse-administered bolus doses, sedatives, and antiemetics the patient received prior to the detection of increased sedation and respiratory depression;
- Vital signs and sedation levels, looking for trends;
- Actions taken to reverse the sedation and respiratory depression;
- Patient outcome.

The group should consider whether any aspect of care was overlooked or might have been done differently to prevent the incident.

At the next staff meeting the team should present their review to their coworkers to pass along what's been learned. This process helps the entire staff feel better about the original incident and can lead to improved patient care.

Success stories

After reviewing his opioid experience, the nurses caring for Mr. Stewart increased his opioid dose without fear of respiratory depression and he was able to go home in two days with controlled pain. Mrs. Lewis was watched closely after her initial dose of opioid to evaluate her pain relief and ability to tolerate the dose. She reported inadequate pain relief and no intolerable adverse effects, so her nurse consulted the physician and was able to increase the amount of her next dose by 50%. Mrs. Lewis reported adequate pain relief with the increased dose. Mr. Thomas was given an NSAID preoperatively and started on IV PCA postoperatively at the lowest end of his prescribed range. He had adequate pain relief and acceptable sedation levels throughout his course of recovery. In all three cases, good nursing decisions demonstrated that fear of respiratory depression need not result in poor pain relief.

Selected references

American Pain Society. *Principles of Analgesic Use in the Treatment of Acute Pain and Cancer Pain.* 3rd ed. Skokie, IL, The Society, 1992.

Deglin, J. H., and Vallerand, A. H. *Davis's Drug Guide for Nurses.* 3rd ed. Philadelphia, F. A. Davis Co., 1993.

Foley, K. M. The "decriminalization" of cancer pain. IN *Advances in Pain Research and Therapy; Vol. 11. Drug Treatment of Cancer Pain in a Drug-Oriented Society,* ed. by C. S. Hill, Jr. and W. S. Fields. New York, Raven Press, 1989, pp. 5–18.

Hord, A., and Kokenes, C. Postoperative pain: a review of management methods. *Hosp. Formulary* 24:28–38, 1989.

Jaffe, J. H., and Martin, W. R. Opioid analgesics and antagonists. IN *Goodman and Gilman's The Pharmacological Basis of Therapeutics,* 8th edition, edited by A. G. Gilman et al. New York, Pergamon Press, 1990, pp. 491–531.

Sinatra, R., and Savarese, A. Parenteral analgesic therapy and patient-controlled analgesia for pediatric pain management. IN *Acute Pain: Mechanisms and Management,* ed. by R. S. Sinatra et al. St. Louis, Mosby-Year Book, 1992, pp. 217–249.

U. S. Agency for Health Care Policy and Research, Acute Pain Management Guideline Panel. *Acute Pain Management: Operative or Medical Procedures and Trauma. Clinical Practice Guideline.* (AHCPR Pub. No. 92-0032) Washington, DC, U.S. Government Printing Office, 1992.

Willens, J. S., and Myslinski, N. R. Pharmacodynamics, pharmacokinetics, and clinical uses of fentanyl, sufentanil, and alfentanil. *Heart Lung* 22:239–251, May–June 1993; Erratum 22:307, May–June 1993.

1. Mr. Jamal, 52 years old, is receiving continuous IV morphine for pain. His respirations are shallow and irregular, and his respiratory rate has decreased to 8/minute. You find that he's arousable but drifts off to sleep during conversation. You understand that
a. his body is mainly relying on his oxygen-driven mechanism to regulate respiration.
b. decreasing levels of PCO_2 are no longer stimulating his respiratory center.
c. the morphine has increased the sensitivity of his respiratory rhythm brain center.
d. the morphine has depressed his cerebral cortex, which primarily regulates respiration.

2. Which of the following situations poses the greatest risk for respiratory depression for a patient receiving opioid therapy?
a. a 25% increase in the opioid dose for an alert patient with poor pain relief
b. supplementation of the opioid with an NSAID around the clock
c. administration of a PRN IV opioid for breakthrough pain in a patient on IV PCA opioid
d. administration of the first dose of the opioid

3. Which of the following patients has the greatest risk for opioid-induced respiratory depression?
a. a three-year-old child, two days postop
b. a 40-year-old male who's never had opioids
c. a 60-year-old woman who's opioid tolerant
d. a 35-year-old male, 30 hours postop

4. A surgical patient is at greatest risk for opioid-induced respiratory depression
a. during the first 24 hours postop.
b. after the first 36 hours postop.
c. after the first 72 hours postop.
d. just prior to discharge.

After reading the preceding article and taking this test, you'll be able to:
- **Identify the relationship between sedation levels and prevention of opioid-induced respiratory depression.**
- **Identify two factors that increase the risk for opioid-induced respiratory depression.**
- **Employ therapeutic assessment and intervention strategies for preventing and managing opioid-induced respiratory depression while ensuring effective pain relief.**

---

5. Mr. Plum, 50 years old, has been admitted in preparation for extensive bladder surgery. He mentions during your admission assessment that he had Demerol (meperidine) 12 years ago after surgery and that "it knocked me out and they had to help me breathe." This indicates that
a. Mr. Plum has opioid tolerance.
b. Mr. Plum's reaction was within normal limits.
c. Mr. Plum is opioid sensitive.
d. Mr. Plum had an allergic reaction to meperidine.

6. Which of the following is currently recommended for assessment of opioid-induced respiratory depression?
a. nurse monitoring of sedation level
b. pulse oximetry
c. blood gas analysis
d. mechanical apnea monitoring

7. Using the sedation scale on page 153, which of the following statements regarding assessment of a patient's sedation is *true?*
a. A sleeping patient's arousability determines the sedation level.
b. It's necessary to awaken sleeping patients with acceptable respiratory rates and depths to determine their sedation level.
c. A patient who is sleeping is considered sedated.
d. A sedation level of 4 is considered acceptable with opioid use.

8. Ms. Archer, 38 years old, is 24 hours postop for total abdominal hysterectomy. She's receiving morphine IV via a combination continuous infusion and PCA bolus for breakthrough pain. While giving her morning care, you note that she frequently drifts off to sleep during conversation but is arousable. Using the scale on page 153, you assess her sedation level to be
a. S.   c. 2.
b. 1.   d. 3.

9. Based on your sedation assessment of Ms. Archer, your most appropriate action would be to
a. contact the physician to obtain an order to decrease the opioid dose by at least half.
b. notify the physician to obtain an order for an opioid antagonist.
c. discontinue the PCA component of Ms. Archer's morphine infusion.
d. arouse Ms. Archer every 15 minutes and have her take deep breaths.

10. Morphine has the fastest onset and time to peak concentration when administered through which route?
a. oral   c. IV
b. IM   d. epidural

11. When NSAIDs are administered in combination with an opioid,
a. the opioid dose can often be reduced.
b. the chance of respiratory depression is enhanced.
c. the patient will experience increased sedation.
d. the patient will have increased pain.

12. To minimize the chance of respiratory depression, which of the following drugs would be the best to use in combination with an opioid to enhance pain relief?
a. promethazine (Phenergan)
b. diazepan (Valium)
c. ibuprofen (Motrin)
d. midazolam (Versed)

13. Mr. Cohn, 60 years old, is recovering from radical prostate surgery and receiving a continuous epidural infusion of fentanyl. He has a history of COPD. When you assess him for pain, he complains of moderate to severe pain and his sedation rating is 2. His pupils are 3 mm. You anticipate that Mr. Cohn's fentanyl dose should be increased within his prescribed range by
a. 5%.
b. 25%.
c. 50%.
d. 75%.

unit

4 Ethical and Legal Issues

Phase 3 · After Reading

Unit 4 addresses a content area important to all health occupations—ethical and legal issues. The focus of this unit is on how health professionals decide what is the "right" thing to do. Why do well-meaning, thoughtful, conscientious individuals sometimes make different decisions about the same ethical issue? Shouldn't there always be one "best" decision, no matter who is deciding?

The unit begins with a chapter from an introductory nursing text. Several journal articles present a variety of clinical situations with ethical and legal implications. Another selection is a chapter from a reference book on ethical and legal issues.

The emphasis in this unit is on goals to accomplish after reading. You will practice a variety of recall and review techniques including note making, outlining, paraphrasing, summarizing, and preparing for tests. All of these techniques allow you to save main ideas and significant details so that they can be reviewed periodically without your having to completely reread the material.

Selection 4-1   *Ethics and Values*

Purpose for Reading

PROCESS GOAL: To organize relevant information for review

Your focus in studying will be preparation for an open-book test. Teachers use in-class, open-book tests to motivate students to study. Tests like this don't require memorization but do reward careful study and careful marking of the text.

OUTCOME GOAL: To complete an open-book test on a textbook chapter with at least 80% accuracy

Health personnel need to be aware of legal issues related to patient care. The nurse's legal role is defined by state nurse practice acts, and the patient's individual rights are also protected by law. Both the nursing profession and federal laws support the patient's right to receive ethical nursing care. With the increasing responsibility for health care that nurses have assumed comes increasing concern about ethical implications. The chapter you will read comes from a textbook for beginning nursing students and offers a general, basic introduction to a complex subject.

Before Reading 1

Goal: Get oriented to the text and assignment
Techniques: Preview new assignment; ask questions

The nursing instructor might introduce this assignment to students as follows:

> Read Chapter 11, "Ethics and Values," to get an idea of the terms used when discussing nursing ethics. You should be able to differentiate among teleology, deontology, and intuitionism and to describe nursing activities related to each statement in the ANA Code for Nurses. Also, be prepared to discuss the role of the nurse as a client advocate. There will be an open-book test in class to check the effectiveness of your studying.

Which of the chapter objectives from the selection most closely relate to the assignment? Put a check mark beside those that seem related.

Chapter Objectives

_____ Explain how to recognize a moral issue.
_____ Define the terms *ethics, bioethics,* and *nursing ethics.*
_____ Discuss sources of ethical problems in nursing.
_____ Explain the difference between decision-focused problems
            and action-focused problems.

_____ Differentiate the following moral frameworks: deontology, teleology, intuitionism, and the ethic of caring.

_____ When presented with an ethical situation, identify the moral principles involved.

_____ Explain the uses and limitations of professional codes of ethics.

_____ Explain how cognitive development, values, moral frameworks, and codes of ethics affect moral decisions.

_____ Discuss the concept of an integrity-preserving compromise.

_____ Describe the elements of selected ethical issues nurses encounter.

_____ Discuss nursing roles and responsibilities with regard to ethics.

Before Reading 2

Goal: Get oriented to the text
Technique: Improve your background knowledge

Several terms are important in nursing ethics, and you might want to look them up in a collegiate dictionary to make sure that you have a general understanding of them. Each of these terms is defined in the assigned chapter, but you will be in a better position to remember the technical definition if you are already somewhat familiar with the word.

Write the ethics-related definition for any word that is new to you:

advocacy
autonomy
beneficence
confidentiality
deontology
ethics
fidelity
justice
nonmaleficence
teleology
veracity
morality
bioethics

During Reading

Goals: Monitor comprehension; monitor reading efficiency
Techniques: Look for main ideas and significant details; adjust reading rate to purpose for reading and to difficulty of the text

From the instructor's assignment, you know that the main topics to master are the technical terms, the teleological and deontological ethical theories, and the nursing code. Although the chapter may seem a little difficult, the objectives provided by the instructor and by the textbook offer clear guidelines for your reading.

Plan to stop periodically to ask yourself whether you have understood the material and to underline main ideas. Keep working on matching your reading rate to your purpose and to the difficulty of the material.

After Reading 1

Goal:	Check initial recall of relevant information
Technique:	Review the whole assignment by self-testing

During your preview, you noticed that not all of the chapter objectives related to the instructor's assignment. Test your recall of the chapter by satisfying the relevant textbook objectives:

Define the terms *ethics, bioethics,* and *nursing ethics.*

Differentiate the following moral frameworks: deontology, teleology, intuitionism, and the ethic of caring.

When presented with an ethical situation, identify the moral principles involved.

Discuss nursing roles and responsibilities with regard to ethics.

After Reading 2

Goal:	Organize relevant information for review
Technique:	Underline and make notes

To prepare for an open-book test, you'll need to make very effective marginal notes so that the chapter will become a reference tool to use during the test. Use the information provided by the instructor to underline and make marginal notes that highlight technical terms, the definitions of the teleological and deontological theories, and the nursing code.

There is no one right way to do this kind of notemaking. Suit yourself, but make it your goal to have legible notes that enable you to find answers without having to reread much of the text.

After Reading 3

Goal:	Test recall of relevant information
Technique:	Answer test questions

What follows is an example of an open-book test. Use it to see how well you made notes to identify relevant information. It is expected that you will refer to the chapter to find the answers. Some questions will be answered directly from information in the text; others will require application of the information. Do not peek at the test until you are sure you are ready to take it!

Open-Book Test

Match each ethical term with the correct definition:

_____ 1. autonomy

_____ 2. beneficence

_____ 3. confidentiality

_____ 4. fidelity

_____ 5. justice

_____ 6. nonmaleficence

_____ 7. veracity

_____ 8. ethics

_____ 9. morality

_____ 10. bioethics

a. keeping one's promise

b. the expected standards of behavior in a group

c. truthfulness

d. consistency, fairness

e. a morally neutral position

f. personal standards of right and wrong

g. self-regulation

h. the duty to do no harm

i. the duty to do good

j. providing for the patient's privacy

k. ethics applied to life and death decision making

11. A classmate asks you to explain utilitarian theory and give an example of it in a nursing situation. In your own words, how would you explain and illustrate this concept?

12. Compare and contrast the basic concepts of the deontological theory and the teleological theory. Why is it useful for nurses to consider these two theories?

Describe a nursing activity that illustrates the following codes from the American Nurses Association Code for Nurses. Write your example in the space provided.

13. *Code 1:*   The nurse provides services with respect for human dignity and the uniqueness of the client, unrestricted by considerations of social or economic status, personal attributes, or the nature of the health problems.

14. *Code 2:*   The nurse safeguards the client's right to privacy by judiciously protecting information of a confidential nature.

15. *Code 3:*   The nurse acts to safeguard the client and the public when health care and safety are affected by the incompetent, unethical, or illegal practice of any person.

16. *Code 5:*   The nurse maintains competence in nursing.

17. *Code 11:* The nurse collaborates with members of the health professions and other citizens in promoting community and national efforts to meet the health needs of the public.

CHAPTER 11

ETHICS AND VALUES

B. Kozier
G. Erb
K. Blais
J. Wilkinson

OBJECTIVES

Explain how to recognize a moral issue.
Define the terms *ethics, bioethics,* and *nursing ethics.*
Discuss sources of ethical problems in nursing.
Explain the difference between decision-focused problems and action-focused problems.
Differentiate the following moral frameworks: deontology, teleology, intuitionism, and the ethic of caring.
When presented with an ethical situation, identify the moral principles involved.
Explain the uses and limitations of professional codes of ethics.
Explain how cognitive development, values, moral frameworks, and codes of ethics affect moral decisions.

.
.
.

Discuss the concept of an integrity-preserving compromise.
Describe the elements of selected ethical issues nurses encounter.
Discuss nursing roles and responsibilities with regard to ethics.

Because nurses deal with the most fundamental human events—birth, death, and suffering—they encounter many ethical issues surrounding these sensitive areas. Nurses must decide what their own moral actions ought to be in these situations, and because of the special nature of the nurse-client relationship, they must support and sustain clients and families who are facing hard moral choices. As client advocates and as continuously present caregivers, nurses must also support clients who are living out the consequences of choices made for and about them by others. Nurses can make better moral decisions by thinking in advance about their beliefs and values and about the kinds of problems they may encounter in caring for their clients.

ETHICS, VALUES, AND MORALITY

The term *ethics* is derived from the Greek *ethos,* meaning custom or character. It has several meanings in common usage. First, it refers to a method of inquiry that assists people to understand the morality of human behavior (ie, it is the study of morality). When used in this sense, ethics is an activity; it is a way of looking at or investigating certain issues about human behavior. Second, ethics refers to the practices or beliefs of a certain group (ie, physicians' ethics, nursing ethics). Third, ethics refers to the expected standards of behavior of a particular group. These standards are described in the group's code of professional conduct. Nurses are expected to maintain certain ethical standards in their nursing practice. (See Codes of Ethics later in this chapter.) **Bioethics** is ethics as applied to life (ie, to life and death decision making). Nursing ethics refers to ethical issues involved in nursing practice.

Values are freely chosen, enduring beliefs or attitudes about the worth of a person, object, idea, or action. Freedom, courage, family, and dignity are examples of values, and form a basis for behavior; a person's real values are shown by consistent patterns of behavior. Once you are aware of your values, they become an internal control for behavior. "Values are significant in choice making" (Salladay

165

TABLE 11–1   Comparison of Morals and Ethics

Morals	Principles and rules of right conduct
	Private, personal
	Commitment to principles and values are usually defended in daily life
Ethics	Formal reasoning process used to determine right conduct
	Professionally and publicly stated
	Inquiry or study of principles and values
	Process of questioning, and perhaps changing, one's morals

& McDonnell 1989, p. 544). Each person has a small number of values.

Values exist in some relationship to one another within a person. A **value system** is the organization of a person's values along a continuum of relative importance. Values underlie **purposive behavior,** which refers to actions that are performed "on purpose" with the intention of reaching some goal or bringing about a certain result. Purposive behavior, then, is based on a person's decisions or choices, and these decisions or choices are based on underlying values.

Morals (or *morality*) is similar to ethics and many people use the two words interchangeably. **Morality** usually refers to *personal* standards of right and wrong. It denotes what is right and wrong in conduct, character, and attitude. Sometimes the first clue to the moral nature of a situation is an aroused conscience, or an awareness of feelings such as guilt, hope, or shame. The tendency to respond to the situation with words such as *ought, should, right, wrong, good,* and *bad* is another indicator. And finally, moral issues are concerned with important social values and norms: they are not about trivial things. They may seem unusually complex or difficult in some undefined way, but this is not necessarily so. See Table 11–1 for a comparison of morals and ethics.

Nurses should distinguish between *morality* and *the law.* Laws frequently reflect the moral values of a society; however, an action can be legal but not moral. For example, an order for "full resuscitation" of a terminally ill client is legal; however, one could still question whether the act is moral. Conversely, an action can be moral but illegal. For example, if a child at home stops breathing, it is moral but not legal to exceed the speed limit en route to the hospital. . . .

Distinction can also be made between *morality* and *religion.* Morality and religion are often closely related. For example, many years ago in the United States, "witches" were burned because of the reli-

gious beliefs of their persecutors. The morality of that practice can be questioned today.

People learn moral reasoning during their **socialization,** the process by which individuals learn the knowledge, skills, and dispositions of their social group or society. Lawrence Kohlberg perceives six stages in the moral development of individuals. . . . [Section omitted.]

NURSING ETHICS

The growing awareness of nursing ethics is mainly a product of social and technologic change and of the nature of nursing itself.

Social Movements   In the 1960s, the civil rights movement and a growing consumerism encouraged people to examine the morality of public institutions, exposing racial and economic discrimination in health care. The feminist movement linked oppression of nurses to discrimination against women in the health care setting and in the workplace, as well as in society as a whole. Currently, the large number of people without health insurance and the escalating cost of health care are raising issues of fairness and allocation of resources.

Technology   Rapidly changing technologies create new issues that did not exist in earlier, simpler times. Before monitors, respirators, and parenteral feedings were available, there was no question about whether to "allow" an 800-gram premature infant to die. If the infant was very premature, there was no way to maintain life. The question has now become, *Should* we always do what we *can* do?

Nurses are accountable for their ethical conduct. In 1991 the American Nurses Association (ANA) published *Standards of Clinical Nursing Practice,* in which Standard V is ethics; see the box on page [167]. Therefore, nurses need to understand their own values related to moral matters and to use ethical reasoning to determine and explain their moral positions. Sometimes nurses are aware of an ethical issue, but nurses also need moral principles and reasoning skills to explain their position. Otherwise they may give emotional responses, which often are not helpful.

Factors Affecting Ethical Decisions

Factors affecting ethical decision-making include nurses' perceptions of their roles and responsibilities, moral theories and frameworks, moral principles, the professional code of ethics, the level of cognitive development of the people involved, and the values, beliefs and attitudes of these people.

Perceptions of Roles and Responsibilities   Nurses are responsible for determining their own actions and

EXAMPLES OF NURSES' OBLIGATIONS IN ETHICAL DECISIONS

- Maximize the client's well being.
- Balance the client's need for autonomy with family members' responsibilities for the client's well-being.
- Support each family member and enhance the family support system.
- Carry out hospital policies.
- Protect other clients' well-being.
- Protect the nurse's own standards of care.

for supporting clients who are making ethical decisions or coping with the results of decisions made by others. A good decision is one that is in the client's best interest and at the same time preserves the integrity of all involved. Nurses have multiple obligations to balance in moral situations. See the box at the top of the next column for examples. . . .

Moral Theories and Frameworks There are four general approaches to moral theory: teleology, deontology, intuitionism, and the ethic of caring. **Teleology** looks to the consequences of an action in judging whether the action is right or wrong. Utilitarianism, one specific teleologic theory, is summarized in the ideas, "the greatest good for the greatest number" and "the end justifies the means."

Deontology proposes that the morality of a decision is not determined by its consequences. It emphasizes duty, rationality, and obedience to rules. For instance, a nurse might believe it is necessary to tell the truth no matter who is hurt. There are many deontologic theories; each justifies the rules of acceptable behavior differently. For example, some state that the rules are known by divine revelation; others refer to a natural law or social contract.

The difference between teleology and deontology can be seen when they are applied to the issue of abortion. A person taking a teleologic approach might consider that saving the mother's life (the end, or consequence) justifies the abortion (the means, or act). A person taking a deontologic approach might consider any termination of life as a violation of the rule, "Do not kill" and, therefore, would not abort the fetus regardless of the consequences to the mother. It is important to note that the approach, or framework, guides making the moral decision; it does not determine the outcome (eg, the person taking a teleologic approach might have considered that saving the life of the fetus justified the death of the mother).

A third framework is **intuitionism,** summarized as the notion that people inherently know what is right or wrong; determining what is right is not a matter of rational thought or learning. For example, a nurse inherently knows it is wrong to strike a client; this does not need to be taught or reasoned out.

Benner and Wrubel (1989) proposed **caring** as the central goal of nursing as well as a basis for nursing ethics. Unlike the preceding theories which are based on the concept of fairness (justice), an ethic of caring is based on relationships. Caring theories stress courage, generosity, commitment, and responsibility. Caring is a force for protecting and enhancing client dignity. Guided by this ethic, nurses use touch and truth-telling to affirm clients as persons rather than objects and to assist them to make choices and find meaning in their illness experiences.

Moral Principles Moral principles are statements about broad, general philosophic concepts such as autonomy and justice. They provide the foundation for **moral rules,** which are specific prescriptions for actions. For example, "People should not lie" (rule) is based on the moral principle of respect or autonomy for people. Principles are useful in ethical discussions because even people who do not agree on which action to take may be able to agree on the principles that apply. That agreement can serve as the basis for an acceptable solution. For example, most people would agree that nurses are obligated to respect their clients (a principle), even if they disagree about whether a nurse should deceive a client about the client's prognosis (action). **Autonomy** (respect for persons) refers to the right to make one's own decisions. Respect for autonomy

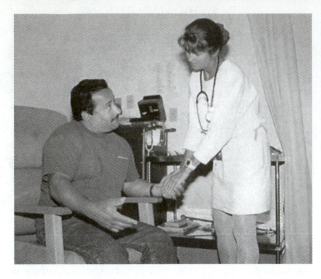

Jorge Zetina, a 47-year-old male, was admitted to your unit yesterday for diagnostic testing to confirm the diagnosis of stomach carcinoma. Mr Zetina's physician has told you that the tumor is malignant, with widespread metastases, but has not informed the patient of his poor prognosis. When you go into Mr Zetina's room, he seems worried and anxious, and then asks, "Did the doctor tell you things aren't going well?"

What would you do?

means that nurses recognize the individual's uniqueness, the right to be what that person is, and the right to choose personal goals. People have "inward autonomy" if they have the faculty and ability to make choices. People have "outward autonomy" if their choices are not limited or imposed by others.

Nurses who follow the principle of autonomy respect a client's right to make decisions even when those choices seem not to be in the client's best interest. Respect for people also means treating others with consideration. In a health care setting, abuses of this principle occur when a nurse disregards clients' subjective accounts of their symptoms (ie, pain). Finally, respect for autonomy means that people should not be treated as "a means to an end" (eg, clients must provide an informed consent before tests and procedures are carried out). . . .

Nonmaleficence means the duty to do no harm. This principle is the basis of most codes of nursing ethics. Although this would seem to be a simple principle to follow in nursing practice, in reality it is complex. Harm can mean deliberate harm, risk of harm, and unintentional harm. In nursing, intentional harm is always unacceptable. However, the risk of harm is not so clear. A client may be at risk of harm during a nursing intervention that is intended to be helpful. For example, a client may react adversely to a medication. Sometimes, the degree to which a risk is morally permissible can be a conflict.

Beneficence means "doing good." Nurses are obligated to "do good," that is, to implement actions that benefit clients and their support persons. However, in an increasingly technologic health care system, "doing good" can also pose a risk of doing harm. For example, a nurse may advise a client about an intensive exercise program to improve general health but should not do so if the client is at risk of a heart attack.

Justice is often referred to as fairness. Nurses frequently face decisions in which a sense of justice should prevail. For example, a nurse is alone on a hospital unit, and one client arrives to be admitted at the same time another client requires a medication for pain. Instead of running from one client to the other, weigh the facts in the situation and then act based on the principle of justice.

Fidelity means to be faithful to agreements and responsibilities one has undertaken. Nurses have responsibilities to clients, employers, government, society, and to themselves. Circumstances often affect which responsibilities take precedence at a particular time.

Veracity refers to telling the truth. Most children are taught to always tell the truth, but as adults the choices are often less clear. Does a nurse tell the truth when it is known that it will cause harm? Does a nurse tell a lie when it is known that the lie will relieve anxiety and fear? Bok (1978) concludes that lying to sick and dying people is rarely justified. The loss of trust in the nurse and the anxiety caused by not knowing the truth, for example, usually outweigh any benefits derived from lying.

Nursing Code of Ethics A code of ethics is a formal statement of a group's ideals and values. It is a set of ethical principles that is shared by members of the group, reflects their moral judgments over time, and serves as a standard for their professional actions. Codes of ethics are usually higher than legal standards, and they can never be less than the legal standards of the profession.

International, national, state, and provincial nurs-

TABLE 11–2 International Council of Nurses Code for Nurses

The fundamental responsibility of the nurse is fourfold: to promote health, to prevent illness, to restore health, and to alleviate suffering.

The need for nursing is universal. Inherent in nursing is respect for life, dignity, and rights of man. It is unrestricted by considerations of nationality, race, creed, color, age, sex, politics or social status.

Nurses render health services to the individual, the family, and the community and coordinate their services with those of related groups.

Nurses and People

The nurse's primary responsibility is to those people who require nursing care.

The nurse, in providing care, promotes an environment in which the values, customs and spiritual beliefs of the individual are respected.

The nurse holds in confidence personal information and uses judgment in sharing this information.

Nurses and Practice

The nurse carries responsibility for nursing practice and for maintaining competence by continual learning. The nurse maintains the highest standards of nursing care possible within the reality of a specific situation.

The nurse uses judgment in relation to individual competence when accepting and delegating responsibilities.

The nurse when acting in a professional capacity should at all times maintain standards of personal conduct which reflect credit upon the profession.

Nurses and Society

The nurse shares with other citizens the responsibility for initiating and supporting action to meet the health and social needs of the public.

Nurses and Coworkers

The nurse sustains a cooperative relationship with coworkers in nursing and other fields. The nurse takes appropriate action to safeguard the individual when his care is endangered by a coworker or any other person.

Nurses and the Profession

The nurse plays the major role in determining and implementing desirable standards of nursing practice and nursing education.

The nurse is active in developing a core of professional knowledge.

The nurse, acting through the professional organization, participates in establishing and maintaining equitable social and economic working conditions in nursing.

Source: International Council of Nurses, *ICN Code for Nurses: Ethical Concepts Applied to Nursing* (Geneva: Imprimeries Populaires, 1973). Reprinted with permission of the ICN.

---

ing associations have established codes of ethics. The International Council of Nurses (ICN) developed and adopted their first code of ethics in 1953. The ICN Code was revised in 1965 and again in 1973 (Table 11–2). The American Nurses Association (ANA) first adopted a code of ethics in 1950; it was revised in 1968, 1976, and 1985 (Table 11–3). In 1980, the Canadian Nurses Association (CNA) adopted a code of ethics; it was revised in 1991 (Table 11–4). Increasingly, professional nursing associations are taking an active part in improving and enforcing standards. Nurses are responsible for being familiar with the code that governs their practice.

Functions of Ethical Codes Nursing codes of ethics have the following purposes:

1. To inform the public about the minimum standards of the profession and to help them understand professional nursing conduct

2. To provide a sign of the profession's commitment to the public it serves
3. To outline the major ethical considerations of the profession
4. To provide general guidelines for professional behavior
5. To guide the profession in self-regulation
6. To remind nurses of the special responsibility they assume when caring for the sick

Because the wording in a code of ethics is intentionally vague, such codes can serve as general guides. They do not give direction for actions to take in specific cases. For example, the first item in the ANA *Code for Nurses* refers to respect for human dignity and states that in caring for clients, nurses should be "unrestricted by considerations of the nature of health problems." Does this mean that it is wrong for a pregnant nurse to refuse to care for a client with active herpes? Or that it is wrong to

TABLE 11–3 American Nurses Association Code for Nurses

1. The nurse provides services with respect for human dignity and the uniqueness of the client unrestricted by considerations of social or economic status, personal attributes, or the nature of health problems.

2. The nurse safeguards the client's right to privacy by judiciously protecting information of a confidential nature.

3. The nurse acts to safeguard the client and the public when health care and safety are affected by the incompetent, unethical, or illegal practice of any person.

4. The nurse assumes responsibility and accountability for individual nursing judgments and actions.

5. The nurse maintains competence in nursing.

6. The nurse exercises informed judgment and uses individual competence and qualifications as criteria in seeking consultation, accepting responsibilities, and delegating nursing activities to others.

7. The nurse participates in activities that contribute to the ongoing development of the profession's body of knowledge.

8. The nurse participates in the profession's efforts to implement and improve standards of nursing.

9. The nurse participates in the profession's effort to establish and maintain conditions of employment conducive to high quality nursing care.

10. The nurse participates in the profession's effort to protect the public from misinformation and misrepresentation and to maintain the integrity of nursing.

11. The nurse collaborates with members of the health professions and other citizens in promoting community and national efforts to meet the health needs of the public.

Source: American Nurses Association, *Code for Nurses* (Kansas City, MO: ANA, 1985). Reprinted with permission.

TABLE 11–4 Canadian Nurses Association Code of Ethics for Nursing*

Clients

I. A nurse treats clients with respect for their individual needs and values.

II. Based upon respect for clients and regard for their right to control their own care, nursing care reflects respect for the right of choice held by clients.

III. The nurse holds confidential all information about a client learned in the health care setting.

IV. The nurse is guided by consideration for the dignity of clients.

V. The nurse provides competent care to clients.

Nursing Roles and Relationships

VI. The nurse maintains trust in nurses and nursing.

VII. The nurse recognizes the contribution and expertise of colleagues from nursing and other disciplines as essential to excellent health care.

VIII. The nurse takes steps to ensure that the client receives competent and ethical care.

IX. Conditions of employment should contribute in a positive way to client care and the professional satisfaction of nurses.

X. Job action by nurses is directed toward securing conditions of employment that enable safe and appropriate care for clients and contribute to the professional satisfaction of nurses.

Nursing Ethics and Society

XI. The nurse advocates the interests of clients.

XII. The nurse represents the values and ethics of nursing before colleagues and others.

The Nursing Profession

XIII. Professional nursing organizations are responsible for clarifying, securing, and sustaining ethical nursing conduct. The fulfillment of those tasks requires that professional nurses' organizations remain responsive to the rights, needs, and legitimate interests of clients and nurses.

*This represents only one element of the code values. For each value noted the CNA Code of Ethics for Nursing provides obligations which provide more specific direction for conduct. In two instances, limitations are also listed which describe exceptional circumstances in which a value or obligation cannot be applied.

Source: Canadian Nurses Association. November 1991. *Code of Ethics for Nursing* (Ottawa: CNA). Reprinted with permission of the CNA.

refuse to care for a client who uses rude language? When making ethical decisions, nurses should consider their code of ethics together with a more unified ethical theory, ethical principles, and the relevant data about each situation.

Cognitive Moral Development Ethics problems require nurses to think and reason in making decisions, judgments, and choices. Reasoning is a cognitive function and is, therefore, developmental. . . .

In resolving ethics problems, one difficulty may be that the people involved in the situation operate at different levels of cognitive reasoning, as well as from different moral frameworks and different individual values. For example, when deciding whether it is right to resuscitate a dying client, a nurse reasoning "by the rules" would think, "According to policy, if there is no DNR (Do Not Resuscitate) order, we must resuscitate." A co-worker, reasoning on the basis of "not hurting others" might think, "Resuscitation will cause the client to suffer needlessly; therefore it is wrong." When trying to achieve consensus, nurses should keep these differences in mind and determine the reasoning of those involved (ie, the client and support persons), asking not only what they believe to be right, but also what process of reasoning led them to that belief.

Values, Beliefs, and Attitudes **Values** are an important aspect of decision making because they influence perceptions and motivation; therefore, it is important that nurses be consciously aware of their own values and the values of the others involved in a given situation. **Beliefs** (opinions) are interpretations or conclusions that we accept as true (Chaffee 1990, p. 187). Beliefs are based more on faith than on fact and may or may not be true.

Beliefs may or may not involve values. For example, the statement, "I believe if I study hard I will get good grades" expresses a belief that does not involve a value. By contrast the statement, "Good grades are really important to me. I believe I must study hard to obtain good grades" does involve a value.

Attitudes are mental positions or feelings made up of many different beliefs and are directed toward a person, object, or idea. They are often judged as good or bad, positive or negative, whereas beliefs are judged as correct or incorrect. The affective aspect of an attitude is the feelings associated with it. Because feelings vary so greatly among people, this may be the most important aspect of an attitude. For example, one client may feel very strongly about the sound from a television set in the next room, whereas another client may dismiss it as unimportant. The cognitive component of an attitude includes the beliefs and factual information associated with it (eg, the knowledge about effective and appropriate nurse-client communication). The behavioral component is the inclination to act as a result of one's attitude. For example, a nurse who disapproves of another nurse's behavior toward a client may think, "If she speaks that way to Mr B again, I shall talk to her."

Types of Ethics Problems

Nurses encounter two broad types of problems: decision-focused problems and action-focused problems. Each requires a different approach (Wilkinson 1993, p. 4).

In **decision-focused problems**, the difficulty lies in deciding what to do. The question is, What *should* I do? For example:

> Because Leon is committed to the sanctity of life, he wishes his client to have artificial nutrition and hydration. As a nurse, Leon also believes in relieving suffering, so when he sees that the tube-feedings are prolonging the client's pain, and even contributing to her discomfort, he wishes to have the feedings discontinued. He is not comfortable with either choice.

In this case, two principles clearly apply, so no matter what the nurse does, an important value must be sacrificed. This is the typical **moral dilemma** that people commonly equate with ethics, sometimes referred to as "being between a rock and a hard place." The nature of a dilemma dictates that there are no easy solutions. However, because the difficulty is personal and internal, nurses can address decision-focused problems by learning to make better decisions by, for example, reviewing their own personal value systems, taking advantage of staff development offerings, and attending ethics rounds.

In **action-focused problems**, the difficulty lies not in making the decision, but in implementing it. In these situations, nurses usually feel secure in their judgment about what is right but act on their judgment only at personal risk. The central question is, What *can* I do? or What risks am I willing to take to do what is right? **Moral distress,** one type of action-focused problem, occurs when the nurse knows the right course of action but cannot carry it out because of institutional policies or other constraints (Jameton 1984, p. 6). This results in feelings of anger, guilt, and loss of integrity on the part of the nurse and can impact client care. For example:

> A resident physician has told the nurses to order complete blood count (CBC) and urinalysis on all clients and to get the results before calling him to the emergency room to examine the clients. The nurses believe this is unethical because it is wasteful and poses unnecessary discomfort and possible risks for clients. However, they do not have the authority or the access to decision-making channels needed to change the situation. So they order the tests, but they feel guilty and upset because they believe what they are doing is wrong.

Unlike decision-focused problems, action-focused problems cannot be resolved by improving one's decision-making skills. Even after a nurse decides what is *right* to do, the issue becomes what the nurse actually can do given the conditions of practice. Research indicates that nurses' actions are influenced by such constraints as verbal threats, fear of losing their jobs or their nursing licenses, fear of physicians, fear of the law or lawsuits, and lack of support from both peers and administrators (Wilkinson 1987/88, p. 21). Action-focused problems require knowledge, experience, communication, and the ability to make integrity-preserving compromises. To deal successfully with these problems, nurses must shift their attention away from "making the right decision" and focus on the factors that are preventing the "right action" (Wilkinson 1993, p. 5).

Conflicts Within Nursing Ethical conflicts also arise from nurses' unresolved questions about the nature and scope of their practice. High-technology and specialty roles (intensive care nurses, diabetes clinicians) have expanded the scope of nursing practice, often causing nursing and medical activities to overlap. This creates value conflicts for nurses. For example:

- Although nurses value health promotion and wellness, many still work in hospitals, and many are involved in high-tech treatment of illness.
- Although the profession values a humanistic, caring approach and emphasizes nurse-client relationships, many nurses spend much of their time attending to the client's machines.

Conflicting Loyalties and Obligations Because of their unique position in the health care system, nurses experience conflicting loyalties and obligations to clients, families, physicians, employing institutions, and licensing bodies. The client's needs may conflict with institutional policies, physician preferences, needs of the client's family, or even laws of the state. According to the nursing code of ethics, the nurse's first allegiance is to the client. However, it is not always easy to determine which action best serves the client's needs. For instance, a nurse may believe the client's interests require telling the client a truth that others have been withholding. But this might damage the client-physician relationship, in the long run causing harm to the client rather than the intended good.

Resolving Ethical Problems

Nurses need to be aware of ethical theories and principles, the nursing code of ethics, and their own hierarchy of values. These components enter into their decision-making process along with the facts of a specific situation. Good decision-making requires nurses to be "aware of the factors that contribute to and/or hinder one's ability to make a choice" (Thompson & Thompson 1990, p. 78). These factors include cultural values, societal expectations, degree of commitment, lack of time, lack of experience, ignorance or fear of the law, and conflicting loyalties.

Responsible ethical reasoning is rational thinking. It is also systematic and based upon principles. It should *not* be based upon emotions, intuition, fixed policies, or precedents. (A *precedent* is an earlier similar occurrence. For example, "We have always done it this way" is a statement using precedence.) However, intuition may actually improve the quality of one's ethical decisions, as shown by a study indicating that "individuals with high levels of intuitive ability make more effective decisions than individuals with low levels of intuitive ability" (Gearhart & Young 1990, p. 49).

[Section omitted.]

SPECIFIC ETHICAL ISSUES

Nurses encounter a variety of ethical issues. In a recent study, respondents reported being involved in issues of client's refusal of treatment, informed consent, discontinuation of life-saving treatment, withholding of information from clients, confidentiality, client competence, and allocation of scarce resources (Cassells & Redman 1989, pp. 467–69).

Acquired Immune Deficiency Syndrome (AIDS) Because of its association with homosexual and bisexual behavior, prostitution, illicit drug use, and inevitable physical decline and death, AIDS bears a social stigma. In a recent study, nurses caring for AIDS clients reported conflicting feelings of anger, fear, sympathy, fatigue, helplessness, and self-enhancement (Breault & Polifroni 1992). According to ANA, the moral obligation to care for an HIV-infected client cannot be set aside unless the risk exceeds the responsibility. "Not only must nursing care be readily available, . . . but nurses must also be advised of the risks and the responsibilities they face in providing care. . . . Accepting personal risk which exceeds the limits of duty is not morally obligatory; it is a moral option" (ANA 1988b, p. 31).

Abortion Abortion is a highly publicized issue about which many people, including nurses, feel very strongly. Debate continues, pitting the principle of sanctity of life against the principle of autonomy and the woman's right to control her own body. This is an especially volatile issue because no public consensus has yet been reached.

Most state and provincial laws have provisions known as *conscience clauses* that permit individual physicians and nurses, as well as institutions, to refuse to assist with an abortion if doing so violates their religious or moral principles. However, nurses have no right to impose their values on a client. Nursing codes of ethics support clients' rights to information and abortion counseling. For example, the CNA's *Code of Ethics for Nursing* 1991 says "Based upon respect for clients and regard for their right to control their own care, nursing care reflects respect for the right of choice held by clients."

Confidentiality   In keeping with the principle of autonomy, nurses are obligated to respect clients' privacy and confidentiality. Clients must be able to trust that nurses will not reveal details of their situation inappropriately but will communicate the information necessary to provide for their health care. Computerized information management in acute care settings makes client data accessible to more people. Nurses should help develop security measures (eg, access codes) and policies to help ensure appropriate use of client data.

Withdrawing or Withholding Food and Fluids   It is generally accepted that providing food and fluids is part of ordinary nursing practice and, therefore, a moral duty. A nurse is morally obligated, however, to withhold food and fluids when it is more harmful to administer than to withhold them (ANA 1988a, p. 2). In addition, "It is morally as well as legally permissible for nurses to honor the refusal of food and fluids by competent patients in their care" (ANA 1988a, p. 3). The *Code for Nurses* supports this statement through the nurse's role as a client advocate and through the moral principle of autonomy.

Termination of Life-Sustaining Treatment   Antibiotics, organ transplants, and technologic advances (eg, ventilators) have helped prolong life. However, the ability to restore health has not kept pace with the capacity to prolong life. Clients may specify that they wish to have life-sustaining measures withdrawn, they may have advance directives on this matter, or they may specify a surrogate decision maker. When these decisions are made, the nurse, as the primary caregiver, must ensure that sensitive care and comfort measures are given as the client's illness progresses (Cassells & Redman 1989, pp. 467–68). A decision to withdraw treatment is not a decision to withdraw care.

Allocation of Health Resources   Allocation of health care goods and services, such as organ transplants, artificial joints, and the services of specialists, has become an especially urgent issue as a result of cost-containment measures and the grow-

ing expense of medical care. For example, the number of office visits and the length of hospital stay are decisions that are increasingly being influenced by administrative policy.

ADVOCACY

An **advocate** is one who pleads the cause of another, and a **client advocate** is an advocate for clients' rights . . . . The JCAHO *Standards Related to Ethics* states "3.2. Nursing staff members have a defined mechanism for addressing ethical issues in patient care" and "3.2.1. When the hospital has an ethics committee or other defined structures for addressing ethical issues in patient care, nursing staff members participate" (1992, p. 3.7.) Also see the box on the ANA standard. The focus of the client advocacy role is to respect client decisions and enhance client autonomy.

According to Kohnke (1982, p. 5) the actions of an advocate are to *inform* and *support*. An advocate informs clients about their rights in a situation,

---

RESEARCH NOTE

Do Nurses Have Ethical Experiences?

In response to a questionnaire sent to 1400 registered nurses, 200 nurses wrote a short description of an ethical situation that occurred in their practice. The most frequently cited dilemmas were those involving quality of life issues and life-sustaining treatment of the terminally ill. The remaining themes from their narratives were: (a) patient's right to know diagnosis and refuse treatment; (b) truth telling and informed consent; (c) difficulty in working with physicians; (d) standards of care; and (e) allocation of resources. Many nurses shared their frustration at not being able to do what they knew was right. Respondents described in great detail the pain endured by both the patient and themselves (eg, "I cried. I am crying now as I write this").

Implications: For nurses, ethical concerns are almost inseparable from concerns about the quality of patient care. Upon graduation from nursing school, nurses are expected to be competent in clinical skills and interpersonal communications, but competence in addressing ethical problems is usually left to on-the-job training or trial and error. Nurses' stories indicate that ethical problems affect them profoundly. More research is needed to help discover what nurses see as the solutions to moral problems in clinical nursing practice. This study supports the need for the nursing work environment to change to support nurses' participation in ethical decision making.

Source: AM Haddad, Problematic ethical experiences: Stories from nursing practice. *Bioethics Forum*, Fall 1993, 9:5–10.

---

and provides them with the information they need to make an informed decision. The first step in informing is to make sure the client agrees to receiving the information. In addition, an advocate must (a) either have the necessary information or know how to get it, (b) want the client to have the information, (c) present information in a way that is meaningful to the client, and (d) deal with the fact that there may be those who do not wish the client to be informed.

An advocate supports clients in their decisions. Support can involve action or nonaction. An advocate must know how to provide support in an objective manner, being careful not to convey approval or disapproval of the client's choices. Advocacy involves accepting and respecting the client's right to decide, even if the nurse believes the decision is wrong. As advocates, nurses do not make decisions for clients; clients must make their own decisions freely. For example: After being fully informed about the chemotherapy treatment, the alternative treatments, and the possible consequences of the available choices, Mr Rae decides against further chemotherapy for his malignancy. The client advocate supports Mr Rae in his decision. Underlying client advocacy are the beliefs that individuals have the following rights:

- the right to select values they deem necessary to sustain their lives
- the right to decide which course of action will best achieve the chosen values
- the right to dispose of values in a way they choose without coercion by others (Donahue 1985, p. 1037).

Nurses who function responsibly as advocates for themselves, their clients, and the community are in a position to effect change. A nurse functioning in this capacity must have an objective understanding of the ethical issues in health care as well as knowledge of the laws and regulations that affect nursing practice and public health. . . .

ETHICS COMMITTEES

Because nurses have more contact with the client and family than other members of the health care team, they know the client better and have access to special kinds of information not available to other health care professionals (Mahon 1990, p. 266). Nurses offer unique perspectives that can greatly improve the quality of the ethical decisions made in health care settings. One important way for nurses to provide input is to serve on institutional ethics committees.

Ethics committees typically review cases, write guidelines and policies, and provide education and counseling. They ensure that relevant facts are brought out, provide a forum in which diverse views can be expressed, reduce stress for caregivers, and can reduce legal risks. These factors tend to produce better decisions than would otherwise be made (Hosford 1986, p. 15).

THE NURSE AS A MORAL AGENT

Nurses should develop the skills necessary to function as **moral agents**—that is, to participate in ethical decision making. Cassells and Redman (1989, pp. 465–66) incorporated these skills as steps of their bioethical decision model. Professional nurses are responsible for acquiring these skills as a part of either their basic or continuing education.

Historically, nurses have looked on ethical decision making as the physician's responsibility. However, no one profession is responsible for an ethical decision, nor does expertise in one discipline (such as medicine or nursing) necessarily make a person an expert in ethics. As situations become more complex, multidisciplinary input becomes increasingly important.

Simply put, morality is the idea that people have choices and are responsible for their actions. Because professionals claim to use their expertise for social good, nurses need to be clear about the ethics of their work in order to conduct it well. Although nursing codes of ethics identify client advocacy as a part of the nursing role, many nurses work in settings that expect accountability but do not support nurses' authority or autonomy to act as advocates or moral agents. There are risks involved in putting advocacy into action (Parker 1990, p. 39). Some nurses have suggested that a viable nursing ethic must include an agenda of sociopolitical reform that empowers nurses to participate in ethical decision making.

CHAPTER HIGHLIGHTS

- Morality refers to what is right and wrong in conduct, character, or attitude.
- Nursing ethics refers to the moral problems that arise in nursing practice and to ethical decisions nurses make.
- Moral issues are those that arouse conscience, are concerned with important values and norms, and evoke words such as *good, bad, right, wrong, should,* and *ought.*
- Ethical problems are created as a result of changes in society, advances in technology, conflicts within the nursing role itself, and nurses' conflicting loyalties and obligations (ie,

to clients, families, employers, physicians, and other nurses).

- Decision-focused problems are those in which it is difficult to arrive at a decision; they can be relieved by improving one's decision-making skills.
- Action-focused problems arise when nurses believe they know the right action but cannot act on their judgment without great personal risk; improved decision-making skills will not relieve the effects of these problems.
- Nurses' ethical decisions are influenced by their role perceptions, moral theories and principles, nursing codes of ethics, level of cognitive development, and personal and professional values.
- Four common moral frameworks (approaches) are teleology, deontology, intuitionism, and caring.
- Moral principles (eg, autonomy, beneficence, nonmaleficence, justice), fidelity, and veracity are broad, general philosophical concepts. Moral rules, by contrast, are specific prescriptions for actions.

- A professional code of ethics is a formal statement of a group's ideals and values that serves as a standard and guideline for the group's professional actions and informs the public of its commitment.

- Nurses are responsible for determining their own actions and for supporting clients who are making moral decisions or for whom decisions are being made.
- Client advocacy involves concern for and defined actions on behalf of another person or organization in order to bring about change.
- The focus of the advocacy role is to inform and support.
- Ethics committees are multidisciplinary bodies that review cases, write guidelines and policies, and provide education and counseling.

Selection 4-2   *Ethical Perceptions of Parents and Nurses in NICU: The Case of Baby Michael*

Purpose for Reading

PROCESS GOAL: **To check your initial recall of relevant information in an article and prepare a summary**

The *Journal of Gynecological and Neonatal Nursing* is a professional journal with a specialty focus. Its readers are primarily clinicians who work in nursing related to birth and the care of newborns. Note the very practical concerns of nurses who care for premature infants as well as the ethical issues facing them and the parents of those infants. You'll use your understanding of the authors' organizational plan to write a summary.

OUTCOME GOAL: **To summarize an article that will add to your understanding of the ethical and legal aspects of health care**

To follow up a classroom lecture on ethical and legal issues in nursing, the instructor might ask students to read a related article and then participate in a clinical conference. Each student would be asked to present a short summary of an article to the group. Then group members would identify and discuss similarities and differences in the articles.

Before Reading 1

Goal: Get oriented to the text
Technique: Ask questions about the information

This journal article looks very technical, with six authors and twelve references. Note that the date the article was accepted and the date it was published are sixteen months apart, which is typical for most journals. Textbook publication takes even longer.

What does the lag time between acceptance and publication tell you about how current the information in the article is?

Where do you think you would find the most current reporting of ethical and legal issues?

Why do you think the address of one of the authors is provided?

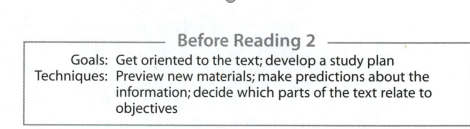

┌───┐
│ ─── **Before Reading 2** ─── │
│ Goals: Get oriented to the text; develop a study plan │
│ Techniques: Preview new materials; make predictions about the │
│ information; decide which parts of the text relate to │
│ objectives │
└───┘

As you preview the article, note that it focuses on one case—the care that an infant received in a neonatal intensive care unit (NICU).

What ethical issues do the authors emphasize in their examination of this case?

How is the section "Nursing Implications" organized?

As you develop your study plan, keep the emotional impact of the topic in mind. You may read more slowly when you are emotionally affected by the material. Keep in mind, too, that your outcome goal is to present a summary of the article to your classmates.

┌───┐
│ ─── **During Reading** ─── │
│ Goal: Monitor comprehension │
│ Technique: Look for paragraph organization │
└───┘

If you have known anyone with a child in an intensive care unit, you know the intensity of the experience. It is amazing to see a healthy baby move and feed and cry. To watch an infant who must work for each breath or who is attached to various machines is agonizing. As you read about Katherine, David, baby Michael, and the nurses and doctors taking care of him, empathize with their desperation and confusion, but remember that your purpose is to summarize and share information with classmates. Mark new words and main ideas as you wish. Focus on the ethical issues that affect the parents and the caregivers, as well as the authors' proposals for dealing with those issues.

After Reading 1

Goal:	Check initial recall of relevant information
Technique:	To restudy, return to an appropriate before-reading or during-reading technique

---

How did you feel after reading this article? Identify your emotions and concerns:

Did your emotional reaction hinder you from understanding the ethical issues and proposed solutions? If you need to return to an earlier phase of the reading process to be sure you have understood the article, do so now.

After Reading 2

Goal:	Check initial recall of relevant information
Technique:	Review the whole assignment by self-testing

To check your recall of the authors' main points, it is often useful to test yourself, basing your questions on the structure of the information. Try answering the following questions, based on the authors' abstract:

1. Identify the parents' problems related to the three ethical issues raised by the authors.

2. What were the issues or dilemmas experienced by the nurses?

3. Explain how Table 2 in the article illustrates what nurses may do to help parents gain a sense of control in difficult situations such as this.

4. Paraphrase (translate into your own words) the following key concept from page 185 of the article: "Nurses have the right and the obligation to participate and support parents in decision making,

and parents have the legal and the moral obligation to participate in the care of and decisions affecting the life of their newborn."

After Reading 3

Goal: Organize relevant material for review
Technique: Learn new terms discovered during reading

Many words used in this article may have been new to you. See how many of the following terms you can match with their meanings. Write the letter of the definition that matches the term in the space provided on the left.

<u>Term</u>

_____ 1. gestation

_____ 2. pneumothorax

_____ 3. neonatologist

_____ 4. do-not-resuscitate order

_____ 5. *sine qua non*

_____ 6. ministration

_____ 7. sepsis

_____ 8. intracranial

_____ 9. surfactant

_____ 10. formidable

_____ 11. premise

_____ 12. assumption

<u>Definition</u>

a. lipoproteins that reduce the surface tension of pulmonary fluids and contribute to the elasticity of lung tissue

b. a supposition

c. the time from fertilization of the egg until birth

d. a written medical order that legally authorizes the omission of resuscitation in the absence of respiration and/or pulse

e. a proposition laid down as the basis of an argument

f. powerful, superior

g. within the cranium or skull

h. Latin for "without which not" meaning something indispensable

i. a collection of air or fluid in the pleural space resulting in collapse of the lung

j. services or assistance given

k. a physician who specializes in the care of the newborn

l. an infected state

After Reading 4

Goal: Organize relevant information for review
Technique: Summarize

The authors' abstract of the article will help you summarize, but it contains only a description of the content; no actual conclusions are mentioned. In order to inform your classmates (and convince your instructor that you read the whole article), your summary should explain each of the main points of the abstract.

1. What are the "ethical challenges" faced by parents and nurses in neonatal intensive care units, as exemplified by this case?

2. What do the authors say about the issues of treatment versus non-treatment, informed consent, and decision making?

3. What is the "integration of crisis intervention techniques and caring processes" that the authors recommend to assist parents?

You can't cover every point in the article without rewriting it. However, you should include enough detail to make your summary clear and interesting. To keep your oral summary focused, write it out before presenting it in class. *Hint:* Try using some of the new vocabulary you learned in your organization of the material for review.

From *JOGNN*, February 1995,
pp. 125–130.

Pamela A. Miya, RN, PhD
Winifred J. Pinch, RN, EdD
Karen K. Boardman, RN, MS, CS
Annabelle Keene, RN C, MSN
Margaret L. Spielman, RN, MEd, MSN
Kathleen L. Harr, RN C, DNSc

A case was used to examine ethical challenges in the neonatal intensive care unit from the perspective of parents and nurses. Discussion focuses on issues of treatment versus nontreatment, informed consent, and decision making. An integration of crisis intervention techniques and caring processes is presented for nurses to assist parents through the neonatal intensive care unit experience.

Accepted: October 1993

Advancements in health care technology present ethical challenges to neonatal intensive-care unit (NICU) nurses as they struggle to provide humane yet effective care to tiny patients and their families. The research teams of Miya, Boardman, Harr, and Keene (1991) and Pinch and Spielman (1989a, 1989b, 1990) met and talked about their independently conducted research. Miya et al. had studied ethical issues facing neonatal nurses, whereas Pinch and Spielman had discussed ethical dilemmas (conflicts) with parents of newborns at high risk. A resultant appreciation of the richness of these descriptive data provided the basis to explore the meaning of both research studies when applied to a specific case. This article describes these ethical concerns in the NICU through a case approach. Implications for neonatal nursing practice are also discussed, based on the work of Aguilera (1990) and Swanson (1991).

Miya et al. (1991) found that NICU nurses perceived that ethical issues and dilemmas related to the care of critically ill infants are inherent to the NICU environment. Among the issues identified were suffering, pain, humane treatment, futile treatment, withdrawing treatment, and quality of life. Additional issues were related to intrapersonal conflict, interpersonal conflict, role conflict, communication, and family rights.

On the surface, parents seem to be faced with multiple critical and troubling ethical decisions about their infants' care and treatment. Surprisingly, Pinch (1990) and Pinch and Spielman (1989a, 1989b, 1990) found that parents generally did not perceive any ethical issues related to neonatal care. Parental perceptions were that health professionals made the majority of treatment decisions. The provision of informed consent was viewed by parents as perfunctory. Table 1 compares the findings from both studies.

The case of baby Michael represents a continuum of ethical issues occurring during the course of NICU hospitalization. (The case has been altered to protect identities.) Selected ethical topics included in this discussion are treatment versus nontreatment, informed consent, and decision making. These topics and subsequent discussions do not represent all ethical issues encountered in NICU's, but they are typical of the results obtained in the above-cited research.

The Case of Baby Michael

Katherine and David Petersen, both 30 years old, were happy about their pregnancy after 5

TABLE 1 Parents' and Nurses' Perceptions of Ethical Issues in the NICU

Parents*	Nurses†
Treatment issues	**Treatment issues**
Focused on pregnancy and birth experience	Doing good versus doing no harm
Did not perceive use of complex techniques or treatments central to ethical debate	suffering, pain, humane treatment
	futile treatment
Felt disconnected from infant	withdrawal of treatment
	treatment versus nontreatment
	ordinary versus extraordinary treatment
Informed consent	**Informed consent**
Nurses were main source of information	Inadequate disclosure of information
Preferred more scheduled time with physician in charge	Truth telling
Intimidated—reluctant to seek information	
Did not perceive serious problems	
Decision making	**Decision making**
Focused on pregnancy and birth	Family rights
Felt no decision making required or were not involved	Conflict
Consent forms—did not involve conflict or pose dilemma	physician
	parents

*Pinch & Spielman, 1990.
†Miya et al., 1991.

years of infertility. They had one adopted child, Kim, who was 3 years old. At 25 weeks gestation, an emergency cesarean section was performed for uncontrollable uterine contractions with fetal distress. The infant, Michael, weighed 700 grams and was admitted to the NICU. A standard treatment protocol was used, and Michael was placed on a ventilator. During the course of treatment, Michael's parents visited several times a day and called frequently. A pneumothorax and systemic infection developed in Michael. His hospital stay was further complicated by a grade III intracranial bleed and cardiac arrest. At one point, the neonatologists approached Katherine and David about a do-not-resuscitate (DNR) order, but the parents wanted their infant to receive every possible chance for life. Before discharge, Michael was weaned from the ventilator and tolerated nipple feedings. He was dismissed from the NICU after 4 months.

Treatment Versus Nontreatment

Treatment for Michael was a sine qua non for his parents. After all, the pregnancy was planned, and they had waited years to conceive a child of their own. To his parents, Michael appeared small and vulnerable; the nurses kept assuring them "Everything will be fine. The baby just has to grow a little." Katherine and David believed this promise and repeated it to themselves over and over again. They clung to the hope it provided and, from a safe distance, watched the ministrations on behalf of their child. The professionals cared for small infants around the clock. They knew what to do and how to do it. In this setting, Michael's care seemed routine, ordinary, and necessary. As the Petersen's looked at the vast array of machines, probes, tubes, needles, medications, and skilled caregivers, they were relieved that such a place was available for their child. In looking at the

other infants in the NICU, they convinced themselves they were lucky. Those other newborns seemed so much worse; their own infant only needed "to grow a little." They wondered how other parents endured the agony. One evening the Petersens overheard another couple softly crying and talking about the uselessness of their baby's ventilator. Katherine and David were stunned by the possibility that Michael's treatment might be unsuccessful. If a child cannot be treated, does the staff give up? This would be a tragic development, but the Petersens believed it could not happen to Michael.

At the time of his birth, nontreatment in Michael's case probably was not a consideration for the nurses. However, treatment versus nontreatment could have become an issue when a pneumothorax and sepsis developed. Although these complications prompted further treatment, the extent to which they were heroic or extraordinary is unclear. The

182

health care team is likely to respond with aggressive management unless there is clear reason not to do so. For nurses, the issue of whether aggressive treatment is humane is ambiguous. When the risks and benefits were balanced, the hope of a positive outcome for Michael probably outweighed the pain and discomfort he suffered.

> **For nurses, the issue of whether aggressive treatment is humane is ambiguous.**

When Michael began to have seizures after intracranial bleeding, the question of treatment loomed even larger. Because the parents' decision was to sustain Michael's life, the nurses were put in the uncomfortable position of inflicting more pain and suffering while carrying out prescribed treatments. Nurses' perspectives may be influenced by previous outcomes of infants like Michael. Sometimes there is a conflict between personal values and professional obligations when caring for critically ill neonates. The nurses may have begun to question the future quality of life for Michael, depending on possible disabilities from his premature birth.

Informed Consent

The Petersens were overwhelmed with requests for permission to carry out various procedures. Beginning with admission to the hospital, there were stacks of forms to sign. The cesarean section required an additional consent form. They also had to consider the research request to use surfactant for Michael, because it was an experimental treatment at the time. The many signatures appeared to be required; however, the Petersens did not believe they were actually granting permission. They thought adding their signatures to the consent form was simply a perfunctory task. The Petersens believed that they lacked sufficient knowledge and comprehension to make informed choices. Would not the staff do what they thought ought to be done, regardless of what parents thought? Although it was not an automatic process, it was matter of fact. The newborn has A, therefore we do X; he has B, now we do Y; then he has C, so next we do Z. The Petersens were confused on so many occasions because there was so much information; when permission was needed, consent seemed a mere formality. At times, only Katherine was involved in the discussions; trying to relate the information to David was difficult.

> **[The parents] believed that they lacked sufficient knowledge and comprehension to make informed choices.**

Most of the time, the nurses were conscientious about discussing Michael, but they were often busy. They encouraged the parents to telephone and ask questions. But what was the right question—not just the correct question—but even, what *was* the question? The Petersens overheard nurses talking about staffing shortages and using "float" nurses from other units. All these infants were very sick; the nurses needed to take care of them and not waste time talking to parents.

The NICU was formidable. With so much equipment and so many monitors in the unit, an important cord or line easily could be disturbed. The unit was not a good place to talk either. The Petersens overheard discussions with other parents and did not want strangers to hear what the doctors had to say about Michael. And the hallway! That was another problem. How could parents act like responsible, mature adults when news was shared in such a public place? The Petersens did not feel like keeping a stiff upper lip. The parents' waiting room was better, but it was still the hospital, and there was little privacy.

It would be good to be *really* able to talk, thought the Petersens, not just about consent forms and Michael's condition. Everyone always wanted to know how the baby was doing and, of course, the Petersens wanted people to care. Katherine needed to talk about her pregnancy and birth experience. Michael's life was a result of those family events. However, it was almost as if he magically appeared in the NICU without any connection to his parents' lives before the premature labor began. Their lives now generally focused on Michael's day-to-day existence. This whole situation might make more sense if only all of the pieces could be put together. It would help to see what went wrong, when it went wrong, and what should have been done differently, along with the whole experience of trying to have a baby.

Nurses caring for infants like Michael often feel caught in the middle of the informed consent process. Nurses see parents making major decisions affecting the lives of their infants based on information the nurses often perceive as inadequate or offering false hope. When parents turn to nurses for information and clarification, the nurses are then unsure of their responsibility about providing additional information or correcting misunderstandings.

Nurses question their role when they perceive the situation as different from that presented by the physician.

The nurses could have questioned whether the Petersens fully understood the potential long-term risks of surfactant, high levels of oxygen and ventilation, total parenteral nutrition, and antibiotics. To what extent is it the nurse's responsibility to ensure that parents understand these risks? Is it unrealistic to expect parents to comprehend fully all this information in a highly stressful crisis? Did Michael's parents truly understand the nature of his medical condition, the proposed interventions, and the consequences of accepting or rejecting them?

Michael's nurses may have become even more concerned after the Petersens were approached about their wishes regarding DNR status. What was the Petersens' understanding of Michael's long-term prognosis and continued aggressive treatment? What were the benefits and burdens for Michael and his parents? The Petersens insisted that everything be done for Michael. They did not perceive "eye and hearing problems" as problematic, but did they fully appreciate the potential for significant brain damage? If this information had been presented by the neonatologist, its impact was minimized by the accompanying remark that "Some of these children may not start kindergarten on time, but they eventually do OK." Was this a misleading statement? Did this offer false hope?

Nurses become distressed when required to provide treatment they think is futile and that inflicts pain or suffering rather than providing benefits for an infant. These situations are even more difficult when it is questionable whether parents have been given adequate information or if they have understood it.

Decision Making

No matter what the Petersens heard and discussed and no matter what happened to Michael, his treatment proceeded as determined by the health care team, leaving Katherine and David feeling helpless and vulnerable. The Petersens raised no objections because they envisioned no objections. Despite a solid general education, a better than usual understanding of current affairs, and a comfortable feeling in most social situations, Katherine and David were not prepared for the NICU. Doctors and nurses are prepared to diagnose, predict, treat, and care. They know what to do and when to do it. They are in control until the infant is discharged. Who are the parents to question this knowledge and authority? Parents must survive and be there when the infant is ready to come home. Parents endure whatever hardships, limitations, and sacrifices are required until the infant has finally grown enough to meet the demands of newborn life. Then the infant is discharged and the decision making reverts to parental control.

> [The infant's] treatment proceeded as determined by the health care team, leaving [the parents] feeling helpless and vulnerable.

Ethical decision making by Michael's nurses was fraught with conflict. Intrapersonal, interpersonal, or role-related conflicts often existed. There were tensions among each nurse's own personal values, beliefs, and behaviors resulting in intrapersonal conflict. As Michael's condition declined, his nurses may have questioned continued treatment. On the other hand, who were the nurses to say what was right for this family? After all, nurses were not the ones who would have to care for Michael the rest of his life.

Nurses also experienced interpersonal conflict. They were troubled by the adequacy of and the manner in which information was shared with the Petersens. Nurses perceived that some neonatologists offered inadequate information and tendered false hope when giving the Petersens information about Michael's prognosis. Nurses were frustrated by the Petersens' decision to continue treatment and full code status when it was obvious that Michael's potential for survival and a meaningful quality of life was negligible.

The nurses' tensions about their roles were heightened when they had to act to promote life but simultaneously inflicted pain. Were they promoting humane care? Were they acting as advocates? Everywhere and every time the nurses looked around the NICU, they were faced with conflict. How can they survive in such a stressful environment?

Nursing Implications

The reactions of Michael's nurses and parents evidenced a common theme of powerlessness or lack of control over what was happening to him. For both parents and nurses in the NICU, coping requires regaining a sense of control and mastery. Nurses think they are valued for the psychosocial interventions they provide (Swanson, 1991). Effectively fulfilling this role promotes empowerment of nurses as they enable parents to assume control over the life of their infant (Erlen, 1991).

The proposed interventions are based on two premises:

TABLE 2   Frameworks for Nursing Interventions

Crisis Intervention Techniques*	Caring Processes†
Help bring present feelings into the open	Knowing—striving to understand an event as it has meaning in the life of another
Help to gain an intellectual understanding of the crisis	Being with—being emotionally present
Explore coping mechanisms	Doing for—doing for the other as one would do for self if at all possible
Reopen social world	Enabling—facilitating the other's passage through life transitions and unfamiliar events
	Maintaining belief—sustaining faith in the other's capacity to get through an event or transition and face a future with meaning

*Aguilera, 1990
†Swanson, 1991

Nurses have the right and the obligation to participate and support parents in decision making, and parents have the legal and the moral obligation to participate in the care of and decisions affecting the life of their newborn. An integration of two frameworks can be used by nurses when assisting parents to progress from nonparticipation to acceptance of the reality and responsibility of parenting their critically ill infant (see Table 2). Aguilera's (1990) framework of crisis intervention and Swanson's (1991) theory of caring provide the basis for the following discussion. Table 2 presents the essential elements of each framework.

Parents experience a series of crises even before their infant's admission to the NICU. They first must integrate and achieve some sense of understanding of their prepregnancy, pregnancy, and birth experiences before successfully dealing with the crisis of a critically ill newborn.

Parents must identify and express their feelings to have the emotional energy necessary to solve problems. Nurses can help parents actualize their experience by providing opportunities to tell and retell their stories. As these stories are told, nurses acquire an understanding of the experience and its meaning for the parents' lives. Nurses listen without judgment or assumptions (Aguilera, 1990; Swanson, 1991).

While listening to parents, nurses convey emotional and physical presence. They are open to the parents' reality and acknowledge that the experience truly matters (Swanson, 1991). Nurses reassure parents that their feelings are normal and allow for individual differences.

Parents need information to understand the crisis process and to implement their parental roles (Aguilera, 1990; Swanson, 1991). The latter need includes information about the infant's behaviors; conditions; medical treatments including risks, benefits, and outcomes; and routine cares. Nurses need to interpret medical terminology for parents and to use lay language when possible. Written materials about the NICU are useful because parents may refer to these at home. A video about the NICU environment and procedures, including sights and sounds, may further enhance parental familiarity. Validation of parental understanding needs to be ongoing.

Once parents have some understanding of the situation, they may be more able to formulate questions and concerns; nurses can encourage parents to write these down. Quiet and private settings promote an atmosphere conducive to the exchange of information.

Parents may be unable to enact parental roles because of their immobilization or the infant's critical condition. Nurses respect these responses while providing competent, skillful care and fostering parental involvement (Aguilera, 1990; Swanson, 1991). At times, nurses may need to be creative in planning activities to include parents in infant care. Parents are supported as they assume more responsibility for decision making and provide physical care for their infants. Before discharge, parents may find it reassuring to stay overnight in a private room with their infant. There parents would assume total care, but nurses would be available for any emergency.

An essential parental role is participation in ethical decision making. Among the many authors who discuss ethical decision making (Aroskar & Davis, 1991; Benjamin & Curtis, 1992;

Jameton, 1984; NAACOG, 1987), there is general agreement that it is a complex process for resolution of conflicts related to values, beliefs, and traditions. Parents want information from the physicians; nurses can facilitate parental access to physicians. Nurses assess parents' understanding, correct misunderstandings, invite questions, and clarify parental values and goals. During problem solving and decision making, nurses help parents explore available options, potential decisions, and probable outcomes. Nurses assist parents to articulate decisions in view of their values, goals, and spiritual beliefs. Parents can be helped to balance burdens and benefits and to decide what is in the best interest of their infant.

Nurses further assist parents in crisis by helping them to identify effective coping mechanisms and support systems (Aguilera, 1990). A multidisciplinary approach to parental support ensures a wide variety of available resources. Selected parents who have had infants in the NICU may provide additional one-to-one support.

Parents must live with the outcome of their decisions. If parents are taking home an infant who requires extensive care, they must be provided with information about available resources for financial, emotional, and social support, and for the provision of care. If parents choose to withhold or withdraw treatment, they need support for this decision and opportunities to parent their child regardless of the outcome, including death.

During the entire relationship between nurses and the family of the critically ill infant, nurses convey their faith in the parents' capacity to get through an event or transition and face a future with meaning (Swanson, 1991). Throughout the NICU residence of the infant, nurses demonstrate a balanced attitude of realistic hope and optimism while helping the parents find meaning in their experience.

In summary, the NICU environment is fraught with ethical dilemmas, as evidenced by the cited studies (Miya et al., 1991; Pinch, 1990; Pinch & Spielman, 1989a, 1989b, 1990). Resolution of these dilemmas can be facilitated by the nurses' use of crisis intervention theory and caring processes.

References

Aguilera, D. C. (1990). *Crisis intervention: Theory and methodology* (6th ed.). St. Louis: C. V. Mosby.

Aroskar, M. A., & Davis, A. J. (1991). *Ethical dilemmas in nursing practice* (3rd ed.). Norwalk: Appleton & Lange.

Benjamin, M., & Curtis, J. (1992). *Ethics in nursing* (3rd ed.). New York: Oxford University Press.

Erlen, J. A., & Frost, B. (1991). Nurses' perceptions of powerlessness in influencing ethical decisions. *Western Journal of Nursing Research, 13*, 397–407.

Jameton, A. (1984). *Nursing practice: The ethical issues.* Englewood Cliffs, NJ: Prentice-Hall.

Miya, P. A., Boardman, K. K., Harr, K. L., & Keene, A. (1991). Ethical issues described by NICU nurses. *Journal of Clinical Ethics, 2*, 253–257.

NAACOG. (1987). *Ethical decision making in OGN nursing practice.* Washington, DC: Author.

Pinch, W. J. (1990). Five families share their views: Ethical decision making in NICU. *Caring, 9*, 12–18.

Pinch, W. J., & Spielman, M. L. (1989a). Ethical decision making for high-risk infants: The parents' perspective. *Nursing Clinics of North America, 24*, 1017–1023.

Pinch, W. J., & Spielman, M. L. (1989b). Parental voices in the sea of ethical dilemmas. *Issues in Comprehensive Pediatric Nursing, 12*, 423–435.

Pinch, W. J., & Spielman, M. L. (1990). The parents' perspective: Ethical decision-making in neonatal intensive care. *Journal of Advanced Nursing, 15*, 712–719.

Swanson, K. M. (1991). Empirical development of a middle range theory of caring. *Nursing Research, 40*, 161–166.

Address for correspondence: Pamela A. Miya, RN, PhD, College of Nursing, University of Nebraska Medical Center, 600 S. 42nd Street, Omaha, NE 68198-5330.

Pamela A. Miya is an assistant professor, College of Nursing, University of Nebraska Medical Center, Omaha.

Winifred J. Pinch is a professor in the School of Nursing and the Center for Health Policy and Ethics, Creighton University, Omaha, NE.

Karen K. Boardman is a mental health clinical nurse specialist, Advanced Practice Nursing Department, University of Nebraska Hospital, Omaha. She is also a faculty associate in the College of Nursing, University of Nebraska Medical Center, Omaha.

Annabelle Keene is an assistant professor in the College of Nursing, University of Nebraska Medical Center, Omaha.

Margaret L. Spielman is a retired assistant professor, School of Nursing, Creighton University, Omaha, NE.

Kathleen L. Harr is vice president for academic affairs and dean of the Nursing Program, Bellin College of Nursing, Green Bay, WI.

Selection 4-3   *Ethical Decision Making*

Purpose for Reading

PROCESS GOAL: **To organize relevant information for recall**

Students in a health occupations program are often required to write a research paper on ethical or legal issues. When doing library research, you will find current journals to be an important resource. You will also find reference books helpful. This selection is part of a chapter called "Ethical Decision Making," from the reference book *Nurse's Legal Handbook*. Since reference books are often kept in the library on reserve, you should choose recent, relevant publications and expect to practice your skimming skills. You will also need to make useful notes because you won't be able to check out reference books and photocopying can be expensive. Therefore, the main technique for organizing information to use when reading this selection is making an outline.

OUTCOME GOAL: **To make an outline of several sections of a reference book and apply the information to patient situations**

Note that this selection is organized for quick reference and ease of reading. While the entire book discusses legal and ethical issues, this particular chapter was selected for its focus on decision making.

Imagine that you want to do research on ethical dilemmas in nursing practice. Use this reference tool to help build your background knowledge of legal and ethical issues. Enjoy the experience of finding connections with what you have already read about ethics and ethical decision making.

```
──────────  Before Reading 1  ──────────
        Goal:  Get oriented to the text
  Techniques:  Preview new materials; improve your background
               knowledge
```

Look through the selection and choose appropriate orientation techniques. Since this reference book provides few study aids, discovering the organization of the chapter may require special effort.

Laypeople often complain about medical jargon—that is, the language of medicine, nursing, laboratory technology, etc. You may feel that you are becoming more comfortable with some of that terminology. This selection contains two more types of jargon—ethical and legal. Search for new words as you preview the selection, and look up some of the words prior to reading if you think that you might not understand a concept without a clear definition.

Before Reading 2

Goals:	Get oriented to the assignment; develop a study plan
Techniques:	Preview new assignment; divide the assignment into manageable parts

You might find it confusing to suddenly move from reading the text to reading a chart. Note the locations of the charts, how many and what kind they are, and how they relate to the other text.

Don't forget that this is a reference book, in which concepts may be even more densely packed than in a textbook. It may take a while to understand the material. Take *brief* breaks after reading for twenty to thirty minutes. You will remember more and be less likely to need to reread a section several times to understand the content.

During Reading

Goals:	Monitor achievement of purpose; monitor reading efficiency
Techniques:	Stop periodically to check achievement of outcome goals; evaluate the efficiency of your study strategies

As you read this selection, keep in mind that you are gathering information related to ethical decision making for a possible research paper. Your goal is to read and outline the introductory paragraphs and the first three sections of the chapter. It may be tempting to outline as you read, but there's good evidence that all notemaking, including outlining, is better done after reading an assignment through once. Having gained a clear understanding of the whole selection, you'll be in a position to take fewer, but more useful notes.

Try reading the selection for understanding, confirming information you've already studied in this unit, in the textbook chapter or in the article on baby Michael. Pause at the end of each section to confirm your understanding and to evaluate the efficiency of your study strategies. Are you concentrating well? If not, would taking a break help? Would it be useful to study at a different time? Do whatever you think is best to ensure that you are using your time effectively.

After Reading 1

Goal:	Organize relevant information for review
Technique:	Outline

To be sure that you have something useful to keep after you return a reference book to the library shelves, you can make an outline. Don't worry too much about formal systems of outline numbering. Instead, indent to show which ideas support other ideas. The more important ideas are those closest to the left margin. Include details if they are essential to your understanding, or if they would be useful in your research.

Use technical terminology in your outline, but put the definitions in your own words. If quoting from the text seems essential, use quotation marks and give page numbers. This applies to all quotations of three or more words in a row! Include the complete bibliographic information in your notes.

Outline the introduction and the sections "Law vs. ethics," "Moral dilemmas," and "Values and ethics." Use a separate sheet of paper.

After Reading 2

> Goal: Organize relevant information for review
> Techniques: Think critically about what you have learned; apply principles to real-life situations

As a test for yourself, use the chart on page 191 of the selection as a guide to identifying other situations that illustrate the ethical and legal issues that occur in nursing. Select examples from the article about baby Michael. An example of a Type 3 situation has been provided for you.

Type 1 Nursing actions are both ethical and legal.	Type 2 Nursing actions *may be considered* ethical but not legal.
Type 3 Nursing actions *may be considered* legal but not ethical. Example: The nurses delivered treatment that seemed futile and was based on a possible misunderstanding by the parents.	Type 4 Nursing actions are neither legal nor ethical.

Every day, nurses make ethical decisions in their nursing practice. These decisions may involve patient care, actions toward co-workers, or nurse-doctor relations. At times, you may find yourself trapped in the middle of an ethical dilemma, caught among conflicting *duties* and responsibilities to your patient, to your employer, and to yourself. And even after you make a decision, you may wonder, "Did I do the right thing?"

There are no automatic guidelines for solving all ethical conflicts. Although such conflicts may be painful and confusing, particularly in nursing, you don't have to be a philosopher to act ethically or to make decisions that fall within nursing's *standards* of practice and ethical *codes*. Nonetheless, you do need to understand the principles of *ethics* that guide your nursing practice.

You are *legally* responsible for using your knowledge and skills to protect the safety and comfort of your patients. At the same time, you are *ethically* responsible for acting as a patient advocate to safeguard patients' rights. For instance, although you are not legally responsible for obtaining a patient's informed consent, you are ethically responsible for notifying the doctor if the patient misunderstands his treatment or withdraws consent. To be an effective advocate, you must know that a patient's consent isn't valid unless he understands his condition, the proposed treatment, treatment alternatives, probable risks and benefits, and relative chances of success or failure.

LAW VS. ETHICS

Ethics is the area of philosophic study that examines *values,* actions, and choices to determine right and wrong. *Laws* are binding rules of conduct enforced by authority. In many situations, laws and ethics overlap. When they diverge, you have to identify and examine the fine lines that separate them.

Relationship Between Law and Ethics When a law is challenged as unjust or unfair, the challenge usually reflects some underlying ethical principal. That's because, ideally, laws are based on what is right and good. Realistically, though, the relation between law and ethics is complex. (See *Nursing ethics and the law.*)

Your role as patient advocate bridges law and ethics. For instance, most medical malpractice suits result from patients' dissatisfaction with the care they received. Such dissatisfaction may arise from a belief that staff members failed to show them respect or ignored or violated their rights. You can be pivotal in preventing such lawsuits by serving as your patient's advocate.

MORAL DILEMMAS

A nurse who must decide whether to follow a doctor's orders to administer an unusually high dose of a narcotic drug faces a *moral dilemma*—an ethical problem caused by conflicts of rights, responsibilities, and values.

Such a dilemma carries with it a great deal of stress. As you grapple with the situation, trying to decide what to do, you'll probably experience psychological and emotional stress, provoked by fear or guilt. In addition, you may experience stress caused by external factors that are political or interpersonal; for example, you may be nervous about confronting the doctor with your doubts because you fear his anger.

Moral dilemmas call for ethical choices in the face of profound uncertainty. At times, you may not know what the right or ethical course of action is. At other times, you may believe completely in the righteousness of a particular action, and yet, for various reasons, find it difficult to act.

A moral dilemma may be further complicated by psychological pressures and personal feelings, especially when any choice is a forced one at best and, in many cases, results in an uncomfortable compromise. Many moral dilemmas in nursing involve choices about justice or fairness, when scant resources (such as bed space or limited staffing) must be divided among patients with equal needs. In other cases, a choice must be made quickly because the patient's medical condition is fluctuating or rapidly deteriorating. By and large, nurses who are compelled to make ethical decisions don't have the luxury of time.

Nursing ethics and the law

The following diagram shows four types of situations that occur in nursing, each with a different relationship between ethics and the law.

Potential moral dilemmas
Certain actions are clearly unlawful and immoral (Type 4). Other actions are ethically or legally ambiguous (Types 2 and 3). In Types 2 and 3, determining whether the action described is legal or ethical may depend on a person's values or religious beliefs or how the law is interpreted. These types of situations present nurses with potential moral dilemmas.

Type 1	**Type 2**
Nursing actions are both ethical and legal.	Nursing actions *may be considered* ethical but not legal.
Example: A nurse gives the right drug by the right route in the right amount to the right patient at the right time—as the doctor ordered.	*Example:* A nurse is caring for a terminally ill patient who is in unendurable pain. The nurse arranges, at the patient's insistence, to help him commit suicide with an overdose of a nonprescribed drug.
Type 3	**Type 4**
Nursing actions *may be considered* legal but not ethical.	Nursing actions are neither legal nor ethical.
Example: A nurse administers a large dose of a pain-relieving drug to an AIDS patient, as prescribed by the patient's doctor, even though she fears it may compromise respiration.	*Example:* A nurse gives the wrong medication to the patient, does not inform the patient's doctor of the error, and does not make an incident report.

Types of Dilemmas

Most moral dilemmas in nursing can be identified according to the following classifications:

- Dilemmas of *beneficence*—dilemmas that involve deciding what is good as opposed to what is harmful; such dilemmas commonly arise when health care providers, patients, or family members disagree over what course of action is in the patient's best interest.
- Dilemmas of *autonomy*—those that involve deciding what course of action maximizes the patient's right of self-determination; these dilemmas are similar to dilemmas of beneficence, especially when someone other than the patient must determine what's best for him.
- Dilemmas of *justice*—dilemmas that involve dividing limited health care resources fairly.
- Dilemmas of *fidelity*—those that involve honoring promises; such dilemmas may occur when a nurse's duties to a patient conflict with her other duties, such as those to the doctor.
- Dilemmas of *nonmaleficence*—dilemmas that involve the avoidance of harm; these arise when a nurse believes other staff members' actions are compromising patient safety, impelling her to "blow the whistle."
- Dilemmas of *confidentiality*—those that involve respecting privileged information; these dilemmas often pit a patient's right to privacy against society's right to be informed of potential threats to public health.
- Dilemmas of *veracity*—dilemmas that involve telling or concealing the truth, such as when a patient is not fully informed of his medical condition.

Types of Decisions

In any of these moral dilemmas, the types of decisions facing nurses usually can be grouped into four categories:

- Active decisions—ethical decisions and moral judgments that lead directly to actions and bring about change
- Passive decisions—decisions that deny, delay, or avoid action and maintain the status quo by denying or shifting responsibility to avoid change
- Programmed decisions—decisions that use

precedents, established guidelines, procedures, and *rules* to resolve anticipated, routine, expected types of moral dilemmas.

- Nonprogrammed decisions—decisions that require a unique response to complex and unexpected moral dilemmas.

Most commonly, a nurse's programmed decisions also are active ones. For example, when a nurse and a doctor tell a patient what to expect in surgery and then ask the patient to sign a **consent form,** they're participating in a programmed decision process that involves ethical and legal practices (such as truth-telling) as well as patients' rights (such as self-determination).

The patient facing surgery—feeling unprepared to make a complex decision—may respond passively, saying, "I don't know what's best. Should I risk the complications of having surgery or the danger of not having it? I'll do whatever you tell me."

In this situation, the doctor and nurse must make a choice. They must either relieve the patient's stress by telling him what's "best" for him, or ensure the patient's autonomy by removing themselves from the decision-making process.

Whenever you're faced with a moral dilemma, you must make moral judgments that lead to decisions about right and wrong courses of action. Even passive decisions—for example, deciding to protect oneself by remaining silent or not taking a stand on an issue—are based on moral judgments. (See *Approaching ethical decisions.*)

VALUES AND ETHICS

Values are strongly held personal and professional beliefs about worth and importance. (The word *value* comes from the Latin "valere"—to be strong.) The remarks that follow are examples of value statements.

- "Nursing is a meaningful profession."
- "Nurses make a difference to their patients by comforting, caring, and teaching."
- "Nurses should be paid more for what they do."
- "The nursing profession must change radically to survive in today's health care system."
- "If you want recognition and respect, don't become a nurse."
- "HMOs put too much pressure on professional health care employees."
- "Doctors should make important health care decisions, not hospital administrators."
- "A new emphasis on preventive medicine will make nursing a more valuable and respected profession."

Not all nurses would agree with every one of these value statements. Value conflicts are common among nurses, doctors, patients, families, and hospital *administrators*.

Clarifying your own values is an important part of developing a professional ethic. A person may become more aware of his values by consciously examining his statements and behavior. . . .

Moral Relativism

The question arises: Are certain values intrinsically best, or are values always a matter of personal interpretation? A theory of ethics known as **moral relativism** holds that there are no ethical absolutes, that whatever a person believes is right, is right for him or her at that moment.

Consider what would happen if everyone practiced moral relativism.

- There would be no objective way to resolve moral dilemmas.
- A person could never question or disapprove of another's moral judgment.
- Professional standards, such as nursing standards, would become meaningless.
- Law and order in society would disappear.
- People and cultures would be unable to grow morally.

Although different people and cultures have different values, moral relativism doesn't provide an adequate basis for ethical decision making. Because you will probably face numerous moral conflicts in the course of your career, you need to develop consistent ethical standards to guide your behavior.

[Nine pages omitted.]

Approaching ethical decisions

When faced with an ethical dilemma, consider the following questions:

- What health issues are involved?
- What ethical issues are involved?
- What further information is necessary before a judgment can be made?
- Who will be affected by this decision? (Include the decision maker and other caregivers if they will be affected emotionally or professionally.)
- What are the values and opinions of the people involved?
- What conflicts exist between the values and the ethical standards of the people involved?
- Must a decision be made and, if so, who should make it?
- What alternatives are available?
- For each alternative, what are the ethical justifications?
- For each alternative, what are the possible outcomes?

---

*S*election 4-4   *Caring for Pediatric Patients with HIV:*
Personal Concerns and Ethical Dilemmas

Purpose for Reading

PROCESS GOAL: **To use appropriate techniques to prepare yourself to take a quiz on an article**

Instructors often use quizzes to discover whether students have done their homework. So, learning how to prepare yourself to do well on quizzes is valuable.

OUTCOME GOAL: **To understand and think critically about reported research as well as to develop an understanding of ethical dilemmas**

People today are very aware of infectious diseases that cannot be cured. While all health care employees have learned how to protect themselves, nevertheless, just as they did seventy years ago before the discovery of antibiotics, they work under risk.

This article addresses the ethical response to known risk. Nurses, like the general public, have questions and concerns about exposure to HIV. This article reports on a survey of nurses' attitudes and concerns. However, its focus is not just risk. Personal values and the professional code affect the care that nurses provide; this article attempts to evaluate how much they affect patient contact and patient care.

This article might be assigned to beginning nursing students to give a context to a discussion of ethical dilemmas. It might also be assigned to students in a pediatrics seminar as a foundation from which to launch a discussion of their feelings about caring for infants with HIV.

> ───── **Before Reading 1** ─────
>
>   **Goals:** Get oriented to the assignment; develop a study plan
> **Techniques:** Preview new assignment; ask questions; divide the assignment into manageable parts; decide when to work on each part

Because you have already read several journal articles and know the format of a research report, you can probably read this report effectively.

Does this article contain all the appropriate features? List them.

How much do you think you can generalize the results of this study, given the number of participants?

Do you understand the difference between HIV and AIDS? If not, do some background reading.

During your preview, note the ethical terms used as headings. Skim these sections for the definitions. Then, look at the figures and tables.

Plan how you will study this article. Decide how to divide the assignment and when you will work on each section. Allow adequate time for a review of the whole article once you've finished working on the parts.

Before Reading 2	
Goal:	Get oriented to the assignment
Technique:	Check for bias in the author or reader

Have you considered your own feelings about working with persons infected with an incurable infectious disease? _____

Is this a major concern for you, affecting your selection of an occupation? _____

How would you feel if your next-door neighbor had AIDS? Would it make a difference if your neighbor were a child or an adult? Male or female?

What personal values most influenced your answers to these questions?

Note: Nurses may not refuse to care for a patient with HIV, AIDS, or any other infectious disease. As you read this article, keep this fact—and your own values—in mind.

During Reading

Goals:	Monitor comprehension; monitor reading efficiency
Techniques:	Stop periodically to underline main ideas; evaluate the efficiency of your study strategies

Read this article with a pencil in hand and a questioning mind. Mark key terms and the authors' findings, and note your own questions. Think about your reading efficiency and make adjustments in your reading rate, when necessary. Keep in mind that your assignment is to prepare for a quiz on the article. The quiz will stress terminology and situations involving ethical dilemmas, as well as evaluate your critical thinking about the article as a whole.

After Reading 1

Goals:	Check initial recall of relevant information; organize relevant information for review
Techniques:	Review the whole assignment by self-testing; make notes; think critically about what you have learned

Think back to the major sections of a research article, and use those categories to test your recall of the contents of this article. If you don't recall something about each of these items, go back to an earlier step in the reading process to fill in the gaps.

Objective

Literature Review

Design, Setting, Participants

Interventions

Results

Conclusions

Make notes on the article. You may choose to make marginal notes or to outline or summarize on a separate sheet of paper.

If you want more information about HIV and AIDS, what are some research techniques you might use?

Think about how you felt while reading the narrative responses from participants in this study. Discuss these reactions with your classmates.

Don't take the test until you are confident that you have done your best to prepare.

After Reading 2

Goal: Test recall of relevant information
Technique: Answer test questions

Article Quiz

A. Match each of the following terms with the best definition of that term.

_____ 1. beneficence

_____ 2. nonmaleficence

_____ 3. justice

_____ 4. autonomy

_____ 5. veracity

_____ 6. confidentiality

_____ 7. principle

_____ 8. AIDS

_____ 9. HIV

a. human immunodeficiency virus; a type of retrovirus that causes AIDS

b. recognition that each person is unique, possesses dignity, and is endowed with freedom and personal responsibility

c. a fundamental truth or law on which others are based

d. the duty to do good

e. the avoidance of infliction of harm

f. acquired immunodeficiency syndrome; a disease involving an immunity defect, manifested by opportunistic infections and a poor prognosis

g. principle of truth-telling

h. condition of limited access to a person or to information

i. treatment based on impartial and fair standards without regard to economic, social, cultural and lifestyle differences

B. Identify the type of ethical dilemma illustrated by each of the following situations. Answer from the health professional's perspective rather than the patient's.

10. A nurse discusses one patient's medical diagnosis with the other patient in the same semi-private room.

    _____

11. A respiratory therapist administers the wrong medication when giving a respiratory therapy treatment.

    _____

12. A dying patient says to the nurse, "Please, can't you tell me what's wrong with me? My doctor won't tell me and my family won't tell me."

    _____

13. A nurse is assigned to care for an injured man accused of killing several people while robbing a jewelry store.

    _____

C. Evaluate the significance of the research described in "Caring for Pediatric Patients with HIV." Identify the strengths and weaknesses of the article, and make suggestions for improvement of the research design.

CARING FOR PEDIATRIC PATIENTS WITH HIV: PERSONAL CONCERNS AND ETHICAL DILEMMAS

From *Pediatric Nursing*, Vol. 20, No. 2, March-April 1994, pp. 171–177.

Jane M. Murphy
Nancy E. Famolare

An informal survey was conducted to determine nurses' professional and personal concerns related to caring for pediatric patients with HIV. Thirty registered nurses participated by responding to written open-ended questions. Risk of exposure in the workplace and fear of transmission to self or family are examples of the issues raised. Many phrased their responses as ethical dilemmas related to the principles of beneficence, nonmaleficence, justice, autonomy, veracity, and privacy/confidentiality. A bioethics consultant's view of many of the issues discussed will immediately follow this article.

Jane M. Murphy, BSN, RN, is staff nurse II at The Children's Hospital in Boston, MA.

Nancy E. Famolare, BSN, RN, is staff nurse II and health educator at The Children's Hospital in Boston, MA.

"Last year I had a needlestick accident even though I was taking proper precautions. The patient tested HIV negative, but for several days I was a mess waiting for the results to come back. I love taking care of my patients, but what if I'm not so lucky next time? I just don't know if it's worth risking my own life."

Nurses in the 1990s are experiencing many conflicts and doubts regarding the care of patients with human immunodeficiency virus (HIV). The issues surface on both a professional and personal level and often present difficult ethical dilemmas. As members of the HIV Resource Group at one of the largest pediatric medical centers in the country, we became aware of many concerns surrounding HIV in recent years. Our interest led us to explore further how nurses felt about caring for HIV-infected children and adolescents. To learn more about this topic, we conducted a small informal written survey using open-ended questions. We formulated the questions based on our practice and knowledge of peer's concerns, and many nurses wrote at length in response.

Although survey results were not obtained through a formal research study, we believe that the information we gathered reflects concerns of nurses in many areas of pediatric care. This article presents issues nurses repeatedly raised in our survey.

Their responses illustrate some of the professional and personal ethical concerns they struggle with in day-to-day practice. The threat of contracting HIV was a prevalent theme. This fear invades the most intimate areas of the nurses' lives, such as decisions regarding sexual relationships and childbearing. Concerns about dying or causing severe illness or death for a family member also surfaced. Survey results and our experiences show that the professional and personal concerns related to caring for pediatric patients with HIV are nearly impossible to separate.

Throughout the article, we use direct quotes from respondents that we found best illustrated and represented the concerns expressed by the majority of survey participants. We do not offer solutions but rather raise questions and present dilemmas that are common to the nurses we surveyed, and most probably, to nurses everywhere. There are no easy or clear-cut answers, yet choices must be made within the realm of nursing practice.

Literature Review

As we reviewed responses of the nurse participants, we wondered how they might correlate with published surveys or research studies. After an extensive literature search, however, we found only a small number of nursing articles on the ethical concerns/issues of nurses related to caring for patients with HIV.

In fact, Larson and Ropka (1991) noted that only 54 nursing research articles have been published about HIV infection from a list of 16,000 citations between May 1987 and June 1990.

A comparison of our findings with four previous studies revealed common themes. The Nurses Service Organization (NSO) surveyed policy holders regarding their concern about the risk of contracting HIV from one of their patients as an occupational exposure (1992). An article in the *NSO Risk Advisor* (1992) about the survey stated, "Almost half of the nurses strongly agreed that they were concerned about contracting HIV from a patient. More than one-third of the nurses were concerned about the risk even if they followed universal precautions" (p. 4).

Scherer, Haughey, Wu, and Miller (1992) surveyed two separate groups of nurses in Erie County, NY, one in 1986 and the other in 1990, to examine nurses' attitudes about caring for patients with AIDS. Half the nurses in both groups stated they were afraid of contracting the AIDS virus from patients. "Half (50%) of the respondents in 1986 were fearful of contracting AIDS and a comparable number (54%) of the 1990 respondents were also fearful" (p. 12). In the 1986 survey, 49% of the nurses said they agreed with the following statement, and in the 1990 survey, 47% agreed: "If I care for individuals with AIDS, I would worry about putting my family, friends, and colleagues at risk of contracting the disease" (p. 11).

Prince, Beard, Ivey, and Lester (1989) surveyed nurses in perinatal departments of five midwestern hospitals to determine knowledge, attitudes, and fears concerning AIDS. "More than 85% indicated a moderate-to-high degree of fear. This fear extended to carrying the virus home to children, relatives, or friends for 35% of the respondents" (p. 365). The authors also note that more than half the nurses (56%) thought they were being exposed to HIV in their day-to-day activities. "When asked to identify their greatest fears about AIDS in their workplace, the nurses' comments centered on (a) fear of caring for AIDS or HIV-positive patients, and (b) not knowing about the AIDS or HIV diagnosis and exposing themselves in an emergency or failing to exercise care in a busy situation. Several nurses indicated they had cared for AIDS/HIV-positive patients and only later learned the serostatus of the individuals" (Prince et al., 1989, p. 367).

VanServellen, Lewis, and Leake (1988) surveyed 1,019 California registered nurses, focusing on nurses' AIDS-related experience, knowledge, fears, and attitudes. Information collected on nurses' attitudes and fears about AIDS or AIDS care included issues such as discomfort at having at-risk persons to care for and perceived personal risk for contracting AIDS. VanServellen et al. (1988) stated, "Despite the fact that the actual risk to nurses is exceedingly small, about a quarter (24.5%) of those surveyed believed they were at high or moderate risk for contracting AIDS because of occupational or environmental exposure in their current work role" (p. 6).

Results of the four surveys cited above are similar to those we found among nurses at our institution. In our survey, however, nurses described their concerns about personal risk of exposure to HIV in more depth and detail, possibly because questions were open-ended. They also phrased many responses as ethical dilemmas.

ANA's publication on nursing and HIV (1988) regarding ethical perspectives in the care of the patient with HIV states, "Compounding the problems is the fear of becoming infected with the virus. Some nurses have a concern of potential transmission of the virus to themselves although the possibility of HIV transmission in the workplace is very, very low. Accidental needle sticks and blood splashes are occupational hazards against which the nurse must take precautions" (p. 7).

In a 1993 article, Carson stated, "As of October 29, 1992, it was known that 32 health care workers, mostly lab technicians and nurses, have been infected with HIV during the course of their work. Twenty-seven were infected when pricked by a needle or cut by a scalpel that had been used on an HIV-infected patient. Four were infected when blood from HIV-infected patients made contact with their mucous membranes or broken skin. One had both types of exposure. Seven of the 32 have developed AIDS" (p. 18).

In recent years, the incidence of HIV in the pediatric setting has increased with women, children, young adults, African-Americans, and Hispanics as the fastest growing groups of those infected (Cassetta, 1993). According to the Pediatric AIDS Foundation, there are "approximately 20,000 children infected with AIDS in America today. It is the ninth leading cause of death among children ages 1 to 4. . . . Among teenagers and young adults ages 15 to 24, AIDS is the sixth leading cause of death. As of September 30, 1992, there were over 10,000 cases of AIDS in people ages 13 to 24 and 46,476 cases between ages 25 to 29" (Cassetta, 1993, p. 16).

Survey Information

Our informal survey was an attempt to obtain information

TABLE 1.   Survey Questions

Professional

1. Have you had the opportunity to work with HIV/AIDS patients and families?
2. As a health care professional, what are your most prevalent concerns regarding the care of an HIV/AIDS patient?
3. As a nurse caring for HIV/AIDS patients, how have your past professional experiences influenced your present level of comfort in working with these patients?

Personal/Social

1. What are your concerns caring for HIV/AIDS patients regarding your own health? Why?
2. How has the knowledge you have acquired working with HIV/AIDS patients influenced your personal relationships with significant others, children, friends, etc.?
3. Do you discuss HIV/AIDS with significant others, children, friends, family, etc.? Do you feel a responsibility to educate others regarding HIV/AIDS?
4. Has working with these patients had any effect on how you deal with others in your personal life?

TABLE 2.   Demographic Characteristics of Survey Participants

Registered Nurse Respondents	n = 30
Age in Years	M = 32.7
	range = 23–48
Marital Status	married = 57%
	single = 43%
Nursing Experience in Years	M = 10.2[a]
	range = 1.5–28
Clinical Specialty	Medical Unit = 7
	Ambulatory Surgery = 5
	Postanesthesia Care = 4
	Inpatient Surgery = 3
	Transplantation = 2
	Surgical Unit = 2
	Perioperative = 1
	Intensive Care = 1
	Not Indicated = 5
Patient Population	Pediatrics all ages = 19
	Adolescents = 6
	School Age = 2
	Infant/School Age = 2
	Infant/Toddler = 1
Worked with patients with HIV and their families	Yes = 97%
	No = 3%

[a]no answer from one respondent

about issues surrounding professional nursing practice and social interactions that had evolved after the experience of caring for patients with a diagnosis of HIV. As we reviewed the results of the survey, we found that respondents were addressing issues that fit within the realm of an ethical dilemma. Mitchell (1990) stated, "In an ethical dilemma there is an irreconcilable conflict that no amount of clarification and application, although helpful, can entirely erase and that eventually results in relinquishing one of the views about what one ought to do, either temporarily or permanently" (p. 427). ANA's publication about nursing and HIV (1988) suggested that professional nurses continually reexamine their own value systems and preconceptions in order to respond appropriately to the needs of HIV-infected individuals.

Questions posed in our survey appear in Table 1. The length of written responses were not restricted. Sixty questionnaires were distributed to nurses working at our hospital, and 50% were returned. Biographical data were manually tabulated. The 30 respondents ranged in age from 23 to 48 years with a mean age of 32.7 (see Table 2). Forty percent of the nurses were 30 years old or younger, and 60% were more than 30 years old (see Figure 1). Fifty-seven percent of the nurses were married, and the remaining 43% were single (see Figure 2). Fifty-three percent had children, who ranged from newborns to adults. The clinical experience of the nurses varied from 1½ to 28 years, with a mean experience of 10.2 years. One respondent did not provide years of clinical practice (see Figure 3).

Surveys were distributed to a variety of settings, including intensive care, postanesthesia care, inpatient surgery, ambulatory surgery, transplantation,

200

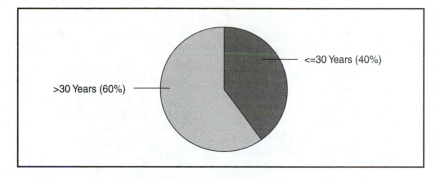

FIGURE 1. Age Factors of Respondents

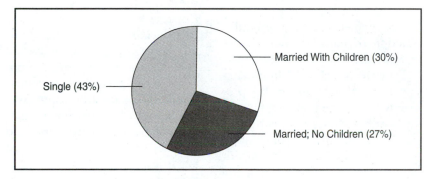

FIGURE 2. Marital Status of Respondents

FIGURE 3. Years of Nursing Experience

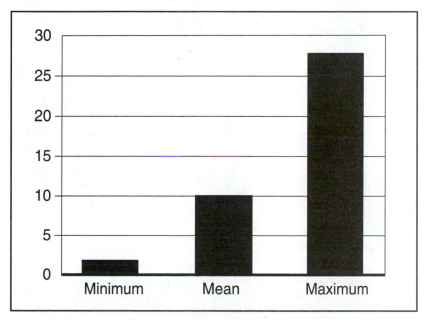

medical units, and surgical units. Patients cared for by the respondents ranged from infants to young adults. Ninety-seven percent of the nurse respondents had worked with patients with HIV and their families (see Table 2).

Confidentiality was insured in a cover letter attached to the request for participation in the survey. We distributed questionnaires to nurse managers throughout the institution and requested that they forward them to some members of their staff. Participation was voluntary, and questionnaires were returned to us via interoffice mail. Although most respondents chose to remain anonymous, some nurses opted to include their names.

Ethical Principles

According to Fry (1986), ethics "is a mode of inquiry that helps one understand the moral dimensions of human conduct" (p. 2). The nurse is held accountable for actions and judgments related to professional ethics as guided by the American Nurses Association's (ANA) *Code for Nurses*. The preamble to the *ANA Code for Nurses* directs the nurse to carry out nursing responsibilities consistent with the ethical obligations of the profession and quality in nursing care (ANA, 1985). The *ANA Code for Nurses* (1985), and Beauchamp and Childress (1989) distinguish ethical principles specifically applicable to health care and relevant to nursing practice to include beneficence, nonmaleficence, autonomy, justice, and veracity, as well as medicolegal concepts, such as privacy and confidentiality.

When we read all the responses to the survey, we realized that many nurses were raising questions related to ethical principles. We further researched nursing ethics and placed like responses from the survey within relevant categories related to these principles. The following sections introduce the reader to six types of ethical concerns raised by the nurses in our survey.

Beneficence

Beneficence is the duty to do good. Ethical questions arise in many situations, namely in preventive, curative, critical, or chronic care settings. Positive acts by the nurse incorporate the obligation to balance the possible goods against possible harms of an action, therefore avoiding acts with undesirable consequences. Nurses promote the welfare of patients through assessing benefit and harm and striving to maximize benefit while minimizing harm.

Nurses identify two different recipients of harm—the nurse and the patient. What is the risk to the nurse of doing good for the patient? Harm to herself through exposure to HIV is addressed by one nurse:

> "I worry about the transmission of HIV from patients. It's very difficult to get the proper equipment in an emergency—my first response is to go to the child, then I realize I have no gloves or goggles on and think, 'Oh God.'"

This situation shows the struggle between adhering to universal precautions to protect oneself and the need for quick response in an emergency. This nurse addresses her concerns about preventing any harm to herself while promoting the physical and psychological well-being of her patients—issues that represent a direct struggle with the principle of beneficence.

On the other hand, harm to the patient through isolation and stigma is illustrated in the following response:

> "I'm concerned with what the use of precautions, the isolation, and the social stigma of continuous glove wearing may represent to the patient and family."

While nurses must carefully analyze and balance the risks and benefits of their actions for the patient, how do they also balance the risks and benefits to themselves? Nurses continuously consider the patient's needs first, but how do they analyze the risk and consider the possible good against the possible harm to themselves?

Nonmaleficence

Nonmaleficence is the noninfliction of harm relating to the traditional rule in medical ethics: "First Do No Harm." In nursing practice, the harm to be prevented, removed, or minimized generally includes pain, suffering, disability, or death from injury, error or disease. In the health care system, a harm can be caused by failure to discharge moral, social, or legal duties to care for or act reasonably toward others. Nurses are in a unique position to protect against harm, as well as avoid causing harm as they provide care.

Under ordinary circumstances, when nursing professionals think of nonmaleficence, it is within the context of protecting the patient.

> "Sometimes I feel like my efforts are futile. There doesn't seem to be a cure in sight, and these children are suffering so much. Why are we putting these children through all this?"

This particular nurse expressed concern for the potential harm to the patient. What is interesting to note is that nurses are also very concerned about avoiding harm or injury to themselves or their families.

> "HIV is a contagious illness that is fatal, and I could pass it on to my family without knowing that I have it. That is my fear. I think the transmission to others is a new concept to deal with. I feel comfortable using precautions to avoid contracting HIV, but the idea that if I'm slack, I wouldn't be the only one who would be affected—that is very difficult to deal with."

This nurse's response illustrates her concern about avoiding harm to herself and her family—an unusual aspect to be considered in a nurse-patient relationship. Concern for self and family leads to a dilemma because nurses usually place the patient above all else. Yet nurses are voicing concerns about their own and their families' welfare and health as a result of caring for a particular type of patient. Since nurses do not tend to place their own needs/fears in the forefront, this type of thinking often leads to a sense of guilt and confusion.

Justice

Justice refers to treatment based upon equitable, impartial, and fair standards without regard to economic, social, cultural, and lifestyle differences. Patient care has historically involved a commitment to the same high quality care provided to each client. The *ANA Code for Nurses* (1985) underscores the principle of justice: "The nurse provides services with respect for human dignity and the uniqueness of the client unrestricted by considerations of social or economic status, personal attributes, or the nature of health problems" (p. 2).

Justice is the expressed principle that all people will be treated fairly. The nurses' responses in our survey acknowledged that patients who are HIV-positive require a tremendous amount of medical and nursing care, as well as emotional support.

202

"It is an incredibly long road for these patients and families, the amount of medical interventions taken is overwhelming, and the emotional stress is draining."

Today's nurses provide care despite the risks of disease, disaster, war, or other adverse conditions. Most do so willingly because they are professionally committed to providing the best possible care to patients. Nevertheless, one nurse said:

"Many patients and families fear they will not receive proper care because of their diagnosis, or that the extra step won't be taken."

In this nurse's opinion, access to care may be perceived as unequal or discriminatory. Another nurse raised the issue of caregivers' attitudes:

"All patients are deserving of the medical care they need. It disturbs me to hear others say "why bother, they are going to die anyway.""

The ethical concern arises when the care provided does not meet the fairness principle inherent in justice based on the patient's HIV status and not on the patient's needs as a human being equal to others.

Autonomy

The principle of autonomy states that each person is unique, possesses dignity, and is endowed with freedom and personal responsibility. By definition, autonomy respects the right of noninterference. The nurse adhering to the principles of autonomy encourages self-directed decision making and recognizes the patient's capacities and perspective, including his or her right to hold views, make choices, and take action based upon personal beliefs and values. Health care professionals do not have the right to proceed with interventions without a patient's consent, and the patient has a right to actively consent or refuse. For a patient's consent to be valid, it must be voluntary and based on understanding. Autonomous, informed decision-making involves adequate disclosure of information, substantial understanding by the patient/family, and voluntary decision/agreement by a competent person.

Nurse respondents expressed both strong fears, as well as strong survival instincts. They questioned the "right" of the patient/family to deny permission to be tested for HIV when another life could be placed in jeopardy.

"What do I do if I sustain a needlestick in the course of my nursing practice and the patient/family refuses permission to test the patient for HIV? This is a very frightening and sobering thought particularly because I work in a high-risk place in the hospital, and the exposure could be potentially lethal for me."

Historically, nurses have assumed a role in which they have placed their own personal safety at risk, for example, during the polio epidemic, in wartime, and in caring for patients with tuberculosis and other infectious diseases.

"In the case that I received a needlestick, my only concern is the necessity of obtaining written permission to test the patient for HIV. In the case of HBV (hepatitis B virus), we can draw blood without written permission. But laws require us to get permission before the testing of HIV!!"

Hunter (1992) cited the first provision of the Massachusetts Law on HTLV-III testing: "No health care provider shall test any patient for the presence of HIV antibody or antigen without first obtaining the subject's written informed consent" (p. 7).

Health care professionals are strong proponents of autonomy or self-determination with a right to noninterference. Autonomous actions indicate that a person should be free to perform whatever action he or she wishes, and in each of the above situations, the forces to recognize the autonomy of the patient/family can be directly opposed to the forces to recognize the autonomy of the nurse. Whose autonomy should be respected? Nurses have long upheld the ethical belief of autonomy as long as the actions produce no serious harm to others. Although nurses could be at risk for HIV infection, do they have a right to insist on testing on another?

Veracity

In ethics, veracity refers to the principle of truth-telling. Veracity is an obligation to tell the truth and not to lie or deceive others. Forms of deception, underdisclosure, and nondisclosure are issues related to veracity. Honest relationships among people ultimately rely on trust, and truth-telling is a valued extension of trust. The *ANA Code for Nurses* (1985) states, "The nurse participates in the profession's effort to protect the public from misinformation and misrepresentation and to maintain the integrity of nursing" (p. 15).

Nurses find themselves educating others outside the workplace, sensing that others use them as resources.

"Although I am knowledgeable since I am a health care provider, I find it hard to

educate others. I do discuss it [HIV transmission] with family and friends. It is my responsibility to educate others. If someone asks me questions, I would be willing to discuss it."

This statement expressed some limitations as to how much information should be given to others to clarify misconceptions. Yet, most nurses believe they have a duty to educate others truthfully even if the subject matter is controversial.

"I worry about my friends who are not practicing safe sex and have greater than one sexual partner. I'm always reminding my single friends about safe sex."

Many survey respondents raised the issue of how much and what type of knowledge they should share with spouses/significant others.

"Friends ask me if I take care of HIV patients, and then they ask if I am afraid to get it or give it to my husband. Some people even feel they wouldn't date a nurse because of her contact with HIV. I must admit I have had a fear in the back of my mind that my husband would have similar feelings if he knew the extent of my exposure to HIV patients."

Should nurses inform their spouses/significant others about the extent of risk they are accepting at work? Do they tend to withhold this type of information? Do they struggle with their moral obligations to tell the truth and their desire to protect their own privacy or protect loved ones from worry?

Confidentiality/Privacy

The *ANA Code for Nurses* (1985) requires nurses to "safe-guard the client's right to privacy by judiciously protecting information of a confidential nature" (p. 4). Privacy is a condition of limited access to a person or limited access to information. A legal right to privacy can be derived from the fundamental democratic rights of life, liberty, and property.

Confidentiality is present when a person discloses information to another with the expectation that the receiver will not divulge the information without permission. Infringement of confidentiality occurs when others are given access to protected information without consent. All hospital facilities publish a patient's bill of rights that defines and supports confidentiality. According to the rule of confidentiality, the patient has a measure of control over information disclosed and not disclosed related to health care issues.

Confidentiality and the patient's right to privacy have always been critical to the nurse-patient relationship. What are the rights of the child who is HIV positive?

"I still have an awful hard time dealing with families who do not want their child to know that they are HIV positive even in the terminal stages. I understand that the parents have made a difficult choice, and we need to respect their right to confidentiality of the diagnosis, but is it fair to the child? Often, they [the children] sense they are going to die. Don't they have the right to 'tie up loose ends' and say goodbyes as adults do?"

In Massachusetts, it is illegal to disclose an HIV diagnosis to a health care provider in another facility without patient/family consent.

"I feel as if I am deceiving my fellow nurses and placing them at risk when I make a VNA referral and the parent refuses to allow disclosure of an HIV diagnosis. Sometimes I find myself hinting at what the diagnosis really is."

Do we have the right to put others at risk by withholding information? Without the information of an HIV diagnosis, what are the risks for the health care providers? This is a difficult dilemma that many nurses face every day.

"I wish that as a nurse we are told in confidence when a patient is HIV positive. I know we should be maintaining universal precautions all the time, but there are incidents, for example, when a child is kicking and screaming, causing an IV to disconnect and allowing blood to leak out. My first instinct is to stop the bleeding and calm the child down before putting on gloves, goggles, and a gown. If I knew the child was HIV positive, my first step would be to protect myself and call for help."

Should patients' rights to confidentiality be respected in the face of potential harm to self or others?

Conclusion

In their response to our informal survey, nurses expressed many similar issues and dilemmas. In written comments, they described a number of concerns and worries regarding work-related exposure risks and many professional and personal ethical concerns. Issues raised in this article are common to many nurses and deserve thoughtful discussion in the workplace and professional literature.

It became clear to us when we read the responses of the nurses surveyed that investigating the ethical components of a situation often leads to conflicting questions without clear-cut answers. Nurses need to learn how to deal with these situations with logical, rational thought, and arrive at the best decision possible for those involved. The nurse's reaction to the ethical dilemma involves a forced choice between two ethically unattractive alternatives. Yet, through the use of appropriate guiding principles of ethics, nurses continue to generate ethically justifiable alternatives.

In their responses, the nurses surveyed described closely related professional and personal concerns often in the same sentence. The issues seemed to be inseparable in their minds. Thus, it appears that the nurses see ethical dilemmas related to the care of patients with HIV to be distinct from other types of ethical dilemmas that are confined to the professional realm. Many nurses have learned to use ethical dilemma resolution techniques to aid in the formulation of opinions and strategies when competing or mutually exclusive ethical obligations arise. Nevertheless, resolution of dilemmas associated with HIV are especially difficult because of the personal concerns related to health risk (ultimately death), and quality of life to nurses and their families. Our article raises some of the prevalent issues voiced directly by a small group of nurses in a hand-written survey and may represent the experiences of many practicing nurses.

Through this article, we hope to stimulate ideas for other articles, as well as ideas for formal nursing research. We also wish to encourage nurses to openly discuss their concerns within their own areas of practice. Ethical issues related to the care of patients with HIV are timely and pertinent to the practice of nursing in the 1990s and into the next century. Health care professionals have barely begun to discuss and analyze the ethical concerns regarding care of patients with HIV.

References

American Nurses Association. (1985). *Code for nurses with interpretive statements*. Kansas City, MO: American Nurses Association.

American Nurses Association. (1988). *Nursing and the human immunodeficiency virus: A guide for nursing's response to AIDS*. Kansas City, MO: American Nurses Association.

Beauchamp, T. L., & Childress, J. F. (1989). *Principles of biomedical ethics* (3rd ed.). New York: Oxford University Press.

Carson, W. (1993, March). AIDS and the nurse—A legal update. *The American Nurse*, p. 18.

Cassetta, R. A. (1993, March). The new faces of the epidemic. *The American Nurse*, p. 16.

Fry, S. T. (1986). Ethical inquiry in nursing: The definition and method of biomedical ethics. *Perioperative Nursing Quarterly, 2*(2), 1–7.

Hunter, C. (1992, November). Statutory regulations of HIV/AIDS disclosure in the medical setting. *Forum Risk Management Foundation of the Harvard Medical Institutions, Inc.,* p. 7.

Larson, E., & Ropka, M. E. (1991). An update on nursing research and HIV infection. *Image, 23*(1), 4–12.

Mitchell, C. (1990). Ethical dilemmas. *Critical Care Nursing Clinics of North America, 2*(3), 427–430.

Nurses Service Organization (NSO). (1992, November). What nurses are saying about HIV. *NSO Risk Advisor,* p. 4.

Prince, N. A., Beard, B. J., Ivey, S. L., & Lester, L. (1989). Perinatal nurses' knowledge and attitudes about AIDS. *Journal of Obstetric, Gynecologic and Neonatal Nursing, 18*(5), 363–369.

Scherer, Y. K., Haughey, B. P., Wu, Y. B., & Miller, C. M. (1992). A longitudinal study of nurses' attitudes toward caring for patients with AIDS in Erie County. *Journal of the New York State Nurses Association, 2*(3), 10–15.

VanServellen, G. M., Lewis, C. E., & Leake, B. (1988). Nurses' responses to the AIDS crisis: Implications for continuing education programs. *Journal of Continuing Education in Nursing, 19*(1), 4–8.

Selection 4-5   *When Language Is an Obstacle*

Purpose for Reading

PROCESS GOAL: **To focus on *after-reading techniques* that aid recall, especially outlining and predicting questions**

This selection is an article taken from a popular nursing journal; it has a legal emphasis, as the list of references suggests. Think of additional examples as you read as a way to aid your recall of the concepts. As a further aid to recall, make an outline of the main ideas in the article, by section.

OUTCOME GOAL: **To develop several questions that might be discussed during a staff development session focusing on this article**

In response to an increasingly litigious work environment, many nursing journals now include a legal column as a regular feature. Andrea Sloan, a nurse-attorney, has written this article about the miscommunication that may arise in a multicultural environment.

Such an article might be posted on a hospital unit bulletin board for staff review. It might also be used as a point of discussion for staff dealing with some of the problems described in the article. Students are also expected to participate in and learn from such review and discussion.

Before Reading

Goals: Get oriented to the text; develop a study plan
Techniques: Preview new materials; ask questions; check for bias in the reader; decide when to work on each part

---

During your preview, you'll have to read more than usual because this author uses only a few headings. The introductory and concluding paragraphs are likely to contain the author's main ideas.

Use the headings to raise questions about the content—for example, "How valid are English-only rules?" Then provide possible answers.

Have you had communication problems because of language differences? It is important to be alert to personal bias as you consider whether language is a block to effective communication. Although you know that individuals are not "dumb" or "ignorant" just because they don't communicate easily in your main language, you may become irritated by your failure to be understood. If you want to communicate with someone but don't speak her or his language, you must problem-solve to overcome this barrier—and your bias.

Make a plan for reading the article.

During Reading
```
        Goal:    Monitor comprehension
   Technique:    Stop periodically to underline main ideas
```

As you read this article, think about making an outline as a way of checking your understanding. Pause periodically to recall what you've learned and to underline main ideas and new terms.

Keep in mind that the author has assumed that her audience is composed of fellow professionals. If you imagine yourself as her colleague rather than as a student or a client when you read, you may have less difficulty understanding the author's viewpoint.

After Reading 1
```
        Goal:    Organize relevant information for review
   Technique:    Outline
```

An informal outline is a tool that will often help you understand and remember information. You can jot your outline in the margins if you have your own copy of the journal or use separate sheets of paper if the journal belongs to a library. Don't worry about using letters and numbers to provide structure for your outline. Just jot down main ideas, keeping the author's ideas in order and looking for organizational relationships. Remember that your intent is to make a brief outline showing the one or two main ideas in each section.

After Reading 2
```
        Goal:    Test recall of relevant information
   Technique:    Predict possible test questions
```

Develop five questions with answers relating to legal issues that could arise from communication problems in the following situation:

> Mrs. K, a Korean woman visiting the United States, has been admitted to the hospital for apparent complications in her late-term pregnancy. Although she speaks no English, her husband, who speaks limited English, is with her.

1.

2.

3.

4.

5.

After Reading 3

Goal:	Test recall of relevant information
Technique:	Answer possible test questions

You may have encountered language-based bias. Regional dialects, accents, and foreign languages are often the subject of jokes and slurs. Based on your own experiences and what you've learned from this article, respond to this biased question: "Why do people come to this country to work when they can't speak English?"

From *RN*, June 1995, pp. 55–57.

Andrea Sloan, RN, JD

The variety of languages spoken by health care providers and patients alike raises a myriad of legal questions. Neither the issues—nor the answers—are clear-cut.

The author is in private practice in McLean, Va. She focuses on health care and employment law, as well as bioethical issues.

Working in an ethnically diverse setting is an enriching experience. But if a language barrier prevents you from understanding a co-worker or patient—or keeps someone from understanding you—your patient's safety could be at stake.

Whether and when an individual may be required to speak English is a sensitive and controversial issue that's bound to raise questions: If English is your second language, for instance, do you have the right to converse with your colleagues in your native tongue? If a health care provider you're working with has limited English skills, are you obligated to intervene? How far must you go to accommodate patients or their family members who don't speak English?

The law isn't always clear on these issues and it by no means affords blanket protection to employees who speak a foreign language on the job—or even those who speak English with a heavy accent. Several important court cases reveal just how murky many aspects of the language issue really are.

Knowing what your professional duty demands and the legal basis for it will help you safeguard patients, lessen your risk of liability, and increase your job security.

The validity of English-only rules

Suppose several nurses on your unit frequently converse in their native language at the nurses station, in the lounge, and in front of patients. This has produced tension among staff and complaints from patients. Can your supervisor require all employees to speak English at all times?

Probably not. Strict English-only rules in the workplace that prohibit workers from speaking a foreign language even while on breaks or at lunch are likely to violate Title VII of the Civil Rights Act of 1965, which prohibits employment discrimination based on national origin.

The Equal Employment Opportunity Commission (EEOC), the agency that administers Title VII, maintains that an individual's primary language is an essential characteristic of national origin. So, courts may view English-only policies as harassment, a burdensome condition of employment, or discriminatory.

However, EEOC guidelines may permit policies that require employees to speak English while they are *on duty*—provided the employer can show that such a policy is a business necessity compelling enough to override any racial impact. Legitimate business needs that courts have recognized include promoting employee efficiency, productivity, and safety; maintaining order and discipline; and responding to customer preference.

The case of an assistant head nurse in California who filed a Title VII action against her employer is one example: The hospital had prohibited the nurse and those she supervised from speaking their native Filipino dialect of Tagalog on the maternity unit where they worked.

The rule was necessary, hospital administrators asserted, because conversations in Tagalog had resulted in preferential treatment for the nurses who spoke it and adversely affected worker morale and supervision. The court found that the language restriction did not violate the nurse's civil rights because it was motivated by a desire to eliminate dissension that could have compromised patient safety.[1]

Foreign accents and patient safety

Let's say you're working with a doctor who has a heavy accent. You have a tough time making out his verbal orders, and he gets angry when you ask him to repeat himself. Patient safety is definitely at issue if communication is hampered by the doctor's accent.

Despite Title VII employee protection, there are instances where an accent may be a legitimate basis for job actions, including firing or refusing to hire someone. In one hotly debated case, a court in Hawaii upheld a decision by Honolulu's motor vehicle department not to hire a clerk because he had a heavy accent: The recruiters believed the applicant's accent would have hampered his ability to communicate with the public—an essential requirement of the job.[2]

While people with thick accents may have a tough time getting hired, the threat of legal action deters most employers from dismissing an employee on that basis. In the case of an attending physician who is not a hospital employee, termination isn't even an option.

Fortunately, there are usually less drastic alternatives. In the case of telephone orders, technology may help. Many nursing units and doctors' offices are equipped with fax machines; some are even

linked by computer networks. The doctor with the accent can be asked to enter the order on the computer or to fax it.

If a fax or computer order isn't an option, confirm the doctor's order by repeating it back to him. Do the same thing with in-person verbal orders. Either way, write the order in the chart and ask for the doctor's signature as soon as possible, or follow your hospital's policy for telephone and in-person verbal orders.

Whatever the situation, you must be firm in requiring that the physician provide comprehensible information. A doctor has a legal duty to give clear, intelligible verbal and written orders. However, heavy accents—or doctors' notoriously poor penmanship, for that matter—do not excuse you from your duty to clarify a poorly communicated order.

Your role as patient advocate is also central here. If you believe a patient is being denied the information he needs to make informed decisions because his doctor cannot communicate effectively, you may have an ethical duty to take action. If you are unsure, discuss the matter with your supervisor, a member of the ethics committee, or a patient care representative.

If you do decide to step in, objectively document the facts of the case and discuss the complaint with your supervisor. If she does not think the matter should be pursued but you still do, forward your complaint to the appropriate department—risk management or quality assessment, for example—or to the medical staff committee.

Keep in mind that nurses should not assume responsibility for providing patients with information necessary for informed consent. That is a legal duty, which, with few exceptions, rests with the doctor.

What if the patient doesn't understand?

A patient who speaks broken English arrives at your outpatient facility shortly after fainting. You ask him whether he's on any medication and he shakes his head No. The doctor writes a prescription and the patient later experiences side effects caused by a drug interaction. It turns out the patient had been taking antibiotics but had not understood your question.

The Americans with Disabilities Act (ADA) and the Rehabilitation Act mandate that federally funded hospitals and other public facilities accommodate people who are *deaf* by finding ways to communicate with them. But the inability to speak or understand English is not considered a disability, and there is no comparable federal law requiring that accommodations be made for such patients.

Some states do have laws that require hospitals to provide interpreters for foreign-speaking patients.[3] But whether you work in one of these states or not, you are still obligated to meet the standard of care. JCAHO standards for ensuring patient rights include meeting their "communication needs."[4] The American Hospital Association's patient's bill of rights also states that hospitals must be sensitive to linguistic differences.[5]

That means you must make a reasonable effort to overcome language barriers. If you do not and the patient does not get the care he needs as a result, you are jeopardizing his safety and leaving yourself open to a negligence suit.

If you encounter a language problem, find out if a family member can translate or help communicate. Because you will be discussing personal medical information, ask the patient for his consent before using any interpreter, family member or not. Document the interpreter's name and relationship to the patient, if any.

When you provide patient education or discharge instructions, ask the patient to repeat what you have said to ensure you are understood. Back up your teaching with written instructions, too, preferably in the language the patient speaks, if possible.

Hospitals should have established procedures for communicating with their non-English speaking patients, such as maintaining and using a roster of employees who are willing to serve as interpreters or working with an outside interpreting service. The policy should also address confidentiality issues and the third party's lack of medical knowledge.

If your hospital doesn't have such a policy, talk to your supervisor or risk manager about developing one. If you care for a large number of foreign-born patients who speak a particular language, such as Spanish, consider taking an intensive language course. Besides finding it easier to communicate with patients, you may discover that learning about another culture has its own rewards.

REFERENCES

1. Dimaranan v. Pomona Valley Medical Center, et al., 775 F. Supp. 338 (C. D. Cal. 1991).
2. Fragante v. City and County of Honolulu, et al., 888 F.2d 591 (9th Cir. 1989).
3. Woloshin, S., Bickell, N. A., et al. (1995). Language barriers in medicine in the United States. *JAMA, 273*(9), 724.
4. The Joint Commission. (1994). 1995 *Accreditation manual for hospitals: Vol. 1. Standards.* Oakbrook Terrace, IL: Joint Commission on Accreditation of Healthcare Organizations.
5. American Hospital Association. (1992). *A patient's bill of rights.* Chicago: Author.

unit
5

Stress

Phases Before, During, and After Reading

This unit reviews the three phases of the reading process. It also provides practice in answering test questions that require you to apply what you have learned to real-life situations. Thus, the focus is on techniques for thinking critically about what you have learned and for quizzing yourself using the same form as actual test questions.

The topic for this unit is stress. Since this is a review unit, it contains only three selections. The textbook chapter is from an introductory textbook for nursing students. One of the journal articles provides a challenging review of the research on implications of dealing with patient stress. The other article analyzes health care workers' response to stress in a way that you may find personally useful.

Selection 5-1   *Stress*

Purpose for Reading

PROCESS GOAL: **To review the techniques for the before-reading and during-reading phases of the reading process**

This selection is typical of a textbook chapter on the subject of stress. It comes from a textbook on medical-surgical nursing used in RN programs and discusses the nursing care of adults. You might use this chapter as your primary resource in studying stress. In addition to reviewing the Before- and During-Reading goals and techniques, you will get practice through taking several tests in thinking critically about the material and in quizzing yourself in the form in which you will be tested.

OUTCOME GOAL: **To demonstrate mastery of course objectives by answering the take-home test questions with at least 78% accuracy**

To reach the outcome goal, you'll need to review the course objectives. The following objectives are typical:

1. Describe how the individual reacts to stressors, according to Selye's theory.
2. Identify interventions to help clients cope with stress.
3. In client situations, evaluate the effectiveness of nursing actions to reduce the effects of stressors.
4. Describe the purpose and use of the Social Readjustment Rating Scale.

Before Reading 1

Goal:	Develop a study plan
Technique:	Decide which parts of the text relate to objectives

---

Compare the course objectives to the Learning Objectives at the beginning of the chapter to identify similarities. Do the chapter objectives clearly include all the course objectives?

Write the number of the course objective (1, 2, 3, or 4) next to the Learning Objective to which it closely relates. Place an X next to any Learning Objective that does not relate to the course objectives.

Course
Objective   Learning Objective

_____   1. Define stressor, stress, demands, primary appraisal, secondary appraisal, coping, and adaptation.

_____   2. Describe the three stages of Selye's general adaptation syndrome.

_____ 3. Describe the coping behaviors used by a patient experiencing stress.

_____ 4. List the variables that may influence the response to stress.

_____ 5. Describe the nursing assessment and management of a patient experiencing stress.

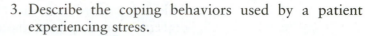

Before Reading 2

> Goals: Get oriented to the text; develop a study plan
> Techniques: Preview new materials; decide which parts of the text relate to objectives

It is important to focus on those parts of the chapter that relate to your course objectives. Preview the chapter headings, marking those that address the objectives and, thus, identifying sections that must be read. Verify that you're planning to read relevant sections by glancing through the take-home test that begins on page 219. Note the concept being tested in each question, but don't try to memorize the wording.

Which course objectives appear in a take-home test question?

Before Reading 3

> Goal: Get oriented to the text
> Technique: Look up significant terms that are not defined in the text

You will find many words that are new to you in this selection. You may want to mark them as you preview the chapter. Then use your medical dictionary to find their meanings.

Before Reading 4

> Goal: Develop a study plan
> Techniques: Divide the assignment into manageable parts; decide when to work on each part

Although you will not need to read all of the chapter to satisfy course objectives or to answer the take-home test questions, this is a long assignment. Make a plan for how much you can accomplish in each study session.

During Reading

Goals: Monitor comprehension and achievement of purpose; monitor reading efficiency

Techniques: Stop periodically to check achievement of outcome goals; adjust reading rate to purpose for reading and to difficulty of the text

---

Read the chapter, periodically referring to the course objectives. Can you address the objectives? Or does the terminology prevent you from effectively understanding the content? Mark any words you still need to look up in a dictionary. Pay particular attention to the boxes and tables, which often illustrate information described in the content.

Mark the sections you decided are not related to the course objectives. If the content is not clearly related to the objectives but is necessary to help you understand the basic terminology, you will need to read those sections. However, you can skip sections clearly unrelated to the course objectives. The course may cover that content at another time or may omit it altogether.

Although this chapter is only nine pages long, don't try to read all of the sections in one sitting. The content is complex, and your reading will be less effective if you try to read too much at one time. Plan one or more breaks, when you at least get up out of your chair and move around. Remember to review what you have read when you resume reading after a break.

After Reading 1

Goal: Check initial recall of relevant information

Technique: Review the whole assignment by answering review questions

---

Answer the review questions on pages 228 and 229 from memory first, then look back in the chapter to confirm or correct your response.

1. _____

2. _____

6. _____

8. _____

Check your understanding of the concept of stress by differentiating among several related terms. Based on your reading of this chapter, define the following basic terms.

1. Stress

2. Stressor

3. General adaptation syndrome

4. Alarm reaction

5. Stage of resistance

6. Stage of exhaustion

7. Coping

8. Fight-or-flight response

After Reading 2

> Goal: Organize relevant information for review
> Technique: Think critically about what you have learned

List five examples of physical and/or emotional stressors found in everyday life. Try to think of examples from your own life first; if necessary, refer to the text for examples.

1. _____
2. _____
3. _____
4. _____
5. _____

Describe how an individual's reaction to one of the stressors listed above may help protect or harm him or her.

Imagine that you are asked by a fellow student to explain the Social Readjustment Rating Scale in Table 5-2 of the textbook chapter on stress. In your own words, describe the purpose and use of the scale.

Just for fun: Tally your own risk level on a separate sheet of paper. Use the Social Readjustment Rating Scale, writing down the number of life events you have personally experienced during the last twelve months and the mean value of each event. Add the total of the mean values and compare that number with those in Table 5-3. What does your finding mean?

Table 5-7 of the chapter on stress presents examples of coping resources. Analyze the information presented in the table so that you can explain how it is organized. For example, how many major types of coping resources are included? What are the subtypes listed under the major ones?

There is one additional study resource in the chapter that has not yet been used. Identify this resource, and suggest how you might use it in your study.

After Reading 3

Goal:	Periodically test recall of relevant material
Technique:	Answer possible test questions

The review questions provided in a textbook can be a helpful study tool. However, they are not always the kinds of questions found on a nursing test. The instructor might assign a take-home test, which may serve as a practice test for class discussion or perhaps be used for a grade. A take-home test is essentially the same as an open-book test. You are expected to take the test out of the classroom and are free to use the textbook for assistance in finding the correct answers. The following questions are examples of application questions nursing students are expected to answer either on a take-home test or on a regular unit test. Note that the questions do not come directly from the reading but ask the student to apply what was read to a specific situation. See if you can select the correct answer. Refer to your textbook for information about the concepts as necessary.

Take-Home Test

Questions 1–3 are application questions; besides choosing the correct answer, provide an explanation or rationale for your choice.

1. While walking across the street, a teenage girl was almost hit by a speeding van. As the van passed, she quickly jumped backward onto the curb next to you. She appears pale and is panting and trembling. In which stage of the GAS is she?
   a. alert
   b. alarm reaction
   c. resistance
   d. exhaustion

2. A pilot was severely injured when his plane crash-landed. Adrenaline was released into his system, and peripheral vasoconstriction helped maintain his blood pressure. However, after thirty minutes, his blood pressure dropped and his cardiac output decreased. With these symptoms, which stage of the GAS had the pilot reached?
   a. alert
   b. alarm reaction
   c. resistance
   d. exhaustion

3. Which of the following nursing actions will be of greatest assistance in reducing the stress experienced by a patient undergoing surgery?
   a. explaining that the surgery is really very simple and nothing to be worried about
   b. asking family members to go home early so that they will not worry the patient during their visit
   c. describing to the patient the usual care given before and after surgery so that he or she will know what to expect
   d. asking a priest to pray with and anoint the patient so that the patient will go to surgery with a clear conscience

4. a. Identify each of these coping resources as occurring in the person (P) or occurring in the environment (E).
   _____ problem-solving skills
   _____ utilitarian resources
   _____ positive beliefs
   _____ social skills
   b. Give an example of each of the coping resources listed above.
   problem-solving skills
   utilitarian resources
   positive beliefs
   social skills

5. Suggest both an emotion-regulating (E-R) and a problem-solving (P-S) coping response to each of these demands.
   a. being diagnosed with AIDS
   E-R _____
   P-S _____
   b. being turned down for a job
   E-R _____
   P-S _____
   c. making an oral book report in class
   E-R _____
   P-S _____
   d. being asked to stay late at your job to close up when you have a quiz the next day and need time to review
   E-R _____
   P-S _____
   e. learning that you have just been awarded a scholarship
   E-R _____
   P-S _____
   f. realizing that you have never read one of the chapters to be covered on tomorrow's exam
   E-R _____
   P-S _____

CHAPTER 5

STRESS: NURSING ASSESSMENT AND ROLE IN MANAGEMENT

Joan Stehle Werner

LEARNING OBJECTIVES

1. Define stressor, stress, demands, primary appraisal, secondary appraisal, coping, and adaptation.
2. Describe the three stages of Selye's general adaptation syndrome.
3. Describe the coping behaviors used by a patient experiencing stress.
4. List the variables that may influence the response to stress.
5. Describe the nursing assessment and management of a patient experiencing stress.

Interest in the study of stress has intensified as investigators have begun to identify its role in relation to physical and emotional health. Most contemporary approaches to the study of stress have been influenced by three different but complementary stress theories. The first theory conceptualizes stress as a *response* to an environmental stressor. This theory was first proposed by Selye, who identified *stress* as a nonspecific response of the body to any demand made upon it.[1] Selye referred to these stress-inducing demands as *stressors*. Stressors can be physical or emotional and pleasant or unpleasant, as long as they require the individual to adapt (Table 5-1). In response to either physical (e.g., burns) or psychologic (e.g., death of a loved one) stressors, a series of physiologic changes occur. Selye called this pattern of responses the *general adaptation syndrome* (GAS).

A second stress theory views stress as a *stimulus* that causes a response. This theory originated with Holmes, Rahe, and Masuda who developed a tool (Table 5-2) to assess the effects of life changes on health.[2,3] *Life changes* are defined as conditions ranging from minor violations of the law to death of a loved one. The major assumption of this theory is that frequent life changes make people more vulnerable to illness (Table 5-3).

A third stress theory focuses on person-environment transactions and is referred to as the *transaction* or *interaction* theory.[4] A proponent of this theory is Lazarus, who emphasized the role of *cognitive appraisal* in assessing stressful situations and selecting coping options. Lazarus and Folkman defined *psychologic stress* as a particular relation-

TABLE 5-1 Examples of Stressors

Physical	Emotional
Noise	Diagnosis of cancer
Amphetamines	Promotion at work
Burns	Watching a loved one die
Running a marathon	Failing an examination
Infectious diseases	Financial loss
Pain	Winning a beauty contest

ship between the person and the environment that is appraised by the person as taxing or exceeding his resources and endangering his well-being.[5] These three stress theories are discussed in more detail in this chapter.

STRESS AS A RESPONSE

Historically, Selye's early research using animals supported his theory that stressors from different sources produce a similar physical response pattern. He called these physical responses to stress the *general adaptation syndrome* (GAS). The GAS is composed of three stages: *alarm reaction, stage of resistance,* and *stage of exhaustion.* Stressors are also likely to result in a local response called *local adaptation syndrome* (LAS). Once the stressor or stimulus is integrated into the central nervous system (CNS), multiple responses occur because of activation of the hypothalamic-pituitary-adrenal axis and autonomic nervous system. The nature of these responses, in which the stimulus and its effects successively cause changes in the nervous, endocrine, and immune

Reviewed by Linda Janusek, RN, PhD. Associate Professor, Loyola University, Chicago, IL.

221

TABLE 5-2 Social Readjustment Rating Scale

No.	Life Event	Mean Value
1	Death of spouse	100
2	Divorce	73
3	Marital separation from mate	65
4	Detention in jail or other institution	63
5	Death of a close family member	63
6	Major personal injury or illness	53
7	Marriage	50
8	Being fired at work	47
9	Marital reconciliation with mate	45
10	Retirement from work	45
11	Major change in health of a family member	44
12	Pregnancy	40
13	Sexual difficulties	39
14	Gaining a new family member (e.g., through birth, adoption, moving in)	39
15	Major business readjustment (e.g., merger, reorganization, bankruptcy)	39
16	Major change in financial state (e.g., a lot worse off or a lot better than usual)	38
17	Death of a close friend	37
18	Changing to different line of work	36
19	Major change in number of arguments with spouse (e.g., either a lot more or a lot less than usual regarding child-rearing, personal habits)	35
20	Taking out a mortgage or loan for a major purchase (e.g., for a home, business)	31
21	Foreclosure on a mortgage or loan	30
22	Major change in responsibilities at work (e.g., promotion, demotion, lateral transfer)	29
23	Son or daughter leaving home (e.g., marriage, attending college)	29
24	Trouble with in-laws	29
25	Outstanding personal achievement	28
26	Spouse beginning or ceasing work outside the home	26
27	Beginning or ceasing normal schooling	26
28	Major change in living conditions (e.g., building a new home, remodeling, deterioration of home or neighborhood)	25
29	Revision of personal habits (e.g., dress, manners, associations)	24
30	Trouble with boss	23
31	Major change in working hours or conditions	20
32	Change in residence	20
33	Changing to a new school	20
34	Major change in usual type or amount of recreation	19
35	Major change in church activities (e.g., a lot more or a lot less than usual)	19
36	Major change in social activities (e.g., clubs, dancing, movies, visiting)	18
37	Taking out a mortgage or loan for a lesser purchase (e.g., for a car, TV, freezer)	17
38	Major change in sleeping habits (a lot more or a lot less sleep, or change in part of day when asleep)	16
39	Major change in number of family get-togethers (e.g., a lot more or a lot less than usual)	15
40	Major change in eating habits (a lot more or a lot less food intake, or very different meal hours or surroundings)	15
41	Vacation	13
42	Christmas	12
43	Minor violation of law (e.g., traffic tickets, jaywalking, disturbing the peace)	11

Modified from Holmes TH, Rahe RH: Social readjustment rating scale, *J Psychosom Res* 11:216, 1967.

systems, is fundamental to understanding the physiologic and behavioral changes that occur in an individual experiencing stress.

Stage of Alarm Reaction

The first stage of the stress response is the alarm reaction of the GAS, in which the individual per-

TABLE 5-3   Life Change Units and Incidence of Major Illness*

Number	Amount of Change	Incidence of Major Illness
0–149	Insignificant	Minimal
150–199	Mild	33%
200–299	Moderate	50%
300+	Major	80%

Modified from Holmes T, Rahe E: The social readjustment rating scale, *J Psychosom Res* 11:213, 1967.
*This table describes the amount of stress as measured by LCUs (life change units), followed by the statistical incidence of disease according to the number of LCUs. The chance of illness is based on the number of LCUs during 1 to 2 years.

ceives a stressor physically or mentally, and the "*fight-or-flight*" response is initiated. When the stressor is of sufficient intensity to threaten the steady state of the individual, it requires a reallocation of energy so that adaptation can occur. This temporarily decreases the individual's resistance and may even result in disease or death if the stress is prolonged and severe.

Physical signs and symptoms of the alarm reaction are generally those of sympathetic nervous system stimulation. These signs include increased blood pressure, increased heart and respiratory rate, decreased gastrointestinal (GI) motility, pupil dilation, and increased perspiration. The patient may complain of such symptoms as increased anxiety, nausea, and anorexia.

Stage of Resistance

Ideally the individual quickly moves from the alarm reaction to the stage of resistance in which physiologic forces are mobilized to increase the resistance to stress. At this time adaptation may occur, involving modification of the external and internal environments. Resistance is high at this time as compared with the normal state. The amount of resistance varies among individuals, depending on the level of physical functioning, coping abilities, and total number and intensity of stressors experienced. For example, a person who has been exercising regularly and is physically fit will have greater ability to adapt to the stress of emergency surgery than a person who is deconditioned and leads a sedentary lifestyle.

Although few overt physical signs and symptoms occur in this stage as compared with the alarm stage, the person is expending energy in an attempt to adapt. This adaptive energy is limited by the resources of the individual. When resources are adequate, the patient may successfully recover from a stressor such as surgery and return to a normal coping state. If adaptation does not occur, the person may move to the next phase of the GAS, which is the stage of exhaustion.

Stage of Exhaustion

The stage of exhaustion is the final stage of the GAS. It occurs when all the energy for adaptation has been expended. Physical symptoms of the alarm reaction may briefly reappear in a final effort by the body to survive. This is exemplified by a terminally ill person who becomes alert and has stronger vital signs shortly before death. The individual in the stage of exhaustion usually becomes ill and may die if assistance from outside sources is not available. This stage can often be reversed by external sources of adaptive energy, such as medication, blood transfusions, or psychotherapy.

Refinements in Selye's Stress Theory

Selye's work addressed the importance of conditioning factors that may affect the stress response. These internal conditioning factors include age, genetic makeup, and previous experience with the stressors, and external conditioning factors such as diet and climate.[6] Selye coined the term *eustress* to refer to stress associated with positive events such as winning a tennis match. However, he never fully explained the health consequences of eustress versus stress. This relationship is currently under investigation by others.

Selye's description of stress focuses on the physiologic changes of the nervous, immune, and endocrine systems that occur as an organism responds to a specific stressor. In his original work, Selye described a triad of responses including (1) adrenocortical activation, (2) thymic involution, and (3) GI ulceration. His work indicates that there is a predictable uniform pattern in the physiologic responses to various stressors. This emphasis is due in part to the fact that Selye used animal models that exhibited a predictable response. As stress researchers began to study humans, the individual variations in response became apparent.

Human research supports different patterns of physiologic responses that occur during stress.[7] Illustrating this view is an early classic study conducted by Lacey and Lacey in 1958.[8] These investigators subjected 42 participants to four mild stressors. Stressors included (1) the cold pressor test, in which one arm is placed in ice water; (2) anticipating the cold pressor test; (3) a mental math problem; and (4) a test of word fluency. A number of physiologic stress responses were assessed. These findings indicate substantial variability in blood pressure, heart rate, pulse pressure, and other measures among subjects in response to the same stressor. The investigators labeled these individual physiologic responses as *individual response stereotypy*. Thus stressors are likely to produce complex and varying profiles of hormonal and tissue changes in different individuals. This may help explain why a variety of the diseases or disorders of adaptation exist. . . .

[Five pages omitted.]

IDENTIFYING STRESSORS OR DEMANDS

Work-Related Stressors

The nurse should become familiar with the types of stressors experienced by various populations and individuals in particular circumstances. For example, work-related stressors are common.[22,23] Some demands are intrinsic to the job, such as poor working conditions, work overload, and time pressures. Other demands stem from the individual's role in the organization (role conflict), career development (overpromotion or underpromotion), relationships at work (difficulties in delegating responsibilities), and the organizational climate (restrictions on behavior). The extensive research on these factors and their effects validates inclusion of occupation and work experience as essential factors in assessment.[24]

Nurses and student nurses have been extensively studied as groups experiencing high levels of stress and burnout. Stressors such as heavy work load, lack of adequate rewards, and lack of participation in decision making have been identified in various practice settings. Knowledge of these stressors is important if nurses do not want to become victims of stress and burnout in the work environment.[25]

Illness-Related Stressors

Another major source of stress relates to illness experienced by a patient, which often causes stress for family members as well as the patient. The nurse needs to assess what aspects of the illness are the most stressful for the patient. These may include such factors as physical health, job responsibilities, finances, and children. This information is valuable because it gives the nurse the patient's perspective on stressors.

Although the nurse and patient generally agree on what stressors are experienced by the patient, the nurse generally rates all items as significantly more stressful than the patient does.[26] These findings emphasize the need for understanding the patient's perception of the situation.

RESEARCH
IMPLICATIONS FOR NURSING PRACTICE

PERSONAL AND WORK STRESS AND BURNOUT IN DIALYSIS NURSES

Citation Lewis SL and others: Personality, stress, coping, and sense of coherence among nephrology nurses in dialysis settings, *Am Nephr Nurs Assoc J* 21:325-336, 1994.

Purpose To examine the relationship among personality types, personal and work-related stress, coping resources, and sense of coherence (SOC) among nephrology nurses in dialysis settings.

Methods Nurses (n = 49) from 13 different dialysis units completed a demographic data form, Perceived and Nursing Stress scales, SOC scale, Coping Resources Inventory, and the Myers-Briggs Type Indicator (MBTI).

Results and Conclusions The results indicated there was a positive correlation between perceived personal stress and work-related stress, especially work load. Conversely, there were negative correlations between (a) both personal and work-related stress with SOC and (b) both coping resources and SOC with burnout. High levels of personal and work-related stress were a result of inadequate coping resources. Regression analysis indicated that the main contributing factors to emotional exhaustion (a major component of burnout) were low SOC, lack of staff support, personal stress, and heavy work load.

Implications for Nursing Practice Chronic stress for the nurse can produce a state of burnout that is incompatible with effective nursing care. Understanding the stressors that affect responses to the work environment will allow for successful interventions to alter the risk of exhaustion and burnout. Increased use of coping resources would facilitate the nurse's management of personal and work-related stressors.

A hospital stress rating scale has been developed based on stressors identified by medical-surgical patients.[27] The five most stressful events in descending order of stressfulness included (1) the possibility of losing sight, (2) the anticipated diagnosis of cancer, (3) the possibility of losing a kidney or other organ, (4) knowing the illness is serious, and (5) the possibility of losing one's sense of hearing.[28]

In a recent study the hospital stressors of patients with acquired immunodeficiency syndrome (AIDS) were identified. Major stressors for all patients were in the areas of loss of independence, separation from significant others, and medication problems.[29] Knowledge of these and other stressors can further assist the nurse in identifying potential and actual sources of stress during hospitalization for a similar group of patients.

TABLE 5-7 Examples of Coping Resources

Coping Resources in the Person

Health, Energy, Morale	*Problem-Solving Skills*
Robust health	Collection of information
High energy level	Identification of problem
High morale	Generation of alternatives

Positive Beliefs	*Social Skills*
Self-efficacy	Communication skills
Spiritual faith	Compatibility

Coping Resources in the Environment

Social Networks	*Utilitarian Resources*
Family members	Finances
Co-workers	Instructional manuals
Social contacts	Social agencies

TABLE 5-8 Examples of Demands and Coping

Demands	*Coping*
Being diagnosed with diabetes	Attending diabetic education classes (P-S) Taking a short vacation (E-R)
Failing an examination	Obtaining a tutor (P-S) Having dinner with friends (E-R)
Being told that more work will be required as part of the job	Learning to use a word processor (P-S) Venting negative feelings about paperwork to spouse (E-R)
Being notified of an appointment for an IRS audit	Reviewing tax records with accountant (P-S) Practicing deep breathing exercises (E-R)
Giving a public speech for the first time	Practicing in front of family members (P-S) Jogging the morning of the speech (E-R)

E-R, Emotion-regulating efforts; *P-S,* problem-solving skills.

COPING

The concept of *coping* has been defined as constantly changing cognitive and behavioral efforts to manage specific external or internal demands that are appraised as taxing or exceeding the resources of the person.[5] Defense processes, such as denial, may also be included as coping processes, since both defensive and coping processes intertwine and are intrinsic to the psychologic integrity of the individual.[30] *Coping resources,* defined as characteristics or actions drawn on to manage stress (Table 5-7), include factors in the person or environment that encompass categories such as (1) health, energy, and morale; (2) positive beliefs; (3) problem-solving skills; (4) social skills; (5) social networks; and (6) material resources.

Coping efforts function broadly in two ways, as *problem-solving* (problem-focused) and *emotion-regulating* (emotion-focused) efforts (Table 5-8). As an individual attempts to deal with demands (internal or environmental) or obstacles that create the demands, the person is said to be using the problem-focused coping efforts. When the individual's effort is concentrated on methods of regulating the emotional response to the problem, the person is said to be using the emotion-focused coping efforts. For example, a patient with diabetes mellitus who learns to give injections is engaged in problem-focused coping. This patient is using emotion-focused coping when the distress of being diagnosed with diabetes is lessened by the thought that it would be worse if the diagnosis had been cancer. Combinations of emotion-focused and problem-focused coping can be used.

As an individual begins to deal with a stressor, modes of coping may include the following:

1. Information seeking (gathering data about the problem and possible solutions to the problem)
2. Direct actions (performing concrete acts to alter self or environment)
3. Inhibition of action (refraining from any action)
4. Intrapsychic processes (reappraising the situation; initiating cognitive activity aimed at improving feelings)
5. Turning to others (obtaining social support)
6. Escaping or avoiding

The choice of coping strategies depends on various factors. Variables that affect an individual's choice of coping strategies include degrees of uncertainty, threat, or helplessness, and the presence of conflict.[31] If uncertainty is high, direct action is less likely to be selected as a coping strategy. If the degree of appraised threat is severe, more primitive coping modes such as panic are more likely to occur. In the presence of conflict, an individual may not be able to take direct actions.

225

Helplessness promotes immobilization. The strategy chosen may also be influenced by the outcome of the cognitive appraisal that categorizes the stressor as harm or loss, threat, or challenge.

Specific strategies labeled as *coping activities* or *processes* have been identified by studying groups of individuals assumed to be dealing with specific stressors.[32] In a study of women with cancer, four problem-focused coping modes were identified: (1) bargaining, (2) focusing on the positive, (3) social support, and (4) concentrated efforts. Three emotion-focused coping processes were also determined: (1) wishful thinking, (2) detachment, and (3) acceptance. The emotion-focused strategies of detachment and wishful thinking and the problem-focused strategy of focusing on the positive were shown to significantly affect various types of emotional distress. Detachment and focusing on the positive helped to mitigate distress, whereas wishful thinking increased emotional distress.[33]

Most of the research to date has focused on types of coping strategies. Findings about which coping strategies are the most beneficial or adaptive are inconclusive.

NURSING MANAGEMENT OF STRESS

Nursing Assessment

The patient faces an array of potential stressors, or demands, that can have health consequences. The nurse needs to be aware of situations that are likely to result in stress and must also assess the patient's appraisal of the situation. In addition to the stress itself, specific coping mechanisms have health consequences and therefore must be included in the assessment.

Although the manifestations of stress may vary from person to person, the nurse should assess the patient for the signs and symptoms of the stress response that occur as a result of changes in the nervous, endocrine, and immune systems. . . .

Three major areas are important in assessment of stress. These areas provide the nurse with a useful guide in the assessment process. The areas include *demands, human responses to stress,* and *coping.*

Demands Stressors, or demands, on the patient may include major life changes, events, or situations, such as changes in family constellation or daily hassles the patient is experiencing. Demands may be categorized as external (environmental) or internal (e.g., perceived tasks, goals, and commitments). Internal demands may also include physical demands resulting from disease or injury. In addition, the number of simultaneous demands, the duration of these demands, and previous experience with similar demands should be assessed. Specific assessment guides for particular types of patients are also available.

Primary appraisal or perception of the demands should be assessed. Demands may be categorized as representing harm or loss, threat, or challenge. Family responses to demands on the patient should also be assessed.[34]

Human Responses to Stress Physiologic effects of demands that are appraised as stressful are mediated primarily via the sympathetic nervous system and the hypothalamic-pituitary-adrenal system. Responses such as increased heart rate, increased blood pressure, loss of appetite, sweating, and dilated pupils are included. In addition, the patient may exhibit some of the diseases of adaptation. . . .

Behavioral human responses include observable actions and cognitions of the patient. Behavioral effects may include responses such as accident proneness, impaired speech, anxiety, crying, and shouting. Behavior in other aspects of life such as occupation may include absenteeism or tardiness at work, lowered productivity, and job dissatisfaction. Observable cognitive responses include self-reports of excessive demand, inability to make decisions and forgetfulness. Some of these responses may also be apparent in significant others.

Coping Secondary appraisal by the patient, or the patient's evaluation of coping resources and options, should be assessed. Resources such as supportive family members, adequate finances, and the ability to solve problems are examples of positive resources (see Table 5-7).

Coping strategies include cognitive and behavioral efforts to meet demands. The use and effectiveness of problem-focused and emotion-focused coping efforts should be addressed (see Table 5-8). These efforts may be categorized as direct action, avoidance of action, seeking information, defense mechanisms, and seeking assistance of others. The probability that a certain coping strategy will bring about the desired result is another important aspect to be assessed.[31]

Nursing Diagnoses

The importance of stress and coping to the nurse is shown by the amount of attention these concepts have received related to nursing diagnoses. A coping-stress-tolerance pattern has been identified as 1 of 11 functional health patterns.[35] This pattern includes the diagnoses presented in Table 5-9. Assessment of the health pattern results in a description of the coping-stress-tolerance patterns of a patient. Stressors can be identified at the individual or family level.

TABLE 5-9 Nursing Diagnoses in Coping-Stress Tolerance Pattern

Impaired adjustment
Caregiver role strain
Ineffective individual coping
  Defensive coping
  Ineffective denial
Ineffective family coping: compromised
Ineffective family coping: disabled
Family coping: potential for growth
Posttrauma response
Relocation stress syndrome
Risk for self-harm
Risk for violence

TABLE 5-10 Conditioning Factors Altering the Stress Response

Age	Personality
Nutrition	Circadian rhythms
Heredity	Previous experiences
Social support	Socioeconomic status
Health	Financial resources

Two specific nursing diagnoses have been identified related to stress: ineffective individual coping and ineffective family coping. *Ineffective individual coping* is defined as an inability to manage internal or environmental stressors appropriately as a result of inadequate resources (physical, psychologic, behavioral, or cognitive). Potential etiologies include disruption of emotional bonds, unsatisfactory support system, sensory overload, and inadequate psychologic resources.[35] *Ineffective family coping: compromised* refers to the usually supportive primary person (family member or close friend) providing insufficient, ineffective, or compromised support, comfort assistance, or encouragement, which may be needed by the patient to manage or master adaptive tasks related to health challenge.[35]

Nursing Implementation

The first step in managing stress is to become aware of its presence. This includes identifying and expressing stressful feelings. The role of the nurse is to facilitate and enhance the processes of coping and adaptation. Nursing interventions depend on the severity of the stress experience or demand. In the multiple trauma patient, the person expends energy in an attempt to physically survive. The nurse's efforts are directed to life-supporting interventions and to the inclusion of approaches aimed at the reduction of additional stressors to the patient. For example, the multiple trauma patient is much less likely to adapt or recover if faced with additional stressors such as sleep deprivation or an infection.

The importance of cognitive appraisal in the stress experience should prompt the nurse to assess if changes in the way the patient perceives and labels particular events or situations (cognitive reappraisal) are possible. Some experts also propose that the nurse consider the positive effects that

result from successfully meeting stressful demands. Greater emphasis should also be placed on the part of cultural values and beliefs enhancing or constraining various coping options.

Since dealing with physical, social, and psychologic demands is an integral part of daily experiences, the coping behaviors that are used should be adaptive and should not be a source of additional stress to the individual. Generalizing about which coping strategies are the most adaptive is not yet possible. However, in evaluating coping behaviors, the nurse should look at the short-term outcomes (i.e., the impact of the strategy on the reduction or mastery of the demands and the regulation of the emotional response) and the long-term outcomes that relate to health, morale, and social and psychologic functioning.

Conditioning factors affect the response to various stressors (Table 5-10). Resistance to stress can be increased with a healthy lifestyle. Some behaviors seem to promote and maintain health. These include the following:

1. Sleeping regularly 7 to 8 hours per night
2. Eating breakfast
3. Eating regular meals with minimal or no snacking
4. Eating moderately to maintain an ideal weight
5. Exercising moderately
6. Drinking alcohol moderately
7. Not smoking (best if have never smoked)

These behaviors help people maintain good health regardless of sex, age, and economic status. These behaviors are also cumulative; that is, the greater the number of these factors habitually practiced by the individual, the better the health.

Good mental health practices are important for good health as well. These practices primarily result in a realistic, positive self-conception, and the ability to solve problems.

Stress-reducing activities can be incorporated into nursing practice. The activities suggested can also be viewed as conditioning factors, because the patient is developing a sense of control with an

TABLE 5-11   Examples of Stress Management Techniques

Techniques	Descriptions
Progressive relaxation	Self-taught or instructor-directed exercise that involves learning to contract and relax muscles in a systematic way, beginning with the face and ending with the feet. The exercise may be combined with breathing exercises that focus on inner self.
Guided imagery	Purposeful use of one's imagination to achieve relaxation and control. An individual concentrates on images and mentally pictures oneself in the scene.
Thought stopping	Self-directed behavioral approach used to gain control of self-defeating thoughts. When these thoughts occur, the individual stops the thought process and focuses on conscious relaxation.
Exercise	Regular exercise, especially aerobic movement, results in improved circulation, increased release of endorphins, and an enhanced sense of well-being.
Humor	Humor in the form of laughter, cartoons, funny movies, riddles, audiocassettes, comic books, and joke books can be used for both the nurse and patient.
Assertive behavior	Open, honest sharing of feelings, desires, and opinions in a controlled way. The individual who has control over one's life is less subject to stress.
Social support	This may take the form of organized support and self-help groups, relationships with family and friends, and professional help.

increase in self-esteem as the practices are incorporated into daily activities. A sense of control is an important mediator in the stress process.[36]

The nurse can assume a primary role in planning stress-reducing interventions. Specific stress-reducing activities within the scope of nursing practice (some of which may require additional training) include relaxation training, cognitive reappraisal, music therapy, exercise, decisional control, massage, and humor (Table 5-11). . . .

In summary, a knowledge of stress and coping theories provides the nurse with useful concepts that are applicable to all phases of the nursing process. Keeping abreast of the current research on this topic is a challenge. The models and concepts proposed are useful to the nurse who chooses to establish a research- and theory-based practice that recognizes the relationships among stress, coping, and health. The nurse should recognize when the patient or family needs to be referred to a professional with advanced training in counseling.

REVIEW QUESTIONS

The number of the question corresponds to the same-numbered objective at the beginning of the chapter.

1. Choose the false statement regarding stress.
   a. It occurs when demands exceed the adaptive resources of an individual.
   b. It occurs only as a result of physiologic stressors.
   c. What is stressful to one individual may not be stressful to another.
   d. It may result from a perceived threat.

2. All the following statements are true about the GAS *except*
   a. it was first defined by Selye and involves stages.
   b. it involves the central and autonomic nervous systems and the pituitary and adrenal glands.
   c. symptoms of the stage of resistance are caused by stimulation of the sympathetic nervous system.
   d. symptoms of the stage of exhaustion may initially mimic those of the stage of alarm reaction.

   .
   .
   .

6. Choose the false statement regarding coping behaviors.
   a. Coping behaviors may include efforts to regulate emotion.
   b. Some coping behaviors are problem-focused efforts.
   c. Denial is a form of coping.
   d. If uncertainty is high, direct action is usually the selected coping strategy.

   .
   .
   .

CASE STUDY

STRESS DURING HOSPITALIZATION

Patient Profile

Mr. R. Ranson, a 20-year-old college student and starting basketball guard, was admitted for an emergency appendectomy the night before his basketball team entered the final playoffs.

Subjective Data

· Has exertional asthma that has been controlled with medication
· Has primarily been eating pizza, doughnuts, and drinking coffee and sodas
· Does not want his family or friends to visit

Critical Thinking Questions

1. Explain the physiologic changes that would be expected in Mr. Ranson during the first 24 hours postoperatively as a result of the demand of surgery.
2. Explain how Mr. Ranson's previous diet may affect his current adaptability.
3. What physiologic and psychologic stressors can be identified or predicted in Mr. Ranson's situation? Describe the possible effects of these stressors on his asthma.
4. What factors will Mr. Ranson's secondary appraisal process focus on?
5. What specific nursing interventions can be included in Mr. Ranson's management that will enhance his adaptability?
6. Based on the assessment data provided, write one or more nursing diagnosis. Are there any collaborative problems?

8. Examples of the signs and symptoms exhibited by the patient experiencing stress include all *except*
   a. anxiety.
   b. forgetfulness.
   c. decreased blood pressure.
   d. impaired speech.

REFERENCES

1. Selye H: The stress concept: past, present, and future. In Cooper CL, editor: *Stress research: issues for the eighties,* New York, 1983, John Wiley & Sons.
2. Holmes T, Masuda M: Magnitude estimations of social readjustments, *J Psychosom Res* 11:219, 1966.
3. Holmes T, Rahe R: The social readjustment rating scale, *J Psychosom Res* 12:213, 1967.
4. Derogatis LR, Coons H: Self-report measures of stress. In Goldberger L, Breznitz S, editors: *Handbook of stress: theoretical and clinical aspects,* ed 2, New York, 1993, Free Press.
5. Lazarus R, Folkman S: *Stress, appraisal, and coping,* New York, 1984, Springer.
6. Selye, H: *The stress of life,* New York, 1956, McGraw-Hill.
7. Calabrese JR, Wilde C: Alterations in immunocompetence during stress: a medical perspective. In Plotnikoff N and others, editors: *Stress and immunity,* Boca Raton, FL, 1991, CRC Press.
8. Lacey JI, Lacey BC: Verification and extension of the principle of autonomic response stereotype, *Am J Psychol* 71:50, 1958.
9. Holmes TH, Masuda M: Life change and illness susceptibility. In Dohrenwend BA, Dohrenwend BP, editors: *Stressful life events: their nature and effects,* New York, 1974, John Wiley & Sons.
10. Leventhal H, Tomarken A: Stress and illness: perspectives from health psychology. In Kasl SV, Cooper CL, editors: *Stress and health: issues in research methodology,* New York, 1978, John Wiley & Sons.
11. Kobasa SC: Stressful life events, personality, and health: an inquiry into hardiness, *J Pers Soc Psychol* 37:2, 1979.
12. Ouellette SC: Inquiries into hardiness. In Goldberger L, Breznitz S, editors: *Handbook of stress: theoretical and clinical aspects,* ed 2, New York, 1993, Free Press.
13. Antonovsky AA: *Unraveling the mystery of health: how people manage stress and stay well,* San Francisco, 1987, Jossey-Bass.
14. Williams SJ: The relationship among stress, hardiness, sense of coherence and illness in critical care nurses, *Medical Psychotherapy* 3:171, 1990.
15. Lazarus RS: Puzzles in the study of daily hassles, *J Behav Med* 7:376, 1984.
16. Kanner AD and others: Comparison of two modes of stress measurement: daily hassles and uplifts versus major life events, *J Behav Med* 4:1, 1981.
17. Lazarus RS, Launier R: Stress-related transactions between person and environment. In Pervin LA, Lewis M, editors: *Perspectives in international psychology,* New York, 1978, Plenum.
18. O'Leary A: Stress, emotion, and human function, *Psychol Bull* 108:363, 1990.
19. Herbert TB, Cohen S: Stress and immunity in humans, *Psychosom Med* 55:364, 1993.
20. Cohen S and others: Psychological stress and susceptibility to the common cold, *N Engl J Med* 325:606, 1991.
21. Spiegel D and others: Effect of psychosocial treatment on survival of patients with metastatic breast cancer, *Lancet* 2:881, 1989.
22. Holt RR: Occupational stress. In Goldberger L, Breznitz S, editors: *Handbook of stress: theoretical and clinical aspects,* ed 2, New York, 1993, Free Press.

23. Karasek R, Theorell T: *Health work: stress, productivity, and the reconstruction of working life,* New York, 1990, Basic Books.

24. Repetti RL: The effects of work load and the social environment at work on health. In Goldberger L, Breznitz S, editors: *Handbook of stress: theoretical and clinical aspects,* ed 2, New York 1993, Free Press.

25. Pines AM: Burnout. In Goldberger L, Breznitz S, editors: *Handbook of stress: theoretical and clinical aspects,* ed 2, New York, 1993, Free Press.

26. Werner JS: Stressors and health outcomes: synthesis of nursing research, 1980–1990. In Barnfather JS, Lyon BL, editors: *Stress and coping: State of the science and implications for nursing theory, research, and practice,* Indianapolis, 1993, Sigma Theta Tau Center Press.

27. Volicer BJ: Perceived stress levels of events associated with the experience of hospitalization: development and testing of a measurement tool, *Nurs Res* 22:491, 1973.

28. Volicer BJ, Bohannon MW: A hospital stress rating scale, *Nurs Res* 24:352, 1975.

29. Van Servellen G, Lewis CE, Leake B: The stresses of hospitalization among AIDS patients on integrated and special care units, *Int J Nurs Stud* 27:235, 1990.

30. Jalowiec A: Revision and testing of the Jalowiec Coping Scale. Proceedings of the thirteenth annual conference of the Midwest Nursing Research Society 13:150, 1989.

31. Moos RH, Schaefer J: Coping resources and processes: current concepts and measures. In Goldberger L, Breznitz S, editors: *Handbook of stress: theoretical and clinical aspects,* ed 2, New York, 1993, Free Press.

32. Taylor SE, Aspinwall L: Coping with chronic illness. In Goldberger L, Breznitz S, editors: *Handbook of stress: theoretical and clinical aspects,* ed 2, New York, 1993, Free Press.

33. Mishel MH, Sorenson D: Revision of the ways of coping checklist for a clinical population, *West J Nurs Res* 15:59, 1993.

34. Halm MA and others: Behavioral responses of family members during critical illness, *Clin Nurs Res* 2:414, 1993.

35. Carpenito LJ: *Nursing diagnosis: application to clinical practice,* ed 6, Philadelphia, 1995, Lippincott.

36. Wallston KA: Assessment of control in health care settings. In Steptoe A, Appels A, editors: *Stress, personal control, and health,* New York, 1989, John Wiley & Sons.

Selection 5-2   *Stress and Anxiety*

Purpose for Reading

PROCESS GOAL: **To focus on achieving your purpose for reading and remembering the material accurately**

The information in this selection summarizes research on stress and anxiety as well as research-validated strategies for reducing stress. The article is from *Nursing Clinics of North America,* a hardbound quarterly journal that focuses on one or two topics each issue. It might be assigned to students who are discussing the concept of stress in a conference group after studying it in the classroom.

OUTCOME GOAL: **To increase your understanding of Selye's contribution to stress research and to learn more about nursing applications of stress research**

In making the assignment, the instructor would probably ask students to read the entire article, focusing on information related to the following course objectives.

1. Describe how the individual reacts to stress according to Selye's theory.
2. Identify interventions to help clients cope with stress.
3. In client situations, evaluate the effectiveness of nursing actions to reduce the effects of stressors.

As extra motivation, the instructor might inform students that a ten-question quiz on the article will be given during the next class period.

Before Reading 1

Goals: Get oriented to the text; develop a study plan
Techniques: Preview new materials; decide which parts of the text relate to objectives

---

During your preview, you may want to pay special attention to the references to see the variety of data supporting this article.

Put a check mark beside the headings that seem to be related most directly to the objectives, and then focus on these sections of text. Put an X beside headings that seem irrelevant to the objectives. Although you have been asked to read the entire article, you can move more rapidly through the sections that do not relate closely to the objectives.

Before Reading 2

Goal:	Get oriented to the text
Technique:	Look up significant terms that are not defined in the text

As an aid to pronouncing the long and technical terms that you may have noticed during your preview, try dividing these words into parts (roots, prefixes, suffixes)—for example, psycho-analyt-ic.

biologic _____

psychosomatic _____

interactional _____

transactional _____

physiologic _____

neurophysiology _____

immediate _____

intermediate _____

neuroendocrine _____

immunocompetence _____

If the meanings of these words or any of the word parts aren't clear, take time to review the definitions. Words misunderstood before reading can cause serious comprehension difficulties during and after reading.

During Reading 1

Goal:	Monitor comprehension and achievement of purpose
Techniques:	Look for main ideas; stop periodically to check achievement of outcome goals and to underline main ideas

Read to fulfill the purpose of learning more about Selye's importance in stress research and to gain information about nursing applications of stress research. Remember that you have identified some sections as candidates for faster, less critical reading.

Remember also that you are reading to prepare for a test. Underline main ideas or jot them in the margins; they will help you review the content.

During Reading 2

Goal:	Monitor reading efficiency
Technique:	Evaluate the efficiency of your study strategies

As you stop periodically to assess your progress in reaching the outcome goals, you should also ask yourself whether you are reading efficiently. Are you reading as rapidly as purpose and difficulty permit? Have you allowed irrelevant thoughts to get you off the track? Remind yourself to be efficient in your studying. If your "irrelevant thoughts" are actually important personal reminders, write them down on a notepad, so that they won't keep popping into your mind. Then you can focus on learning.

After Reading 1

Goal:	Organize relevant information for review
Technique:	Make notes and jot down questions

To review and clarify the author's densely packed findings, focus your notemaking on these sections: the introduction, "Biologic Response," "Biologic Research," "Nursing Research on Stress Incidence, Treatment, and Prevention," "Implications for Nursing Research and Practice," and "Summary." These sections relate most closely to the course objectives.

Your notes should reflect main ideas and significant details, as well as the author's organization.

After Reading 2

Goal:	Test recall of relevant information
Techniques:	Review notes without rereading the text; answer possible test questions

---

When you are satisfied with your understanding of the article, complete the following test. Don't reread the article, but feel free to review your notes before taking the test.

When you feel prepared, turn the page and begin the test.

Comprehension Test

Choose the best answer from the choices that follow each question.

1. According to Lisa Robinson in "Stress and Anxiety,"
   a. anxiety and stress are equally difficult to describe.
   b. anxiety is felt as an early stage of the stress response.
   c. Freud first wrote about stress in 1926.
   d. stress is defined as a response rather than a stimulus.
2. Selye placed the following into the biologic context:
   a. the term *arousal* that is associated with anxiety
   b. the general adaptation syndrome (GAS)
   c. contemporary research in behavioral sciences
   d. the term *stress*, which was originally an engineering and physical one

3. One possible criticism of Selye's work is that it
   a. did not explain individual variations in response to stress.
   b. was the springboard for much contemporary research.
   c. neglected the physiologic aspects of stress.
   d. took place in the 1940s.
4. One interesting finding of research on stressors and hospitalized or diseased patients is that
   a. the management of anxiety was best done by women.
   b. sources and intensity of patient anxiety were incorrectly assessed by nurses.
   c. the language of stress and coping emerged as biased and confusing.
   d. the effect of preparatory information was insignificant.
5. Anxiety is an appropriate subject of study for nurses because it is related to
   a. necessary descriptive work that must be done.
   b. one component of the postulated stress response.
   c. patient comfort, a central concern of nursing.
   d. unquestioned validity and reliability.
6. The best time for stress management is
   a. before stress occurs.
   b. when stress is occurring.
   c. immediately after the stressor is perceived.
   d. at the optimal junction.
7. Reframing and redefinition are techniques for
   a. eliminating stress.
   b. assuming a passive, victim-like role.
   c. coaching the patient to avoid stressors.
   d. changing one's understanding of the source of stress.
8. Learning to limit the threatening, hence stressful, actions of others is one example of a/an
   a. cognitive response.
   b. behavioral response.
   c. emotional response.
   d. physical response.
9. One example of an adaptive emotional coping response is
   a. endorphin production.
   b. relaxation.
   c. laughter.
   d. assertiveness.
10. According to the author of the article "Stress and Anxiety," focused coping can lead to an increase in feelings of
    a. futility.
    b. relaxation.
    c. immunocompetence.
    d. self-efficacy.

After completing the test, go back to your outline and to the article to locate the information required by each question. Does your outline contain the "right answers"? What about your underlining and marginal notes?

Since the questions come from noteworthy areas of the text, use this as an opportunity to improve your notes. Feel free to change your answers at this stage, too.

From *Nursing Clinics of North America*, **Vol. 25, No. 4, December 1990, pp. 935–943.**

Lisa Robinson, PhD, RN, FAAN, CS*

*Professor and Coordinator, Graduate Program in Psychiatric Nursing, Department of Psychophysiological Nursing, School of Nursing; and Assistant Professor, Department of Psychiatry, School of Medicine, University of Maryland, Baltimore, Maryland

Address reprint requests to:
Lisa Robinson, PhD, RN, FAAN, CS
421 Parsons Hall
University of Maryland
622 West Lombard Street
Baltimore, MD 21201

Stress and anxiety have been studied abundantly by nurses for several decades. These topics have been popular in the health-related literature for even longer. The concept of anxiety arose from psychoanalytic theory and was pivotal to that discipline from the time that Freud first wrote about it in 1926. In the 1930s the concept was linked to psychosomatic disease when it was recognized by many prominent theorists that anxiety played a pivotal role in disease. Their belief was that specific emotions such as anxiety, anger, and rage were associated with specific diseases, such as gastric ulcers, asthma, and ulcerative colitis. This focus gradually shifted to a more generic one, where the ideas of anxiety and disease specificity were replaced by a research interest in stress and vulnerability to disease. Contemporary research has revealed that the stress response is, in fact, a prolonged psychophysiologic reaction. Its initial phase manifests itself through felt anxiety, which is the subjective manifestation of arousal.[19] This stage of the stress response precedes both coping and further psychophysiologic change when one is confronted by a threat.

Stress is apparently more difficult to define and describe than was anxiety. The literature demonstrates marked differences in its conceptualization. Stress is defined as both a stimulus and response. Stimulus definitions focus on events in the environment such as natural disasters, noxious conditions, illness, or personal calamity. These conceptualizations usually are generated by scientists in psychological disciplines. Response definitions that have been prevalent in the biological and physiologic literature refer to a state of stress in which a person is described as reacting to stress, or being under stress.

Because of the demonstrated linkages between person and environment, an interactive definition best describes stress. Lazarus and Folkman conclude that psychological stress "is a particular relationship between the person and the environment that is appraised by the person as taxing or exceeding his or her resources and endangering his or her well being. This appraisal is succeeded by a series of physiological responses that will be described."[14]

Biologic Response

In the 1920s Cannon studied the physiologic responses to emotional arousal. While he emphasized the adaptive function of the "fight or flight" reaction, Cannon suggested somewhat speculatively that physiologic processes were influenced by emotional states. The latter, which physiologists termed "arousal," would in psychological terms be associated with self-reports of human subjects and be termed "anxiety."[4] In the 1940s Selye expanded the earlier work and placed the concept of stress, which was originally an engineering and physical term, into the biologic context. Selye's classical formulation of stress is a physiologic state manifested by the general adaptation syndrome (GAS) of stereotypical physiologic responses. The stress manifested by the GAS is a nonspecific response of the body to any adaptive demand made on it. The criticism of Selye's work was that it did not account for variation in human response based on individual vulnerabilities. His work, however, was the springboard for much contemporary research in both the physiologic and behavioral sciences.[20]

Contemporary stress research focuses on psychobiologic (endocrine, immunologic, and psychological) phenomena including performance, cognitive functioning, emotional life, and social functioning in experience with a stimulus or situation that is appraised as aversive or unpleasant. Increasing attention is focused on the way that people cope with stressful events. Nursing research explores clinical interventions and preventive actions aimed at neutralizing adverse health effects secondary to stressful encounters. Vingerhoet and Marcelissen describe nine bases of stress research: (1) biologic; (2) the (classic) psychosomatic; (3) life events; (4) interactionistic or transactional approaches; (5) life-style and behavior; (6) group differences in vulnerability; (7) the sociocultural (macro) factors and vulnerability; (8) work and organizational stress research; and (9) intervention and prevention.[23] The four most salient to nursing, the biologic, psychosomatic, life event, and interactionistic or transactional approaches, will be summarized as the bases of stress theory.

Biologic Research

Cannon and Selye were classic physiologic investigators of stress. Cannon demonstrated that psychological stimuli could activate the physiologic system of an organism, in particular the sympathetic division of the autonomic nervous system, causing the release of adrenaline and noradrenaline by the adrenal medulla. Selye emphasized the role of the adrenal cortex secreting corticosteroids. He identified theories about the relationship between short-term stress reactions and their outcomes: the diseases of adaptation.

The biologic approach focused mainly on short-term somatic reactions of organisms to aversive stimulation. Lacking in this work was attention to the "black box" that characterized the human response to stress, i.e., the perception that an event was or was not aversive.

Psychosomatic Approach

The psychosomatic model suggests that specific diseases, i.e., asthma, hypertension, hives, ulcerative colitis, acne, and even cancer, are caused by specific intrapsychic conflict. A hypothesis generated by Graham[10] and later by Derogatis et al.[8] posited that specific attitudes were linked not only with cause, but with the clinical courses of diseases. The psychosomatic model highlighted the roles of anger and anxiety in disease. This model had its roots in psychoanalysis and acted as a foil against the biologic models that gained prominence. From the psychosomatic tradition came two lines of contemporary research: personality as an etiologic factor and specific psychological states predisposing to disease. Personality variables that are now studied are sensation seeking, hardiness and neuroticism. It is hypothesized that certain personality features make a person more or less resistant to stress, and these characteristics determine the outcome of a stressful interaction.

Life Events

In the social sciences the most influential line of research has been that associated with Holmes and Rahe on the relationship between "life events" and illness. Many theorists criticize the study of life events in the tradition of Holmes and Rahe because it does not take into account the evaluation of the event by the subject. This evaluation comprises significant features such as negative or positive, unexpected or anticipated, and ability to control.[22]

Interactional/Transactional Approach

This model helps to explain the influence of individual differences, and it gets at the moderating and mediating variables of outcomes. Lazarus and Folkman[14] have provided much of the research for this model. Appraisal and coping are the two central concepts. Appraisal refers to the evaluation of the situation in which two considerations are paramount: what is at stake? and what can I do about it? If the subject feels a discrepancy between the demands of the situation and his capabilities to do something about it, then a state of stress develops. Coping refers to the process of managing external and internal demands that tax or exceed the resources of the person. Lazarus and associates maintain that coping is a process that can be described in terms of a relationship between the person and the specific environment.[14] They reject the trait approach of coping, and instead maintain that coping is a dynamic process, determined by the nature of the stressor.

Current research has begun to refocus on the process of coping rather than on stress. Although the psychological component of the psychophysiologic response to stressful events still is unclear in its linkages to illness, the physiologic processes are more clearly demonstrated and understood.

PHYSIOLOGIC COMPONENTS OF THE STRESS RESPONSE

While the stress response can be organized by systems, it can also be viewed through a temporal context. There are three phases: immediate, intermediate, and long term.

Immediate Physiologic Processes

The automatic nervous system is activated when an individual perceives a threat or demand from the environment. In the stress response the hypothalamus stimulates the sympathetic fibers. The body prepares for "fight or flight," increasing its likelihood of survival. The effects of sympathetic stimulation occur within 2 to 3 seconds and last between 5 and 10 minutes. Sympathetic nerve fibers release the catecholamines epinephrine and norepinephrine. Anxiety is experienced and can be observed both through a person's verbal report, as well as clinical signs, including perspiration, tremulousness, and rapid pulse and breathing.

Intermediate Response

Within 2 to 3 minutes following perception of the stressor epinephrine and norepinephrine are secreted. These neurotransmitters travel to the end organs where they maintain the processes already initiated. These sympathetic effects are maintained for 1 to 2 hours. The adrenal medulla does not continue its response but is reactivated only after the central nervous system triggers the sympathetic nervous system again. The catecholamines also stimulate gluconeogenesis, which provides the body with additional energy.

Long-term Response

Three pathways of the endocrine system perpetuate the long-term effects of stress: the adrenocorticotropic, the thyroxine, and the vasopressin pathways. The adrenal cortex secretes two types of corticoids: mineralocorticoids and glucocorticoids. Aldosterone, a mineralocorticoid, raises the systemic blood pressure. Cortisol, which is representative of the three glucocorticoids, is pivotal to the breakdown of fats and proteins for energy. Their prolonged secretion, however, has negative effects. The effects of thyroxine are not observed until it peaks at about the 10th day following the stressful event, and the effect may last 6 to 8 weeks. Thyroxine increases the body's metabolism as much as 60% to 100%. Vasopressin is released from the posterior pituitary gland and elevates blood pressure.

Neurophysiology of Thought and Emotion in the Stress Response

The earliest theories of emotional processes relevant to stress and coping posited the significance of emotional arousal or drive tension. Folkman and Lazarus's studies have facilitated the understanding that coping is not only a response to such tension but is strongly influenced by the act of appraisal. It is not so clear, unfortunately, what the neurophysiologic linkages are between the perception of an event, its appraisal as stressful, and the decision to cope by problem solving or management of emotions. In fact, the actual response is not a simple linear one. There are multiple feedback loops between the initial appraisal and later reappraisals. They are moderated by cognitions, which involve activation of the limbic system and one special component of it, the hippocampus. Not far from the hippocampus is the amygdala. Recent research indicates that the hippocampus may be the site of simple recall, whereas the rearrangement of memory images, as in imagination, may be mediated by the amygdala. Both, however, depend on the intricate network of sensory connections.[17] The final products that reach the memory areas for storage are highly abstract and many synaptic connections removed from the original stimulus. Nonetheless, these abstractions are chemically recalled from the limbic system up to the cerebral cortex where transformations of electrical and chemical impulses that result in cognition occur. They are the basis of thought and emotion, which are components of the stress response associated with arousal and cognitive appraisal.

Interaction of Neuroendocrine Influences on Immunocompetence in the Stress Response

Of interest to such investigators as Bartrop[2] and Stein et al.[21] has been the influence of distressing events such as death and survivor bereavement on the ability of the body to fight off illness. It has been demonstrated that the stress of these events is associated with alteration in the body's ability to marshall its cellular and humoral forces against invading pathogens.

Antoni[1] and others have been exploring the relationship of stress and immunocompetence. Antoni has outlined a framework that indicates the relationship among chronic psychological emotional stress, accompanying neurohormonal changes, and loss of immunocompetence. He posits that a person's appraisal of a stressor triggers a series of specific physiologic responses in the nervous, endocrine, and immune systems. He defines two types of stress responses: the sympathoadrenomedullary system (SAM) and the hypothalamic-pituitary-adrenocortical system (HPAC). The SAM response, influencing

238

engagement with the stressor, releases norepinephrine into the circulation to initiate the fight or flight response. The HPAC response is associated with helplessness, hypervigilance, and conservative withdrawal from the stressor. This pattern elevates levels of cortisol that have been associated with suppression of the immune response, including activity of T cells, macrophages, and natural killer cells.

Nursing Research on Stress Incidence, Treatment, and Prevention

Nurse researchers have investigated stress and coping since the 1960s. At that time, the research did not use these terms, but it focused on patients' adjustment to stressful situations. Nurses such as Dumas and Anderson from Yale School of Nursing, under the influence of Skipper and Leonard, were investigating preparatory information and its effect on recovery postsurgery. The focus was on management of anxiety.[9] The decade of the 1970s, however, yielded a larger volume of investigations, and the following decade saw the emergence of the language of stress and coping.[24] As sociologic models of stress and strain emerged,[15] nursing adopted them and shifted its clinical focus to types of stressors found in various clinical situations and disease states.[7,11] An interesting finding of some of these studies was that the stressors that nurses associated with patients' anxiety were not so felt by patients, nor were the intensity of the patient's reactions what the nurses expected.

The 1980s also yielded a more sophisticated level of nursing research that focused on processes. Some investigations looked at methodologic problems in analyzing stress and coping studies.[18] Johnson, who had been studying the effect of preparatory information on patient's anxiety, shifted her attention to the underlying processes that enhance coping. She and Lauver examined the premises of four theories (emotional drive, self-regulation, cognitive appraisal, and self-efficacy) to understand how interventions affect the observed coping outcomes.[13] The investigators developed hypotheses from these four theories and tested them in a study of the effects of a preparatory information intervention on coping with radiation therapy for cancer. Emotional drive theory, which is emerging from the psychoanalytic tradition, suggests that patients with high anxiety will be highly anxious before and after the threatening event. Preparatory information should help these patients to lower their anxiety and to focus on information that is given. Moderately anxious patients will be able to think what the experience will include and how to cope with it. This mental work is called "work of worry." The theory suggests that a moderate level of anxiety creates an effective level of motivation in preparation for an impending experience. Patients with low level of anxiety are not motivated to prepare for the stressful experience. Janis suggests that information will help to focus highly anxious patients, decreasing their anxiety; it will not affect the coping of moderately anxious patients, and it will motivate patients with low anxiety to engage in the work of worry, causing them to be less anxious postoperatively.[12]

Self-regulation is a cognitive theory developed out of the ego psychology tradition. It relies on information processing. A central concept of self-regulation theory is the schema, a cognitive structure of complex knowledge that is abstracted from experience. The components of an experience to which the schema directs the person's attention have emerged as important variables in the coping process.[14] Based on self-regulation theory, preparatory informational interventions are expected to have a positive effect on coping outcomes because they decrease the discrepancy between expectations and actual experience and they increase patients' understanding of their experience. Johnson and Lauver write that "coping outcomes are important because only through measuring outcomes can caregivers determine whether interventions achieve the expected effects on patients' behaviors and responses. Studies only of coping processes or outcomes make limited contributions because they address just one part of the entire model of coping." Outcomes of coping are directly related to the functions of coping, which are two: to problem solve and to manage emotions. These two functions serve patients by minimizing stressful events and facilitating their return to normal activity. In their study, Johnson and Lauver selected prostate cancer patients coping with radiation therapy. They were exposed to information delivered by tape-recorded messages. Outcome measures reflected the two functions of coping. Emotional distress was measured by the *Profile of Mood States*. The indicator of maintenance of usual life activities was the recreation and pastime category from the *Sickness Impact Profile*.

The process of coping based on Janis's theory required patients' anxiety to be measured at entry into the treatment situation and serial times thereafter. The process variables relevant to self-regulation theory were the similarities between expectations and experience, and understanding of the experience. The findings did not support Janis's emotional drive theory: Patients with high anxiety remained so; those with moderate or low anxiety maintained those levels of affect. Other studies of anxiety have also not supported Janis's findings. In fact, current knowledge suggests that clinicians not focus the patient's attention on the emotional or reactive dimensions of a stressful situation. Johnson and Lauver found that explanations of coping outcome derived from self-regulation theory, using the outcome measure of return to normal activities, were supported. Recent work of Folkman and Lazarus also suggests that support of cognitive efforts in coping are more efficacious and can, in fact, alter negative affect. These findings corroborate Beck's theory that affect follows cognition.[3]

The linkages between stress and disease are still unclear, but investigators increasingly are interested in this association. The early psychosomatic theorists included rheumatoid arthritis in their foci of study in which specific emotion was linked to specific disease outcomes. A contemporary investigation by Crosby has examined this disease from another perspective. The purpose of Crosby's study was to determine the relationship between stress factors, emotional stress, and rheumatoid arthritis disease activity. The investigator used the *Daily Hassles Scale* to identify daily stress factors and several measures of anxiety to observe emotional stress. Disease activity was observed by measuring the erythrocyte sedimentation rate and completion of an instrument developed by the investigator to measure rheumatoid arthritis activity. The theoretic framework for the study reflected the increasing complexity of information that has evolved about stress.[6] The investigator states that:

Understanding how an emotional response is translated into a phys-

ical response becomes clearer if one applies a concept of cybernetics known as the *feedback loop*. The concept should be interpreted as a loop in which one event triggers a second event that, in turn, feeds back to the origin. The feedback loop is a concept applicable to understanding the stress response. When subjected to stressful stimuli, one perceives stress factors and initiates coping strategies that may result in adaptation or partial adaptation. Partial adaptation yields a state of residual stress, which is subsequently transmitted to the hypothalamic-pituitary axis and sympathetic nervous system. The sympathetic nervous system prepares the individual to confront the residual stress by dilating the pupils, shunting blood to vital organs, and increasing the heart rate. Such physiologic responses require the release of hormones from the adrenal glands including epinephrine, norepinephrine, and cortisol. The hormones continue to be released, at varying levels as long as the stress signal is present. This is an example of a psychophysiologic feedback loop that involves the mind through perception and the body through hormone release. The loop will persist until an intervention occurs and the stress signal is reduced or eliminated.

Crosby's hypotheses were that a positive correlation between emotional stress level and rheumatoid arthritis activity would be demonstrated and that a positive correlation between the number and the severity of daily stress factors and the emotional stress level would be evident. Her hypotheses were supported by the data.

Implications for Nursing Research and Practice

The crucial link in the stress theory, the process by which stress is transformed into illness, remains unclear and unproven. In fact, the precise nature of stress itself eludes definition, and there

is no consensus on what it includes.[16] Therefore, much descriptive work remains to be done. On the other hand, one component of the postulated stress response, i.e., anxiety, is measured with unquestioned validity and reliability, and has been for many many decades. It is important to nursing because it exemplifies the domain of interest: patient comfort.

It continues to be crucial to nursing practice that interventions to decrease patient discomfort be described and evaluated. This work should continue even as a more robust description of stress is awaited. What to do about discomfort should continue to be investigated from the viewpoints of both what patients feel discomfort about and what nursing measures help patients to feel less discomfort.

These questions, of course, encompass the nature of stressors and of coping. No matter how the nomenclature changes with the scientific vogue, patient states and nursing actions to alter those states are pivotal to nursing research and practice. Of particular interest yielded from contemporary investigations is the divergence between what nurses believe patients think and feel and what patients actually report as important to them. After this, interventive processes to facilitate patient comfort are of primary importance.

A strong theoretic base plus contemporary nursing research reveals several junctures within the stress response where intervention may moderate or modify stress. The optimal juncture for stress management is prior to its presentation. Prevention is accomplished through prediction and rehearsal. When candidates for confrontation with stressors can be coached to identify those potential stressors and to describe behaviors to either modify the

240

stressors or alter their responses to them, stress may be decreased or avoided. Perception of the stressor can be altered through two techniques: reframing and redefinition. In the former mental operation, the perceiver alters the meaning of the stressor in its potential context. For instance, the person who is facing surgery might be coached to view the period of hospitalization as only 5 days within that person's year. Another useful technique is redefinition. Using the same example, the patient can be coached to view self as the person who *owns* the symptom to be surgically manipulated; he has also contracted with a surgeon to perform the needed procedure. Thus, the patient is an actor, and a powerful actor in the drama. The patient takes responsibility for what follows rather than assuming a passive, victimlike role. Stress is reduced by maintenance of the person's awareness of self as competent and self-determining.

Once the stressor has implicated the perceiver, other behavioral responses may be used to moderate the stress response. Most of them are coping strategies. They can be grouped as behavioral, physical, cognitive, and emotional responses that are all aimed toward adaptation. Two behavioral coping responses are assertiveness and limit setting. When individuals can overcome their closely held inhibitions about assertiveness, they are able to take stands that support their positions, empowering them in stressful transactions. Limit setting goes hand in hand with assertiveness. People who tolerate abuse of any kind, or allow themselves to be taxed beyond their felt resources, are stressed because they do not experience self-control. That situation imposes a threat. By learning to limit behaviors by others that impose this stress, the individual experiences

self as increasingly competent and capable of self-care.

Physical responses that have the potential to alter stress include the judicious inclusion of healthy foods such as the basic four food groups and a healthy, socially gratifying setting in which to eat. Exclusion of unhealthy foods such as sodium, caffeine, and cholesterol can also modify the potential for stress.

Exercise is another physical means of coping with stress. Exercise causes muscles to relax after the work period, leading to a sense of calm. Exercise also augments the effect of vitamins C and E in improving immune functioning.[5]

Another behavioral coping response is relaxation. Neither patients nor nursing colleagues can be expected to relax on command because the direction to do so immediately intensifies effort. But self-directed progressive relaxation can be taught over a period of weeks. Once an individual learns the sequence and practices it, progressive relaxation can be used effectively whenever the individual experiences tension.

The last set of adaptive coping responses are cognitive and emotional. Included in these categories are the use of humor and cognitive restructuring. Humor as therapy has been popularized by Vera Robinson in the nursing literature and Norman Cousins in the lay literature. Clearly the capacity to perceive fun and to laugh alleviates stress. Some literature suggests that like intense exercise, laughter causes the secretion of endorphins. Endorphins in circulation lead to feelings of satisfaction, which are the antithesis of experienced stress.

Finally, cognitive restructuring is mentioned again. It is a category composed of reframing and redefinition. While it is effectively used in preparation for stressful

encounters, it is equally useful in countering the stress response already under way. Cognitive restructuring involves altering one's view of the stressor or modifying one's view of self in relation to it. Generally speaking, the person who is able to view self in control or who can give up control of that which is uncontrollable, will experience less stress than the person who either feels victimized or continues futile efforts to manage external events that are not amenable to control.

Prediction and rehearsal can help people to prepare to encounter stressors in a more relaxed manner. Once the imposition of stressors elicits the stress response, the latter can be modified through the use of adaptive coping responses that tap the behavioral, physical, cognitive, and emotional dimensions of the individual's life. Such focused coping empowers, leading to an increased feeling of self-efficacy and fulfillment.

SUMMARY

Anxiety is the psychophysiologic signal that the stress response has been initiated. The stress response's by-product, stress, is difficult to define. The response has multiple dimensions that have yielded research with many foci. Most salient to nursing are investigations of psychobiologic variables, the influence of life events, and the interactional model of the stress response.

The stress response can be viewed as an interactional process that causes psychophysiologic reactions that are immediate and can occur up to and including physiologic events 3 weeks after confrontation with the stressor. The literature suggests that neuroendocrine alterations in response to confrontation with a stressor may influence immunocompetence.

Intervention and prevention studies of stress focus on pharmacotherapy, psychotherapy, behavioral techniques, personality engineering, relaxation training, and biofeedback. Nursing research on stress has proliferated in the 1980s. Implications for nursing intervention include coping strategies that fall into four categories: behavioral, physical, cognitive, and emotional.

REFERENCES

1. Antoni M: Neuroendocrine influences in psychoimmunology and neoplasia: A review. Psychol Health 1:3–24, 1987
2. Bartrop R, Lazarus L, Luckhurst E, et al: Depressed lymphocyte function after bereavement. Lancet 1:834–836, 1977
3. Beck A: Cognitive Therapy and the Emotional Disorders. New York, International Universities Press, 1976
4. Cannon W: The Wisdom of the Body. New York, WW Norton, 1932
5. Chatsworth E, Nathan R: Stress Management: A Comprehensive Guide to Wellness. New York, Ballentine Books, 1984
6. Crosby L: Stress factors, emotional stress and rheumatoid arthritis disease activity. J Adv Nurs 13:452–461, 1988
7. Dennis K: Dimensions of client control during their hospitalization. Nurs Res 36:151–156, 1987
8. Derogatis L, Abeloff M, Melisaratos N: Psychological coping mechanisms and survival time in metastatic breast cancer. JAMA 242:1504–1508, 1979
9. Dumas R, Anderson B, Leonard R: The importance of the expressive function in preoperative preparation. *In* Skipper J, Leonard R (eds): Social Interaction and Patient Care. Philadelphia, JB Lippincott, 1965
10. Graham D: Psychosomatic medicine. *In* Greenfield N, Sternbach R (eds): Handbook of Psychophysiology. New York, Holt, Rinehart and Winston, 1972
11. Gurlis J, Menke E: Identification of stressors and use of coping methods in chronic hemodialysis patients. Nurs Res 37:236–239, 1988
12. Janis I: Psychological Stress: Psychoanalytic and Behavioral Studies of Surgical Patients. New York, Wiley, 1958
13. Johnson J, Lauver D: Alternative explanations of coping with stressful experiences associated with physical illness. Adv Nurs 11:39–52, 1989
14. Lazarus R, Folkman S: Stress, Appraisal, and Coping. New York, Springer, 1984
15. Pearlin L, Schooler C: The structure of coping. J Health Social Behav 19:2–21, 1978
16. Pollock K: On the nature of social stress: Production of a modern mythology. Social Sci Med 26:381–392, 1988
17. Restak R: The Brain, New York, Bantam Books, 1984
18. Roberts J, Browne G, Streiner D, et al: Analyses of coping responses and adjustment: Stability of conclusions. Nurs Res 36:94–97, 1987
19. Schwartz G: Biofeedback and physical patterning in human emotion and consciousness. Am Scientist 63:314–324, 1975
20. Selye H: The Stress of Life. New York, McGraw-Hill, 1976
21. Stein M, Keller S, Schleifer S: Stress and immunomodulation: The role of depression and neuroendocrine function. J Immunol 135:827, 1985
22. Thoits P: Dimensions of life events that influence psychological distress: Evaluation and synthesis of the literature. *In* Kaplan H (ed): Psychosocial Stress: Trends in Theory and Research. New York, Academic Press, 1983, p. 33
23. Vingerhoet A, Marcelissen F: Stress research: Its present status and issues for future development. Social Sci Med 26:279–292, 1988
24. Volicer B: Patients' perceptions of stressful events associated with hospitalization. Nurs Res 23:235–238, 1974

Selection 5-3 *Analyzing Job Demands and Coping Techniques*

Purpose for Reading

PROCESS GOAL: **To review the techniques of the *before-reading* and *during-reading phases*, with special emphasis on applying principles outlined in an article to issues in your own life**

For this selection, instead of focusing on specific reading techniques, you will review and apply the results of your reading. The article was selected from the journal *Nursing Management,* which focuses on administration and management of nursing service. The article's title provides a clue to its focus: "Analyzing Job Demands and Coping Techniques." The intended audience of "nursing leaders" can readily apply the article's principles to their own jobs. Even if you do not yet have a health-related job, you can apply the ideas to the demands of your present job and your schoolwork.

OUTCOME GOAL: **To write a statement showing how the ideas in this article apply to your own life**

Nurses and allied health professionals work with real individuals who seldom look or act exactly like people described in a textbook. Real people have complex problems and concerns. Therefore, practitioners must be able to take facts and concepts and apply them in individual situations, including the work setting.

Before Reading 1

Goals: Get oriented to the text; develop a study plan
Techniques: Preview the assignment; divide the assignment into manageable parts; decide when to work on each part

---

Preview the article, noting the authors' different backgrounds. Next, read the abstract and Exhibits I and II to get oriented to the authors' ideas. Then read the headings, thinking about the authors' pattern of organization.

After your preview, develop a study plan, using techniques that have worked well for you previously.

—————— **Before Reading 2** ——————

> Goal: Get oriented to the text
> Technique: Look up significant terms that are not defined in the text

As you prepare to read this article, note that there are a few medical terms scattered throughout. If the words seem important to the research, mark them for later dictionary searches. You may find that some are not critical to understanding the actual subject of the article.

—————— **During Reading** ——————

> Goal: Monitor comprehension
> Technique: Look for main ideas, significant details, and paragraph
>   organization

An experienced reader approaches research articles differently than he or she reads general informational articles. Research articles describe a process as well as results or findings. The discriminating reader of research recognizes good and bad research techniques and good and bad recordings of the results by asking certain questions at each step of the research report:

> Who are the researchers? Does their background relate to the
> subject being studied?
> Is the problem clearly stated? What is the hypothesis? Are there
> sufficient numbers included in the study?
> How were the data collected? How are they analyzed? Are the
> conclusions clearly related to the study? Is there any obvious bias
> or error in the study?
> Is there a recommendation for further study or replication of the
> study?

As you read this research study, ask yourself similar questions.

—————— **After Reading 1** ——————

> Goal: Organize relevant information for review
> Technique: Make notes

Design a chart that reflects the authors' organizational pattern so that you can make notes about the research findings. Use a separate piece of paper.

Hint: Which organizational pattern do the authors use: sequence, listing, cause/effect, comparison/contrast, or definition?

———— ⚷ ————

After Reading 2

Goal: Organize relevant information for review
Technique: Think critically about what you've learned

Interview at least four people, asking them the three questions used in this research study (use your own words if you prefer):

1. What was your worst experience in nursing?
2. How did you manage the incident?
3. What advice would you give to another nurse in a similar situation?

Space is provided here for four interviews; however, feel free to speak with more individuals if your interest and time allow. Be sure each person agrees to provide responses for your survey.

After you have collected your interview data, analyze the information by noting similarities and differences in the comments. Are there any similarities with the concerns mentioned in the article? Did you note any use of the pronouns "I" and "they" in the comments? If so, how were they used? What types of activities are being used to relieve stress, and how often are they used?

Remember to respect and protect the privacy of the participants. (In other words, do not use the names or otherwise reveal the identities of the people you have interviewed.)

Be sure to note exactly how you asked each question along with the responses. You might use a format like this to record your questions, responses, and analysis of the interviews:

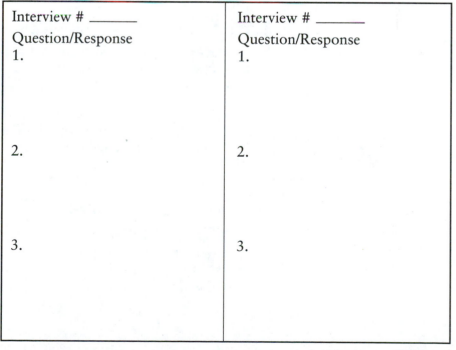

Interview # _____	Interview # _____
Question/Response	Question/Response
1.	1.
2.	2.
3.	3.

Continued

Interview # _____ Question/Response	Interview # _____ Question/Response
1. 2. 3.	1. 2. 3.
Analysis of Interviews	
Similarities among Interviews	Differences among Interviews

After Reading 3

Goal: Organize relevant information for review
Technique: Apply principles to real-life situations

From your own experience, identify other occupations for which you might recommend duplication of the research project in order to validate or confirm the findings.

On a separate sheet of paper, write a paragraph analyzing one of your own stressful experiences, work-related or otherwise. How might you use the authors' results to decrease your stress?

ANALYZING JOB DEMANDS AND COPING TECHNIQUES

From *Nursing Management*,
Vol. 26, No. 2, February 1995,
pp. 51–53.

Barbara A. Petermann
Pam Springer
Judy Farnsworth

Abstract: Surviving the stressful days nurses encounter in today's healthcare environment involves sophisticated coping skills. This qualitative study found nurses responded with the use of "I" or "they" approaches to stressful situations. Nursing leaders are offered strategies for identifying and relating to these two groups of staff.

Barbara A. Petermann, MSN, RN, CNAA, is Associate Chief of Staff/Nursing at Boise Veterans Affairs Medical Center; Pam Springer, MS, RN, is Program Director, Associate of Science Nursing Program; and Judy Farnsworth, PhD, RN, is Associate Professor, Baccalaureate of Science Nursing Program, Boise State University, in Boise, Idaho.

Sally was expecting a busy day at work. Over the last years the patient population had changed: they came in sicker and went home sooner. Since Diagnosis Related Groups (DRGs) had changed hospitals' payment, patients were more fragile; brittle conditions deteriorated suddenly.

After shift report, Sally received her assignment. She had five patients: a man 2 days post radical neck dissection with a tracheostomy and pedicle graft who had just returned to the unit; a woman who would soon arrive from the post-anesthesia care unit; a man ready for discharge; and two elderly women, one nonresponsive who required frequent repositioning and one recuperating from a recent total hip replacement.

Sally quickly assessed each patient. One patient, 2 days post radical neck dissection, was pale and clammy; his blood pressure was low, and his pulse rate had increased to 110. His dressing was stained with bright blood. After completing the assessment, she called the patient's physician. Several calls and 20 minutes later, she learned the doctor had just left the hospital. By the time she finally reached him, the patient's vital signs had worsened. Sally had already increased his IV rate, and now, after speaking with the physician, she started processing the new order for blood. About the same time, the post-anesthesia unit called—

her new patient was ready to be transferred back to her room.

Sally apprised the charge nurse of her workload problems and requested assistance. The charge nurse learned that Nursing Service would have to call someone extra in. Meanwhile, the staff on the unit would have to handle the situation. It looked to Sally as if she was in for another one of "those crazy evenings."

A typical day

A day like Sally's leaves most nurses wondering not only if they have done all they would *like* to do, but also if they have done all they *had* to do to keep patients safe. The only sure thing about today's work environment is that the job done yesterday probably looks very different today. Decreased economic reimbursement, along with advanced technologies, have significantly reduced hospital admissions and lengths of stay. The impact of these changes has been an increase in the number of very ill hospitalized patients who require more nursing skill.[1] Previous literature has studied stress and frustration in nursing primarily as concepts relating to dissatisfaction and turnover.[2] In addition to identifying the processes involved in turnover, this research addresses the relationship between stress, frustration and the nursing work environment.

Few studies have identified the actual demands and high expectations placed upon nurses, nor

Exhibit I

Purposes:	To discover what nurses, themselves, believe to be the stressors they encounter in their work environment and to identify how they deal with those stressors.
Location:	Pacific Northwest
Time Frame:	Over a 9-month period in 1992
Population:	16 female registered nurses
Tool:	Open-ended interview with questions developed by the researchers. Inverviews lasted approximately 30 minutes.
Sample:	Twenty-two interviews were conducted of which 73% (16) were usable.

have they addressed how nurses cope with those demands. Most studies have been quantitative in nature; a nurse's "real" experiences have not been described. A study was conducted to research these factors in more depth. (See Exhibit I.)

Following a qualitative design, 16 registered nurses (RNs) working on surgical or medical units in the acute-care setting were randomly selected from a list of RNs obtained through the State Board of Nursing. (See Exhibit II.) The nurses were interviewed during off-duty time. Once the informed consent was signed, demographics were recorded. The nurse was asked three open-ended questions: to describe her very worst experience in nursing, how she managed the incident and the advice that

Exhibit II

Sample Characteristics

Number of Nurses: 16 female registered nurses

Age: M = 41.5 years (SD = 9.2 years)

Years in Nursing: M = 15 years (SD = 9.6 years)

she would give to another nurse in a similar situation. Each interview lasted approximately 30 minutes and was audiotaped, then transcribed verbatim and entered into a computer program. Investigators read the interviews numerous times to identify recurring themes in the data. The themes were coded and analyzed.

To ensure internal validity, an outside expert analyzed three randomly selected interviews and validated the same dominant themes. In addition, the internal validity was strengthened by presenting the results to the respondents, who confirmed the findings.

Identifying stressors

All of the RNs described days that included stressors similar to Sally's: personal expectations, frequent interruptions, limited numbers of staff and demands imposed by others. The following types of situations developed into stressors.

- *Time-consuming procedures:* "Well, I started out with four patients, which really isn't bad for a 3–11. But two were getting blood and one of the ladies got an epidural so I had to do sed [sedation] (sic) and respiratory checks."

- *Patient's condition deteriorated rapidly:* "You know everything happens all at once, or if you have a patient who crashes on you. . . ."

As these events continued, the nurse was unable to mobilize resources to deal with the unraveling situation, to regain composure or to complete the assignment adequately. One nurse said: "I don't deserve this. Either I get some help, or something is going to happen."

In addition to describing a bad day, the nurses identified demands of their jobs.

- *High personal expectations:* ". . . and I just knew I should be able to handle it and why can't I handle it?"
"Sometimes I think I put a lot of pressure on myself because I give myself a hundred things I want to do. . . ."
- *Limited resources or staff:* "It gets really frustrating when I have to leave one patient to go to another patient I thought I had just helped. . . ."

The nurses described several other stressors: demanding ethical issues arising in the current healthcare environment, increased use of technology and demands placed on them by others.

These findings are consistent with results from other studies. Huey and Hartley found that 60% to 70% of RNs in their sample were dissatisfied with the administrative support, their salary and the nurse to patient staffing ratios.[3] In a study of 1,044 staff nurses, Prescott and Bowen concluded that workload and staffing were the major reasons nurses became dissatisfied and left their jobs.[4] They also cited the lack of support from administration. In another study, when nurses were asked to choose the most time-consuming and exhausting activities of a normal day, they listed caring for high acuity patients and charting as most time-consuming; decreased staffing, negative staff attitudes, demanding families and no time for breaks or lunch were the most exhausting.[5]

Responding to demands

An unexpected finding was how the nurses perceived and responded to "crazy" day stressors. Responses fell into two groups: "I" and "they." Recalling a specific stressful day, the "I" group took ownership for work stressors, held realistic expectations of themselves, prioritized workloads and practiced self-care techniques as a coping strategy. In contrast, the "they" group listed similar components but were unable to recall a specific situation or day. These individuals believed that others had failed to fix the stressors. This group did not demonstrate any self-care practices.

Twelve (75%) of the group fit into the "I" category and could pinpoint exact details of a specific bad day without difficulty. Like Sally, the day started as a typical day; then something went awry. They reported that not all days were bad days and often thought, "tomorrow would be better." This group took control and managed their stressful days. They either changed how they perceived the situation or seemed to come to terms with it:

"I try not to get too freaked out about it, and you know, I just do the best I can. Some days I do a good job, and some days I just muddle through like everybody does."

They learned:

"I've learned that you're not superwoman. You take your priorities, you list them and that's what you do."

They managed:

"I got help. I had to go out and say to people—we are having a crisis."

Another characteristic of the "I" group was positive self-care practices.

"I have to say, 'Hey, I'm Number One.' If I'm feeling stressed and freaked out and just overburdened, then I'm not going to do a good job. I will just sit down and take a 30-minute break."

They used this time to reassess demands, adjust priorities and plan patient care. Nurses demonstrated self-care through adequate rest, good diet and exercise. One "I" respondent believed in taking responsibility for oneself and one's actions, something she thought many nurses did not do.

Several nurses also chose to work part-time to facilitate more balance in their lives. As a result, they were more rested when they came back to work and able to deal with everyday problems. The "I" group also acknowledged that their personal expectations were at times unrealistic.

The remaining 25% of the respondents fit into the "theys." This group listed components that made up a "crazy" day but were unable to recall a specific situation or day. Rather, one nurse stated:

"I don't know. I can't think of a particular situation, but we usually feel like this. You know that every day is the same for me."

These individuals appeared to cope by blaming others for not fixing their stressful days. They considered their working situations less than ideal. These nurses thought someone or something beyond them hindered them in work success. They felt that management was out of touch:

"If they'd just come to work once in a while in white."

"I see nurses making decisions about nurses who don't have a clue about what nursing is any more. . . ."

These nurses wanted someone else to fix their situation. In contrast to the "I" nurses, they seemed to feel powerless to make changes in their work environment. They felt out of control and they expressed feelings of helplessness and powerlessness:

"I'm personally powerless to do something about it."

"I never see anything done."

"I can't do anything about it."

The "they" group of nurses reported no self-care practices, or any positive coping or self-care techniques. None of the nurses in this group reported taking time to get away and regroup.

Coalescence and encouragement

Nursing leaders need to recognize the existence of these two groups, differentiate between the two and learn how to relate to each nurse. By obtaining the right mix of staff, managers can develop a strong work team while still recognizing each member as an individual.

Clarifying coping strategies will provide the nurse manager with vital information to differentiate the two groups. Once managers determine patterns, strategies can be implemented to form the best team possible. Allowing "I" staff to grow while providing them with supportive leadership appears to be what they need. Nurse managers should be comfortable in freeing and supporting staff to resolve the problems they face.

Working with the "theys" may be more challenging. Nurse managers need to assess their effect on the morale and productivity of the unit staff. Nurse managers should ask: Would these nurses benefit from employee assistance counseling to deal with stressors? Does the nurse manager really hear and respond to staff concerns? Would changing the employees' work environment encourage them to take more responsibility? When hiring new employees, one interview question used in the study will help identify coping skills: "Tell me about the worst day you've had at work. Tell me how you handled it."

Teamwork is essential to delivering quality care in this cost-conscious environment. By identifying the uniqueness of employees and using appropriate strategies, managers should be able to positively affect patient care and staff satisfaction.

References

1. Butler, J., and R. Parsons, "Hospital Perceptions of Job Satisfaction," *Nursing Management*, 20:8:45–48.
2. Landstrom, G., D. Biondi, and D. Gillies, "The Emotional and Behavioral Process of Staff Nurse Turnover," *The Journal of Nursing Administration*, 19:9:23–28; Norbeck, J., "Perceived Job Stress, Job Satisfaction, and Psychological Symptoms in Critical Care Nursing," *Research in Nursing and Health*, 8:3:253–259; Pagel, I., and M. Whittman, "Relationship of Burnout to Personal and Job Related Variables in Acute Care Pediatric Settings," *Issues in Comprehensive Pediatric Nursing*, 9:2:131–143; and Prescott, P., and S. Bowen, "Controlling Nursing Turnover," *Nursing Management*, 18:6:60–66.
3. Huey, F., and S. Hartley, "What Keeps Nurses in Nursing," *The American Journal of Nursing*, 88:2:181–188.
4. Prescott, P., and S. Bowen, *loc.cit.*
5. Simms, L., M. Erbin-Resman, A. Darga and H. Coeling, "Breaking the Burnout Barrier: Resurrecting Work Excitement," *Nursing Economics*, 8:3:177–187.

unit 6

Review and Practice in Critical Thinking

In this unit, you will review selections in earlier units and complete activities that will require you to think critically about the material.

The techniques for reviewing are similar to those for previewing. To review, think about and then look in the places where you're most likely to be reminded of the main ideas, the author's organization, and your own reactions to the material. Re-previewing the selection and looking over the related activities you completed should refresh your memory adequately. You should do this for each activity in this unit.

To do the critical thinking required in this unit, you'll need to call on all your powers of analysis and reasoning. Use the following list of questions as a mental checklist when you are analyzing material critically:

- What is the central issue?
- What are the underlying assumptions?
- Is the evidence given valid?
  - Are stereotypes or cliches used?
  - Are emotional or biased arguments used?
  - Are the data adequate and verifiable?
  - Are important terms clearly defined?
  - Are the given data relevant?
  - Is the problem or issue correctly identified?
- Are the conclusions acceptable?
  - Is the conclusion accurate?
  - Is the conclusion applicable?
  - Is there any value conflict?

Tappen, R. (1989). *Critical thinking in nursing leadership and management: Concepts and practice* (p. 128). (2nd ed.). Philadelphia: FA Davis.

Responding to the activities in this unit will require your best efforts. Whether you're asked to make an oral report or to write a paper, draft your response, revise it until it says exactly what you think, and then prepare an edited final version. The length of your response will vary with the question, but a complete answer to most of the questions will require multiple paragraphs.

Unit 2: Orientation to the Health Professions

Selection 2-1, the first chapter of *Introduction to Physical Therapy,* begins Unit 2. It serves as a typical example of introductory chapters in textbooks.

> Apply the criteria for a profession (Fig. 1-1 in Selection 2-1) to what you know about radiologic technology from "The Birth of a New Profession" (Selection 2-2). Evaluate whether each of the five criteria does or does not apply. Include a statement of your conclusion about whether radiologic technology is or is not a profession.

Selection 2-2, "The Birth of a New Profession," provides a review of the history of radiologic technology. Note the lengthy list of references consulted by the authors while doing their research.

> If you wanted to read further about some aspect of the history of radiologic technology, how would you go about locating the listed references? List the references available in your library. How might you locate the books and articles that are not currently available in your library?

Selection 2-3, "Blessed Are the Flexible . . .," offers the editorial opinions of a prominent nursing writer.

> Curtin refers to nurses metaphorically as "gyroscopes." That is, she implies a comparison between gyroscopes and nurses. Explain what you think she means by this comparison, and suggest another metaphor that you think works equally well. Explain your choice.

Selection 2-4, "Chattering Hopes and Advices," presents Florence Nightingale's suggestions for caring for seriously ill patients.

> What kind of patient does Nightingale have in mind as she offers her advice? Where would such patients be cared for today? How would you change Nightingale's advice to fit what you know about the care of the sick?

Selection 2-5, "Using an Index," includes indexes from five nursing textbooks that might be used to master course objectives on patient teaching. The index pages apparently didn't address the objective on principles of learning.

Which index entries would you consult to make sure that none of the textbooks contains information on principles of learning? List at least three terms or phrases that you would look for, and explain how each might be useful in finding the information you seek.

Selection 2-6, "Cultural Considerations," includes two articles from a special issue of the journal of the National Student Nurses' Association devoted to culture. Look at the list of references provided by each author, and note the difference in the number of references included.

Does the number of references affect the credibility of an author? What can you conclude about the ethnicity of the authors? Does an author's ethnicity affect his or her credibility when writing on culture or ethnicity?

Unit 3: Pain

Selection 3-1, "Care of Patients with Pain," introduces the topic of pain management to nursing students. Reread the section on placebos (pp. 104–105), paying particular attention to the four bullets marking the guidelines for using the placebo response (p. 105). The guidelines are apparently offered to counteract abuses of the placebo response, which the author does not detail.

Use your critical thinking skills to explain possible abuses that might lead to the need for each one of the guidelines.

Selection 3-2, "Nurses Plunged Me Into the Pain Cycle; Nurses Pulled Me Out," reports the author's personal experience with pain in two health care facilities.

Using only the most current information is an important guideline for researchers in the allied health sciences. Why, then, has an article published in 1988 been included here? Take a position about whether the article should have been included as one of the selections on pain, and then defend your position with three arguments based on the Critical Analysis Questions on page 251.

Selection 3-3, "Nurses' Judgments of Pain in Term and Preterm Newborns," is the article that introduced you to formal research design.

Imagine that you are in charge of staff development for a hospital and that the topic of pain management for newborns has been identified as one on which the staff needs more information. Use the information in the article to outline a staff development session.

Selection 3-4, "Review of Literature . . . with Focus on Mexican-Americans," summarizes many different research studies and suggests areas for additional investigation. Respond to both of these activities:

On page 143, center column, the authors identify four areas for additional qualitative studies and four for additional quantitative studies. Choosing either the qualitative or the quantitative option, suggest a group on which additional research should be conducted and explain why in terms of the four areas.

Explain why you think qualitative or quantitative research into the reactions to pain of members of various subcultures is not appropriate, giving reasons related to each of the four areas.

Selection 3-5, "Avoiding Opioid-Induced Respiratory Depression," teaches readers how to "prevent, assess, and manage respiratory depression" (p. 149).

Using the box on page 152 titled "Nine Ways to Prevent Opioid-Induced Respiratory Depression," create a narrative about a patient who did not suffer respiratory depression as a result of effective care. Use at least seven of the nine methods in your narrative.

Unit 4: Ethical and Legal Issues

Selection 4-1, "Ethics and Values," is the textbook chapter that introduces Unit 4. It discusses the terminology of medical ethics.

Choose an issue that involves an ethical dilemma, such as abortion rights versus the right to life or euthanasia versus natural death. Write two one-paragraph summaries on the topic, one from the teleologic perspective and one from the deontologic perspective.

Selection 4-2, "Ethical Perceptions of Parents and Nurses in NICU: The Case of Baby Michael," presents a patient situation and discusses related ethical issues. You studied the situation and completed several activities related to problems experienced by baby Michael's parents and the nurses who cared for him.

One issue not addressed in this article but of concern to medical ethicists is that of allocation of resources for patients like Michael. List the pros and cons of allocating so many dollars for hospital care and for staff and equipment costs to keep this baby alive. Once your list is complete, take a position for or against such allocations and explain your position in writing.

Selection 4-3, "Ethical Decision Making," is a chapter from a reference book that deals with both ethical and legal concerns of nursing. This particular chapter defines and gives examples of ethical dilemmas faced by nurses. The following situation is such a dilemma:

A student nurse has been told by the instructor not to give *any* medicine that she has not prepared herself. One day, while the student is helping a patient, the head nurse hands the student a filled syringe and says "Give your patient this shot because I'm too busy right now to do it myself." What options does the student nurse have? What are the possible consequences of each action?

Selection 4-4, "Caring for Pediatric Patients with HIV: Personal Concerns and Ethical Dilemmas," addresses some of the concerns of nurses who care for patients with HIV or AIDS. Because there is currently no cure for this infectious disease, ethical and legal issues arise.

Analyze the similarities and differences between the following statements:
1. Every patient, regardless of diagnosis, race, religion, or sexual orientation, has the right to the same quality of care from nurses and any other hospital personnel.
2. Every patient has the right to the same level of care.

Selection 4-5, "When Language Is an Obstacle," provides another example of an issue that has ethical and legal implications for both nurses and the patients in their care. Sometimes communication is a problem for reasons other than language.

Compare and contrast three patients as to their communication problems and the approach you would take to assist them.
1. An 80-year-old man who became deaf within the last year
2. A 52-year-old man who has had a stroke and can only say "Oh boy, oh boy" and "Darn it, darn it"
3. A 22-year-old woman who recently became blind

Unit 5: Stress

Selection 5-1, "Stress," was selected from a textbook for students enrolled in a nursing program. The chapter addresses a concept that is important for nurses and of interest to the general public.

Using Table 5-8 on page 225 as an example, create a list of other demands on a student and identify several activities that might help such a person cope with the stress. Indicate whether any of these coping activities could be of assistance to you in your busy life.

Selection 5-2, "Stress and Anxiety," describes stress as defined by several theorists and as it applies to nursing.

Draw an illustration that might be included in a textbook to help explain Selye's theory of stress. Feel free to refer to any or all of the selections in this unit.

Selection 5-3, "Analyzing Job Demands and Coping Techniques," is an article describing how different nurses cope with the demands of their work. The authors describe the research they have done, draw conclusions, and make suggestions for administrators supervising nurses.

Critical thinkers don't accept or reject new information until they fully understand it. As you read this article, how did you evaluate the conclusions drawn in the section entitled "Coalescence and encouragement"? What do you see as strengths and weaknesses of the conclusions drawn by the authors?

Consultations

Unit 1   The Reading and Remembering Process

Selection 1-1. The Reading and Remembering Process

	Before Reading 1 (pp. 3–4)
Goal:	Get oriented to the text, the author, the assignment, and the scope and organization of the information
Technique:	Preview new materials and assignment

1. How many phases are there in the reading process? What are they called?

   There are three phases in the reading process: Before, During, and After Reading.

2. How many process goals are there in each phase?

   Phase 1 (Before Reading) has two process goals; phase 2 (During Reading) has two; phase 3 (After Reading) has three.

	Before Reading 2 (p. 4)
Goal:	Develop a study plan
Techniques:	Divide the assignment into manageable parts; decide when to work on each part

Your plan doesn't have to be exactly like anyone else's. However, if it doesn't suit your schedule, it isn't going to work. Since there are three phases in the reading process, you might find that reading about one phase at a time will help you stay alert and interested.

	After Reading 2 (p. 5)
Goal:	Check initial recall of relevant information
Technique:	Review the whole assignment by answering review questions

1. Match each goal or technique with the appropriate phase in the reading process.
   a. Before reading
   b. During reading
   c. After reading

   b Adjust reading rate to purpose for reading and to difficulty of the text
   a Develop a study plan
   c Periodically test recall of relevant material
   c Underline, make notes, outline, summarize, and/or jot down questions
   c Predict and answer possible test questions

2. Which of the techniques used during and after reading specifically relate to the recursive nature of the reading process?

   The techniques that suggest returning to an earlier phase relate to the recursive nature of the reading process. If I find myself not understanding during reading (Goal 3, Technique 3) or if I can't remember what I've read right after reading (Goal 5, Technique 2), I'll need to return to an earlier stage in the process. This could happen at any point in the process, but it is particularly likely at these two points.

3. Do any of the goals or techniques seem unclear to you? If so, do your best to write a question that you could ask your teacher.

   We can't predict what your questions may be, but be sure to ask them in your next class!

Note: The answers to After-Reading activities, which are like quizzes, are not generally found in this Consultations section. These first two are included here to help you get a feel for this section. This section will indicate when answers can be found in the *Instructor's Resource Manual.*

Unit 2   Orientation to the Health Professions

Selection 2-1. Introduction to Physical Therapy

Before Reading 1 (pp. 18–20)

Goal: Get oriented to the text
Technique: Preview new materials

You probably picked up most of these facts:

2. The author's background, credentials, and family

   Michael Pagliarulo has a doctorate in education and a degree as a physical therapist. He teaches therapy in Ithaca, New York. He has taught an introductory course in physical therapy for more than ten years. He gives credit to his Italian immigrant parents for their hard work and values; he thanks his wife and three children for support during the writing of the textbook.

Features used: *Title Page, Dedication, Preface, Acknowledgements*

3. The organization of the book

The book is divided into two main sections: profession and practice. Each section is somewhat chronological. The chapters have an outline and list of key terms; study questions are at the end of each chapter. The chapters in the second part have the same structure: case studies follow a general presentation of each topic. Throughout, the author uses a "people first" orientation and refers to physical therapists as females.

Features used: *Preface, Table of Contents, Chapter 1*

Before Reading 2 (pp. 20–21)

Goal: Get oriented to the assignment
Technique: Preview new assignment

Did you put a check beside these features?

__√__ Title

_____ Objectives

__√__ Key word list or glossary

__√__ Headings

__√__ Bulleted items (list items introduced with a • instead of a number) *(Box 1-1 is full of these.)*

__√__ Words in **bold** type *(There are lots of these; do they always appear on the Key Terms list?)*

__√__ Words in *italic* type

_____ Photos

_____ Graphs or charts *(None. There are boxes and a figure though.)*

_____ Summary

__√__ Review questions

__√__ Other features: *Besides the list of references cited in the chapter, the author includes several suggested readings. The chapter outline at the beginning of the chapter may substitute for objectives.*

Before Reading 3 (p. 21)

Goal: Get oriented to the assignment
Technique: Preview new assignment

Chapter Outline	Review Question Number
Definition	1
Physical Therapy as a Profession	2, 3

This assignment only requires you to find answers to three questions. If you are interested in learning about the whole history of physical therapy, you might decide to read the whole chapter. You can save some time, however, by reading only the sections that relate to the review questions.

After Reading (p. 22)

Goals: Check initial recall; organize relevant information for review

Techniques: Self-test; make notes and underline

Of course, your answers will not be the same as these samples, but they should contain similar information.

1. How does the "definition" of physical therapy differ from the "philosophical statement" as defined and described, respectively, by the APTA?

    The "definition" includes a long list of the aspects of the practice of physical therapy. The "philosophical statement" is more of a generalized description of the profession, including the goal of promoting optimal health and function.

2. Describe the practice vs profession of physical therapy, and identify the documents that describe each.

    The profession of physical therapy is described in the APTA's philosophical statement. It stresses a professional goal of promoting optimal health and function. The model for a definition provided by the APTA includes lists that describe the activities and functions performed by physical therapists.

3. Define "profession" and apply its five characteristics to physical therapy. Is it a profession?

    Three characteristics generally recognized as describing a profession are specialized knowledge, social value, and recognized autonomy. Two additional characteristics, lower on the hierarchy than the first three, are lifetime commitment and professional organization. Pagliarulo indicates that physical therapy satisfies each of these criteria as a profession.

Note: Review the answers you have written. If your answers look remarkably similar to these, then you have made an error that is easy to make—but could have serious consequences. Copying from another source is called plagiarism, which means you have used someone else's ideas and words without giving proper credit. To avoid plagiarism, you can use quotation marks around the author's words or you can paraphrase. Paraphrasing involves translating the author's words into your own but keeping the same meaning. Using even three words in a row from the original material can, according to some sources, be called plagiarism.

Whether you quote or paraphrase, you must credit the sources you use. For example, you might paraphrase the last sentence in the third answer above in this way: *Faulkner and Stahl suggest that Pagliarulo thinks physical therapy meets all five criteria for a profession.*

Selection 2-2. The Birth of a New Profession

Before Reading 1 (pp. 35–36)

Goal: Get oriented to the assignment
Techniques: Preview new assignment; check for bias in the author

---

1. This article is the *3rd* of a total of *7* articles in the series.

2. What is the authors' level of expertise in this topic? Does their presentation seem biased or balanced?
   Jack and Angie Cullman are both retired radiologic technologists who collect x-ray memorabilia and write about the field from their home in Rochester, New York. They lived through much of the period covered by the article, and they definitely seem to be experts. On the other hand, they don't appear to have slanted the information just because they know a lot. The presentation seems balanced.

3. What historical period is covered by the *series* of articles?
   The series commemorates the centennial of radiology: 1895–1995.

4. Over what time span did "the birth of a new profession" occur? In other words, what period of time is covered by this particular article?
   The profession of radiologic technologist seems to have been "born" from the 1920s to the 1960s; the dates in the second and following headings cover this time span.

5. What changes in the profession can you infer from the photographs?
   Figure 1 doesn't reveal many changes, but the operators in the 1930s were nurses (wearing caps) who were NOT wearing protective shields.

Before Reading 2 (pp. 36–37)

Goal: Get oriented to the assignment
Technique: Improve your background knowledge

Compare what you learned with what other students learned. "Right" answers aren't the goal here; learning more about the topic is the goal, and other students can be an excellent source of additional information. For the sake of comparison, here is an example of an answer from a nursing instructor:

> My grandfather was five years old in 1895. I have these associations to the decades: Roaring 20s, Great Depression in the 1930s, World War II in the 1940s, television becoming more common in homes during the 1950s, and the Vietnam War and hippies as emblems of the 1960s.

After Reading 2 (pp. 37–38)

Goal:	Periodically test recall of relevant information
Technique:	Answer possible test questions

Answers to possible test questions can be found in the *Instructor's Resource Manual.*

Selection 2-3. Blessed Are the Flexible

Before Reading 3 (pp. 44–45)

Goal:	Get oriented to the text
Technique:	Make predictions about the information

Does your sentence say something similar to this?

> *Curtin seems to be saying that change is inevitable, though difficult. Nurses have always been involved in change that can benefit patients, and they will continue to be if they remain flexible.*

Even if you didn't get the same idea of Curtin's thesis, don't be discouraged. You're learning to use previewing. Use what you learned from your preview and your effort to state her main point to help you get ready to read.

After Reading 2 (p. 46)

Goal:	Organize relevant information for review
Technique:	Look up and learn new terms discovered during reading

---

Using a dictionary to learn word parts and definitions takes some work, but it's worth it! Learning about the prefix, root, and (less frequently) the suffix can help you remember a new word, and you'll know the building blocks of thousands of other words.

You may need to look up each separate word part. (*Hint:* Prefixes are listed in most collegiate dictionaries followed by a hyphen, as in ac-; suffixes are treated similarly but with the hyphen at the beginning, as in -or.)

	Word Meaning	Prefix Meaning	Root Meaning	Suffix Meaning
accommodate	adjust, make suitable	ac-: toward	commodare (Latin): to make fit	
innovator	one who introduces change	in-: into	novus (Latin): new	-or: one who makes
incredulous	skeptical, not believing	in-: not	credo (Latin): believe	-ous: having or possessing
obsolete	out-of-date, no longer in use	ob-: reverse of	solere (Latin): used to	
gyroscope	device for determining direction		gyr (Greek): ring, circle -scope (Greek): instrument for viewing or observing	
dictum	a saying, a pronouncement		dicere (Latin): to say	
*status quo**	the condition that currently exists		status (Latin): state	quo: in which
interventions	actions taken to modify a situa-tion		intervenire (Latin): to come between	

*Be sure you looked up the two-word Latin phrase rather than the English word *status*.

Selection 2-4. Chattering Hopes and Advices

> ───── **Before Reading 2 (pp. 51–52)** ─────
> Goal:　Get oriented to the text and the author
> Techniques:　Improve your background knowledge; make
> 　　　　　　predictions about the information

1. When was Florence Nightingale born? How old was she when she died?

   Nightingale lived from 1820 to 1910; she was 90 when she died.

2. When and where did the Crimean War take place? What was Nightingale's role in it?

   The Crimean War took place between 1853 and 1856 on the Crimean peninsula (now part of Russia). Russian forces were fighting British, French, Turkish, and Sardinian troops. Because it was the first war covered by newspaper correspondents with access to the telegraph, the suffering and death among the troops were of great concern in Britain. Nightingale was asked to use her methods to improve sanitation and establish nursing facilities. Her efforts reduced the mortality rates dramatically.

3. What are Nightingale's major contributions to the development of nursing?

   Florence Nightingale raised nursing from the status of an occupation pursued only by women of no training and "low moral character" to one with rigorous educational and ethical standards.

4. Label each event as happening BN (before Nightingale was born), DN (during her lifetime), or AN (after her death):

   __BN__ Invention of the hot air balloon (1783)

   __BN__ Declaration of Independence (1776)

   __AN__ U.S. statehood for Alaska (1959)

   __DN__ First flight by the Wright brothers at Kitty Hawk (1903)

   __AN__ First associate degree programs in nursing (1952)

   __DN__ U.S. Civil War (1861–1865)

Note: Several sources suggest that *Notes on Nursing* was the first textbook for nurses. According to Nightingale, in the Preface of the book, this was not her purpose: "The following notes are by no means intended as a rule of thought by which nurses can teach themselves to nurse, still less as a manual to teach nurses to nurse. They are meant simply to give hints for thought to women who have personal charge of the health of others" (p. 3).

After Reading 2 (pp. 55–56)

Goal:	Organize relevant information for review
Technique:	Learn new terms discovered during reading

Although your sentences will be unique, you might want to compare them with Nightingale's use of these words. The page numbers are shown.

1. extant (page 58)
2. bane (pages 58)
3. cursory (page 58)
4. seraphic (page 59)
5. *viva voce* (page 60) (The italics are used to signal a foreign phrase.)
6. obstinately (page 60)
7. benevolent (page 61)
8. lachrymose (page 61)
9. vegetate (page 62)

10. pluck (noun) (page 62) (If your sentence has to do with removing feathers, you looked up the definition of the verb, not that of the noun!)

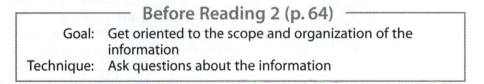

After Reading 3 (p. 57)

Goal:	Organize relevant information for review
Technique:	Think critically about what you have learned

The *Instructor's Resource Manual* contains an example of a response to this activity. Your paragraph may reflect a very different reaction to Nightingale's ideas.

Selection 2-5. Using an Index

Before Reading 2 (p. 64)

Goal:	Get oriented to the scope and organization of the information
Technique:	Ask questions about the information

The following terms, singly or in various combinations, are the most useful to scan for in the indexes: *patient, client, health, teaching, learning,* and *education.* Some other helpful terms used in the indexes you'll consult are *communications* and *health promotion.*

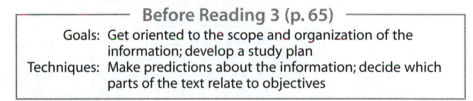

Before Reading 3 (p. 65)

Goals:	Get oriented to the scope and organization of the information; develop a study plan
Techniques:	Make predictions about the information; decide which parts of the text relate to objectives

Although your page numbers may differ from those listed below, any major differences suggest a need for more scanning practice.

- Identify the significance of the nurse's role as a health teacher.
  Craven, 493–495; Sims, 109; Smith-Temple, 8.

- Give examples of these three types of learning: cognitive, psychomotor, and affective.
  Craven, 504.

- Recognize certain principles of learning and the effect of each on health teaching.

- Identify external factors affecting the teaching/learning process.
  Craven, 490–493.

- Describe four major steps in the teaching process.
  Craven, 499–502.

- Recall relevant factors to be considered in the assessment of a patient's learning needs.
  Craven, 495–497; Lewis, 1461; Sims, 4; Smith-Temple, 8.
- Write appropriate learning objectives for specific situations.
  Craven, 499; Lewis, throughout.
- Apply various teaching methods in patient care situations.
  Craven, 504–505.
- Recognize the appropriate use of teaching aids.
  Craven, 500–501; Smith-Temple, 8.
- Select methods of evaluating the teaching/learning process.
  Craven, 505.
- Identify the influences of cultural diversity on the teaching plan.

Before Reading 4 (pp. 65–66)

    Goal: Develop a study plan
Technique: Decide when to work on each part

Use the order given as a basis of comparison. There is no one right answer in this process!

___1___ R. Craven & C. Hirnle. *Fundamentals of nursing* (2nd ed.).

Explain: *This text seems to have a whole chapter on teaching/learning with many relevant parts. It's the most comprehensive and important source.*

___3___ S. Lewis, I. Collier, & M. Heitkemper. *Medical-surgical nursing* (5th ed.).

Explain: *The entries in this text are mostly related to patient care situations. This source will probably provide specific details about teaching but not general information.*

__omit__ J. Needham. *Gerontological nursing.*

Explain: *There are many other sources with more than one general entry on this topic.*

___4___ L. Sims, D. D'Amico, J. Stiesmeyer, & J. Webster. *Health assessment in nursing.*

Explain: *There are only a couple of references that seem to relate to the topic, although this text might be useful in specific patient care situations.*

___2___ J. Smith-Temple & J. Johnson. *Nurses' guide to clinical procedures* (2nd ed.).

Explain: *Although the relevant materials only take up four pages, several objectives are addressed here.*

Don't panic because none of the indexes seems to have entries related to learning principles or the influences of cultural diversity on the teaching plan. You may come across the information as you read. If you don't, it would be music to your teacher's ear to hear a question like this: "Can you suggest a reference for learning principles?" Your teacher's reply might indicate plans to lecture on the topic soon or provide some other sources to consult.

Selection 2-6. Cultural Considerations

> **Before Reading 1 (p. 73)**
> Goals: Get oriented; develop a study plan
> Techniques: Preview new materials; decide when to work on each part

Did you notice that the article by Louie, although longer, has subheadings that might make it easier to read and more useful as an analytical tool? On the other hand, if the cultures of Asian-Americans and Pacific Islanders are very unfamiliar to you, you'll have to do some background work before you start.

The article by Douglas is shorter and may cover more familiar material. However, it lacks subheadings, which makes both previewing and notemaking more challenging.

> **After Reading 4 (pp. 75–76)**
> Goal: Test recall of relevant information
> Technique: Answer possible test questions

Answers to the possible test questions can be found in the *Instructor's Resource Manual*.

Unit 3 Pain

Selection 3-1. Care of Patients with Pain

> **Before Reading 1 (p. 88)**
> Goal: Get oriented to the text
> Techniques: Preview new materials; ask questions about the information

1. The chapter is 17 pages long.
2. There are eight objectives listed on the chapter's first page.
3. The evaluation of the difficulty level of the chapter depends on your familiarity with the topic and your motivation to learn the topic—as well as the author's choice of content and language. Note that the material is mostly words; there are some graphics, but not many. There is some technical vocabulary. Besides the nine vocabulary words on the chapter opener page, some terms

used in the objectives may be new: *physiologic/psychological, stimuli, subjective, interventions,* and *analgesics.* This chapter's coverage of pain concepts is not as technical as some, but it introduces the concepts of pain in a comprehensive way.

Before Reading 2 (pp. 88–89)

Goal: Develop a study plan
Technique: Decide which parts of the text relate to objectives

---

Page Number(s)	Objective
Page 94, under the heading "Physiology of Pain"	1. Define pain.
Page 95, in the section "Perception of and Reaction to Pain"	2. Describe physiologic and psychological reactions to pain stimuli.
You may have trouble with this one. The table on page 101 covers acute and chronic pain, but that's only two. . . .	3. Compare and contrast three different types of pain.
Five myths are discussed on page 97.	4. Describe common biases and myths about pain.
The section "Assessment of Pain" goes from page 96 to page 100; it includes subsections on subjective and objective data.	5. Assess pain in assigned patients, fully appreciating the subjective nature of pain.
The table on page 104 lists eleven interventions not involving pain medication.	6. List at least seven nursing interventions other than the administration of analgesics for the relief of pain.
The "When appropriate" column in the table on page 104 is useful here. And the section "General Nursing Measures" on pages 101–106 is probably also relevant.	7. Select nursing interventions appropriate for each type of pain experience.
This objective calls for the application of theory to actual patients; the two "Clinical Case Problems" at the end of the chapter (on pages 106–107) offer a chance to practice your evaluation skills—even if you don't have any patients yet.	8. Evaluate the effectiveness of measures used for the management of pain in assigned patients.

After Reading 1 (p. 91)
Goal: Organize relevant information for review
Technique: Make notes

There are lots of examples; here are a few with which to compare your choices.

Pattern	Section	Page Number
comparison/ contrast	physiologic/psychological reactions	p. 95
	signs of superficial and deep pain	p. 99
	Table 10-1: "Acute and Chronic Pain"	p. 101
cause/effect	causes of pain	p. 95
	"Medical and Surgical Treatment"	p. 100
process/time order	gate control theory	p. 96
	Nursing Care Plan 10-1	p. 103
listing	factors affecting pain reaction	p. 95
	"Biases and Myths about Pain"	p. 97
	"Subjective Data" lists factors for pain assessment	pp. 97–98

Being aware of these kinds of patterns while you read can help you organize the material mentally for better comprehension and retention. The next time you read textbook material, actively look for such patterns and use them to help organize information for recall.

After Reading 2 (p. 92)
Goal: Organize relevant information for review
Technique: Underline

Did you find sentences expressing a main idea in most paragraphs? Here are examples from the first two paragraphs:

<u>Dictionary definitions of pain usually describe it as a feeling of distress, suffering, or agony that is caused by stimulation of specialized nerve endings scattered throughout the body</u>. Pain is a universal symptom, which means that it is not specific to any one disease or type of injury. Its purpose is to act as a warning that tissues are being damaged and to motivate the sufferer to remove or withdraw from the source of the pain or otherwise seek relief.

Anyone who is trying to help a person cope with pain must be careful not to be judgmental and decide whether the pain actually exists. We can define pain in a somewhat detached and limited way for the purposes of study and communication, but <u>the person experiencing pain is the most reliable source of information about how it feels, where it is located, and what provides relief.</u>

The first paragraph has other general sentences relating to a definition of pain, but the first sentence contributes most to the objective "Define pain." Although the second and third sentences provide additional information, they don't seem to be as important to remember as far as the author is concerned. How can you be sure?

In the "Study Outline," beginning on page 107, the author has provided a guide to what are, in her opinion, the main ideas and significant details. For example, the main ideas in the five paragraphs in the section entitled "Reception and Transmission of Pain Signals" are listed in the outline.

Use the Study Outline as an answer key showing the author's thinking about what's important. Compare her thoughts with yours. For every sentence you underlined that matches an outline entry, put a check mark next to that entry. When you finish, look back at the outline entries that are not checked. Did the author organize material differently in the outline than in the text? Did you think something was important while she did not? What is your explanation for the differences?

After Reading 3 (pp. 92–93)

Goal:	Check initial recall of relevant information
Technique:	Review the whole assignment by self-testing

One possible set of responses to the objectives, expressed in terms of their location in the "Study Outline" on pages 107–110, is in the *Instructor's Resource Manual*.

Selection 3-2. Nurses Plunged Me Into the Pain Cycle; Nurses Pulled Me Out

---

Before Reading 2 (pp. 111–112)

Goal:	Get oriented to the text
Techniques:	Preview new materials; look up significant terms that are not defined in the text

---

Does your answer look something like this?

The author is identified as a *nurse* who uses a *comparison/contrast* pattern to present her experiences with *pain in two different facilities*.

If you didn't choose comparison/contrast as the pattern, you probably chose cause/effect. Both are used in this author's article, but the contrast between the two facilities is the main point.

After Reading 1 (pp. 112–113)

Goal:	Check initial recall of relevant information
Technique:	Review the whole assignment by self-testing

Were you able to get this much information immediately after reading, without looking back at the article?

The pain cycle experienced by the author at the orthopedic hospital began with medications that were delivered late, so her body began to increase its demand for pain relief. With repeated late, inadequate analgesia, the patient began concentrating only on her pain and her anxiety, so that pain medication couldn't be as effective as it should have been. In the rehabilitation facility, the medications were always on time, with dosages increased to meet the patient's peak needs, such as when she was having therapy. As the patient became more confident, she was able to use diversions such as relaxation and TENS to decrease the frequency and amount of medication.

After Reading 2 (pp. 113–114)

Goal:	Organize relevant information for review
Technique:	Make notes

Did you choose most of these topics for your chart?

Orthopedic Hospital	Rehabilitation Facility	Psychological Factor
fear of "trouble-maker" label	initial expression of concern met with smile, analgesia	training and cultural guidelines for acceptable responses
medications often late	medications delivered on time	previous experience with pain
pain endured until "nothing else existed in the world"	patient able to use temporary diversions: relaxation, TENS, hobbies	coping mechanisms
"neglect drove me inward"	methodical approach to delivering medication produced confidence in patient	mental health

Continued

Orthopedic Hospital	Rehabilitation Facility	Psychological Factor
exaggerated sympathy from and helplessness of nurses	objective signs used by nurses to counter stoic behavior	training and cultural guidelines for acceptable responses
fear of loss of compassion, respect	patient is partner in developing schedule and goals	mental health
"perfect patient" is one who is passive, depressed, withdrawn	patient's increasing confidence that medications would be delivered on time resulted in her using less medication	mental health

After Reading 3 (p. 114)

Goal: Organize relevant information for review
Techniques: Look up and learn new terms discovered during reading; think critically about what you have learned

Do you agree with the following response?

The nurses in the orthopedic hospital seemed to be showing "exaggerated sympathy" rather than "empathy." They did not demonstrate the objective awareness of another's feelings that might have led them to take appropriate, empathic actions, as indicated in Taber's Cyclopedic Medical Dictionary. *Instead, they had a sympathetic, affective reaction and did not take steps to correct the patient's pain problems.*

After Reading 4 (p. 115)

Goal: Organize relevant information for review
Technique: Look up and learn new terms discovered during reading

The correct answers to the vocabulary quiz are in the *Instructor's Resource Manual.*

Selection 3-3. Nurses' Judgments of Pain in Term and Preterm Newborns

Before Reading 1 (pp. 120–121)

Goal: Get oriented to the text
Technique: Make predictions about the information

Journal's Outline Format	Author's Headings and Subheadings

Objective ——————— Purpose of the Research
                                   Literature Review

Design ——————— Methods

Setting ——— Population and Setting

                                 Instrumentation

Participants ———   The instrument

                                    Establishing validity and consistency

Interventions ——— Procedure

                                 Results

Main Outcome   Hypothesis 1

   Measures   Hypothesis 2

Results ——— Discussion and Nursing Implications

                                 Limitations

                                 Recommendations for Further Research

Conclusions ——— Conclusions

                                 Acknowledgment

                                 References

    You haven't read the article, so it's hard to be sure about these connections. It appears that the journal editors and the author use different words for the same things: *objective* versus *purpose,* for example. The review of literature and the list of references cited are not included in the journal's summary outline.

After Reading 1 (pp. 122–123)

Goal: Check initial recall of relevant information
Technique: Review the whole assignment by self-testing

Suggested responses to this activity are in the *Instructor's Resource Manual.*

Selection 3-4. Review of Literature on Culture and Pain of Adults with Focus on Mexican-Americans

---

Before Reading 1 (pp. 132–133)

Goal: Get oriented to the text
Techniques: Preview new assignment; make predictions about the information

---

Introductory paragraphs:
   Purpose is to review literature on Mexican-Americans' response to pain and draw implications for future.

Conceptual framework: culture and pain
> *"Nurses and other health caregivers in the United States often characterize various ethnocultural groups according to their reaction to pain and their ability to tolerate pain."*

Definition of terms
Transcultural pain studies
> *"Cross-cultural studies have demonstrated that White Americans of Northern European origin react to pain stoically and as calmly as possible, choosing to withdraw if pain becomes intense. This response to pain has become the cultural model or norm in the United States. It is the behavior expected and valued by health caregivers."*

Pain response in Mexican-Americans
> *"Mexican-Americans are often described as complainers who want immediate relief for their pain. Yet studies of Mexican-American culture and cross-cultural studies of the pain experience and responses of Mexican-Americans do not support this characterization."*

Evaluation of pain response by nurses
> *"Nurses and patients assess pain differently regardless of cultural background. Both nurses and physicians tend to underestimate and undertreat the pain of their patients when compared to patients' assessment of pain. However, the ethnicity and culture of the patient influence the extent of difference between the patient's and nurse's assessments. The culture of the nurse also influences the inference of patients' physical pain and psychological distress."*

Implications for transcultural nursing practice
Recommendations for future research
Conclusion

Which sentences in the abstract are *not* related to one of the headings?
> *"The purposes of this paper are to review the literature on culture and pain in adults, and specifically on Mexican-American beliefs about pain, and nurses' responses to patients' pain."*

This is an important sentence because it tells the three purposes of the paper. If the authors had included a heading called "Introduction" at the beginning of the article, you would have written this main idea with that heading.

Which headings are not explained in the abstract?
> *You'll have to read four sections of the article to get the authors' main ideas: "Definition of terms," "Implications for transcultural nursing practice," Recommendations for future research," and "Conclusion."*

During Reading 1 (p. 134)

    Goal: Monitor comprehension
    Technique: Stop periodically to check achievement of goals and to
                underline main ideas

In the section titled "Implications for transcultural nursing practice," the first paragraph of the section has many generalized, broad sentences. It's hard to know which one to pick. Did you choose the first sentence? It is too general to be really helpful in remembering this article. The last sentence in the paragraph is probably too specific. Perhaps this sentence from the middle of the paragraph best expresses the idea that the authors would like you to remember:

> "In making an assessment of a Mexican-American and his or her potential response to pain, the cultural beliefs, values and practices of the client must be assessed with respect to illness, suffering and pain."

The second paragraph explains a two-step process of assessment, with lots of examples for each step. Did you underline these two sentences?

> 1. "An assessment of actual responses to pain should include gathering data on what a particular behavior and/or vocalization might mean in response to pain."
> 2. "Secondly, an assessment of actual response to pain should include gathering data on the function of particular behaviors and vocalizations . . ." (You don't need to underline the example if you understand the concept.)

The third paragraph begins with a sentence that carries the assessment a step further:

> "The management of the patient's pain should include an assessment of the type of intervention the person desires."

Did you include this additional sentence from the middle of the paragraph? Or did you consider family and support networks as part of the desired intervention?

> "The role of the family or social support network in providing any of these interventions should be assessed as well and accommodations made for family, friends and clergy to provide interventions."

Which sentences did you underline in "Recommendations for future research"?

The first paragraph, again, has many general sentences, most of which seem to warn of the difficulties of this type of research. Perhaps this is the sentence the authors would want the reader to remember:

> "Nurses who wish to pursue research of the kind reviewed here should be aware of the methodological problems that characterize these studies and make cross-cultural comparisons difficult."

The second paragraph opens with a broad statement about cross-cultural research; the third sentence focuses on the topic of this article:

> "Suggested areas for study involving Mexican-Americans and Anglo-Americans include both qualitative and quantitative approaches to the development of knowledge."

You might also have underlined this sentence:

> "Finally research is needed which focuses on development of pain assessment tools that nurses can use with different cultures and

development of reliable and valid research tools that can be used in cross-cultural populations."

```
┌──────────────── After Reading 1 (pp. 134–136) ────────────────┐
│      Goal:   Check initial recall of relevant information      │
│   Technique:   Review the whole assignment by self-testing     │
└────────────────────────────────────────────────────────────────┘
```

To check your work, reread the abstract at the beginning of the article and the sentences you underlined in the "Implications" and "Recommendations" sections. A paraphrase of the underlined sentences is available in the *Instructor's Resource Manual*.

```
┌──────────────────── After Reading 2 (p. 136) ────────────────────┐
│      Goal:   Organize relevant information for review             │
│   Technique:   Think critically about what you have learned       │
└────────────────────────────────────────────────────────────────────┘
```

Depending on your familiarity with the pain literature, you may have found many names you know. Margo McCaffery, the author of the "wherever, whenever" definition of pain, is represented as a coauthor with N. T. Meinhart.

Selection 3-5. Avoiding Opioid-Induced Respiratory Depression

```
┌──────────────────── Before Reading 1 (p. 145) ────────────────────┐
│      Goal:  Get oriented to the text                               │
│   Techniques:  Preview new assignment; make predictions about the  │
│                information; estimate the difficulty of the material │
└──────────────────────────────────────────────────────────────────────┘
```

The most extreme adverse effect of respiratory depression is death. That risk is significant enough for health care providers to look for ways to avoid it.

The second author of this article, Margo McCaffery, is known for her definition of pain, which is cited in the textbook chapter you read as the first selection of this unit. Both authors are nurses who work as consultants, so their income depends on their expertise. It is not surprising that the *American Journal of Nursing* selected experts in the field to write an article of this significance.

Did you notice the introductory anecdotes and the readable, conversational style? Readers, who are addressed as "you," are assumed to be nurses, not students. Thus, you might expect a challenging level of technical difficulty.

┌─────────────── **After Reading 1 (pp. 146–147)** ───────────────┐
│   Goal: Organize relevant material for review
│ Technique: Look up and learn new terms discovered during
│   reading
└──┘

1. What (exactly) do these abbreviations stand for? Where can you look up such abbreviations?

    COPD: *chronic obstructive pulmonary disease* (for example, emphysema)

    NSAID: *non-steroidal anti-inflammatory drugs* (If you can't provide examples of NSAIDS, you haven't gotten enough information yet.)

    PACU: *post anesthesia care unit*

    PCA: *patient controlled analgesia*

    PRN: *pro re nata* (Latin for "as needed")

    Although NSAID was defined in the article (in the box on p. 152), PCA was introduced in the first selection of this unit, and COPD is in a recent college dictionary, most abbreviations like these require you to look in a medical dictionary.

2. Use the chart on opioid characteristics on page 151 to answer these questions:

    a. Which opioid has the quickest onset time using the intravenous route?

    Fentanyl seems to be the fastest with any route, but IV is faster than epidural.

    b. Which opioid takes the longest to reach peak effectiveness? Using which route?

    By far the longest time to peak effectiveness is obtained with morphine through an oral route, although it has a slow onset.

    c. If the goal is delayed onset of analgesia, which medication and route would you recommend?

    The slowest onset could be achieved by using oral morphine, but epidural morphine is almost as slow.

3. If the "incidence of clinically significant respiratory depression in hospitalized adults receiving opioids in therapeutic doses is approximately 0.09%," how many people are affected?

    c. *9 of 10,000 (0.09% = 0.0009 = 9/10,000)*

4. What is your response to the second objective: "Identify two factors that increase the risk for opioid-induced respiratory depression"?

    The risk of respiratory depression is greater for patients who are opioid naive (that is, have not taken opioids for a week or more) and for those who are opioid sensitive, which is hard to identify except from previous history.

┌─────────────── **After Reading 2 (pp. 147–148)** ───────────────┐
│   Goal: Test recall of relevant information
│ Technique: Answer test questions
└──┘

The following list of answers is offered only as a basis for comparison and discussion with your classmates: a, d, b, a, c, a, a, d, a, c, a, c, b. You are not eligible for the continuing education units offered by the journal, and these answers are not to be considered official or necessarily correct.

If you have a different answer, can you support it with a clear reference from the article? If so, can you convince others of your position? Can you give evidence showing that the other answer choices for that question are incorrect?

Unit 4   Ethical and Legal Issues

Selection 4-1. Ethics and Values

> ―――――― **Before Reading 1 (pp. 160–161)** ――――――
> Goal: Get oriented to the text and assignment
> Techniques: Preview new assignment; ask questions

The lack of similarity between the chapter objectives and the headings in the textbook chapter makes the choices difficult here. There seem to be four objectives that fit the assignment closely.

<u>Chapter Objectives</u>

_____   Explain how to recognize a moral issue.

___√___   Define the terms *ethics*, *bioethics*, and *nursing ethics*.

_____   Discuss sources of ethical problems in nursing.

_____   Explain the difference between decision-focused problems and action-focused problems.

___√___   Differentiate the following moral frameworks: deontology, teleology, intuitionism, and the ethic of caring.

___√___   When presented with an ethical situation, identify the moral principles involved.

_____   Explain the uses and limitations of professional codes of ethics.

_____   Explain how cognitive development, values, moral frameworks, and codes of ethics affect moral decisions.

_____   Discuss the concept of an integrity-preserving compromise.

_____   Describe the elements of selected ethical issues nurses encounter.

___√___   Discuss nursing roles and responsibilities with regard to ethics.

> ―――――― **After Reading 2 (pp. 162–163)** ――――――
> Goal: Organize relevant information for review
> Technique: Underline and make notes

The box that follows shows a sample of notemaking on part of the selection text. This style of marginal notes uses abbreviations to identify ideas for subsequent review. For example, "nprr" stands for "nurses' perceptions of their roles and responsibilities," and "good dec = cbi, pi" summarizes the sentence "A good decision is one that is in the client's best interest and at the same time preserves the integrity of all involved." If you like the idea of reviewing without rereading the text, develop your own style of abbreviations or shorthand. Putting only abbreviations in the margins forces you to test yourself mentally to find out if you really know the content.

---

6 **Factors Affecting Ethical Decisions**

nprr
mt, f
mp
c/e
cd
vba
　　Factors affecting ethical decision-making include [1.] nurses' perceptions of their roles and responsibilities, [2.] moral theories and frameworks, [3.] moral principles, the professional [4.] code of ethics, the [5.] level of cognitive development of the people involved, and the [6.] values, beliefs and attitudes of these people.

1. nprr
d + s
Perceptions of Roles and Responsibilities Nurses are responsible for determining their own actions and for supporting clients who are making ethical decisions or coping with the results of decisions made by others. A good decision is one that is in the client's best interest and at the same time preserves the integrity of all involved. Nurses have multiple obligations to balance in moral situations. . . .

good
dec=
cbi, pi

2. mt,
f=4
① T=c
u=gg
Moral Theories and Frameworks There are four general approaches to moral theory: teleology, deontology, intuitionism, and the ethic of caring. Teleology looks to the consequences of an action in judging whether that action is right or wrong. Utilitarianism, one specific teleologic theory, is summarized in the ideas, "the greatest good for the greatest number" and "the end justifies the means."

②
D=d,r, r
　　Deontology proposes that the morality of a decision is not determined by its consequences. It emphasizes duty, rationality, and obedience to rules. For instance, a nurse might believe it is necessary to tell the truth no matter who is hurt. There are many deontologic theories; each justifies the rules of acceptable behavior differently.

For example, some state that the rules are known by divine revelation; others refer to a natural law or social contract.

T vs. D
ex ab
　　The difference between teleology and deontology can be seen when they are applied to the issue of abortion. A person taking a teleologic approach might consider that saving the mother's life (the end, or consequence) justifies the abortion (the means, or act). A person taking a deontologic approach might consider any termination of life as a violation of the rule, "Do not kill" and, therefore, would not abort the fetus regardless of the consequences to the mother. It is important to note that the approach, or framework, guides making the moral decision; it does not determine the outcome (e.g., the person taking a teleologic approach might have considered that saving the life of the fetus justified the death of the mother).

③
I=pk
　　A third framework is intuitionism, summarized as the notion that people inherently know what is right or wrong; determining what is right is not a matter of rational thought or learning. For example, a nurse inherently knows it is wrong to strike a client; this does not need to be taught or reasoned out.

④
c=R
　　Benner and Wrubel (1989) proposed caring as the central goal of nursing as well as a basis for nursing ethics. Unlike the preceding theories which are based on the concept of fairness (justice), an ethic of caring is based on relationships. Caring theories stress courage, generosity, commitment, and responsibility. Caring is a force for protecting and enhancing client dignity. . . .

stress
c, g, c, r

After Reading 3 (pp. 163–164)
Goal: Test recall of relevant information
Technique: Answer test questions

The answers to the open-book test are in the *Instructor's Resource Manual*.

Selection 4-2. Ethical Perceptions of Parents and Nurses in NICU: The Case of Baby Michael

---
Before Reading 1 (pp. 176–177)
Goal: Get oriented to the text
Technique: Ask questions about the information

What does the lag time between acceptance and publication tell you about how current the information in the article is?

The article was printed 16 months after being submitted to the journal. While the information in journals is usually more current than that in textbooks, the lag time may not allow the inclusion of the most recent research findings.

Where do you think you would find the most current reporting of ethical and legal issues?

Newspapers, popular magazines, and TV news programs offer the latest information about legal and ethical issues, but they often do not supply complete, accurate details. Some college and public libraries contain legal departments that receive monthly updates regarding court and legislative decisions.

Why do you think the address of the author is provided?

The authors want readers to be able to correspond with them about the content of the article.

Before Reading 2 (p. 177)
Goals: Get oriented to the text; develop a study plan
Techniques: Preview new materials; make predictions about the
              information; decide which parts of the text relate to
              objectives

What ethical issues do the authors emphasize in their examination of this case?

The abstract and headings focus on issues of treatment versus nontreatment, informed consent, and decision making. Table 1 (on p. 182) outlines the same issues for two groups: parents and nurses.

How is the section "Nursing Implications" organized?

The abstract suggests that the selection provides an "integration of crisis intervention techniques and caring processes." Table 2 (p. 185) lists examples of those two types of interventions.

After Reading 2 (pp. 178–179)
Goal: Check initial recall of relevant information
Technique: Review the whole assignment by self-testing

Compare your answers to these:

1. To identify the parents' problems related to the three ethical issues raised by the authors, did you use a combination of Table 1 (p. 182) and the material under each heading?

   Treatment issues facing the parents involved failure to understand complex treatment methods, a feeling that the procedures must be routine, and a wish to believe that the need to "grow a little" was all that was wrong with Michael.

   Informed consent issues related to the facts that the nurses became the parents' primary source of information, that there wasn't a private place to talk about the consent form they were filling out, and that they thought the forms were only a "formality"—not realizing the seriousness of what they were doing.

   Decision making was almost impossible for the parents, who felt ill-equipped to deal with the NICU.

2. The nurses' issues or dilemmas can also be summarized using Table 1 and the material under each heading.

   The nurses faced many ethical dilemmas over treatment issues. They had to inflict pain in order to follow orders and the parents' wishes. Knowing about possible disabilities raised questions about quality of life.

   Informed consent also raised many issues for the nurses, especially since the parents may have based their decisions on false hopes. Deciding whether to tell the parents the truth put a strain on the nurses.

   The nurses also experienced conflict in decision making, as their personal values were called into question with regard to treatment and the adequacy of information available to the parents.

3. Your explanation of how Table 2 (page 185) illustrates what nurses may do to help parents in such situations should resemble the following:

   Table 2 summarizes two frameworks that nurses can use together to help parents in this kind of situation. Crisis intervention techniques and caring processes allow nurses to provide support while helping family members identify their own coping mechanisms.

4. Is your paraphrase something like this? (A true paraphrase does not use even three words in a row from the original.)

   Ethically and legally, nurses must provide the support needed by parents in the decision-making process. Parents must be enabled to care for and make decisions about their babies.

Could you have come up with similar self-test questions on your own?

After Reading 3 (p. 179)
Goal:	Organize relevant material for review
Technique:	Learn new terms discovered during reading

Did you use a dictionary to look up any of the words? Had you already circled them during reading?

   1. c; 2. i; 3. k; 4. d; 5. h; 6. j; 7. l; 8. g; 9. a; 10. f; 11. e; 12. b

---
After Reading 4 (p. 180)
Goal:	Organize relevant material for review
Technique:	Summarize

A sample summary can be found in the *Instructor's Resource Manual*.

Selection 4-3. Ethical Decision Making

Before Reading 1 (pp. 187–188)
Goal:	Get oriented to the text
Techniques:	Preview new materials; improve your background knowledge
---

Because the chapter lacks such organizational clues as objectives or a summary, making a list of the headings will probably help you see the organizational plan.

Introduction: a general discussion of ethics
Law vs. ethics: a distinction between legal and ethical matters
Moral dilemmas
　　Types of dilemmas (definitions and examples)
　　Types of decisions (definitions and examples)
Values and ethics
　　Moral relativism

Note: This list is also an informal outline of the chapter's contents because the minor headings are indented under the main ones. Using indentations to show relative importance is an important outlining technique.

After Reading 1 (pp. 188–189)

Goal: Organize relevant information for review
Technique: Outline

Your outline might look something like the following one.

Partial Outline of "Ethical Decision Making"

Chapter 8: Ethical decision making. Nurse's Legal Handbook (1996) (pp. 275–288). (3rd ed.). Springhouse, PA: Springhouse Corporation.

Introduction:

A conflict of duties may be resolved by using nursing standards and codes and by understanding the principles of nursing ethics.

Law vs. ethics:

Ethics is the branch of philosophy that studies values and actions. Laws are "rules of conduct" that are enforced.

A law that is challenged usually reflects a conflict with a principle of ethics.

Nurses who serve as patient advocates may help reduce legal actions by patients who are dissatisfied with their care.

Moral dilemmas:

A moral dilemma occurs when there are no clear choices for resolving an ethical problem.

> *Stressful; not easy to know what to do*
>
> *Choices made with uncertainty*
>
> *Psychological and time pressures*

Common types of nursing dilemmas include beneficence (good vs. harm), autonomy (self-determination), justice (fair distribution of resources), fidelity (keeping promises), nonmaleficence (avoiding harm, whistle-blowing), confidentiality (privacy), and veracity (truth-telling).

Dilemmas addressed by nurses can be categorized as active or passive; programmed by rules or nonprogrammed and requiring a unique response.

> *Consent form—active; delay of decision—passive*

Values and ethics:

Values are personal and/or professional beliefs about what is important.

Clarifying personal values is "an important part of developing a personal ethic" (p. 192).

Moral relativism, which says that there are no moral absolutes, may result in conflicts.

After Reading 2 (p. 189)
Goal: Organize relevant information for review
Techniques: Think critically about what you have learned; apply principles to real-life situations

---

You may have chosen different examples to illustrate the types of nursing actions, which is fine. Compare your choices with these and the ones listed in the selection. Are they similar?

Type 1 **Nursing actions are both ethical and legal.** *Teaching baby Michael's parents how to care for him after he leaves the hospital.*	**Type 2** **Nursing actions** *may be considered* **ethical but not legal.** *Increasing baby Michael's medication to provide him with additional pain relief without a doctor's order to do so.*
Type 3 **Nursing actions** *may be considered* **legal but not ethical.** The nurses delivered treatment that seemed futile and was based on a possible misunderstanding by the parents.	**Type 4** **Nursing actions are neither legal nor ethical.** *Telling baby Michael's parents that the prescribed treatment is causing their child needless pain and that they should stop all treatment.*

Do you understand the differences among the types of nursing actions? If not, you may want to reread sections of the chapter and discuss the various types with other students or with your instructor.

Selection 4-4. Caring for Pediatric Patients with HIV: Personal Concerns and Ethical Dilemmas

---
Before Reading 1 (pp. 193–194)
Goals: Get oriented to the assignment; develop a study plan
Techniques: Preview new assignment; ask questions; divide the assignment into manageable parts; decide how and when to work on each part

---

Does this article contain all the appropriate features? List them.
In this informal study, the following features are present:
  problem recognition (in general terms only)
  a participant population (30 nurses, employed in diverse roles in one hospital)

a review of the literature
a listing of survey questions
a description of the data collection method
a narration of types of ethical concerns, with participants' comments
a summary of the significance of the results
a suggestion for further study to be conducted
There is no statement of hypothesis.

How much do you think you can generalize the results of this study, given the number of participants?

Because this study was conducted in one city, in one hospital, with a participant population of 30, it would be inappropriate to generalize the results to the general population of nurses.

After Reading 1 (pp. 195–196)

Goals: Check initial recall of relevant information; organize relevant information for review

Techniques: Review the whole assignment by self-testing; make notes; think critically about what you have learned

---

Do your notes clearly identify and help you recall the objective of the research; the design, setting and participants; the interventions (in this case, the survey questions and data collection methods); the results; and the conclusions?

If you want more information about HIV and AIDS, you may consider looking up these acronyms in a medical dictionary or encyclopedia. Remember that this is a relatively new disease, so the source must be a recent publication to have an accurate description.

Your school library is likely to have an index such as CINAHL (Current Index to Nursing and Allied Health Literature), which you can use to find current articles about AIDS, including ones on medical, nursing, and home health care for the person with AIDS. If you don't know how to use the index, the librarian will help you.

Your library may also have books about new infectious diseases, including AIDS, which may prove helpful.

Although on-line sources of information are very interesting, it is important to think critically about information from these sources because no editors or evaluators have reviewed and approved it for publication.

After Reading 2 (pp. 196–197)

Goal: Test recall of relevant information
Technique: Answer test questions

Answers to the quiz are located in the *Instructor's Resource Manual.*

How did you do on this quiz? If you didn't do well, can you identify weak points in your study habits? Plan to improve your performance next time. If you did really well, think about how you prepared for the quiz, and keep up the good work.

Selection 4-5. When Language Is an Obstacle

After Reading 1 (p. 207)
Goal: Organize relevant information for review
Technique: Outline

Your outline might look something like this one. However, what is most important is that it include sufficient, accurate information to remind you of the important points the author makes in the article.

Outline

Sloan, A. (1995). When language is an obstacle. RN, 58(6), 55–57.

Introduction:

  Language barrier may place patients at risk.

  Knowing the legal basis for professional communications helps patients, decreases lawsuits, and maintains jobs.

The validity of English-only rules:

  Employee guidelines are acceptable if business requirements override the discriminatory implications.

Foreign accents and patient safety:

  Accents that hamper communication may require creative alternatives, such as fax or E mail, to ensure patient safety.

  The physician has a duty to patients to give unambiguous orders and to communicate sufficiently in order to give patients their right to informed consent.

  The nurse's role as patient advocate may require the nurse to act.

What if the patient doesn't understand?

  Patients have the right to information despite their inability to speak English.

  Nurses must make a reasonable effort to overcome a language barrier.

  Hospital policies should identify methods that will help overcome language barriers.

After Reading 2 (pp. 207–208)
Goal: Test recall of relevant information
Technique: Predict possible test questions

Compare your questions with those of other students to get an idea of the range of possible responses. The following questions and answers will give you an idea of how a nursing instructor might respond to the assignment.

1. How can Mrs. K's questions about her condition be answered?

   The nurse might check the hospital's list of translators. Some of these people are available to come to the hospital; others may help by telephone (the nurse would have to speak to the translator and then hand the telephone to the patient for translation; obviously, this takes more time). Another possibility is to ask Mrs. K's husband or a Korean-speaking visitor to translate. If no Korean-speaking person is available to translate, perhaps Mrs. K or her husband speaks another language for which a translator can be found.

2. How can Mrs. K's nurse ensure that she gives informed consent for any procedures recommended by the doctor?

   When a nurse recognizes that a patient doesn't understand the surgery or medical procedure recommended by the physician, including its risks and benefits and alternative treatments, the nurse has the responsibility to call this to the attention of the doctor. The nurse may watch the patient sign an informed-consent form, but if the consent is not truly informed, the nurse has not met the obligation to the patient.

3. How can a nurse be an effective patient advocate for a patient like Mrs. K, who doesn't speak English?

   As a patient advocate, the nurse works closely with the doctor to assure that Mrs. K understands before she gives her permission for a procedure. The physician has the responsibility to continue working with the translator until the patient understands.

4. What are the advantages and disadvantages of using Mrs. K's husband as a translator for her?

   Since a translator is needed for Mrs. K, it might be convenient to use her husband to translate. However, as with any translator, there is the risk that errors might be passed on when the person translating doesn't understand the message. The risk of error is greater when medical jargon is used, since the translator might not understand the terminology. Also, Mrs. K's right to privacy may be compromised. She may not feel as free to express her feelings when a family member is privy to what she says. In addition, she may not be able to keep certain information private if a family member translates for her.

5. What would be the advantages and disadvantages of using as a translator a female housekeeping staff member who speaks Korean?

   Using a woman as a translator may avoid some problems, but the staff member may have limited knowledge of medical terms in English.

───────── **After Reading 3 (p. 208)** ─────────

Goal:	Test recall of relevant information
Technique:	Answer possible test questions

A response to the biased question "Why do people come to this country to work when they can't speak English?" is given in the *Instructor's Resource Manual.*

Unit 5 Stress

Selection 5-1. Stress

> ## Before Reading 1 (pp. 214–215)
> Goal: Develop a study plan
> Technique: Decide which parts of the text relate to objectives

Course Objective	Learning Objective
1	1
1	2
2	3
2, 3	4
3	5

Note that the fourth course objective does not match a learning objective, but the Social Readjustment Rating Scale appears on page 222.

> ## Before Reading 2 (p. 215)
> Goals: Get oriented to the text; develop a study plan
> Techniques: Preview new materials; decide which parts of the text relate to objectives

Did you check the following headings?

√ Stress as a Response

    Stage of Alarm Reaction

    Stage of Resistance

    Stage of Exhaustion

    Refinements in Selye's Stress Theory

Identifying Stressors or Demands

    Work-Related Stressors

    Illness-Related Stressors

√ Coping

√ Nursing Management of Stress

    Nursing Assessment

        Demands

Human Responses to Stress
Coping
Nursing Diagnoses
Nursing Implementation
Review Questions

All three course objectives are addressed in take-home test questions.

After Reading 1 (pp. 216–217)
Goal: Check initial recall of relevant information
Technique: Review the whole assignment by answering review questions
---

Answers to review questions: 1. b; 2. c; 6. d; 8. c

Definitions:

1. Stress: *the nonspecific response of the body to any demand placed upon it*
2. Stressor: *a stress-inducing demand; an event that stimulates the stress response*
3. General adaptation syndrome: *a stimulus/response pattern to stress, consisting of three stages*
4. Alarm reaction: *the first stage of the GAS, which shows such symptoms as increased pulse and respiratory rates, elevated blood pressure, increased cardiac output, pupil dilation, increased perspiration, muscle tension, and diminished peripheral circulation*
5. Stage of resistance: *the second stage of the GAS, during which the physiological forces are maintained to support function. The adaptive energy that facilitates this stage may be limited, causing the person to move into the stage of exhaustion.*
6. Stage of exhaustion: *the third stage of the GAS, when the individual no longer has the resources to maintain adaptation. Death may be the result if assistance is not available.*
7. Coping: *the process by which a person deals with stress. The cognitive aspects of coping include the thought and learning necessary to identify the source of stress. The noncognitive aspects focus on relieving discomfort.*
8. Fight-or-flight response: *the reaction of the body to stress through action of the sympathetic nervous system and the adrenal medulla*

After Reading 2 (pp. 217–218)
Goal: Organize relevant information for review
Technique: Think critically about what you have learned

Examples of physical/emotional stressors are listed in Table 5-1 (page 221).

Does your description resemble this?

The stressor would help the individual if it caused him or her to move away from a harmful stimulus or if it kept the affected person alive until aid could be obtained. It would hurt the individual if the result were a somatic illness.

Does your explanation of the Social Readjustment Rating Scale look something like this one? If many details are missing in your explanation, you probably are not spending enough time studying the table or reviewing the related text.

One stress theory, developed by Holmes, Rahe, and Masuda, states that multiple life changes may result in a greater risk of illness. To measure this risk, they designed the Social Readjustment Rating Scale—a chart of common events with a risk value assigned to each event. An individual first identifies on the list a series of events he or she may have recently experienced. By totaling the number value for each event, the individual can ascertain whether he or she is at minimal, moderate, or major risk of major illness.

Compare your analysis of the table with this example:

Table 5-7, Examples of Coping Resources, presents two main types of coping resources: in the person and in the environment. There are four subtypes of personal resources: (1) health, energy, and morale, (2) positive beliefs, (3) problem-solving skills, and (4) social skills. There are two subtypes of environmental resources: social networks and utilitarian resources (such as money).

Which resource did you identify?

The case study provided on page 229 has not yet been used. It might be useful after reading and studying the unit. A study group might be helpful to answer the questions and to create additional situations. Practice in applying the information will aid in preparation for application exam questions.

After Reading 3 (pp. 218–220)

Goal:	Periodically test recall of relevant information
Technique:	Answer possible test questions

Answers for the take-home test are provided in the *Instructor's Resource Manual.*

Selection 5-2. Stress and Anxiety

Before Reading 1 (p. 231)

Goals:	Get oriented; develop a study plan
Techniques:	Preview new materials; decide which parts of the text relate to objectives

---

√ Introductory paragraphs

    √ Biologic Response

    √ Biologic Research

    X Psychosomatic Approach

    X Life Events

    X Interactional/Transactional Approach

X Physiologic Components of the Stress Response

    X Immediate Physiologic Processes

    X Intermediate Response

    X Long-term Response

    X Neurophysiology of Thought and Emotion in the Stress Response

    X Interaction of Neuroendocrine Influences on Immunocompetence in the Stress Response

    √ Nursing Research on Stress Incidence, Treatment, and Prevention

    √ Implications for Nursing Research and Practice

√ Summary

√ References

Before Reading 2 (p. 232)

      Goal: Get oriented to the text
  Technique: Look up significant terms that are not defined in the text

---

How do your divisions compare with these?

    bio-log-ic
    psycho-soma-tic
    inter-ac[t]-tion-al
    trans-ac[t]-tion-al
    physio-log-ic
    neuro-physio-logy
    im-medi-ate
    inter-medi-ate
    neuro-endo-crine
    immuno-compet-ence

Do you need to review the meaning of any of these word parts?

After Reading 2 (pp. 233–235)

    Goal: Test recall of relevant information
  Techniques: Review notes without rereading the text; answer possible test questions

---

Compare your answers to the test with the correct ones:

1. b (in the first introductory paragraph on page 236)
2. d (in same paragraph as question 1)
3. a (in same paragraph as question 1)
4. b (in the first paragraph following the subheading "Nursing Research . . .") on page 239.
5. c (in the first paragraph following the heading "Implications for Nursing Research and Practice")
6. a (second sentence in the fourth paragraph following the heading "Implications for Nursing Research and Practice")
7. d (in the fourth paragraph, fifth sentence following the heading "Implications for Nursing Research and Practice")
8. b (in the fifth paragraph following the heading "Implications for Nursing Research and Practice")
9. c (in the third paragraph following the heading "Implications for Nursing Research and Practice")
10. d (in last paragraph preceding "Summary")

Selection 5-3. Analyzing Job Demands and Coping Techniques

After Reading 1 (p. 244)

Goal: Organize relevant information for review
Technique: Make notes

Does your chart resemble this one? Or did you find another way to make notes about the contrasting groups?

"I" Group	"They" Group
1. Took ownership of work stressor; could pinpoint exact details of a specific bad day	1. Were unable to identify specific stressful events
2. Recognized that not all days were bad days	2. Felt that every day was the same
3. Held realistic expectations of themselves	3. Coped with stress by blaming others for failing to fix stressors
4. Prioritized work and made adjustments when necessary	4. Believed that someone or something beyond themselves hindered their work success (e.g., felt that management was out of touch)

Continued

"I" Group	"They" Group
5. Practiced self-care techniques (e.g., took a 30-minute break); acknowledged unrealistic personal expectations	5. Did not demonstrate self-care practices
6. Often held the expectation that "Tomorrow will be better."	6. Wanted someone else to fix the situation

---

After Reading 3 (p. 246)

Goal: Organize relevant information for review
Technique: Apply principles to real-life situations

Almost any occupation can have stressors. Occupations that allow less independence for workers have been documented as creating higher levels of stress than those in which the individual can exercise more control by making more decisions independently. Students may experience significant stress levels, especially when they have work and/or family responsibilities in addition to their studies.

Bibliography

Orientation to the Health Professions

Selection 2-1. Pagliarulo, M. (1996). *Introduction to physical therapy* (5 front matter pages, pp. 1–6, 14–15, 289, 299). St. Louis: Mosby.

Selection 2-2. Cullinan, J., & Cullinan, A. (1995). The birth of a new profession. *Radiologic Technology, 66,* 179–183.

Selection 2-3. Curtin, L. (1996). Blessed are the flexible . . . . *Nursing into the 21st century* (pp. vi–vii, 211–214). Foreword by Margretta Madden Styles. Springhouse, PA: Springhouse.

Selection 2-4. Nightingale, F. (1969). Chattering hopes and advices. Chapter 12 in *Notes on nursing: What it is, and what it is not* (pp. 95–105). New York: Dover.

Selection 2-5. Craven, R., & Hirnle, C. (1996). *Fundamentals of nursing* (2nd ed.) (pp. I-6, 12, 33). Philadelphia: Lippincott.

Lewis, S., Collier, I., & Heitkemper, M. (1996). *Medical-surgical nursing* (5th ed.) (pp. I-37, 62, 63, 81). St. Louis: Mosby.

Needham, J. (1993). *Gerontological nursing* (p. 391). Albany, NY: Delmar.

Sims, L., D'Amico, D., Stiesmeyer, J., & Webster, J. (1995). *Health assessment in nursing* (pp. 752, 756). Menlo Park, CA: Addison-Wesley Nursing.

Smith-Temple, J., & Johnson, J. (1994). *Nurses' guide to clinical procedures* (2nd ed.) (pp. 728, 730, 743). Philadelphia: Lippincott.

Selection 2-6. Douglas, C. Y. (1995). Cultural considerations for the African-American population. *Imprint, 42*(2), 57–59.

Louie, K. B. (1995). Cultural considerations: Asian-Americans and Pacific Islanders. *Imprint, 42*(2), 41–46.

Pain

Selection 3-1. deWit, S. (1992). Care of patients with pain. Chapter 10 in *Keane's essentials of medical-surgical nursing* (3rd ed.) (pp. 205–222). Philadelphia: W. B. Saunders.

Selection 3-2. Owen, A. S. (1988). Nurses plunged me into the pain cycle; nurses pulled me out. *RN, 51*(8), 22–25.

Selection 3-3. Shapiro, C. R. (1993). Nurses' judgments of pain in term and preterm newborns. *Journal of Gynecological and Neonatal Nursing, 22*(1), 41–47.

Selection 3-4. Calvillo, E. R., & Flaskerud, J. H. (1991). Review of literature on culture and pain of adults with focus on Mexican-Americans. *Journal of Transcultural Nursing, 2*(2), 16–23.

Selection 3-5. Pasero, C. L., & McCaffery, M. (1994). Avoiding opioid-induced respiratory depression. *American Journal of Nursing, 94*(4), 25–31.

Ethical and Legal Issues

Selection 4-1. Kozier, B., Erb, G., Blais, K., & Wilkinson, J. (1995). Ethics and values. Chapter 11 in *Fundamentals of nursing: Concepts, processes, and practice* (pp. 200–216). Menlo Park, CA: Addison-Wesley.

Selection 4-2. Miya, P. A., Pinch, W. J., Boardman, K. K., Keene, A., Speilman, M. L., & Harr, K. L. (1995). Ethical perceptions of parents and nurses in NICU: The case of Baby Michael. *Journal of Gynecological and Neonatal Nursing 24*(2), 125–130.

Selection 4-3. Ethical decision making. Chapter 8 in *Nurse's Legal Handbook* (3rd ed.) (pp. 275–279). (1996). Springhouse, PA: Springhouse.

Selection 4-4. Murphy, J. M., & Famolare, N. E. (1994). Caring for pediatric patients with HIV: Personal concerns and ethical dilemmas. *Pediatric Nursing, 20,* 180.

Selection 4-5. Sloan, A. (1995). When language is an obstacle. *RN, 58*(6), 55–57.

Stress

Selection 5-1. Werner, J. S. (1996). Stress. Chapter 5 in S. Lewis, I. Collier, & M. Heitkemper (Eds.), *Medical-surgical nursing: Assessment and management of clinical problems* (5th ed.) (pp. 70–72, 78–83). St. Louis: Mosby Year Book, Inc.

Selection 5-2. Robinson, L. (1990). Stress and anxiety. *Nursing Clinics of North America, 25,* 935–943.

Selection 5-3. Petermann, B. A., Springer, P., & Farnsworth, J. (1995). Analyzing job demands and coping techniques. *Nursing Management,* February, 51–53.